Programming Techniques
Volume 4

Bits and Pieces

Blaise W. Liffick, Editor

BYTE BOOKS™
"BOOKS OF INTEREST TO COMPUTER PEOPLE"

Programming Techniques.

CONTENTS: v. 1. Program Design.—v. 2. Simulation.—v. 3. Numbers in Theory and Practice.—v. 4. Bits and Pieces.

1. Electronic Digital Computers—Programming. 2. Computer Simulation. 3. Mathematics—Data Processing. I. Liffick, Blaise W.

QA76.6.P7518 001.64'2 78-8649

ISBN 0-07-037828-2(V. 4)

Bits & Pieces

TABLE OF CONTENTS

FROM THE EDITOR

Programming Techniques is a series of books specifically designed to help make programming easier and more enjoyable for the personal-computer enthusiast. This is done by providing articles which detail successful techniques for designing and implementing programs. Each book is a collection of the best articles on the selected subject from past issues of BYTE, The Small Systems Journal, plus new material which has not appeared in print before. This provides the reader with vital information from previous BYTE issues which might have been missed, new material that has not appeared in the magazine, plus a book covering one specific theme for quick, easy reference.

The first volume in this series, **Program Design** (ISBN 0-931718-12-0), provides a look at several different methods for designing programs more efficiently and effectively. Included in the topics covered are structured-program design, modular-programming techniques, program-logic design, designing tables, and binary-tree processing.

Volume 2 is **Simulation** (ISBN 0-931718-13-9). Its purpose is to familiarize the reader with both a general overview of the vast area of computer simulation as well as details of specific types of simulations. The term simulation can cover a lot of territory, but for this book only three categories were chosen: artificial intelligence, motion, and experimentation.

Numbers in Theory and Practice (ISBN 0-07-037827-4) is the third volume of the series. It covers many areas of numbers and computational methods for microcomputers. It serves as an introduction to number systems, floating-point numbers, numerical methods, random number generators, and the mathematics of computer graphics. There are many practical programs included, as well as numerous references for further study of the subject.

Volume 4 is **Bits and Pieces**, not an altogether whimsical title. This is perhaps the most advanced book of the series thus far, delving into some of the more difficult topics of programming. In many instances it gets down to the most fundamental levels of programming microcomputers, covering topics only slightly removed from the actual hardware of the machine, such as stacks and interrupts. At other times, the discussions cover the other end of the spectrum, detailing the use of executives, or sophisticated operating systems on microcomputers.

The three sections of this volume, **Software Systems, Data Handling,** and **Advanced Techniques,** bring together up-to-date information on some of the more complex problems and applications facing the microcomputer programmer. Since the subjects covered are diverse, they will all help you become a more effective microcomputer programmer.

Blaise W. Liffick
Editor

Software Systems

About This Section

Anyone who has been involved in computing for long is at least somewhat familiar with the history of computers. It has been an interesting history, although, for the most part, it spans less than 50 years. During that time, four basic generations of computers can be identified, with the microcomputers being the most recent development.

Many people have pointed out how similar the development of the microcomputer has been to the previous development of the minicomputer. Recall that the minicomputer came about as a result of the large-scale machines being too fast for the relatively slow peripheral input/output devices such as printers. The minicomputers were designed to interface between the large-scale machines and the peripherals, keeping the large machines from wasting time. It took some time before these "peripheral data processors" were recognized for their own potential as general-purpose computers.

Similarly, the microprocessor was developed as a process controller. It was several years before anyone actually put one to use to drive what we now call a microcomputer. Again paralleling the minicomputer, the microcomputer began as a single-user machine, running one program at a time, essentially without an operating system. The microcomputer has been considered too slow to handle sophisticated system software. This criticism, along with it not having enough main memory, was also previously leveled at the minicomputer, but anyone familiar with the industry knows that the minicomputer is now a well-respected machine.

As this section clearly shows, many people in the industry have apparently misjudged the capabilities of the microcomputer as well. With the speed of microprocessors increasing, and the size of memory on the rise, perhaps there is little the microcomputer will not ultimately be able to do. The articles included here make it obvious that the areas of multiprogramming, multiprocessing, and time-sharing are not the exclusive realm of larger machines.

A Real-Time Executive for Your Microcomputer

Wayne Crutchley

Many personal computer owners today are seeking new and better uses for their microprocessors. Often starting with a basic system capable of displaying and programming memory, playing various keyboard games, or running some version of BASIC, the serious computer enthusiast begins to extend this package into a specially customized system. This specialized system may include such features as expanded memory, disk- or tape-operating systems, special input/output (I/O) peripherals for analog-to-digital conversion, music, speech, graphics, or any amount of various computer applications. All of these additions may amount to a seemingly endless job, involving continuous work towards completion of the system.

Where is the end to this continuous design and upgrading? When will the system be complete so that it need not be revised, but simply used? For many designers, there is no end; moreover, total satisfaction and completion will never be achieved on any system. However, for many others, the ultimate system design may be envisioned early in their personal computer adventure and, through well-planned and dedicated work, may eventually be achieved on a permanent basis.

This presentation discusses one such variation of a completed, custom-designed microprocessor system, which has as its heart a *real-time priority interrupt executive.* Real-time processing is used today in a number of applications, large and small, with many different combinations of hardware and software systems. This system, like all the others, contains the basic components that are present in all real-time operating systems, and this article will illustrate these basic components and principles through the description of this version of the executive.

There are three basic aspects of the real-time executive:

- real-time program execution
- priority scheduling and reentrancy
- interrupt processing

Combining these three components into an integrated system results in an executive operating system with great capabilities. For commercial use, such an operating system excels in such applications as process control or data acquisition (the main applications of the system presented here). For the personal computer owner, it can provide both real-time or process-control capabilities, as well as batch or multiple-user terminal processing.

For example, envision the following home computer system equipped with a real-time executive; this system could be simultaneously performing the following tasks for the personal computer user:

- controlling home or office utilities on a real-time basis (heat, electricity, appliance control, security, etc)
- monitoring status of these utilities with video display or hard-copy printout
- supporting multiple-terminal or keyboard inputs from various users
- supporting high-speed peripherals like disks or digital cassettes, along with operating systems to run major programs such as compilers, assemblers, or word processing programs
- supporting interfaces to specialized or experimental peripherals such as musical, vocal, or test equipment
- recording periodically acquired data and system date and time
- supporting system debugging or on-line machine-language programming utilities
- maintaining data-link communication to a similar microprocessor system or to a higher-level system at a remote location

Is it feasible to expect this kind of performance from a microcomputer? The answer to this is an unconditional *yes*. A large fraction of the total processing capabilities of many personal and commercial microcomputer systems is often wasted, such that the total power of a microprocessor is sometimes underestimated. For example, consider the question: What task consumes most of the total real time of a microprocessor system? If the subject is the typical personal computer system, the answer is that most of the time (up to 99% or more) is spent looping or waiting for a keyboard input or some other event from the external world to key the next sequence of events. This implies that almost all of the computer's processing power (and, similarly, the owner's investment) may be wasted. The presentation of the following real-time executive will attempt to explain how much of this wasted processing power may be harnessed to create a system with powerful capabilities that will enable a user to get the most out of his or her personal computer.

Real-Time Executives

A real-time executive is a program, or operating system, capable of handling a large number of tasks more or less simultaneously on a priority basis. These tasks may include program scheduling, interrupt servicing, peripheral communication, and others. To dispel a myth which some personal computer owners may have concerning real-time processing, the real-time executive does much more than merely keep time, as the term *real-time* may suggest. Timekeeping is merely one of the tasks (normally a relatively insignificant one, in comparison to the total system task) that the executive may perform.

The real-time priority executive gets its name from the manner in which program execution takes place within the system. The heart of the system is a clock-driven interrupt to the microprocessor that causes the system to execute certain programs periodically and interrupt less important programs according to a well-defined set of priorities. In almost all cases, the clock interrupt will be a precise, crystal-controlled or 60 Hz time base such that various program executions will be performed accurately enough to do time-based functions like keep time and date. (This, however, is not an absolute requirement, merely a convenient feature.) In addition to the clock interrupt, the system receives various other interrupts that are generally associated with certain peripheral devices which request attention.

Since multiple events will be continuously occurring, both from external devices and from internal programs, the executive must be able to handle and service the events in the proper sequence. The idea that the processor is performing tasks simultaneously is, of course, not true, but it *does* appear to be that way, as it is humanly impossible to perceive the speed at which the computer performs tasks on a multilevel system.

Priority

The executive must handle a large number of tasks, since the total amount of work to be completed varies and since tasks are requested asynchronously from the external world. To handle these tasks, the executive must have a way of scheduling the sequence in which it performs certain programs when there are more than one to perform at any given time. The sequence in which the executive will execute programs will depend on the priority of each program, which is set by the computer operator at the time the program is linked to the executive.

The necessity of priority is due to the importance of a particular task relative to any other tasks on the system. For example, assume a program such as a BASIC interpreter is linked to a real-time executive, and the user has just initiated a BASIC program which involves a long calculation that may take several seconds, or even minutes, of the processor's time to complete. There will be plenty of processor time in the next few seconds or minutes to perform the BASIC calculation; however, before the calculation is completed, it is likely that some other task will be scheduled to execute on the system. For example, someone may request program service from another keyboard, a message may be received from a data link, or a regularly scheduled program, such as security monitoring, may be enabled for immediate execution. Naturally, the more important programs should not have to wait on a less critical function, such as a BASIC calculation, which is normally expected to take some time anyway, and therefore can wait. The BASIC calculation is then said to have a lower priority than, for example, the security program.

Another example on a more critical time basis would be the servicing of a high-speed peripheral, such as a disk or tape interface. When the ready-interrupt signal from such a device occurs, it is critical that it be serviced immediately to avoid losing the data. Therefore, this type of program is even more important than the regularly scheduled type of program and must have a still higher priority.

As we can see, there exists a need for the executive to treat programs on a priority basis. There also exists the need for different degrees of importance. How are these different degrees of importance measured? What are the ground rules for the executive in handling these different degrees of priority? For the executive presented here, the degree of priority is measured by the *level* of the program, and the ground rules for the handling of the programs at the different priority levels are shown figures 1, 2, and 3.

These simple illustrations represent the real-time executive as a group of water reservoirs, labeled level 0 thru level 3. (Level 0 has the highest priority and level 3, the lowest.) These reservoirs represent the various priority levels of the executive, which contains the current tasks to be performed. In the computer, this reservoir network is actually a list or *stack* of programs in the processor's main memory; hence the name *job stack*.

The water contained in the reservoirs is analogous to the current requested workload of the executive. The valves that control the water into and drain the water out of these reservoirs are analogous to the interrupt service

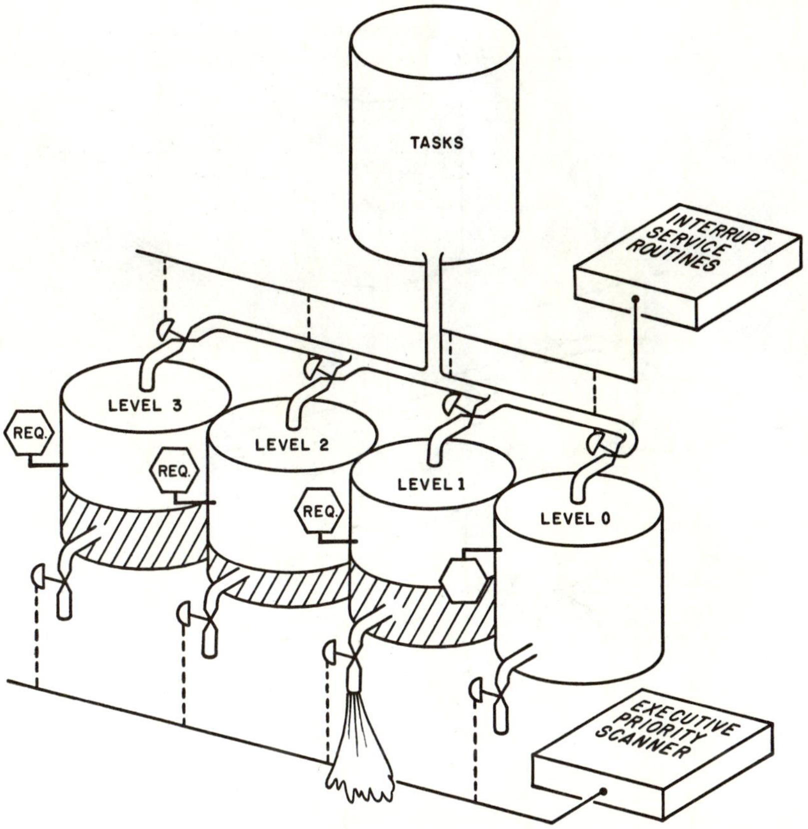

Figure 1: *Visualizing the real-time executive. In figures 1 thru 3, the water reservoirs represent programs assigned to a given priority level, and the valves regulating flow out of the reservoirs represent the executive priority scanner. Here, levels 1, 2, and 3 all have work to be completed, and the priority scanner is allowing level 1 (the highest priority not empty) to drain (or execute).*

routines and the priority scheduler, respectively.

Figures 1 thru 3 show a series of sequential events, which illustrate the rules of priority within the real-time executive. In figure 1, a current workload exists at levels 1, 2, and 3. Level 0 is shown completed or empty at this time. Of all the levels that have a workload, level 1 has the highest priority. Therefore it is being serviced, or "drained," while the programs at the other levels are awaiting execution.

After a time period proportional to the total amount of workload originally contained in level 1, the level will be completed. At this time, the executive will compare the priorities of all the levels requested. Level 2 now has the highest priority, and it will be the next to be serviced, as shown in figure 2. While level 2 is being serviced, an interrupt occurs, resulting in the interrupt service routine of some particular device to request a program to execute at level 0. This status is shown in figure 3.

At this point, program execution is temporarily suspended on level 2 in order to service the higher-priority level 0. Note

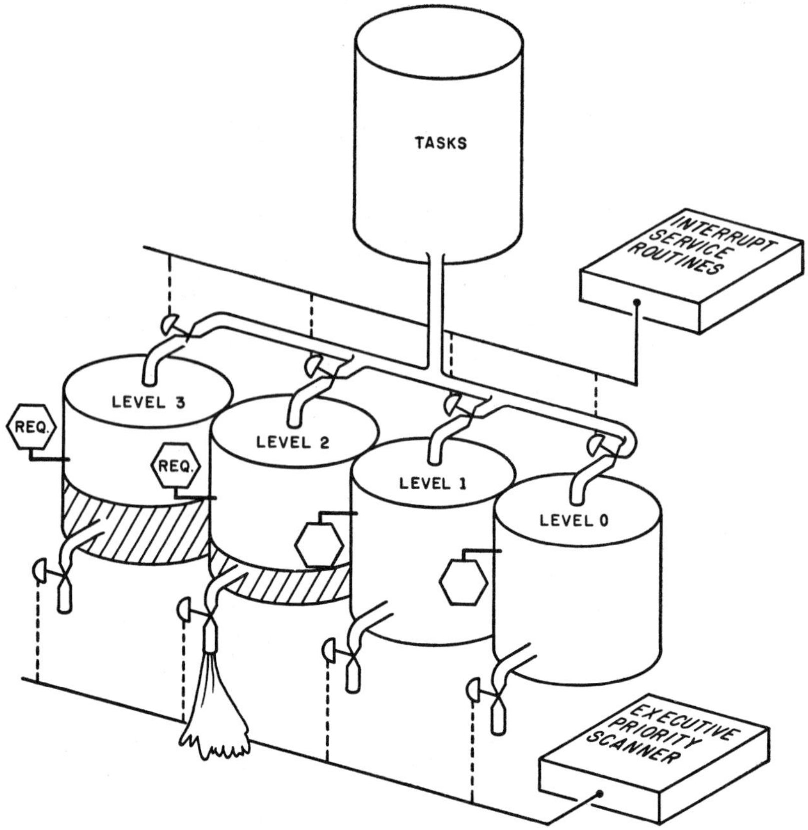

Figure 2: *Visualizing the real-time executive. Here, level 1 has finished its execution and level 2, the next in line, is now being serviced. The priority principle always forces the executive to service the highest of requests at any particular moment.*

that a special flag is set at level 2, indicating that it was interrupted. The purpose of this flag will be explained subsequently.

Eventually level 0 will be completed (assuming no further tasks are immediately added at this level), and the executive will again be free to compare priorities. This time, level 2 still has the highest priority; however, the *suspended* flag exists at this level. This flag indicates that the current requested workload at level 2 has already been started but interrupted before completion. In this special case, the executive will reenter the program at the point of interruption, after restoring all registers and status for that program. (Each level, of course, has a separate space allocated for storage of its working registers, status, and program counter; the space is unique to that level only.)

When any interrupt occurs on the system, all interrupt service routines that will eventually lead to a task request must always save the processor status for a current level and set the appropriate flags. This is so the eventual return to the interrupted level (and program) will be made exactly where the program left off, with the exact processor status at the time of the interrupt. (This basic concept is known as *reentrancy*, which will be further explained later.)

The simple example shown in figures 1 thru 3 illustrates only one of the many possible sequences and situations which may occur during real-time executive scheduling. It should be noted that the interrupt service sequence, described above, can also occur in a multiple-level or chain-reaction manner. For example, assume that while level 2 is in the suspended state and level 0 is being serviced, as above, another interrupt occurs on the system, resulting in tasks being requested on the system at level 1. For this case, during the interrupt service routine, both level 2 and level 0 have job requests, and both are in the suspended state. (All processor status data for each level is saved in areas unique to each level.) Upon completion of the particular interrupt service routine, priorities of all requested tasks will be compared (including both interrupted and new tasks). The task with the highest priority will always be entered (or reentered) first. In this case level 0 would be reentered.

To any active program, any interrupt on the system will be essentially unnoticed, since the program will always be entered (or reentered) with all processor-status data intact. Hence, as far as individual programs are concerned, they all run simultaneously, each program using processor time on a priority basis, whenever it is available, to complete their individual tasks. The operation of the priority principle may be summarized as follows: a program at any particular priority level will be allowed to execute only when all programs at a higher level are complete. In figures 1 thru 3 we see the processing of jobs by a priority interrupt system as the control of water into and out of reservoirs, each of which represents a priority level for the jobs (water) contained within. Normally the processor is sitting with all "reservoirs" empty, waiting for a task to be requested. When one or more tasks arrive, they will be finished immediately, and the processor will be ready for more tasks. The total amount of time that the processor spends with tasks to be completed at any level, as compared to the total available time, is referred to here as the *job loading* and will be discussed later.

For the home microprocessor system described earlier, this job loading should average out to approximately 50% or less. However, this does not mean that at all times there will be 50% processing capability unused. For example, during the long BASIC calculation described earlier, which may take several seconds or even minutes, the job loading will be 100% until the calculation is complete. Assuming that before the calculation was initiated, the processor had a 55% job loading, then during the calculation, this 55% of the processor time will still be devoted to its normal tasks, and 45% will be put towards the calculation. The greater the normal job loading is, the longer the calculation will appear to take (although the actual amount of processor time will always be the same).

During the calculation, any program at a lower priority than the BASIC routines will not be allowed to run, or will be suspended until the calculation is complete. Thus, the priority system gives the user a method of distributing or budgeting the total processor time. These descriptions basically explain the priority principles used in the real-time executive. Many questions may arise at this time, such as: How should it be determined at what level to place any particular program? What happens when more than one program on a level is requested at the same time? How do interrupt service routines request tasks to be run in the executive? How do I link my own custom programs to the real-time executive? These and similar questions will be dealt with in later sections.

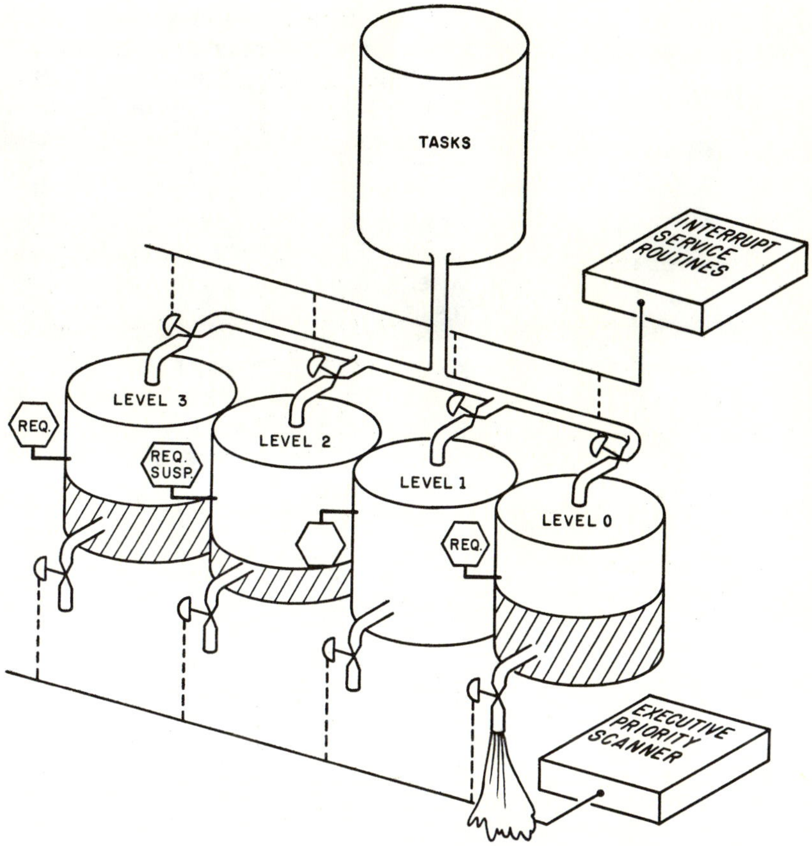

Figure 3: *Visualizing the real-time executive. Here, during the servicing of level 2 (in figure 2), an interrupt occurs, resulting in new tasks flowing into level 0. Therefore, level 2 is suspended, and a special "suspended" flag is set. Level 0 is now being serviced, and when it is finished, level 2 will restart. Level 2 is then said to be "reentered."*

Program Scheduling

One of the ways in which programs become *enabled*, or requested to execute in the real-time system, is through the *scheduler*, which is an integral part of the real-time executive. The scheduler is linked to the real-time clock interrupt, and includes the clock-interrupt service routine as one of its program segments. On most practical real-time systems, it is desirable to have certain programs run on a regular, cyclic basis; for example, once per second, once per 100 ms, etc. For the personal computer user, these programs may perform the following functions: security monitoring, utilities monitoring, video updating, timekeeping, etc. This type of program execution mode is referred to here as *polling*.

The clock-interrupt service routine will have access to a set of tables, one that points to various programs to be executed, and another that is essentially a list of programs grouped in order of their priority of execution. For the executive presented here, these tables are called the *poll table* and *executive job stack*, respectively.

The executive job stack contains certain information about each program and ties the program to a certain *level* and *program number*. The level determines the relative priority of a program. Also, only one program from a given level can be running, scheduled, or interrupted by the executive.

The function of the poll table is to group programs (defined as level-number/program-number pairs) according to the frequency with which they will be executed. Each group within the poll table contains three items: an execution time that determines the frequency of execution of the programs in that group, an active timer initiated to the execution time (periodically decremented until it signals execution of the programs at a count of zero), and a list of pointers to the executive job stack of the programs to be run at this interval.

At each clock interrupt, each active timer is decremented by 1, and, when any one expires, the associated programs linked to that poll group are enabled to execute. Before returning to the interrupted program, the interrupt routine will scan the executive job stack to check the status of programs. If any of the newly enabled programs are found to be at a level higher than the interrupted program, the interrupted program will be left suspended, and program control will be given to the newly scheduled task. Otherwise, the interrupted program will be resumed.

Thus it can be seen how normally scheduled programs of a higher level can interrupt lower-level programs through the actions of the clock-interrupt routine, thus maintaining priority for all scheduled programs.

As shown above, the scheduler is merely a sophisticated network of timers, which are counted down and monitored at precise intervals through the actions of the real-time clock interrupt. The expiration of any of these timers causes a program or group of programs to be enabled and eventually executed on a priority basis by the executive.

Interrupt Processing

Another way that programs are enabled to execute is through interrupts from peripheral devices. Many different variations of interrupt routines are possible and are generally customized to the particular device concerned. All interrupt service routines must, however, be linked to the executive in some organized fashion. For this particular executive, this is done by making various major utility subroutines available for use, such that custom interrupt routines are easily written. The implementation section deals with this subject in further detail.

At this time, one point should be made concerning priority: the levels, as described in the previous sections, refer to the software levels of priority only. There exists another level of execution which has a higher level of priority than even the highest software level. This is the *interrupt level*. Any program running at the interrupt level will have absolute control of the processor and cannot be interrupted or suspended in any way.

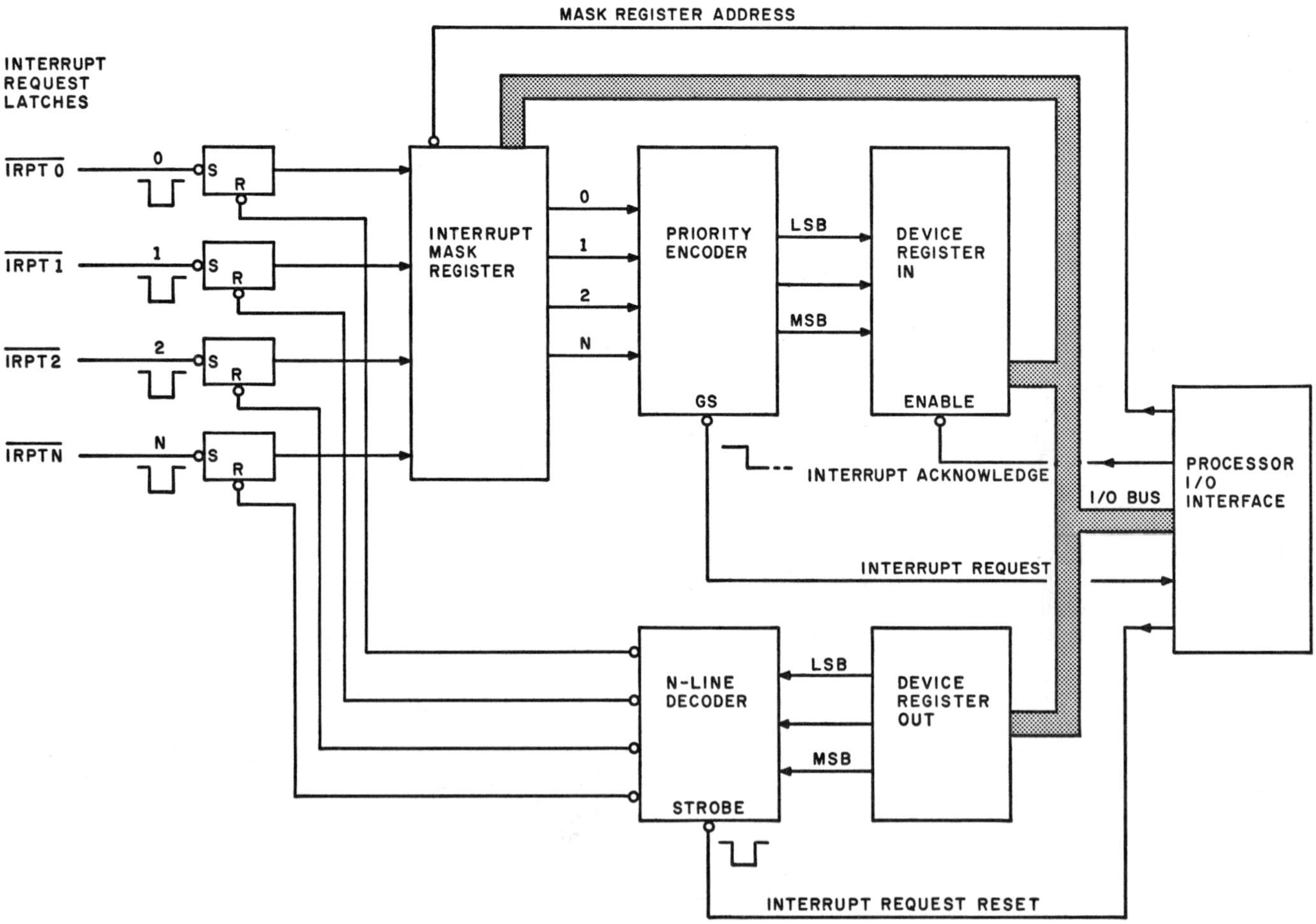

Figure 4: *A block diagram of a hardware priority interrupt system. Priority detection is done by the encoder, which selects one of the N lines and encodes it into a binary representation of the selected line. Latched interrupt requests are reset when they are acknowledged by the processor through the device register-out port. A mask register is shown here to provide software control to disable any interrupts not used or not needed.*

(Naturally all interrupts are disabled for this program mode.)

For best operation on any real-time system, another priority chain should be implemented to handle interrupts. This priority chain is done with the hardware, which interfaces the processor with the external interrupting devices. A hardware block diagram of this priority chain is shown in figure 4. This diagram may be applicable to a number of different microprocessors.

The heart of this system is a hardware priority encoder (such as the 74147 or 74148 integrated circuit), which encodes 1 of N lines from peripheral devices into a binary code that identifies the pending device. A priority circuit is used here for the case when more than one interrupt occurs before the processor has a chance to acknowledge any of them. In this instance, the one with the highest priority will be serviced first (analogous to the procedures for software priority-level service). Optionally, the priority detection may be accomplished by software at the interrupt level. This requires directly reading the latched requests and using an algorithm to determine priority; this scheme, however, is not dealt with here.

All of the latched interrupt requests are gated through an *interrupt mask register* before being presented at the encoder input. This enables the processor to switch off unused interrupts, or those that are not needed at the moment. After acknowledging any interrupt, the processor must reset the latched request so that it will not be interrupted again by the same event. This is accomplished by the *device register out* port, used by the processor to cause a pulse that strobes the reset on a given individual request latch, thus freeing the latch to receive another interrupt once the current interrupt has been serviced. Normally, this request reset will be a hardware function.

Since figure 4 is meant as a general block diagram, it may not be the best application, exactly as shown, for all microprocessors. However, it is the basis of a viable scheme that will fulfill the real-time executive's needs. For variations of such designs, it is recommended that hardware priority detection be used over software methods, due to the speed advantages. Also, encoding (that is, N lines encoded to a binary number) should be used to allow expansion to a large number of devices. Finally, a mask register is recommended for greater flexibility in dealing with peripheral interrupts.

It should be made clear at this time that the hardware priority levels are not necessarily related to software levels, but are merely a method of distinguishing a further and higher level of importance. For example, a device that has hardware priority level 0 (ie: highest priority) can be linked to an interrupt service routine which may eventually cause a program to be enabled at software level 3, say, or vice versa. In this case, the hardware device and the software program servicing the device have totally different priorities. The hardware priority system is merely a way in which a secondary priority system may be implemented at the hardware level. This allows better control of interrupt devices, since the executive has little control over hardware interrupts, other than enabling and disabling them. The hardware priority interrupt scheme is very important when using high-speed peripherals on the system. However, it is perhaps not as important as it is useful, when only slower devices are used.

Real-Time Executive Example

A working version of the real-time executive is presented in this section. The assembled source listings, along with other diagrams, are used to illustrate its structure and operation. This particular version is being used as the executive for a commercial process-control design that handles tasks in excess of those in the home system described earlier. Used and tested in a home system, it was found to be extremely easy to work with and to interface. This makes it ideal for the personal computer system. This software's initial test applications have shown that the real-time executive and the particular microprocessor used have powerful capabilities when they are linked to efficient system programming.

The listings presented here show the final assembled and debugged programs. The listings that cover some of the table structures, however, have been abbreviated to save space, but the initial portions of the tables illustrate the overall structure so it may be extended by the reader.

This version is assembled at hexadecimal address 1000 and occupies ½ to ¾ K bytes, depending on the length of the executive job stack, poll tables, and stack areas. The version currently includes eight priority levels, with four programs per level; however, it can easily be expanded to provide up to 16 levels, with as many as 16 programs per level, a capacity which, of course, will take up more memory space. The Z80 is used for

```
1000             ;
1000             *
1000             *
1000             *
1000             *
1000             ******************************************
1000             *
1000             *
1000             *
1000             * PRIORITY INTERRUPT REAL TIME EXECUTIVE
1000             * SYSTEM POINTERS & EQUATES
1000             *
1000             *
1000             *
1000             ******************************************
1000             *
1000             *
1000             *
1000             *
1000 00          XAL     DB   0          CURRENT LEVEL (B7=ACTIVE FLAG,B0-3=LVL#)
1001             *
1001 00          XLVL    DB   0          LVL POINTER DURING XJS SCAN
1002             *
1002             *
1002 00 00       XPGM    DW   0      XJS PGM ADDR DURING A LEVEL SCAN
1004             *
1004 00          XRSC    DB   0      RESCAN FLAG, SET TO -1 WHEN XJS RESCAN IS REQ.
1005             *
1005             XMSK    EQU  08         NORM IRPT MSK
1005             *
1005             XMSC    EQU  03         MSK DURING RTC SRVC
1005             *
1005 00          XME     DB   0          EXT USER MSK BITS
1006             *
1006                     DS   24         XEXC STACK
101E             XSTK    EQU  $
101E             *
101E 00 00       XTMP    DW   0      XEXC TMP SAVE
1020             ;
1020             *
1020             *
1020             *
1020             ************************************
1020             *
1020             *     EXECUTIVE JOB STACK
1020             *
1020             * FOR EACH PGM, FORMAT AS FOLLOWS:
1020             * BYTE 0 - B7 PGM ENABLE BIT
1020             *          B6 PGM SCHEDULED BIT
1020             *          B5-B0 SPARES
1020             *
1020             * BYTE 1,2 = L,H PGM ADDR
1020             *
1020             ************************************
1020             *
1020             XJS:    EQU  $       START XJS
1020             0:      EQU  $       STRT L0
1020 00                  DB   0       L0,P0
1021 00 00               DW   0
1023             *
1023 80                  DB   080         L0,P1
1024 00 00    U          DW   XDBG        DEBUG PGM
1026             *
1026 00                  DB   0       L0,P2
1027 00 00               DW   0
1029             *
1029 00                  DB   0       L0,P3
102A 00 00               DW   0
102C             *
102C FF                  DB   -1          END L0
102D             *
102D             1:      EQU  $       STRT L1
102D 00                  DB   0       L1,P0
102E 00 00               DW   0
1030             *
1030 00                  DB   0       L1 P1
1031 00 00               DW   0
1033             *
1033 00                  DB   0       L1 P2
1034 00 00               DW   0
1036             *
1036 00                  DB   0       L1 P3
1037 00 00               DW   0
1039             *
1039 FF                  DB   -1          END L1
103A             *
103A             2:      EQU  $       STRT L2
103A 00                  DB   0       L2,P0
103B 00 00               DW   0
103D             *
103D 00                  DB   0       L2,P1
103E 00 00               DW   0
1040             *
1040 00                  DB   0       L2,P2
1041 00 00               DW   0
1043             *
1043 00                  DB   0       L2,P3
```

Listing 1: *System pointers and executive job stack. The system pointers and "equates" tables show the global temporary storage area used by the executive. The executive job stack XJS shows the program format used for entries in the executive job stack. The levels are labeled as "0:" "1:", "2:", etc. These levels may be relocated to anywhere in memory.*

this version of the real-time executive, as this processor has many advantages over most other 8-bit microprocessors for this particular type of system. Despite the advantages of the Z80, many of the more powerful microprocessors available today could also handle the real-time executive very well. The principles of real-time priority processing are as equally applicable to these other processors.

Generally, the following features of the Z80 have been the most advantageous for the real-time executive and associated software:

- generally powerful instruction set
- flexible input/output (I/O) capabilities (eg: register indirect, block I/O)
- excellent hardware interrupt capabilities (eg: Z80 mode-2 interrupt)
- high-speed operation

In particular, the I/O capabilities of the Z80 have been shown to be the most useful for multilevel processing, where common I/O subroutines are shared by multiple levels on a reentrant basis. This allows easy, efficient means of writing and interfacing I/O software to multilevel programs. The hardware interrupt system allows easy implementation of a hardware priority-interrupt chain, giving ultimate flexibility in creating or relocating interrupt service routines. The restart vectors are then freed for other uses.

Software-Table Structure

System pointers (listing 1)

The first half of listing 1 shows the global system pointers for the executive. These pointers are highly important. They are responsible for keeping track of the master executive status (ie: where it is) at all times. Among the more important of these pointers:

XAL	Current active executive level
XMSK, XMSC	Interrupt mask register enable bits
XSTK	Executive active stack area

Executive job stack (XJS, listing 1)

The second half of listing 1 shows the start of the executive job stack. All user programs linked to the executive must be listed in the job stack. This particular stack is listed in order of priority. However, it does not need to be; any level of the executive job stack can be added or relocated to anywhere in

```
1088              1660 ,
1088              1662 *
1088              1664 **************************
1088              1665 *
1088              1668 *    LEVEL CONTROL TABLES
1088              1669 *
1088              1670 *     8 BYTES PER TABLE
1088              1680 *     1 TABLE PER LVL
1088              1690 *
1088              1693 **************************
1088              1695 *
1088              1700 XLT    EQU  $      STRT LVL TBLS
1088              1710 *
1088 20 10        1720        DW   0.     L0 XJS
108A 00           1730        DB   0      STATUS (B7,LVL REQ B6,LVL IRPT'D)
108B A6 12        1740        DW   XST0       STK ADDR
108D 00 00        1750        DW   0      SP SAVE
108F 00           1760        DB   0      SPARE
1090              1770 *
1090 2D 10        1780        DW   1:     L1 XJS
1092 00           1790        DB   0      STAT
1093 C6 12        1800        DW   XST1   STK
1095 00 00        1810        DW   0      SP
1097 00           1820        DB   0
1098              1830 *
1098 3A 10        1840        DW   2:     L2 XJS
109A 00           1850        DB   0      STAT
109B E6 12        1860        DW   XST2   STK
109D 00 00        1870        DW   0      SP
109F 00           1880        DB   0
10A0              1890 *
10A0 47 10        1900        DW   3.     L3 XJS
10A2 00           1910        DB   0      STAT
10A3 20 14        1920        DW   XST3   STK
10A5 00 00        1930        DW   0      SP
10A7 00           1940        DB   0
10A8              1950 *
10A8 54 10        1960        DW   4:         L4 XJS
10AA 00           1970        DB   0          STAT
10AB 20 14        1980        DW   XST4       STK
10AD 00 00        1990        DW   0          SP
10AF 00           2000        DB   0
10B0              2010 *
10B0 61 10        2020        DW   5.         L5 XJS
10B2 00           2030        DB   0          STAT
10B3 40 14        2040        DW   XST5       STK
10B5 00 00        2050        DW   0          SP
10B7 00           2060        DB   0
10B8              2070 *
10B8 6E 10        2080        DW   6.         L6 XJS
10BA 00           2090        DB   0          STAT
10BB 68 14        2100        DW   XST6       STK
10BD 00 00        2110        DW   0          SP
10BF 00           2120        DB   0
10C0              2130 *
10C0 7B 10        2140        DW   7.         L7 XJS
10C2 00           2150        DB   0          STAT
10C3 90 14        2160        DW   XST7       STK
10C5 00 00        2170        DW   0          SP
```

```
10C9              2210 ,
10C9              2220 *
10C9              2225 **************************
10C9              2226 *
10C9              2228 *     POLL TIME TABLES
10C9              2230 *
10C9              2235 **************************
10C9              2238 *
10C9              2240 XT01   EQU  $
10C9              2250 * TBL FOR 0.1 SEC MIN POLL PGMS
10C9              2260 *- 0.1 SEC: -
10C9 01           2270        DB   1      0.1 SEC
10CA 01           2280        DB   1      ACTIVE TIMER
10CB 00           2290        DB   000    L0,P0
10CC 10           2300        DB   010    L1,P0
10CD 20           2310        DB   020    L2,P0
10CE 30           2320        DB   030    L3,P0
10CF 40           2330        DB   040        L4,P0
10D0 50           2340        DB   050        L5,P0
10D1 60           2350        DB   060        L6,P0
10D2 70           2360        DB   070        L7,P0
10D3 FF           2370        DB   -1     END GROUP
10D4              2380 *- 0.5 SEC: -
10D4 05           2390        DB   5      0.5 SEC
10D5 01           2400        DB   1      TIMER
10D6 00           2410        DB   0          NOP
10D7 11           2420        DB   011    L1,P1
10D8 21           2430        DB   021    L2,P1
10D9 31           2440        DB   031    L3,P1
10DA FF           2450        DB   -1     END GROUP
10DB              2460 *
10DB 00           2470        DB   0      END XT01
10DC              2480 *
10DC              2490 *
10DC              2500 XT10   EQU  $
10DC              2510 *      TBL FOR 1.0 SEC MIN POLL PGMS
10DC              2520 *- 1.0 SEC: -
10DC 01           2530        DB   1      1.0 SEC
10DD 01           2540        DB   1      TIMER
10DE 02           2550        DB   002    L0,P2
10DF 12           2560        DB   012    L1,P2
10E0 22           2570        DB   022    L2,P2
10E1 32           2580        DB   032    L3,P2
10E2 42           2590        DB   042        L4,P2
10E3 43           2600        DB   043        L4,P3
10E4 52           2610        DB   052        L5,P2
10E5 53           2620        DB   053        L5,P3
10E6 62           2630        DB   062        L6,P2
10E7 63           2640        DB   063        L6,P3
10E8 72           2650        DB   072        L7,P2
10E9 73           2660        DB   073        L7,P3
10EA FF           2670        DB   -1     END GROUP
10EB              2680 *- 60.0 SEC. -
10EB 3C           2690        DB   60     60.0 SEC
10EC 01           2700        DB   1      TIMER
10ED 23           2710        DB   023    L2,P3
10EE 33           2720        DB   033    L3,P3
10EF 41           2730        DB   041        L4,P1
10F0 51           2740        DB   051        L5,P1
```

Listing 2: *The level-control and poll-time tables. The level-control table XLT is used to keep track of each level's status individually. It also contains pointers to the stack area and to the job stack for that level. The poll-time tables XT01 and XT10 contain data that point to the programs to be scheduled at that particular poll interval.*

memory with a simple 2-byte change. For each program there is a 3-byte entry in the executive job stack. The first byte contains the program-enable and status bits (the program can be manually enabled or disabled by the user by altering these bits). The next 2 bytes contain the address of the program.

Level-control tables (XLT listing 2)

These tables contain the status byte and the pointers associated with each individual level. Through the use of static and dynamic pointers in this table, the executive is able to execute, suspend, and reenter the different levels while maintaining complete status for the levels. The first 2 bytes point to the beginning of the executive job stack for that level (this address may be modified by the user to relocate or create a new level). The third byte is a status byte that contains level flags (level interrupted, level requested, etc). The fourth and fifth bytes point to an area of memory that will be used as the stack area for that level. The stack pointer is initialized to this address each time a new program is executed on that level. (Each level naturally has its own stack area.) This address may also be modifed to allow for different stack requirments for different levels. When the level is interrupted or suspended, the sixth and seventh bytes are the save address for the current stack pointer. All other status is saved directly on the stack. The last byte is currently unused and is included to make the table length exactly 8 bytes for simpler indexing purposes.

Poll-time tables (listing 2)

These poll-time tables are divided into two major segments, those that are scanned 10 times per second, and those that are scanned once per second. Thus, the various poll groups within each segment may have a minimum resolution (or minimum poll time) of 0.1 second and 1.0 second, respectively. (This

```
10F5                ;
10F5                *
10F5                ***************************
10F5                *
10F5                *    PROGRAM - XRTI
10F5                * DIRCT RTC IRPT HANDLER
10F5                * 1) SCANS POLL TBLS
10F5                * 2) SCHEDULES PGM XQT
10F5                * 3) EXITS TO XSCN
10F5                *
10F5                ***************************
10F5                *
10F5 CD 13 13       XRTI:   CALL XUT0       SAVE ALL STAT
10F8 FB                     EI
10F9 AF                     XOR  A
10FA 32 58 11               LD   (F:),A SET PASS1
10FD 21 C9 10               LD   HL,XT01 .1 SEC TBL
1100 7E             A:      LD   A,(HL)
1101 A7                     AND  A
1102 28 3D                  JR   Z,2:   IF END TBL
1104 23                     INC  HL
1105 35                     DEC  (HL)   COUNT DN
1106 28 09                  JR   Z,5:   IF EXPIRED
1108 3E FF                  LD   A,-1
110A 23             9:      INC  HL
110B BE                     CP   (HL)
110C 20 FC                  JR   NZ,9:
110E 23             6:      INC  HL     ADV TO NXT GROUP
110F 18 EF                  JR   A:
1111                *
1111 2B             5:      DEC  HL     GET POLL
1112 7E                     LD   A,(HL)
1113 23                     INC  HL
1114 77                     LD   (HL),A RESET
1115 3E FF                  LD   A,-1
1117 32 04 10               LD   (XRSC),A  SET RSCN FLG
111A                *
111A 23             8:      INC  HL
111B 7E                     LD   A,(HL)   GET PGM,LVL
111C FE FF                  CP   -1
111E 28 EE                  JR   Z,6:   JP END GROUP
1120 E5                     PUSH HL         SAV POLL INDX
1121 21 88 10               LD   HL,XLT
1124 4F                     LD   C,A    SAVE LLPP
1125 1F                     RRA         A=(LVL*8)=DISPL IN LVL TBL
1126 E6 78                  AND  078    EXTR LVL # BITS
1128 5F                     LD   E,A
1129 16 00                  LD   D,0
112B 19                     ADD  HL,DE  FORM STRT ADDR IN XJS
112C 5E                     LD   E,(HL)
112D 23                     INC  HL
112E 56                     LD   D,(HL)
112F 23                     INC  HL     HL=LCW ADDR
1130 CB FE                  SET  7,(HL) SET LVL REQ
1132 79                     LD   A,C    =PGM #
1133 E6 0F                  AND  0F     B0-3,CA=0
1135 4F                     LD   C,A
1136 17                     RLA         *2
1137 81                     ADD  C      *3
1138 6F                     LD   L,A
1139 26 00                  LD   H,0    HL=DISPL FM LVL STRT
113B 19                     ADD  HL,DE
113C CB F6                  SET  6,(HL)  SET PGM SCHL'D
113E E1                     POP  HL         =POLL INDX
113F 18 D9                  JR   8:
1141                *
1141 3A 58 11       2:      LD   A,(F:)
1144 A7                     AND  A
1145 20 13                  JR   NZ,XSCN   IF END PASS 2,THEN DONE
1147 21 59 11       3:      LD   HL,E:  TIMER
114A 35                     DEC  (HL)   CNT DN
114B 20 0D                  JR   NZ,XSCN  NOT YET
114D 3E 0A                  LD   A,10
114F 77                     LD   (HL),A   RESET
1150 32 58 11               LD   (F:),A     "   PASS 1
1153 21 DC 10               LD   HL,XT10
1156 18 A8                  JR   A:     SCAN 1 SEC POLL TBL
1158                *
1158 00             F:      DB   0      PASS FLG
1159 01             E:      DB   1      ACTV TIMER
115A                :       END  XRTI
```

Listing 3: *The clock-interrupt routine, XRTI. This routine counts down the timers in the poll tables and sets the program ready bits in the job stack for those programs of a poll group that are ready for execution.*

breakdown is done to minimize overhead in the table-scanning routines.) Within each of the two segments, there may exist any number of poll groups, each of them having their own individual poll time, which is always a multiple of the minimum poll time. The first 2 bytes of each poll group are the actual poll time, followed by the active timer. Next comes a list of program pointers of variable length, that is terminated by a byte containing a-1. For each of the program pointers in the group, one program in the job stack will be scheduled at that group's poll time. The program pointer bytes are divided into a high and low 4-bit nybble. The high nybble identifies the level in the job stack, and the low nybble points to a program on that level. This arrangement allows flexibility in assigning varying amounts of poll time to any program on any level of the job stack.

Interrupt-vector tables (XIVT, listing 7)

This table is pointed at by the Z80 mode-2 interrupt register. Any of the eight interrupts connected to this system will cause the processor to perform an automatic indirect call to one of the eight addresses listed in this table. The hardware priority encoder on this system is configured such that devices 0 thru 7 will cause a hexadecimal F0, F2, F4, ... FE to be placed on the processor data bus to be used as the low-order byte of an interrupt table address. The high-order byte is given by the value in the I register, meaning that this table can be easily moved to any page of memory. Currently existing in the table are vectors for the real-time clock interrupt (ie: device 4) and two keyboard interrupts (ie: devices 6 and 7). The vector for device 0 is reserved for the digital cassette or disk interrupt, and the rest are unused. It should be noted that this table can be easily expanded to accommodate up to 128 interrupt vectors (ie: 256 bytes).

Program Structure

The general program structure of the real-time executive is shown in figures 5 and 6 in a Warnier-Orr structured diagram. The following paragraphs describe the four major program segments contained in the executive.

Clock-interrupt routine (XRTI, listing 3)

This program is the direct address to which the real-time clock interrupt is vectored; that is, the hardware interrupt caused by the real-time clock causes this routine to execute. It will first save all processor-status data (subroutine XUTO) and then search for poll groups that require servicing (those with an actual timer value of zero). Upon finding a group that is ready, its poll timer will be reset. Those programs that the group points to will be scheduled by setting the appropriate bit (bit 6) in the job stack control word for that program. After scanning all poll tables that require service, XRTI will exit to the program XSCN. If any programs have been scheduled, a special *rescan flag* will be set. The purpose of the rescan flag will be explained later.

Priority-scanning routine (XSCN, listing 4)

This routine is responsible for performing the priority decisions in the executive. It will scan the level-control tables, searching for a level requiring service. XSCN will be enabled by the rescan flag (which would have been set by XRTI, if any programs were scheduled) or will be cancelled if the flag is not set.

Upon finding any level that has a task pending, priorities will be compared to the current active level. This is normally the level that was suspended at the time the interrupt was received in order to determine whether to service the level immediately or return to the interrupted program. XSCN always starts its scan at level 0 and sequentially advances to the lower levels, thus servicing the highest levels first. When a level request is found and priorities allow, the XSCN routine will exit to XLSC, the next program to execute, setting the proper pointers and status data.

Level-scanning routine (XLSCS, listing 5)

This program will scan one individual level searching for programs that have been enabled by the clock-interrupt routine. It is not concerned with priority since it has already been given the go-ahead by XSCN to execute this level. If the "level interrupted" flag is set, then program control will be returned to whichever program was interrupted, after restoring all status data. If the flag is not set, XLSC will scan this level's job stack for enabled programs and enter them with the stack pointer set at the level's stack area. Eventual return from the programs will be vectored back to XLSC, which will continue to execute the enabled programs one by one until they have all been run. When the level is complete, it will return to XSCN, which will find the next level to scan on a priority basis, and in turn come back to XLSC, to scan the next level, again using the XLSC routine.

In this manner, the executive works its way from the highest level to the lowest, completing all programs on each level. If it is in the middle of a scan and new programs become enabled at higher levels (which have already been scanned), the current scan is aborted and a new one is begun at the highest priority level. This action is initiated by the rescan flag, which is monitored at each interrupt.

Eventually, the executive will complete all levels and have no more work to do. At this time it will go into the executive "no operation" loop and wait for an interrupt to request more tasks. The job

```
115A                 ,
115A                 *
115A                 ***************************************************************
115A                 *
115A                 *    PROGRAM - XSCN
115A                 *
115A                 * 1)  SCANS LVL CTRL TBLS
115A                 * 2)  ENTERS XLSC ON PRIORITY BASIS WHEN LVL IS ACTIVATED
115A                 *     -ENTRY FM XRTI-
115A                 *
115A                 ***************************************************************
115A                 *
115A 3A 04 10        XSCN:  LD   A,(XRSC)
115D A7                     AND  A
115E 20 09                  JR   NZ,2:  IF RSCN RQD
1160 3A 00 10               LD   A,(XAL)
1163 CB 77                  BIT  6,A
1165 20 4E                  JR   NZ,XRTN    IF THIS LVL IRPTD
1167 18 1B                  JR   XNOP
1169                 *
1169                 XSC2   EQU  $          RESCAN XJS
1169 AF              2:     XOR  A
116A 32 04 10               LD   (XRSC),A RESET
116D 3E 80                  LD   A,080
116F 21 88 10               LD   HL,XLT     INIT XLT INDX
1172 32 01 10        C:     LD   (XLVL),A  SET SCAN ACTV,L0
1175 22 1E 10               LD   (XTMP),HL  SAV INDX
1178 7E                     LD   A,(HL)
1179 FE FF                  CP   -1
117B 20 0F                  JR   NZ,7:  IF NOT END
117D                 *
117D 21 00 10               LD   HL,XAL
1180 AF                     XOR  A
1181 77                     LD   (HL),A
1182 23                     INC  HL
1183 77                     LD   (HL),A   SET XAL,XLVL INACTV
1184                 *
1184 31 1E 10        XNOP   LD   SP,XSTK
1187 FB                     EI
1188 00                     NOP
1189 00                     NOP
118A 18 FB                  JR   XNOP+3
118C                 *
118C 23              7:     INC  HL
118D 23                     INC  HL      =STAT ADDR
118E CB 6E                  BIT  5,(HL)
1190 20 04                  JR   NZ,XSC1    IF LVL SUSP
1192 CB 7E                  BIT  7,(HL)
1194 20 0D                  JR   NZ,8:  IF LVL REQ
1196 3A 01 10        XSC1   LD   A,(XLVL)
1199 3C                     INC  A
119A 2A 1E 10               LD   HL,(XTMP)
119D 11 08 00               LD   DE,08
11A0 19                     ADD  HL,DE      ADV XLT INDX
11A1 18 CF                  JR   C:      SRVC NXTLVL
11A3                 *
11A3                 *
11A3                 *
11A3 3A 00 10        8:     LD   A,(XAL)
11A6 CB 77                  BIT  6,A
11A8 28 45                  JR   Z,XLSC      IF LVL NOT IRPTD
11AA E6 0F                  AND  0F
11AC 47                     LD   B,A
11AD 3A 01 10               LD   A,(XLVL)
11B0 E6 0F                  AND  0F
11B2 B8                     CP   B
11B3 38 3A                  JR   C,XLSC      IF CURR ACTV LVL HAS LOWER PRIORITY
11B5                 * ELSE FALL THRU XRTN
11B5                 *
11B5                 XRTN   EQU  $           NORM RET TO IRPTD PROGRAMS
11B5 F3                     DI
11B6 31 1E 10               LD   SP,XSTK
11B9 3A 05 10               LD   A,(XME)
11BC F6 08                  OR   XMSK
11BE D3 02                  OUT  02
11C0 3A 04 10               LD   A,(XRSC)
11C3 A7                     AND  A
11C4 C2 69 11               JP   NZ,XSC2     IF XEXC WAS THE ONE IRPTD, RSCN XJS
11C7 3A 00 10               LD   A,(XAL)
11CA E6 0F                  AND  0F          RESET IRPT BIT
11CC F6 80                  OR   080         ACTV
11CE 32 00 10               LD   (XAL),A
11D1 CD 4D 12               CALL XLAD
11D4 23                     INC  HL
11D5 23                     INC  HL
11D6 CB B6                  RES  6,(HL)      LVL IRPTD
11D8 23                     INC  HL
11D9 23                     INC  HL
11DA 23                     INC  HL
11DB 5E                     LD   E,(HL)
11DC 23                     INC  HL
11DD 56                     LD   D,(HL)      DE=SP
11DE EB                     EX   DE,HL
11DF F9                     LD   SP,HL
11E0 D9                     EXX
11E1 E1                     POP  HL
11E2 D1                     POP  DE
11E3 C1                     POP  BC
11E4 D9                     EXX
11E5 FD E1                  POP  IY
11E7 DD E1                  POP  IX
11E9 E1                     POP  HL
11EA D1                     POP  DE
11EB C1                     POP  BC
11EC F1                     POP  AF
11ED FB                     EI
11EE C9                     RET              BACK T0 IRPTD PGM
11EF                 *
11EF                 *
```

Listing 4: *The priority-scanning routine, XSCN. This routine performs the priority decisions in the executive. It will scan the level control tables and, on a priority basis, find the level that is the next to be serviced.*

loading, as mentioned in previous sections, is directly related to how much time the processor spends in this loop.

Miscellaneous Routines

XEXC (listing 6) — Routine that causes a normal return to the executive. Return is accomplished by a program jumping to the beginning of the routine when it has finished its task. XEXC reads the executive status flags and reenters the executive at the appropriate place, depending upon whether there is a level scan active, a rescan requested, or no levels active.

XIN (listing 6) — Cold-start initialization routine. This routine resets all flags and pointers for a safe entry into the executive. It also initializes the Z80 interrupt register and writes the proper interrupt mask to the hardware. This is the only place the executive should be entered from a cold start or after linking an object program into the executive.

XUTO (listing 7) — Executive subroutine for saving the working registers, processor status data, and stack pointer for any particular level. This subroutine normally is used by the interrupt service routines to save status data at the interrupt level. On entry, the Z80 registers contain the data to be saved, and the pointer XAL contains the level under which it is to be saved. The routine returns with all registers and stack pointer saved, level flags set, and the stack pointer set to the executive stack. After calling this routine, the user program is then free to alter any registers or stack data without destroying any status data of the interrupted program.

XENP (listing 7) — Enable-program routine. This routine allows a user program to access the job stack and schedule programs on demand, independent of the clock routine. Thus, programs may be enabled to execute based on external events rather than through the scheduler. On entry, the first call parameter of the calling routine contains the level and program number (identical to the poll table format) to be enabled. Naturally, when enabling a program through XENP, the status data of the current program is saved and a priority comparison is done such that priority is maintained, even in this mode of scheduling. In this way, a program that is running on a low level may enable a higher-level program, resulting in the higher-level program running and completing before returning from the XENP call to the lower-level caller. This feature is absolutely necessary in some instances, although not always critical — all in all, a good feature.

XEN2 (listing 7) — Similar to XENP, except that interrupt status is not saved and return is always made immediately to the caller. This is generally used by routines

```
11EF            4580 ;
11EF            4582 *
11EF            4584 ********************************************
11EF            4586 *
11EF            4588 *      PROGRAM - XLSC
11EF            4589 *
11EF            4590 * 1)  SCANS 1 LVL, XTMP = LVL ADDR
11EF            4600 * 2)  ENTERS PGMS WHEN ENABLED,AND SCHL'D
11EF            4610 * 3)  EXITS TO XSCN WHEN LVL COMPLETE
11EF            4620 *
11EF            4623 ********************************************
11EF            4627 *
11EF 2A 1E 10   4630 XLSC:  LD   HL,(XTMP)  GET LVL ADDR
11F2 5E         4640        LD   E,(HL)
11F3 23         4650        INC  HL
11F4 56         4660        LD   D,(HL)
11F5 23         4670        INC  HL
11F6 ED 53 02 10 4680       LD   (XPGM),DE  SAV XJS INDEX
11FA CB BE      4690        RES  7,(HL)  LVL REQ
11FC CB 76      4700        BIT  6,(HL)
11FE 20 3B      4710        JR   NZ,1:  IF THIS LVL WAS IRPT'D
1200 2A 02 10   4720 XLS1   LD   HL,(XPGM)
1203 7E         4730        LD   A,(HL) =PGM STAT WD
1204 23         4740        INC  HL
1205 5E         4750        LD   E,(HL)
1206 23         4760        INC  HL
1207 56         4770        LD   D,(HL)
1208 23         4780        INC  HL
1209 22 02 10   4790        LD   (XPGM),HL
120C FE FF      4800        CP   -1
120E CA 96 11   4810        JP   Z,XSC1     IF END LVL
1211 17         4820        RLA
1212 30 EC      4830        JR   NC,XLS1   NOT ENABLED
1214 17         4840        RLA
1215 30 E9      4850        JR   NC,XLS1   NOT SCHED
1217 2B         4860        DEC  HL
1218 2B         4870        DEC  HL
1219 2B         4880        DEC  HL
121A CB B6      4890        RES  6,(HL)   PGM SCHED BIT
121C 2A 1E 10   4900        LD   HL,(XTMP)
121F 23         4910        INC  HL
1220 23         4920        INC  HL
1221 23         4930        INC  HL
1222 4E         4940        LD   C,(HL)
1223 23         4950        INC  HL
1224 46         4960        LD   B,(HL)
1225 69         4970        LD   L,C
1226 60         4980        LD   H,B    HL=STACK ADDR
1227 F9         4990        LD   SP,HL
1228 EB         5000        EX   DE,HL
1229 F3         5010        DI
122A 3A 05 10   5020        LD   A,(XME)
122D F6 08      5030        OR   XMSK
122F D3 02      5040        OUT  02
1231 3A 01 10   5050        LD   A,(XLVL)
1234 F6 80      5060        OR   080
1236 32 00 10   5070        LD   (XAL),A   SET THIS LVL CURRENT,AND ACTV
1239 FB         5080        EI
123A E9         5090        JP   (HL)
123B            5100 *
123B CB 6E      5110 1:     BIT  5,(HL)
123D C2 96 11   5120        JP   NZ,XSC1    SKIP IF LVL SUSP.
1240 CB B6      5130        RES  6,(HL)     LVL IRPTD
1242 CB FE      5140        SET  7,(HL) LVL REQ
1244 3A 01 10   5150        LD   A,(XLVL)
1247 32 00 10   5160        LD   (XAL),A    SET THIS SCAN LVL ACTV
124A C3 B5 11   5170        JP   XRTN
124D            5180 *
124D            5190 *
124D            5200 * SUBR XLAD, CALC XLT ADDR FM A(LVL#)
124D            5210 *
124D E6 0F      5220 XLAD   AND  0F      B0-3
124F 17         5230        RLA
1250 17         5240        RLA
1251 17         5250        RLA          *8
1252 5F         5260        LD   E,A
1253 16 00      5270        LD   D,0
1255 21 88 10   5280        LD   HL,XLT
1258 19         5290        ADD  HL,DE
1259 C9         5300        RET
125A            5310 *
```

Listing 5: *The level-scanning routine, XLSC. This routine does the actual scanning of any particular level. It is entered from XSCN, which has already determined priority and authorized XLSC to scan a given level. Depending on the status of the level, this routine will either enter the level (if scheduled), skip the level (if suspended), or reenter the level (if interrupted).*

that are running at the interrupt level, having already suspended the interrupted program, saved the status data, and taken priority from the executive.

Efficiency

Does the executive load down the processor considerably with its priority scheduling? How much time does it consume? Is it efficient? In approximating the executive's efficiency by summing up the execution times of the various loops required to schedule and enter programs, the following can be calculated:

Assuming an executive with eight levels, at four programs per level (thirty-two total), using the Z80 (2.5 MHz):

Clock routine, poll table scanning	2.7 ms
Priority level scanning and execution	5.5 ms
TOTAL	8.2 ms

These figures may vary slightly depending on the exact arrangement of job stack and poll tables. The total time is 8.2 ms; for thirty-two programs scheduled once per second, the executive loading is 0.82 percent, and for thirty-two programs scheduled at 100 ms, the loading is 8.2 percent.

Depending on the poll intervals, a system with thirty-two programs will have an executive loading somewhere between the above two numbers. (Typically, the result should be very close to 0.82 percent, since in a typical home system, very few programs will be required to run at ten times per second. Also the total number of programs would be much less than thirty-two, giving a direct proportional reduction in overhead. Thus, the above figures can be considered as a maximum for most home computer systems.

Implementation Examples

Now that we have the basic real-time system to handle programs on a priority basis, we must give the system some practical tasks to perform. This section will describe the interface to the executive using general examples of the most common programs and peripherals which may be found on a typical home computer system.

The objective of this executive design, as far as software is concerned, is to be able to easily interface new or existing programs without having to write special coding to do so. From the hardware point of view, the general interface philosophy is to parallel the previous ready, strobe, or status lines from the peripheral devices as interrupt inputs to the hardware priority chain. The already existing input and output ports to these devices are still used to communicate to the real-time system, as well as to previous systems, with no changes required other than the loading of different software.

```
125A                 5320 ;
125A                 5322 *
125A                 5324 **************************
125A                 5326 *
125A                 5330 *       NORMAL RET TO EXEC
125A                 5340 *
125A                 5345 **************************
125A                 5347 *
125A F3              5350 XEXC:  DI
125B 3A 00 10        5360        LD   A,(XAL)
125E CB 7F           5370        BIT  7,A
1260 CA 84 11        5380        JP   Z,XNOP     IF NO LVL ACTV
1263 CB BF           5390        RES  7,A
1265 32 00 10        5400        LD   (XAL),A    SET INACTV
1268 31 1E 10        5410        LD   SP,XSTK
126B FB              5420        EI
126C 3A 04 10        5430        LD   A,(XRSC)
126F A7              5440        AND  A
1270 C2 69 11        5450        JP   NZ,XSC2    IF PGMS REQ WHILE AWAY
1273 3A 01 10        5460        LD   A,(XLVL)
1276 CB 7F           5470        BIT  7,A
1278 CA 84 11        5480        JP   Z,XNOP     IF SCAN NOT ACTV
127B C3 F2 11        5490        JP   XLSC+3     CONT SCAN
127E                 5500 *
127E                 5510 *    - STACK AREA -
127E                 5520 *
127E                 5530        DS   40         LONGER STK FOR KB RTNS
12A6                 5540 XST0   EQU  $
12A6                 5550 *
12A6                 5560        DS   32
12C6                 5570 XST1   EQU  $
12C6                 5580 *
12C6                 5590        DS   32
12E6                 5600 XST2   EQU  $
12E6                 5610 *
12E6                 5620 *
12E6                 5630 *
12E6                 5640 **** - NOTE XST-3,4,5,6,7  PLACED IN PAGE 4
12E6                 5650 *
12E6                 5660 ;
12E6                 5662 *
12E6                 5665 ***********************************
12E6                 5670 * PROGRAM - XIN
12E6                 5672 * COLD START INITILIZATION ROUTINE
12E6                 5674 *
12E6                 5676 ***********************************
12E6                 5678 *
12E6 F3              5680 XIN    DI
12E7 AF              5690        XOR  A
12E8 21 00 10        5700        LD   HL,XAL
12EB 77              5710        LD   (HL),A
12EC 23              5720        INC  HL
12ED 77              5730        LD   (HL),A   XLVL
12EE 23              5740        INC  HL
12EF 23              5750        INC  HL
12F0 77              5760        LD   (HL),A    XRSC
12F1 ED 5E           5770        IM   2
12F3 21 F0 13        5780        LD   HL,XIVT  IRPT TABLE
12F6 7C              5790        LD   A,H
12F7 ED 47           5800        LD   I,A    SET IRPT PAGE #
12F9 3A 05 10        5810        LD   A,(XME)
12FC F6 08           5820        OR   XMSK       SET IRPT MASK
12FE D3 02           5830        OUT  02
1300 21 88 10        5840        LD   HL,XLT     STRT AT TOP OF LVLS
1303 7E              5850 1:     LD   A,(HL)
1304 FE FF           5860        CP   -1
1306 CA 5A 12        5870        JP   Z,XEXC     DONE
1309 23              5880        INC  HL
130A 23              5890        INC  HL
130B AF              5900        XOR  A
130C 77              5910        LD   (HL),A     CLR LVL STATUS
130D 11 06 00        5920        LD   DE,6
1310 19              5930        ADD  HL,DE      ADV TO NXT
1311 18 F0           5940        JR   1:
1313                 5950 *
```

Listing 6: *The normal-return and cold-start routines, XEXC and XIN. XEXC is the normal return to the executive after any program has finished execution. This routine reads the executive status and enters the executive at the proper point. XIN is the cold-start initialization routine, which is the only point from which the executive should be entered after loading the executive into memory or after running other software. It initializes pointers and flags in the executive, insuring a safe execution.*

```
1313                5960 ; XEXC UTIL, SAVS STAT & SP, SETS LVL IRPTD
1313                5970 *
1313 F3             5980 XUT0   DI
1314 22 6E 13       5990        LD   (1:),HL      TMP SAV
1317 E1             6000        POP  HL
1318 22 70 13       6010        LD   (2:),HL      SAV XUT0 RET
131B 2A 6E 13       6020        LD   HL,(1:)      RESTORE HL
131E F5             6030        PUSH AF
131F 21 00 10       6040        LD   HL,XAL
1322 CB 7E          6050        BIT  7,(HL)
1324 CB BE          6060        RES  7,(HL)
1326 20 0C          6070        JR   NZ,3:        IF LVL ACTV
1328 3E FF          6080        LD   A,-1
132A 32 04 10       6090        LD   (XRSC),A
132D 31 1E 10       6100        LD   SP,XSTK
1330 2A 70 13       6110        LD   HL,(2:)
1333 E9             6120        JP   (HL)         BACK TO CALLER
1334 CB F6          6130 3:     SET  6,(HL)       LVL IRPTD
1336 2A 6E 13       6140        LD   HL,(1:)      RESTORE
1339 C5             6150        PUSH BC           CONT, SAV REG
133A D5             6160        PUSH DE
133B E5             6170        PUSH HL
133C DD E5          6180 0:     PUSH IX
133E FD E5          6190        PUSH IY
1340 D9             6200        EXX               SAV AUX REG
1341 C5             6210        PUSH BC
1342 D5             6220        PUSH DE
1343 E5             6230        PUSH HL
1344 D9             6240        EXX
1345 3A 00 10       6250        LD   A,(XAL)
1348 CD 4D 12       6260        CALL XLAD         HL=LVL ADDR
134B 3A 05 10       6270        LD   A,(XME)
134E F6 08          6280        OR   XMSC
1350 D3 02          6290        OUT  02           SET XEXC MSK+EXT BITS
1352 23             6300        INC  HL
1353 23             6310        INC  HL
1354 CB F6          6320        SET  6,(HL)       LVL IRPTD
1356 44             6330        LD   B,H
1357 4D             6340        LD   C,L
1358 23             6350        INC  HL
1359 23             6360        INC  HL
135A 23             6370        INC  HL
135B EB             6380        EX   DE,HL
135C 21 00 00       6390        LD   HL,0
135F 39             6400        ADD  HL,SP
1360 EB             6410        EX   DE,HL        DE=SP,HL=SAV ADDR
1361 73             6420        LD   (HL),E
1362 23             6430        INC  HL
1363 72             6440        LD   (HL),D
1364 31 1E 10       6450        LD   SP,XSTK
1367 2A 70 13       6460        LD   HL,(2:)
136A E5             6470        PUSH HL           =RET
136B 60             6480        LD   H,B
136C 69             6490        LD   L,C          HL=LCW ADDR
136D C9             6500        RET               BACK TO CALLER
136E                6510 *
136E 00 00          6520 1:     DW   0            TMP HL SAV
1370 00 00          6530 2:     DW   0            RET SAV
1372                6540 *
1372                6550 ;
1372                6560 ****************************************
1372                6570 *
1372                6580 * 1)  XENP,ENABLE PGM RTN
1372                6590 *          CALL XENP
1372                6600 *          DB   0LP  L=LVL#, P=PGM#
1372                6610 * 2)  XEN1 (SAME AS XENP, BUT A HAS 0LP.
1372                6620 *
1372                6630 * -XENP,XEN1 ENABLE AT PGM LVL,& RET TO CALER ON PRIO BASIS
1372                6640 * 3)  XEN2,SAME AS XEN1,BUT RET IMMED,(FOR IRPT LVL SERVC)
1372                6650 *
1372                6655 ****************************************
1372                6657 *
1372 E1             6660 XENP:  POP  HL
1373 7E             6670        LD   A,(HL)
1374 23             6680        INC  HL
1375 E5             6690        PUSH HL           ADV RET
1376 32 83 13       6700 XEN1   LD   (0:),A
1379 CD 13 13       6710        CALL XUT0         SET LVL IRPT SAV STAT
137C CD 84 13       6720        CALL 2:           SET PGM BITS
137F FB             6730        EI
1380 C3 69 11       6740        JP   XSC2         RESCAN XJS
1383                6750 *
1383 00             6760 0:     DB   0            TMP SAV FOR 0LP
1384                6770 *
1384                6780 2:     EQU  $            SUBR SETS PGB ENBL BITS
1384 21 83 13       6790        LD   HL,0:
1387 ED 6F          6800        RLD               A=LVL#
1389 CD 4D 12       6810        CALL XLAD         GET LVL ADDR
138C 5E             6820        LD   E,(HL)
138D 23             6830        INC  HL
138E 56             6840        LD   D,(HL)
138F 23             6850        INC  HL           DE=XJS ADDR
1390 CB FE          6860        SET  7,(HL)       LVL REQ
1392 21 83 13       6870        LD   HL,0:
1395 ED 6F          6880        RLD               A=PGM#
1397 E6 0F          6890        AND  0F
1399 47             6900        LD   B,A
139A 17             6910        RLA               *2
139B 80             6920        ADD  B            *3
139C 6F             6930        LD   L,A
139D 26 00          6940        LD   H,0          HL=DISPL TO PGM
139F 19             6950        ADD  HL,DE
13A0 CB F6          6960        SET  6,(HL)       SET PGM SCHLD
13A2 C9             6970        RET
13A3                6980 *
13A3                6990 *
13A3 32 83 13       7000 XEN2   LD   (0:),A       SAV 0LP
13A6 CD 84 13       7010        CALL 2:
13A9 3E FF          7020        LD   A,-1
13AB 32 04 10       7030        LD   (XRSC),A     RESCN XJS
13AE C9             7040        RET
13AF                7050 *
```

```
13D7                7510 ;
13D7                7512 ***********************************************************
13D7                7514 *
13D7                7520 * Z80 IRPT VECTOR TABLE (STARTS AT END OF PAGE BOUNDRY)
13D7                7530 *
13D7                7535 ***********************************************************
13D7                7538 *
13D7                7540        ORG  XAL+03F0     TOP OF PAGE 3
13F0                7550 XIVT   EQU  $
13F0                7560 *
13F0 E6 12          7570        DW   XIN          0
13F2                7580 *
13F2 E6 12          7590        DW   XIN          1
13F4                7600 *
13F4 E6 12          7610        DW   XIN          2
13F6                7620 *
13F6 F5 10          7630        DW   XRTI         RTC
13F8                7640 *
13F8 E6 12          7650        DW   XIN          4
13FA                7660 *
13FA E6 12          7670        DW   XIN          5
13FC                7680 *
13FC 00 00      U   7690        DW   KBI0         KYBD 0
13FE                7700 *
13FE 00 00      U   7710        DW   KBI1         KYBD 1
1400                7720 *
1400                7730 *
1400                7740 *
1400                7750 **** - REST OF XEXC STACK -
1400                7760 *
1400                7770 *
1400                7780        DS   32
1420                7790 XST3   EQU  $
1420                7800 XST4   EQU  $
1420                7810 *
1420                7820        DS   32
1440                7830 XST5   EQU  $
1440                7840 *
1440                7850        DS   40           FOR KB RTNS
1468                7860 XST6   EQU  $
1468                7870 *
1468                7880        DS   40           FOR KB RTNS
1490                7890 XST7   EQU  $
1490                7900 *
1490                7910 *

XAL  1000   XLVL 1001   XPGM 1002   XRSC 1004   XMSK 0008   XMSC 0008
XME  1005   XSTK 101E   XTMP 101E   XJS  1020   XLT  1088   XT01 10C9
XT10 10DC   XRTI 10F5   XSCN 115A   XSC2 1169   XNOP 1184   XSC1 1196
XRTN 11B5   XLSC 11EF   XLS1 1200   XLAD 124D   XEXC 125A   XST0 12A6
XST1 12C6   XST2 12E6   XIN  12E6   XUT0 1313   XENP 1372   XEN1 1376
XEN2 13A3   XRLE 13AF   XSUS 13B8   XSU1 13BC   XREN 13C4   XRE1 13C8
XIVT 13F0   XST3 1420   XST4 1420   XST5 1440   XST6 1468   XST7 1490
```

Listing 7: *Enable-program and save-registers routines, XENP and XUTO, and the Z80 mode-2 interrupt table, XIVT. Routine XENP is an enable program routine that allows user programs to index the job stack and thereby enable program execution regardless of the real-time clock scheduler. Priority is maintained by this routine. XUTO saves the status data of an interrupted program. The level indicator variable XAL points to the level for which the status data will be saved. XIVT is the Z80 mode-2 interrupt-vector table. It contains the addresses of the direct-interrupt service routines linked to each interrupt line.*

REAL-TIME CLOCK INTERRUPT		See Figure 6	
+			Set Level Pointer = 0
		Rescan Request	Start New Scan
	Level Active	+ (0,1)	
	(0,1)	No	
Normal Return	+	Rescan Request	Reenter
		(0,1)	"XLSC", Continue Scan
To Executive	Level Not	No-Operation Loop	
	Active		
	(0,1)		
+			
	Set level 0, Inactive (1,1)		
	Reset Rescan Flag (1,1)		
Initialization	Initialize IRPT Register (1,1)		
	Update Hardware IRPT Mask (1,1)		
	Clear Level Status Word (1,1)		
	Exit to "XEXC" (1,1)		
	Save Status (XUTO)	Debug in use	Skip
+	(1,1)	(0,1)	
	Read Keyboard		
	Save Character		
	(1,1)		
		+	
	Character = "CTRLP"		
	(0,1)		
Keyboard(N)		Debug not in use	Enable Debug Program
Interrupt			
	+	(0,1)	Skip
			Reset Keyboard request (1,1)
		Keyboard	
		Input	Index to requesting
		Request	Level number (1,1)
		(0,1)	Reset level
	Character $\neq$ "CTRLP"		Suspended Flag (1,1)
	(0,1)		
		+	Rescan Job stack (1,1)
			(XSCN)
		No	
		Keyboard	Return to
		Input	Interrupted
		Request	Program
		(0,1)	

Figure 5: *A Warnier-Orr diagram of the real-time executive program structure. This diagram shows the three possible dynamic entry points to the executive and an example of a common peripheral interrupt device (keyboard). The "normal return to executive" entry at top is from programs that have finished executing and are returning program control to the executive.*

	Save Interrupt Status (1,1)	Index Program pointer (1,p+1)	Set Rescan Request Schedule program (p,p)		
	Advance Poll Timers Group (1,1)	Not End, Poll (1,1)	Next p (p,p)		
	Poll timer expired (0,1)	+			
	+	End Poll Group			
	None Expired (1,1)	(1,p) Skip	Skip		
		Initialize Level Index (1,1)	Level suspended (0,L)	Next L	
			+	Current Active Level Higher	Reenter Current Active Level
Real Time Clock Interrupt	Rescan Request (0,1)	Level Request (1,L)	Level Interrupted (0,L)	+ Not Higher	Restore This, Levels Status Re-enter this Level
		+	+		
	+		Level Ready	Program enabled (1,p) +	Set new stack (1,1) Execute new program
		No Level Request (1,L)	Next L	Program not enabled	NEXT p
	No Rescan Request (0,1)	Level active Now (0,1)	Reenter interrupted program (0,1)		
		+ No level active now (0,1)	No-operation loop		

Figure 6: *A Warnier-Orr diagram of the real-time clock interrupt structure. This diagram shows the general sequence of events occurring within or subsequent to the real-time clock interrupt. (This figure is a continuation of figure 5.)*

Interfacing keyboards

Hardware:

Figure 7 presents two variations of a typical keyboard/computer interface. The keyboard will be connected to the processor I/O bus and read through a typical input instruction. The lower bits of the port will have the ASCII code for any key, and one of the high-order bits (usually the most significant bit) will be the *key-pressed* strobe signal. Alternatively, for remote keyboards there may be a serial interface from a remote station to the computer, with a serial receiver (usually a UART) connected to the I/O bus or buffered through an I/O port. In this case, the interface is similar except that the *data-available* status signal of the serial receiver is used to generate the *key-pressed* strobe, which is also connected to the most significant bit of the input port. It is very easy to interface these keyboards to the real-time system. The hardware configuration is left exactly as is (thereby not interfering with the original mode of operation), and an extra line is added from the strobe bit to the interrupt-request latch, thus paralleling the most significant bit of the input port. The strobe signal on some systems may need further conditioning before being presented to the interrupt-request latch. This, however, depends upon the hardware setup used to set and reset the interrupt request. This arrangement allows the same keyboard to be used in either mode of operation, without need of any hardware changes to switch from one mode to another. Batch-mode operation will be required to run with interrupts disabled; otherwise, the keyboard-interrupt line will have to be disconnected for this mode.

Software:

The appropriate software interface to the keyboards shown in figure 7 would be a subroutine that accepts inputs from either keyboard on the system. Usually

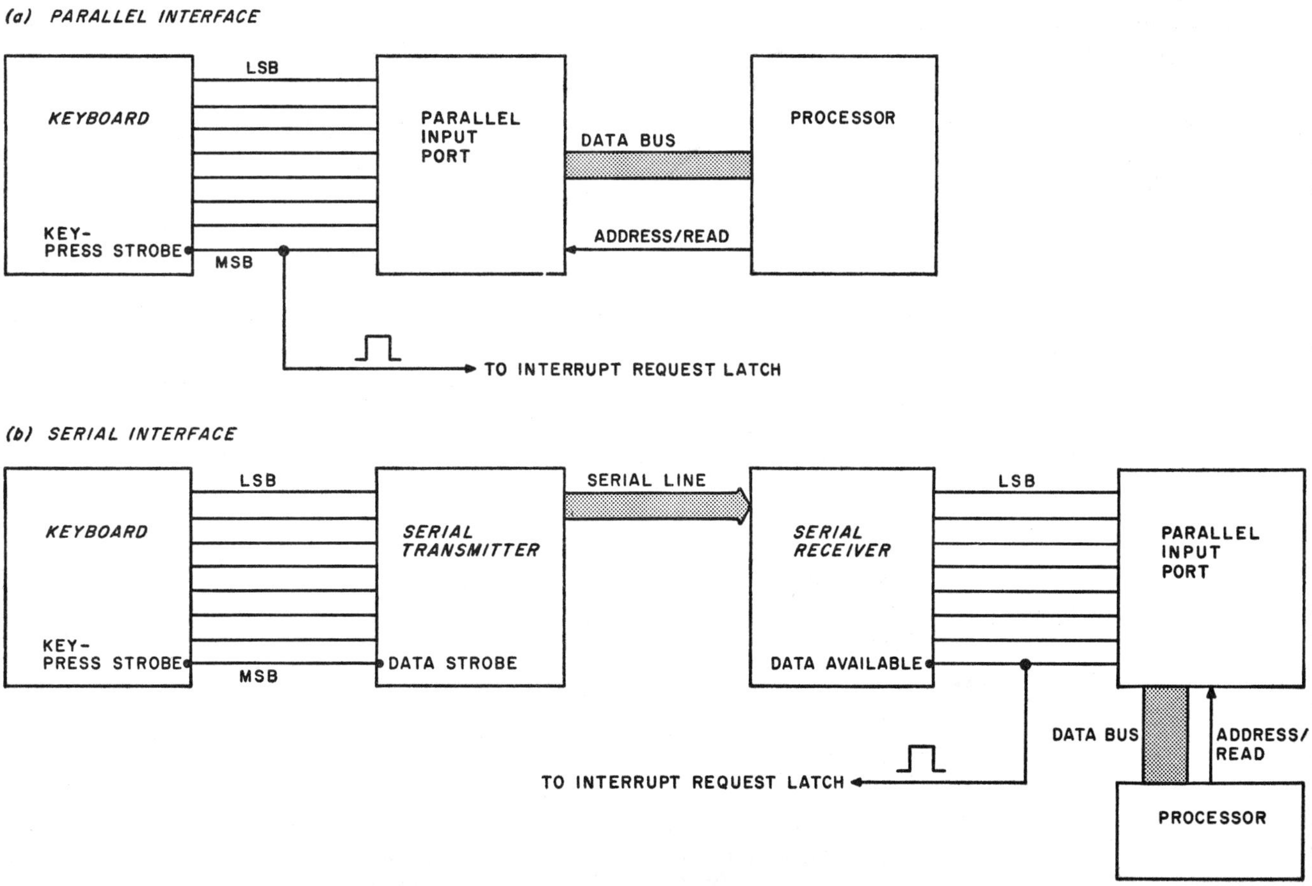

Figure 7: *Two block diagrams showing possible keyboard interfaces to the real-time executive. In both the parallel (a) and serial (b) cases, the keyboard can be interfaced to the executive using the already existing key-pressed or data-available signals to generate the keyboard interrupt. Paralleling these signals allows the same hardware configuration to be used for both real-time and batch modes of operation.*

```
162E                ;
162E                ****************************************
162E                * SUBR, IP FM KYBDS ON REAL TIME BASIS
162E                *
162E                * -USE  CALL   INKB
162E                *        DB     N      N=KYBD#
162E                *
162E                * -OR:  CALL  INK1   A=KBD#
162E                *
162E                *        USES A,BC
162E                ****************************************
162E C1             INKB:  POP  BC
162F 0A                    LD   A,(BC)    KB#
1630 03                    INC  BC
1631 C5                    PUSH BC        ADV RTRN
1632 01 64 16       INK1   LD   BC,0·     KB TBLS
1635 E6 03                 AND  03
1637 07                    RLCA           *2
1638 81                    ADD  C
1639 4F                    LD   C,A
163A 30 01                 JR   NC,$+1
163C 04                    INC  B         ADD A TO BC
163D C5                    PUSH BC        SAV TBL ADDR
163E 03                    INC  BC
163F 0A                    LD   A,(BC)
1640 17                    RLA            TST B7
1641 38 19                 JR   C,A:      IF CHAR READY NOW
1643 0B                    DEC  BC        ELSE RCL INDX
1644 3A 00 10              LD   A,(XAL)
1647 CB FF                 SET  7,A       SET ACTV
1649 02                    LD   (BC),A    SET ENBL,AND USER LVL#
164A 01 5C 16              LD   BC,A:     BC=IRPT RET ADDR
164D C5                    PUSH BC
164E CD 13 13              CALL XUT0      FORCE LVL IRPTD
1651 CB EE                 SET  5,(HL)    SUSP. LVL
1653 21 00 10              LD   HL,XAL
1656 CB B6                 RES  6,(HL)    DE-ACTV CUR LVL
1658 FB                    EI
1659 C3 96 11              JP   XSC1      ON TO NXT LVL IN XJS
165C                *
165C                A:     EQU  $         IRPT RET ADDR
165C C1                    POP  BC        TBL ADDR
165D 03                    INC  BC
165E 0A                    LD   A,(BC)    =CHAR FM KBD
165F F5                    PUSH AF
1660 AF                    XOR  A
1661 02                    LD   (BC),A    RESET CHAR RCV FLG
1662 F1                    POP  AF        RCL CHAR
1663 C9                    RET            BACK TO CALLER
1664                *
1664                * -KYBD TBLS,2 BYTES PER TBL
1664                *
1664                INKT   EQU  $
1664                0:     EQU  $         TBLS STRT
1664 00                    DB   0         KB0,LVL FLG
1665 00                    DB   0         CHAR SAV
1666                *
1666 00             1:     DB   0         KB1,LVL FLG
1667 00                    DB   0         CHAR SAV
166C                ;
166C                ***************************************************
166C                *
166C                *  DIRECT INTERRUPT HANDLER FOR ALL KEYBOARDS (8:)
166C                *  KEYBOARD 0 - KBI0
166C                *  KEYBOARD 1 - KBI1
166C                *
166C                ***************************************************
166C                *
166C                KBI0   EQU  $         KB0 DIRECT IRPT HANDLER
166C CD 13 13              CALL XUT0      SAV STAT
166F 3E 00                 LD   A,0
1671 0E 00                 LD   C,0       A=KB# , C=DA
1673                8·     EQU  $         COMMON ENTRY FOR ALL KYBDS
1673 21 64 16              LD   HL,0·
1676 E6 03                 AND  03        MSK KBD #
1678 07                    RLCA           *2
1679 85                    ADD  L
167A 6F                    LD   L,A
167B 30 01                 JR   NC,$+1
167D 24                    INC  H
167E ED 78                 IN   (C),A     READ CHAR
1680 23                    INC  HL
1681 CB FF                 SET  7,A       SET STRB IN CASE MISSED
1683 77                    LD   (HL),A    SAV CHAR
1684 2B                    DEC  HL
1685 FE 90                 CP   090       CHK CTRL P
1687 20 0D                 JR   NZ,7:
1689 3A 00 00     U        LD   A,(XDBF)
168C A7                    AND  A         CHK FOR DBUG IN USE
168D 20 07                 JR   NZ,7:
168F E5                    PUSH HL        SAV INDX
1690 3E 01                 LD   A,01      L0,P1
1692 CD A3 13              CALL XEN2      ENABLE DBG PGM
1695 E1                    POP  HL        RCL INDX
1696 CB 7E          7:     BIT  7,(HL)
1698 20 03                 JR   NZ,9:     IF KBD ENBLD
169A C3 B5 11              JP   XRTN      BACK TP PGM IF NOT
169D                *
169D CB BE          9:     RES  7,(HL)    ACK CHAR RCVD
169F 7E                    LD   A,(HL)    LVL #
16A0 CD 4D 12              CALL XLAD      GET USER LVL#
16A3 23                    INC  HL
16A4 23                    INC  HL
16A5 CB AE                 RES  5,(HL)    LVL SUSP
16A7 FB                    EI
16A8 C3 69 11              JP   XSC2      DO XJS RSCN
16AB                *
16AB                *
16AB                KBI1   EQU  $         KB1 DIRCT IRPT HANDLER
16AB 3E 01                 LD   A,01
16AD 0E 05                 LD   C,05
16AF 18 C2                 JR   8:        ENTER RTN
16B1                *
```

Listing 8: *The real-time keyboard input routine. This routine is given in two parts. The first part, INKB, suspends the current level and enables the keyboard input. The second part, KBIO, is the direct-interrupt handler for the keyboards. This routine reads the keyboard, saves the character, and eventually returns to INKB on a priority basis through the executive.*

this subroutine is called with a register pointing at the keyboard number or the device address of the keyboard to be read. When a key is pressed, the routine returns with a register or memory location containing the ASCII code for the key pressed. These subroutines work by reading the status of the strobe bit, looping until true, and returning with a register set to the value read last. Usually, for well-structured software, there will be only one such routine that all higher programs use. Therefore, to make a simple interface of new or existing software to the real-time executive, we create a similar routine that functionally replaces it. All calls in the existing software to the old routine would be replaced by calls to the real-time keyboard routine. The higher-level programs can therefore run the software with *no changes required*. These programs will be unaware that the keyboard routine has been changed.

We cannot create a real-time program that loops on a keyboard strobe. It would waste too much time, or it could be interrupted and miss the strobe signal. How, then, do we handle a keyboard input on a real-time basis?

Listing 8 shows the keyboard program and its associated interrupt service routine, which is functionally identical to the looping keyboard input routine. This routine handles any number of keyboards and users "simultaneously" on a real-time basis. It always returns to the proper user with the received ASCII key and with all registers and status data restored (except for the accumulator, which contains the received key, and the BC register pair, which contains the address of the keyboard table).

This routine is split into two parts. The first part, INKB, indexes the appropriate keyboard table, sets enable flags in this table, saves all status data, and then suspends the current level. Program control is then given to the executive, which will continue with the other levels on the system, bypassing the level that is requesting the key; this last level stays in the suspended state. Thus, the program that called the keyboard routine will also be suspended, just as if it were looping on a key-strobe signal.

The second part, KBIO, is the actual keyboard interrupt service routine. This routine saves the status of the program that was interrupted when the key was pressed, indexes its own appropriate keyboard table, and checks to see which level is requesting a key from this keyboard. If no levels have made a request, then the routine simply returns to the interrupted program. If some level is waiting on this keyboard, the keyboard will be read, the input-key data will be saved in the table, the requesting level will be reenabled, and then the routine will be exited to a rescan of the executive levels. The rescan will eventually result (as priorities allow) in the original suspended key-requesting level being reentered with all status data restored. Reentry is back to the routine INKB, which then loads the saved key from the table and returns to the caller. The calling program continues on, unaware that this has occurred and is content with the key data just received.

One additional note: this particular interrupt routine has an extra bit of coding that is used to enable the executive debug program upon receiving a Control-P. This function is done at the interrupt level to give an absolute priority to the debug program (thus providing a type of "panic button" recovery from any routine without disturbing the real-time system). This coding does not interfere with the normal keyboard-input function and has other uses that will be discussed later.

Foreground/Background Programs

As shown in the previous section, we now have a method to use many of our existing programs on a real-time basis by implementing a real-time keyboard routine, which is the functional equivalent of previous batch-type keyboard routines. In addition to this I/O interface, the program itself must be linked to the executive and given a priority.

There are two types of programs discussed in this section, referred to here as *foreground* and *background* programs. As used here, foreground refers to programs that are continuously enabled and are running on a regular basis. Sometimes referred to as polled or cyclic programs, these types will perform their tasks at regular intervals through the scheduler. They normally will not be associated with external devices such as keyboards or peripherals which require status looping or interrupts. Examples of these programs (from the system described earlier) are: security monitoring, analog input monitoring, timekeeping, etc. The linking of these programs is simple and straightforward, merely requiring the user to assign a priority level to the program, enter its starting address in the job stack at that level (make sure that the exit point of the program is to XEXC of the executive), assign a poll time in one of the poll tables, and set the enable bit in the job stack.

Background programs are referred to here as those that may be required to be suspended (eg: waiting for a peripheral) or simply disabled for a period of time. They may also be those that are of lesser importance in terms of execution speed, and perhaps those that take considerable time themselves to execute. An example would be the BASIC calculation described earlier.

Background programs must also be given a priority and placed in the job stack. However, poll times are not given to these programs, since they are not to be scheduled regularly. Examples of these are: disk or tape operating systems that handle programs such as high-level languages, text editors, assemblers, etc; keyboard input utilities such as system debugging; or other programs that service peripherals and operate in an unscheduled manner.

One necessary requirement of background programs is a means for them to be initially enabled and eventually disabled when completed. This must be done by a user-initiated action that causes the execution of a routine that eventually enables the program. A special button that activates the program request by being polled or by causing an interrupt can be used for this operation, although a more logical device is the keyboard. Use of the keyboard, however, requires special provisions, since it is also used for normal operator communication and data entry, which must not be confused with function selection. A good example of how to implement this feature is shown in listing 8, where the Control-P is used to enable the debug program, which is a background executive utility.

By implementing such a scheme at the interrupt level, global priority may be given to a keyboard to enable or disable background programs, regardless of whether the keyboard is or is not currently servicing a function. A proposed scheme is to extend the example of listing 8 and use a separate control key for each major background program on the system, thus allowing users at different terminals to enable and use these background programs (provided they are not already in use at another terminal).

Priority Assigning

Now that the two major types of programs have been identified, how do we determine what priority to assign these programs? Priority should be selected according to how the user wishes the system to operate, with respect to the priority rules presented earlier. Normally priority will not be extremely critical, unless the programs themselves consume a very large amount of time or are critical in respect to the execution interval. As an example, an assembler which consumes large amounts of time must be put in a low-priority region. However, also within this low-priority region are programs that may be simultaneously resident with the assembler. It must be determined which one should be completed before the others are allowed to run. Since they all have a relatively low priority, it is not a critical decision and is determined by the designer's own preference, based on the average amount of time each program will take, as well as various other system configuration aspects.

Foreground programs should always be put in the medium priority region above any background programs that are likely to consume a lot of time. These are the programs that are expected to execute once per second, for example. Medium priority foreground programs may not be executed at exactly the time interval specified by their poll time, since these levels are subject to being interrupted by higher levels. As a result, execution is delayed past the poll time by an amount equal to the total execution time of all the interrupting programs.

Foreground programs required to run at exceedingly close tolerances to their poll time should be placed at the highest priority levels. Those foreground programs performing operations on which lower-level programs rely should also be placed at the highest levels. For example, assume there is an analog input routine that reads a multiplexed analog-to-digital converter and saves the data in memory for subsequent use by other programs. Assume, also, that both the analog input routine and the programs that use its data are run once per second. Naturally, the analog read program should execute first so that the data used by the other programs will be the most current readings. Therefore, the priority of the analog-read program should be set higher than that of the other programs.

For programs on the same level, which has the highest priority? Does priority even exist on any individual level? For this executive, all programs on a given level have equal priority. However, a slight difference in their execution mode may be thought of as a type of priority. Due to the manner in which the executive routine XLSC scans an individual level for task requests, the programs listed first in the job stack will be executed first in most instances. Hence the first programs have a higher priority. However, this is a limited priority in that it does not allow a program listed first, for example, to interrupt a program listed lower. Any time a program starts to execute on a level, it must be complete before any other program is allowed to run. The rule then for priority on an individual level is "first come, first served" unless the programs arrive simultaneously; in this case, the first listed in the job stack will be the first to run.

As indicated, a foreground program with a certain poll time should not be placed on the same level or on a lower level than a background program that is likely to consume more time than the poll interval of the foreground program. Otherwise, polling of the program may be skipped due to an overload at higher levels. Another point is that programs scheduled at frequent intervals should be of short duration in comparison to the interval; otherwise, the executive simply lacks time to execute all of the work at that level or lower.

Reentrant Programming

To obtain the highest efficiency possible in custom user software, reentrant type programming should be used. To illustrate reentrancy, consider a typical subroutine such as a software-multiply algorithm, a subroutine likely to be used by many programs running on different levels. Assume that this subroutine uses temporary or scratch-pad storage during its execution to store an intermediate result. If the program is interrupted, and if the scratch pad is the working register of the processor, then the data will be saved by the interrupt service routine and subsequently restored upon reentering the subroutine at a later time. If the scratch area is the processor stack, then that too will be restored upon return, with still no problem. If the scratch area is a particular memory location used only by that subroutine, then the data will be there when the program returns. On the other hand, suppose while the original user of the multiply routine is suspended, a higher level uses the same multiply routine. The scratch-pad memory area has then been destroyed as far as the original user is concerned; this original user will eventually return from the multiply routine with the wrong result.

If other types of subroutines are the topic, more disastrous types of errors could occur. The above subroutine, which uses an absolute memory area for temporary storage, is not reentrant and could cause problems if linked to the executive and used by multiple levels.

Reentrancy is discussed here to aid the user in writing real-time programs and subroutines. Also, be cautioned when linking any existing software to the executive: existing programs are probably written in a non-reentrant manner, since the programmer probably did not anticipate their use on a multilevel system. Therefore, it is advisable to carefully examine existing software before linking it to the executive.

How can reentrancy always be maintained when writing new software? As a means for temporary saving of data on most systems, the following are a few ideas that may be helpful:

- Use the working registers as much as possible.
- Use the processor stack.
- Use index registers to point at memory areas unique to the level.
- Only call a particular subroutine from one level.
- Disable interrupts when the data is saved and reenable when retrieved.

The first three points are recommended as being the most efficient for almost all microprocessors. Restricting subroutine usage is, of course, inefficient; if multiple levels need a particular routine, then a separate version of that routine must be coded for each level and called from that level exclusively. Disabling the interrupts should be used only as a last resort. A particularly poor solution, it leaves interrupts disabled for extended periods of time and can adversely affect system operation, particularly when high-speed, interrupt-driven devices are being disabled.

Peripheral Interface

This section will discuss the interface of a high-speed peripheral, such as a disk or digital cassette,to the real-time executive. In these cases, we are talking about devices that will generally have the highest priority on the system and will be the major user of processor time at the interrupt level.

The first requirement of any device is that it be interrupt driven, using one or more of the ready-status signals to generate the interrupt. The second is that a reasonable amount of hardware sophistication exists such that software is not required to control every menial function of the device. (If it is software controlled, then it may still be used with the executive; however, the system will be subject to sustained periods with interrupts disabled.)

To illustrate the general procedures the executive software would use in a typical system, the example of a simple disk operating system is used. (Details of the actual driving routines are omitted, since they may vary widely from one disk operating system to another.) Assume the reading of a data block from the disk; a generalized example of the communication of a disk system to the executive is as follows:

- First, the user will request the high-level programs of the disk operating system to be enabled (with a particular control key, for example).
- The user enters the required information for the desired file through the keyboard.
- A routine of the disk system calculates the required sector of the beginning of the block on the disk, based on its various tables and directory information. This information, along with a buffer pointer and byte count, is initialized and ready for input.
- A low-level subroutine issues a seek command to the disk controller for the required track and sector. It then suspends its current level and returns program control to the executive.
- Upon receipt of the disk-ready interrupt signal, the connected interrupt service routine saves the current status data and points to the input buffer and byte count. The routine then loops on the ready status signal reading the required block to the memory buffer, one byte at a time, until the byte count has decremented to zero. This is all done with interrupts left *disabled* so as not to miss any of the incoming data.
- When the block is read, the priority level that was using the disk is reenabled, and control is given back to the executive (which will then scan priorities).

- As priorities allow, the original suspended level is reentered. The new data in the buffer is then transferred, manipulated, checked, etc. The above is then repeated, starting with step 3, every time a block is read from the disk.

This description is very generalized, with many details left to be filled in depending on the particular disk system. The major point is that the disk will actually be read or written at the interrupt level, and the operating system that initializes, sends commands, and manipulates the data is run at a medium or higher software level of the executive.

On this type of system, events will occur at the interrupt level for durations of 5 to 20 ms, depending on the block size and data transfer rate, indicating that even the highest software level will be subject to at least this amount of timing delay. Also note that by assigning the disk-system background programs to high-priority levels, the return from the buffer input routine may be made almost instantly, such that sequential sectors of a disk may be read without having to issue separate commands for each sector read.

For a high-speed, digital-cassette system, a similar procedure is applicable, except that instead of reading an entire record at the interrupt level, only a single byte is read. Thus, during any data transfer, an interrupt will occur every 1 to 2 ms, at which time the service routine will read or write 1 byte to or from a buffer, and return. When the entire buffer is finished, the background program will be reenabled to perform the data manipulation.

Printer/Communications Link

This interface is similar to the digital cassette: only a single byte is transferred at the interrupt level and the higher-level driver programs are run at a medium- or low-priority level. It is the task of the higher-level program to initially format the buffer and initialize the byte count (in the case of sending a message), or to reserve a buffer space and initilize pointers (in the case of receiving a message). This leaves the most simple tasks to be performed at interrupt level — merely reading the device, indexing the buffer, saving the data, and returning. Actually, there is no need to save full status when interrupted, since the processor will only require a few general registers to perform the tasks above. At the completion of the message the original calling level is reenabled. Naturally, as with the high-speed peripherals, most of the work is done by the background program that handles the data.

Direct Memory Access Interface

The description of a direct memory access (DMA) interface completes this presentation. This kind of interface involves a relatively complex hardware configuration and therefore may not be as practical as the previously described interfaces for the home computer.

Basically, DMA uses the external device to request direct access to the system's address and data busses, while cutting off the processor from these busses. The device is then free to transfer data to or from memory, independent of the processor. The advantage, of course, is the efficiency and speed of the operation; the drawback is the amount of hardware needed.

The interface to the executive is very similar to the disk interface mentioned earlier and relies on the DMA controller to be interrupt-driven.

A high-level program in the executive will initiate the procedure by requesting a DMA transfer (usually done with an I/O command). The program and level are then suspended, and the processor waits for the DMA interrupt. The DMA controller takes over completely at this point by commanding the device to seek the required data, read it, and then, one byte at a time, perform a DMA transfer to external memory. When the entire sector or block is read, the DMA interrupt gives control back to the executive, which causes the original user program to be activated and reentered on a priority basis.

The DMA type of operation is most applicable for the case of the *intelligent terminal* type of I/O peripheral, which has its own separate processor to control the device and the DMA operation. Most efficient, this type of operation is the ultimate for peripheral interface to the executive. Although it is a very convenient feature, it is not usually necessary for the typical home computer system, where normal I/O interface methods suffice.

Summary

Real-time processing has many applications with respect to the home computer system. To further enhance a simple real-time system, a priority executive may also be implemented, giving significantly powerful capabilities to the relatively small and inexpensive personal computer system.

For those users who are seeking a permanent home computer, the real-time executive offers the ideal operating system, because it allows the computer to be used in the normal dedicated use simultaneously with various monitoring functions. Such a system will allow this particular user to obtain the most from his personal computer investment.

For the designer or experimenter who uses his computer strictly in the workshop, the benefits of a real-time executive may not be as great. However, the inventive designer could undoubtedly find a number of uses for the executive in his workshop as an experimental or practical aid.

The executive presented here, unfortunately, only lays the groundwork for a complete and practical system, and much work is left to the end user, who must interface and write his own custom programs to put the executive to work. But hopefully, this presentation will enlighten some owners of personal computers to the powerful capabilities these machines possess and will encourage them to implement or experiment with real-time executives to explore the capabilities of their system. ■

Multiprogramming Simplified

Irwin Lahasky

Multiprogramming is the ability of the computer's operating system to handle and execute several programs concurrently. In this article, I have set out to explain in a simple fashion the concept of how the operating system of a computer handles more than one job (ie: program) at one time. Only the essential elements are included in this simple model, which is based on a typical large-scale computer's programming environment. The same general concepts are of course applicable as well to the much smaller memory regions of the typical personal computer.

The operating system, through its various control programs, keeps track of the amount and location of available memory and the specific memory regions allocated to programs currently in memory. As programs (ie: tasks) are read into the computer, certain information associated with them is stored by the computer. The name of the program and the location where the above information about the program is stored is placed on a list called the job, or task, queue. (See figure 1.) As memory becomes available, programs to be executed are loaded into memory (figures 2a and 2b) according to their size and arrival time (ie: how long they have been waiting). Information regarding these programs, such as name and location, is placed on the ready queue. As processing continues, programs are categorized as either active, ready or waiting. Only one program at a time can be active.

The operating system maintains a special memory location for each program in memory which contains the next sequential instruction (NSI) to be executed for that program. This memory location is called the NSI cell. As a pro-

Job Queue	Active Queue	Ready Queue	Waiting Queue	NSI Cells
A–100 K				
B–150 K				
C– 50 K				
D–150 K				
E–100 K				

Program Counter = xxxxxx

Figure 1: When a program is entered into the multiprogramming computer, it is first put onto a job queue. The jobs are typically stored in the order they are entered, and each queue entry has all the essential information about the job.

Job Queue	Active Queue	Ready Queue	Waiting Queue	NSI Cells
		A		A 100,000
		B		B 200,000
		C		C 350,000
D–150 K				
E–100 K				

Program Counter = xxxxxx

Figure 2a: Enough memory is available to fit the first three programs into the ready queue so they can await execution. The next sequential instruction (NSI) cell for each of the programs is initialized to the location of the first instruction in the corresponding program.

* Address 000,000	Operating System Programs	Address 99,999 *
* Address 100,000	Program A	Address 199,999 *
* Address 200,000	Program B	Address 349,999 *
* Address 350,000	Program C	Address 399,999 *
* Address 400,000	Unused	Address 449,999 *

Figure 2b: A representation of where the programs are actually stored in memory. Addresses 0 thru 99,999 (in decimal notation) are used by the operating system of this example.

Job Queue	Active Queue	Ready Queue	Waiting Queue	NSI Cells
	A			A 100,000
		B		B 200,000
		C		C 350,000
D–150 K				
E–100 K				

Program Counter = 100000

Figure 3: Program A is moved into the active queue to be executed. The next-sequential-instruction pointer is moved from the appropriate NSI cell to the program counter upon activation.

Job Queue	Active Queue	Ready Queue	Waiting Queue	NSI Cells
	A			A 100,000
		B		B 200,000
		C		C 350,000
D–150 K				
E–100 K				

Program Counter = 100002

Figure 4: The program counter is here incremented by 2, since the first instruction of program A is a 2-byte instruction. This has no effect on the related NSI cell.

gram is loaded into memory, the address of the first instruction to be executed for that program is moved into this NSI cell. A special NSI register, the program counter, is maintained by the hardware containing the address of the next-sequential-instruction to be executed for the currently active program. When a program becomes active, the next-sequential-instruction pointer is moved from its NSI cell to the program counter of the computer; this will of course be dynamically changing for the currently active program. As instructions for the active program are executed the value of the program counter is typically incremented by the length of the current instruction being executed to reflect the address of the next instruction address that is to be executed. When branches occur, the program counter is redefined completely. This process is repeated until the program is either completed or interrupted by an outside service request from a real-time clock or input/output (I/O) operation. If the active program has been completed, its memory allocation is freed and becomes available for reallocation. If it was interrupted it will be placed on the waiting queue and its next-sequential-instruction pointer will be defined by the old program counter value at the time of interrupt. The highest priority program in the ready queue will be given active status, its NSI cell will be moved to the program counter, and instruction execution will be resumed at its NSI address.

As I/O requests are serviced, programs will be moved from the waiting queue to the ready queue, and will be returned to active status when their turn comes. Example: Program A (100 K bytes), program B (150 K bytes), program C (50 K bytes), program D (150 K bytes) and program E (100 K bytes) are read into the computer and placed on the job queue. (See figure 1.) 350 K bytes of memory are available beginning at address location decimal 100,000. Addresses 0 thru 99,999 may contain operating system programs. Program A is loaded into locations 100,000 to 199,999, its NSI pointer is set to its first instruction to be executed (address 100,000), and it is placed in the ready queue. Program B is loaded into locations 200,000 to 349,999, its NSI pointer is set to its first instruction address of 200,000, and it is placed second in the ready queue. Program C is loaded into locations 350,000 to 399,999, its NSI pointer is set to 350,000 and it is placed third in the ready queue. 50 K bytes remain available in memory from addresses 400,000 to 449,999, but this is insufficient for either of the remaining programs (D and E), which require 150 K and 100 K bytes, respectively. Therefore this memory will remain temporarily unused. (See figures 2a and 2b.)

If there is no entry in the active queue, the first program in the ready queue, program A, is moved to active status. Its NSI cell is moved to the program counter (as shown in figure 3), and execution will begin at the status address. Program B now becomes first on the ready queue and program C second. As the instruction at location 100,000 is fetched and executed, the address in the program-counter value changes as instructions are executed.

Assuming the first instruction is 2 bytes long, the next sequential instruction to be executed becomes 100,002. (See figure 4.) After the execution of the instruction at location 100,000 is completed, the instruction pointed to by the program counter (at location 100,002) is fetched for execution, and the program counter is changed to 100,004. This is done because the second instruction is also 2 bytes long.

Processing continues in this manner until an interrupt in processing is encountered, such as a request to read data into the program from an input device or a request to write data to an output device. In this case, time is required to get or write the external data, and control is transferred to another program in the following manner. For the purpose of our example, let us assume that program A issued a read instruction located at address 158,266, and that this instruction type is 6 bytes long. The program counter which had been pointing to address 158,266 will be incremented by 6 to 158,272 (figure 5). An interrupt is generated by this I/O instruction.

The program counter contains the address where execution is to be resumed for program A (158,272). The program counter is stored in program A's NSI cell, and program A is placed last on the waiting queue. The next program in the ready queue is moved to active status, its NSI cell is moved to the program counter, and processing is continued at the (now different) address in the program counter. (See figure 6.)

As jobs are completed and their memory allocation is freed, programs waiting on the job queue are loaded into available locations. Their NSI cells are initialized and they are placed last on the ready queue.

Job Queue	Active Queue	Ready Queue	Waiting Queue	NSI Cells
			A	A 158,272
		B		B 200,000
		C		C 350,000
D–150 K				
E–100 K				

Program Counter = 158,272

Figure 5: When program A reaches memory location 158,266, a read instruction is encountered that is 6 bytes long. The program counter is incremented by 6 to 158,272. While the read operation takes place, program A is removed from the active queue and put into the waiting queue. The current value of the program counter is then stored in the A NSI cell as shown here.

Job Queue	Active Queue	Ready Queue	Waiting Queue	NSI Cells
			A	A 158,272
	B			B 200,000
		C		C 350,000
D–150 K				
E–100 K				

Program Counter = 200,000

Figure 6: The next program on the ready queue is moved to the active queue after an interrupt. The appropriate NSI cell is moved to the program counter (re)starting the program on its way.

Job Queue	Active Queue	Ready Queue	Waiting Queue	NSI Cells
	A			A 158,272
		B		B 248,208
D–150 K				
		E		E 350,000

Program Counter = 158,272

Figure 7: At this point program C has finished and has been removed from memory. There is not enough room for program D but there is for program E, which is loaded into memory and the ready queue. Program E's NSI cell is set to its first instruction's location. Program A's read operation has finished and program A is again in the active queue. The programs will continue to shift in and out of the active status as they are interrupted, until the entire series, and any that are read in later, is completed.

Programs are loaded into memory according to their position on the job queue, their memory needs, and availability of core. If program C, which occupies 50 K bytes, finishes first, its memory allocation of 50 K bytes plus the 50 K bytes which is unused (total 100 K bytes) is not sufficient for program D (which needs 150 K bytes) even though program D is next in line on the job queue. The 100 K bytes of available memory is sufficient for program E, so it is loaded into locations 350,000 thru 449,999. Its NSI cell is then set to 350,000 and it is placed last on the ready queue. (See figure 7.)

This idea of multiprogramming has developed over a number of years of conventional computing systems, ranging from the simplicity of two interacting programs on small machines to the larger contexts of many jobs executing simultaneously on the biggest machines. It is an example of how creative programming and design of systems software can make a machine do more than what the hardware designer intended.■

Introduction to Multiprogramming

Mark Dahmke

Multiprogramming has usually been considered out of reach of the average personal computer experimenter using a small- or medium-scale computer. Actually, anyone with a processor above the level of an 8008 can operate a multiprogram or multiuser system. The original purpose of multiprogramming was to allow more than one user to take advantage of a computer simultaneously. This increased the productivity of the machine by allowing programs to run while other programs were awaiting user input, access to a disk, etc.

This may seem to conflict with the advantages inherent in microprocessor based systems (ie: single-user systems and low cost). However, there are many instances where the ability to run more than one program at a time may be advantageous. Note that the statement "more than one program may run at a time" does not mean simultaneous execution. That is the definition of multiprocessing (more than one processor on the bus), not multiprogramming.

To describe multiprogramming more effectively, I shall refer to a more well-known function in computers: real-time interrupts. Suppose we are using a microcomputer to manage the environment in a small office building. Normally we want to continually poll (ie: scan) the sensors that are distributed throughout the building and adjust heating, cooling and lights on the basis of temperature and time of day. Let us say that during normal operation, someone in the building wants to change the temperature of an office.

One way to do this is to have a video terminal and keyboard attached to the system that generates an interrupt when a keyboard request is made. Upon receiving the interrupt, the computer saves the status of the current program and enters or transfers control to the keyboard read routine. As soon as the user has made the desired change, the system loads the olds or transfers control to the keyboard read routine. As soon as the user has made the desired change, the system loads the old status information and returns to the original program. This same interrupt technique could be used to design a time-shared system that would allow several terminals to be hooked up to a processor. Each terminal would generate an interrupt, and whichever program was active would be put in a wait state. This arrangement only works well for a few terminals, though. You can imagine what would happen if everyone happened to press a key at the same time.

Figure 1 shows timing comparisons of several modes of operation already discussed. In figure 1a two independent

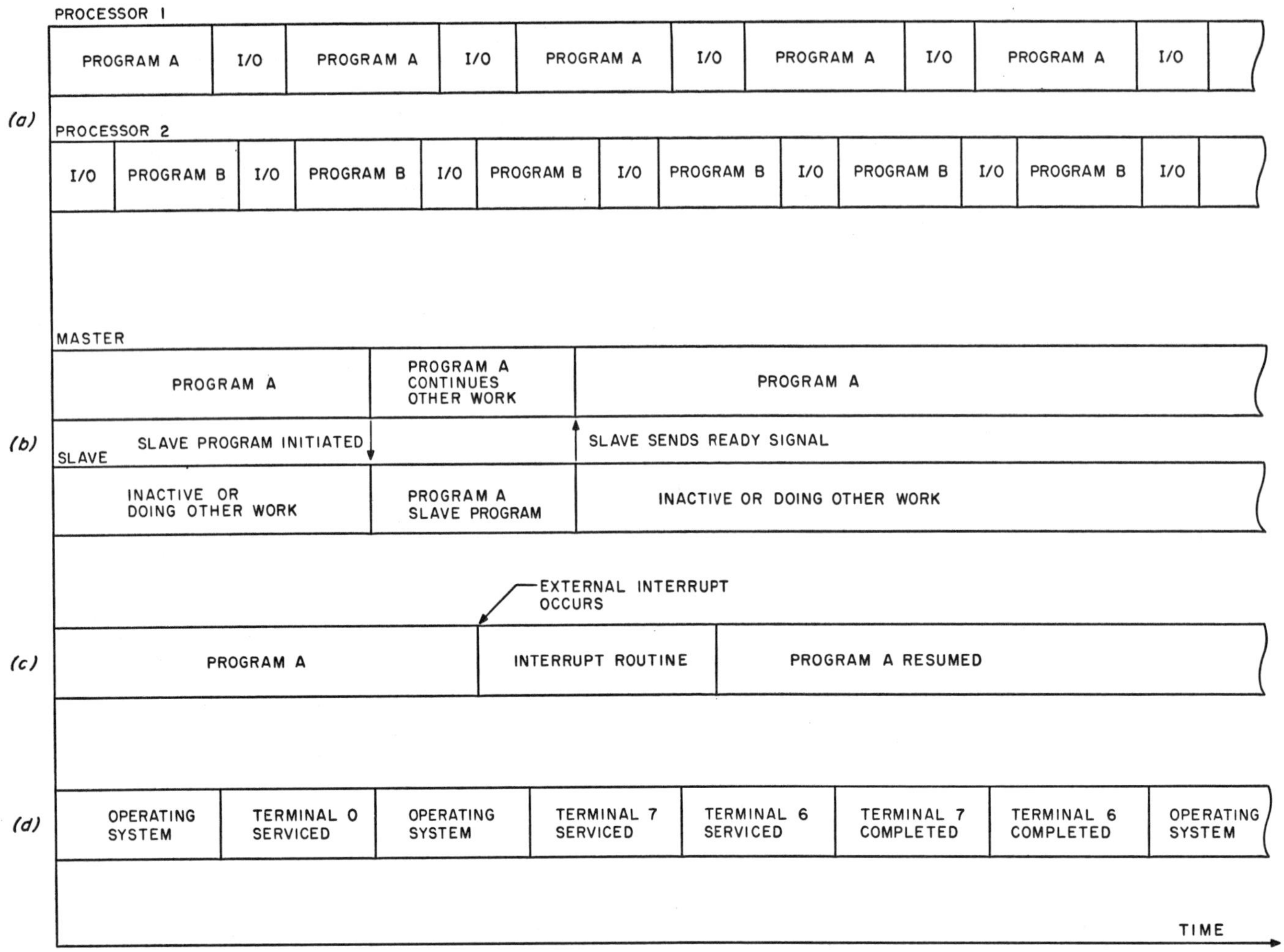

Figure 1: Timing diagrams for four different system organizations. Figure 1a is a multiprocessing example using two independent processors. Figure 1b is a multiprocessing example using two processors connected in a master-slave configuration. Figure 1c is a single processor with one level of interrupt. Figure 1d is a single processor with eight levels of interrupts. Each of the eight levels is activated by one of eight terminals.

processors are shown, each doing something different and neither interfering with the other. This is known as multiprocessing. The processors may or may not be sharing input/output (I/O) terminals or memory.

In figure 1b two processors are shown in a *master-slave* arrangement. Perhaps the slave processor performs floating point arithmetic or some complex I/O function. The master processor can give the slave processor commands via an interrupt and continue other processing until the slave informs it that it has finished the desired operation.

Figure 1c shows a single processor with an interrupt being applied. The processor temporarily gives control to the routine specified by the interrupt hardware and begins executing it. When complete, it returns control to the main program. Figure 1d shows the multiterminal timeshare system. Usually the interrupt hardware contains provisions for daisy chaining or giving priority to the interrupts as they come in. Thus, if terminal 6 applies an interrupt and the processor is busy with terminal 7, terminal 6 is not allowed to interrupt the processor until terminal 7 is finished.

Using multiprogramming is like using real-time interrupts. A multiprogrammed system uses interrupts, but in a more efficient way. Imagine a simple two-program situation. Suppose program A is running and no other programs have been started. Then a user initiates (ie: loads) another program called B. How will program B gain control of the system so that it might start to execute?

The process of passing control from one program to the next is usually handled by an operating-system module referred to as an *interrupt call* routine. Normally, to save the programmer the trouble of making sure that this routine gets called at regular intervals, the routine is usually imbedded in many of the I/O

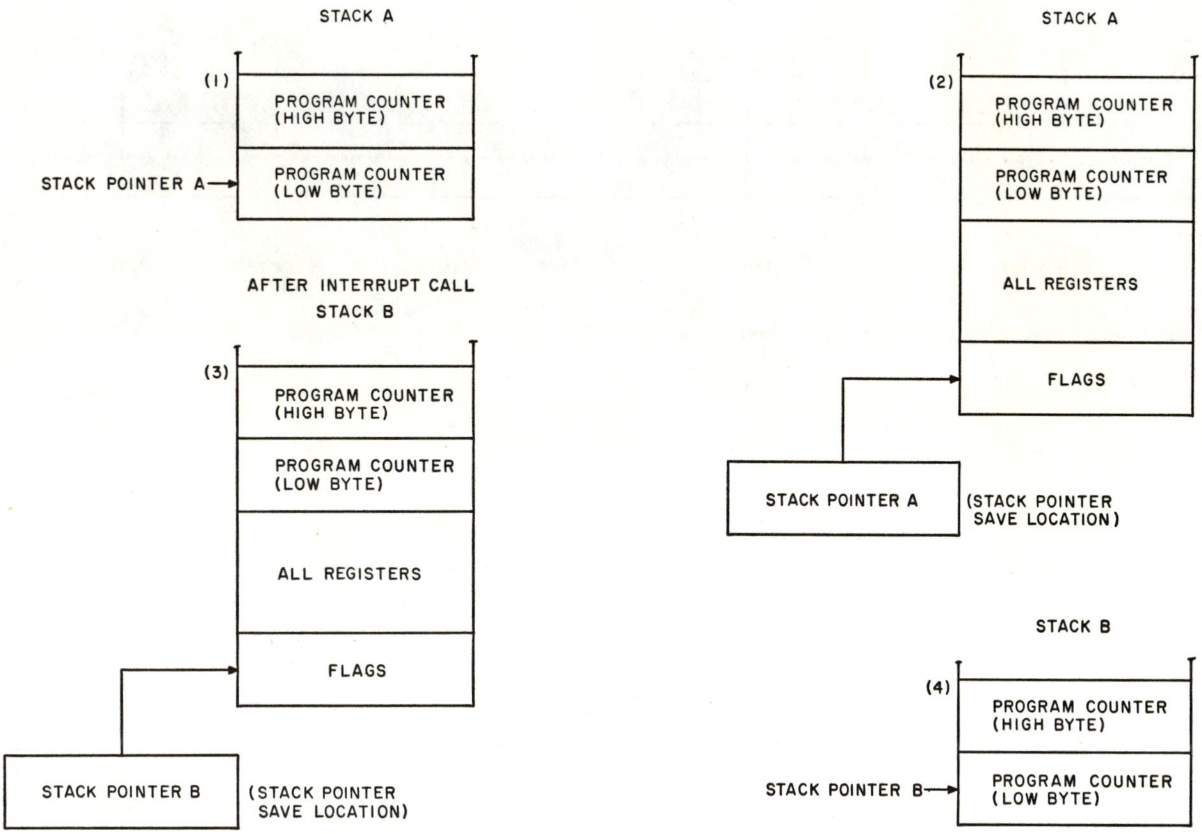

Figure 2: Arrangement of all stacks and stack pointers at each interval of an interrupt call routine.

driver routines or other standard utility subroutines on a system. Note that this technique will in no way upset any of the flags or registers of the routine it is called from.

This interrupt call program will:

1. Determine if any other programs are waiting to execute.
2. If so, save all registers and flags on the stack and save the address of the current program's stack pointer in a special table in memory.
3. Load the new program's stack pointer from the table, pop all registers and flags off the stack.
4. Return to the new program.

Loading the new stack pointer raises some interesting questions. If program B has not yet begun, how could its registers have been pushed onto its stack? Figure 2 shows the stacks of both programs as they would be at each step in the previously described interrupt call routine. Part of the job of the routine that initialized program B is to set up a dummy stack and stack pointer such that the program counter address on the top of the stack contains the entry point of program B. Thus, when the interrupt call routine reaches step 4, it will execute a return instruction, then pop the entry point address off the stack and begin executing program B. When the interrupt routine is called again, it will see that program A is waiting and will save

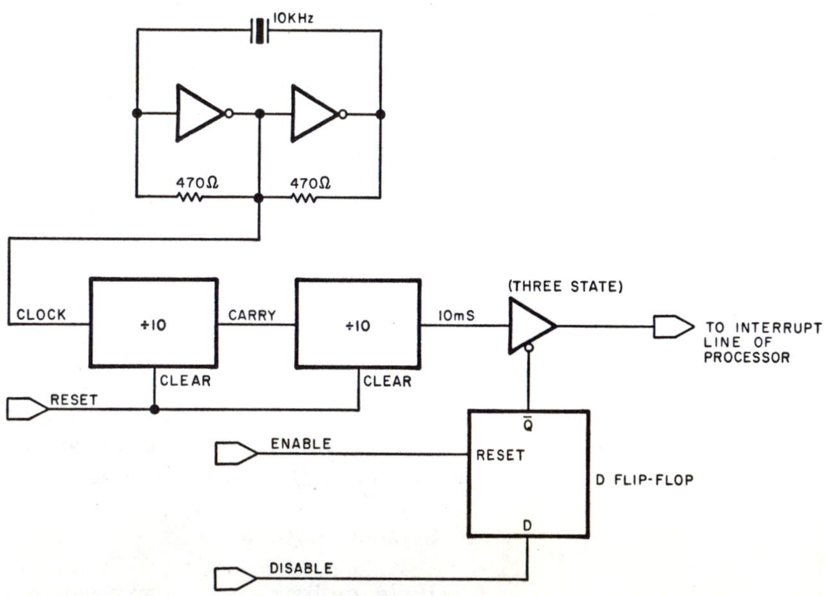

Figure 3: Simple hardware interrupt timer set for 10 ms intervals.

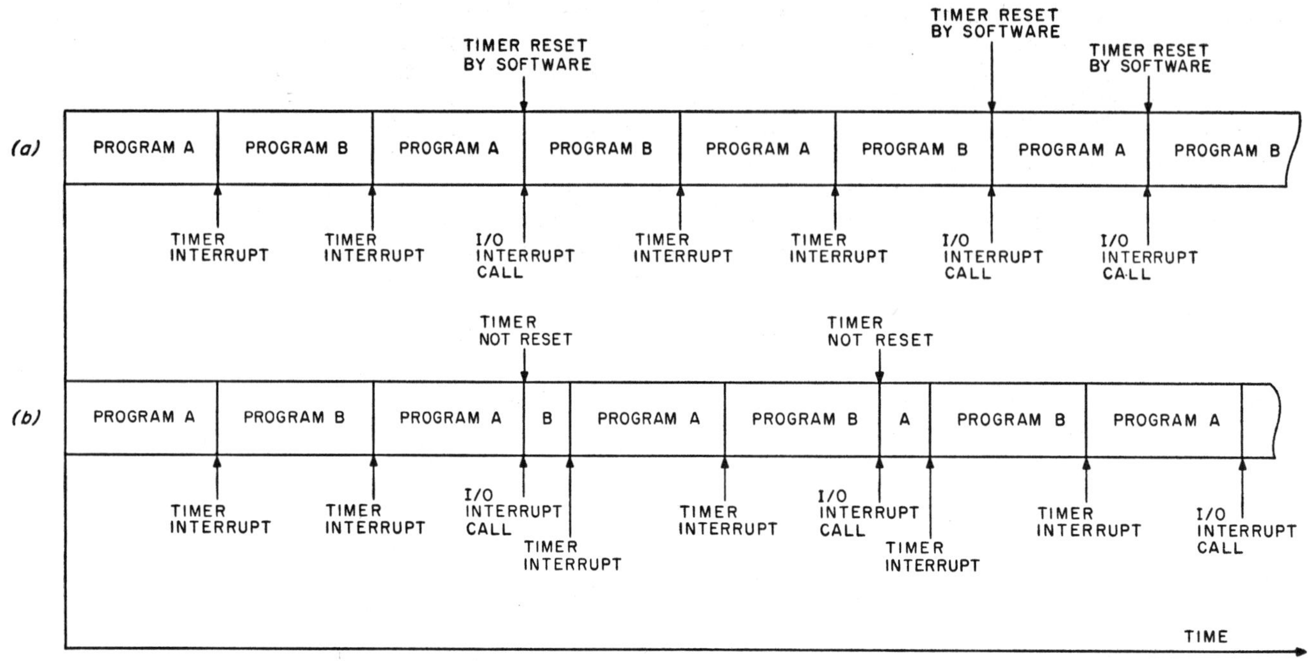

Figure 4: Interrupt timing example of figure 1 reviewed with the addition of a hardware timer. The timer may be used in two ways. The example in figure 4a resets the timer on each interrupt call. This allows each program to receive its full 10 ms time slot. The example in figure 4b does not reset the timer. Therefore, a hardware interrupt occurs every 10 ms.

all of program B's registers and flags, swap stack pointers and return to program A at the point where it was first interrupted.

All this activity will take place every time the interrupt routine is called, but if one of the programs gets caught in an infinite loop, the interrupt call routine may not get called. The simplest way to avoid this kind of problem is to add some hardware to provide external timed interrupts. As shown in figure 3, the interrupt timer is set to provide an interrupt every 10 ms. A reset line is provided in the event that the interrupt routine is manually called through the software method. The timer may be reset to give the program its full 10 ms. A disable line is provided to allow the user to turn off the timer for special applications (eg: software timing) in which the processor must not be interrupted.

Figure 4 shows our previous example of figure 1, but with the extra hardware-generated interrupts added. In figure 4a some software interrupts are mixed in with the hardware interrupts. The timer is reset after each call to the interrupt routine. Figure 4b is the same except that the timer is not reset after each call.

A Complete System

There are limitless ways to develop a computer system that will be easy to use. A look at the current market shows this to be true, perhaps even to a greater extent on the small systems level. I will not attempt to describe all possible variations available on a multiprogramming system, but I will try to give as generalized a view as possible.

First, we must consider what is necessary to make a useful system. The following are essential:

1. Some form of operating system that allows simplified user communications (eg: BASIC, DOS, CPM).
2. Convenient mass storage I/O (eg: cassette or disk).
3. Sufficient memory to handle all programs.

Another consideration might be the internal architecture of the processor, but that is another level of problem.

Figure 5 shows the memory layout of a typical multiprogramming system. To maintain a simple system, I have combined the operating system with the time-sharing routines that support all terminals, such as video displays, keyboards and teletypewriters. This means that each time the operating system gains control, through an interrupt call or timer interrupt, it will complete its own activity and then transfer control to the timesharing program for the remainder of the time slot. If the operating system is given highest priority, the response times of the terminals should not suffer. The operation of the time-share program can be treated as a multiprogram system in miniature, where each terminal is given a time slot, or it may be designed to simply scan the terminals, choosing a new terminal each time it is given control.

Controlling I/O

Many programmers have discovered the convenience of vectoring all I/O through one subroutine; this simplifies programming greatly and makes system changes much easier. Typically, one subroutine will accept an operand, if necessary, and an operator function code passed from the main program and will decide which I/O function to perform. In my hypothetical computer, this approach will be used. Note that in some large computer systems, the I/O driver programs can only be accessed by executing a special kind of interrupt call that informs the operating system that the user's program desires to perform some kind of input or output operation. The operating system then takes charge, performs the I/O for the program in question, and returns pointers, telling where the input data was stored in memory or that the requested output function has been completed.

This type of I/O handling is necessary because the I/O controllers are extremely complex and are capable of performing an entire I/O operation without processor intervention. In fact, it would be very inefficient to make the processor of a large system perform these menial tasks when it could be working on more important programs. In microcomputer systems we are not normally concerned with the optimization of I/O functions and it does not hurt performance to have the processor perform most of the I/O. Consequently, the I/O driver routines in the system I am describing will not be considered as part of the operating system. They are just utility subroutines that may be called by the user's program.

Defining the Necessary Tables

With only two programs very few, if any, tables are needed to tell the interrupt routine which program was active at the instant the system was interrupted and which program is next in line. But imagine a system capable of supporting ten or more programs: some form of priority scheduling will be needed, as well as a table to hold all of the stack pointers of the inactive programs.

To handle the list of programs (herein referred to as tasks), we must define a *task-control table* that keeps track of a number of pointers and descriptors. First, each entry will begin with the task number that uniquely defines each task. Next, we will include the priority of the task on an arbitrary scale of 0 to 10. It will then get the processor before a task of lower priority: 10 is highest. If two tasks have the same priority, the first one in line in the task-control table will get control. The task-control table must also keep track of the last value of the stack of each task and whether or not the task may be interrupted, as in the case of critical timing loops.

Another important status byte that must be kept is the *current activity indicator.* This byte contains the task number of the currently active task. Now let us assume that we have three different tasks running and all have been initialized (ie: stored in the task-control table). The first task has a task number of 0 and a priority of 10. Generally the operating system is given the task number 0 designation. Since the operating system and the time-sharing program that controls the user terminals are considered one big program in this example, task 0 is also the designation of the time-share system. Task 1 is a program that one of the users submitted (ie: initiated) from a terminal; it has a priority of 10. Task 2 was also loaded and initiated by a user through the time-share terminals, and it has a priority of 10.

Imagine that the time-share program calls the I/O driver program to write a

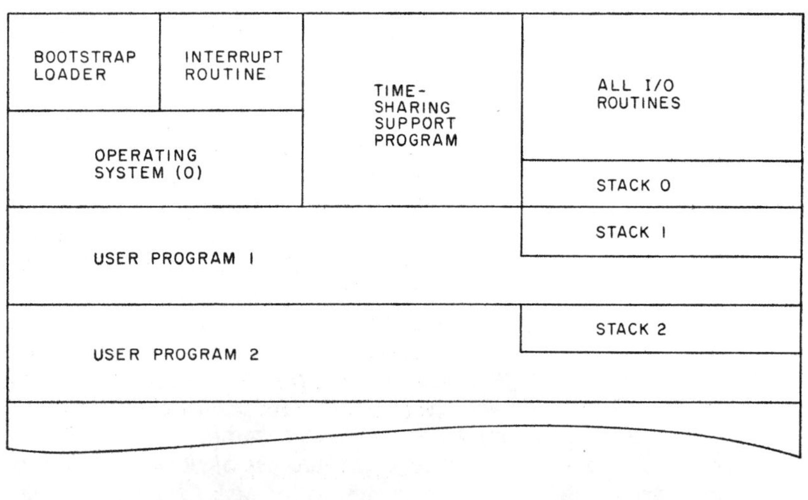

Figure 5: System geography of a typical multiprogramming system with space for the operating system and two other programs.

character out to a terminal. Since there could be many terminals connected to the system, how does the program know which one to write to? It would be very inefficient to have different routines for each device, but the only way that a program could tell the I/O driver which specific display to write to is for the calling program to know the physical address of that terminal. Passing the actual address of the device ruins the neatness of the I/O routine, though. It is more convenient to specify the function to be performed (1 = write to video display; 2 = read keyboard; 3 = write to cassette; 4 = read cassette).

The solution is to have another entry in the task-control table called a *communications control-block* pointer that points to the location of the communications control block for the particular task. Since each task is given its own block, the user may define his or her own functions and addresses. Thus each program may have its own video display, keyboard, cassette interface and disk. The communications control block contains a list of function numbers, the address of the I/O port or memory-mapped port, and the address of the I/O subroutine that will perform the operation. Figure 6 shows the arrangement of all tables.

Starting and Stopping

To initialize a new task, the user adds entries to the appropriate tables through a console command, causing a dummy stack and stack pointer to be created. To

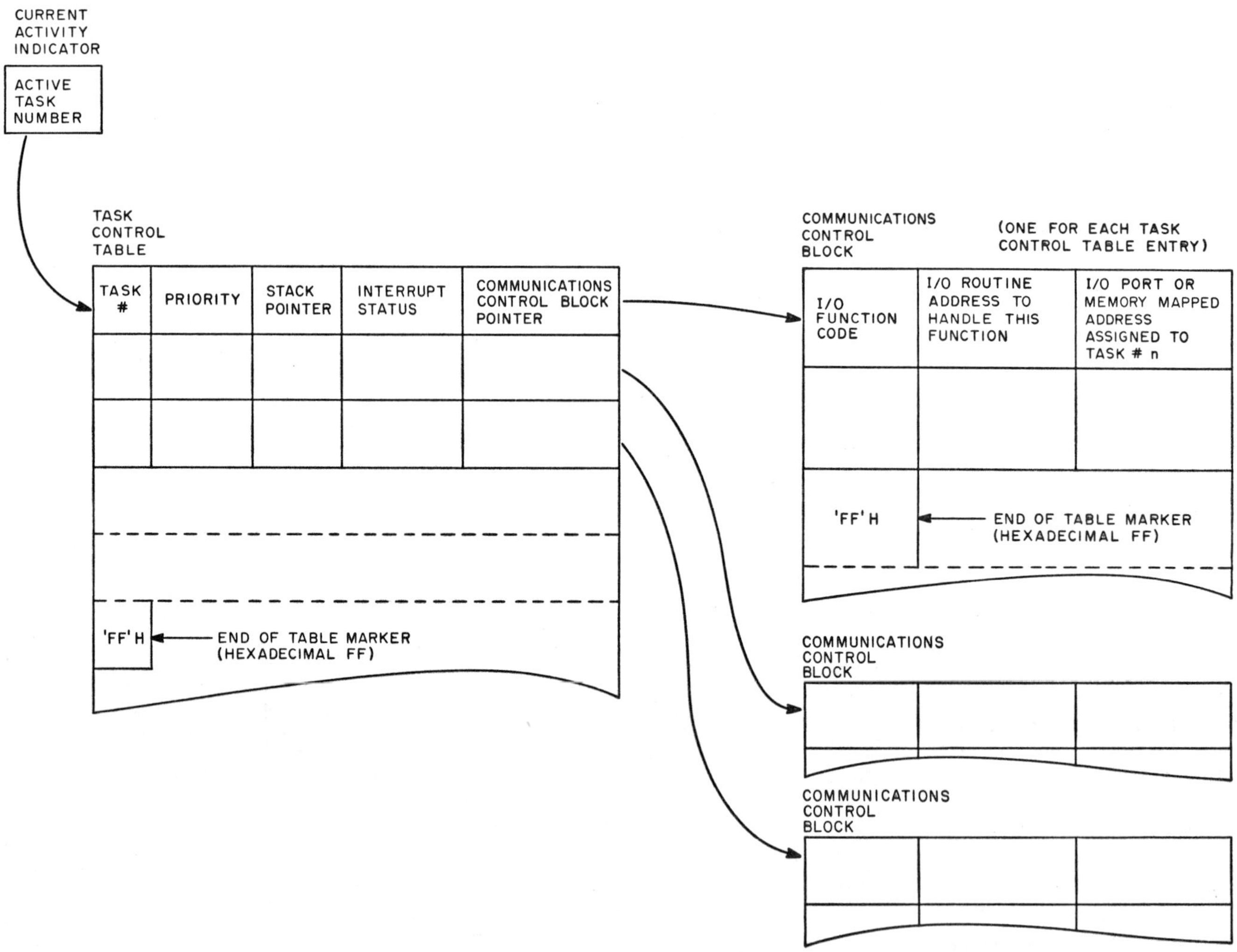

Figure 6: Control table organization. The current activity indicator contains the task number of the active task. The task-control table contains the task number, task priority, last value of stack pointer, interrupt status flag (1 for yes, 0 for no interrupts), and the pointer to the task's communications control block. The communications control block contains the input/output (I/O) function code, address of I/O driver routine associated with the function code, and the I/O port or memory mapped address assigned to the task for the particular function. One entry is provided for each function code used in the task. The owner of the task may add entries to the communications control block for specialized I/O driver requirements.

stop a task, the last thing done in the task is to call a subroutine that would remove its task control table entry. This is equivalent to a CALL EXIT in FORTRAN found on many larger systems.

Example

The easiest way to show how all tables and pointers affect each other and the system is to observe them during a short period of machine activity. As we begin, task 0 (the operating system and time-share routines) has control, and a timer interrupt is occurring. There are two other tasks in memory: task 1 has priority 5 and task 2 has priority 4.

First, as the interrupt routine is entered, it saves all registers and flags of task 0 on stack 0 and saves the task 0 stack pointer in the task 0 task-control table entry. (See figure 7.) Next, it scans the task-control table for the task of next highest priority, moves the new task number (task 1) to the current activity indicator, moves the task 1 stack pointer from the task-control table to the processor's stack pointer, pops all of task 1's registers and flags off of stack 1, and executes a return, which has the effect of popping the program counter and jumping to that address.

Task 1, while executing, encounters a call to the I/O driver routine with a request for a keyboard input. (See figure 8.) When the I/O driver routine is entered, it scans the task-control table to find the communication control-block pointer entry for task 1 (ie: the routine determines which task called it by looking at the current activity indicator), then scans the communication control block for the function number entry corresponding to the one passed by the main program. Even though the computer may have five or more keyboards attached to it, the port address found in the communication control block gives it the address of the keyboard assigned to task 1.

Since the keyboard read routine is a common one, the address referred to in the communication control block points to a subroutine located within the operating-system area. Note that if the user had need for some special I/O subroutine, he could locate it in his own memory area and put the address in his communication control block as another function code.

Returning to the example, the keyboard read subroutine is called from the I/O driver, reads the keyboard port assigned to task 1, and returns to the I/O driver with the ASCII code. The I/O driver returns to the main program with the ASCII code in a register or memory location. In figure 9 the next timer interrupt has occurred, so control returns to the interrupt-handler routine. Again, the interrupt routine saves all registers and flags of task 1 on stack 1, looks at the current activity indicator to see which program was last active, saves the stack pointer in the task 1 task-control table entry, scans the task-control table for the next highest priority task, and finds

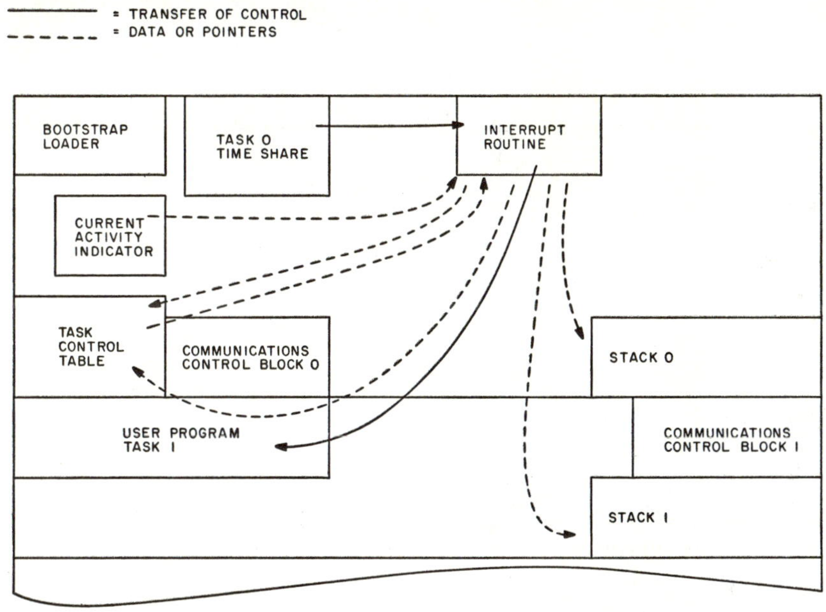

Figure 7: Task 0 has control of the processor and has just been interrupted. The interrupt routine looks at all pointers, saves the status, and then transfers control to task 1.

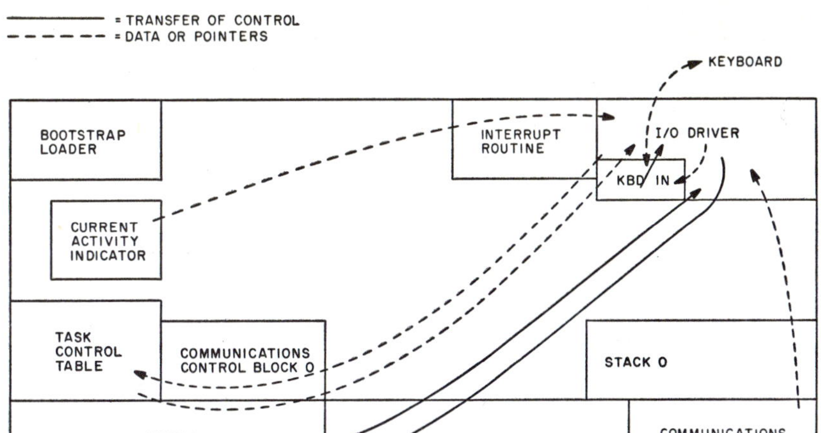

Figure 8: Task 1 has requested keyboard input from its assigned keyboard. When the input is completed, the I/O driver returns control to task 1.

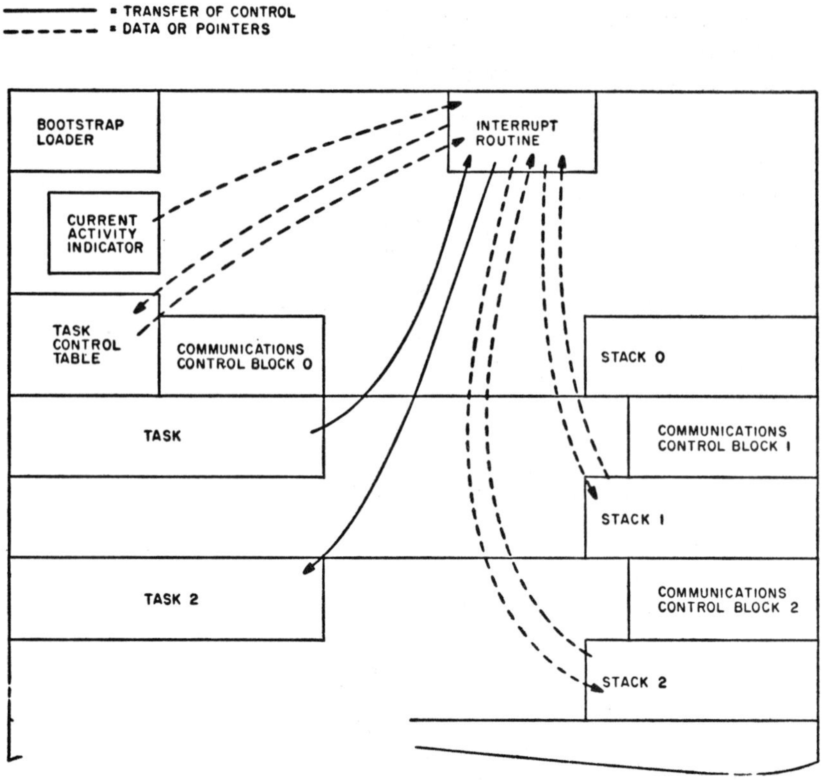

Figure 9: Task 1 has been interrupted and turns control over to the interrupt routine. Control is then passed to task 2.

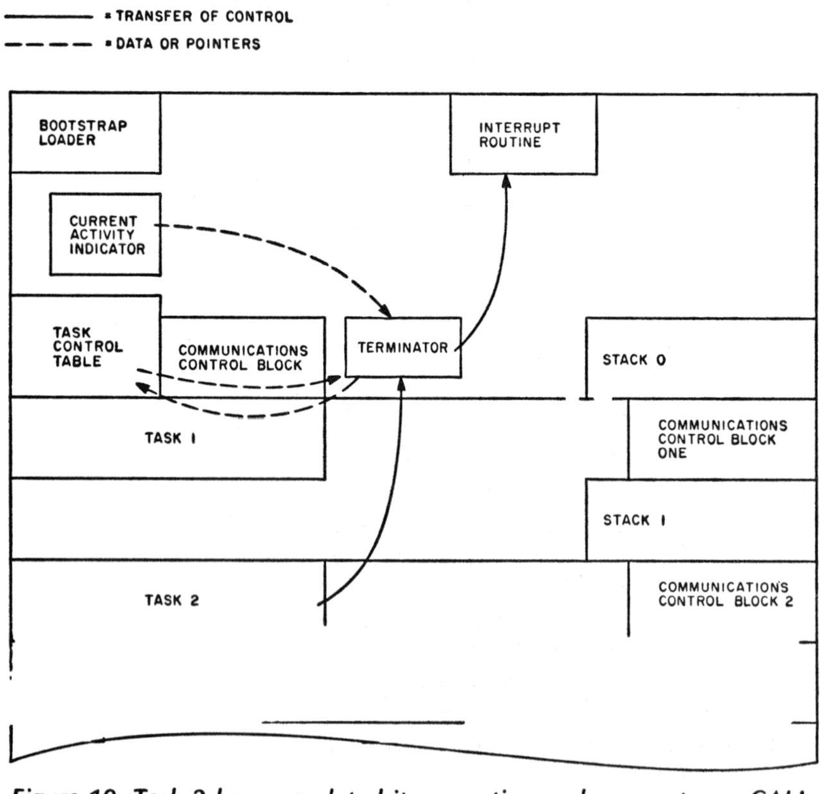

Figure 10. Task 2 has completed its execution and encounters a CALL EXIT. Control is given to the terminator routine which performs some cleanup operations and removes the task 2 entry from the task-control table, effectively destroying the task. Control is then given to the interrupt routine which again scans the task-control table to find the next task awaiting execution.

that task 2 should get control. The stack pointer for task 2 is loaded from the task-control table, all registers and flags are popped off of stack 2 and again a return is executed that causes task 2 to take control.

In the next step (shown in figure 10), task 2 has encountered the equivalent of a CALL EXIT or STOP command and has finished processing. This CALL EXIT calls a terminator routine which again finds out via the current activity indicator who called it and simply eradicates the task-control table entry for that task. To keep things neat, all succeeding table entries are moved up one notch. Then, control is returned to the interrupt handler, which will find the next task in line. In this case, since no other tasks of lower priority are waiting, control is returned to the highest priority task 0.

Error Handling

On a single program system, error handling is something that the user can watch for manually. When several programs are running, the system must have routines to handle errors rapidly so that other programs will not be slowed down or destroyed. There are many common errors that are relatively easy to deal with. Executing an invalid op code or forgetting to put in the second or third byte of a multibyte op code can be handled through a simple system restart (through the interrupt-handler routine) without losing continuity. But what about a program loop that accidentally destroys part or all of another user's program? On an IBM 360, all memory blocks assigned to a task are given a unique 4-bit protect key, which is the same as the task number. This key is stored in external hardware.

One approach might involve having two external 16-bit registers that could be loaded by the interrupt routine with the high and low memory addresses of the active task. Every time the address bus has a valid address on it, it is tested against these registers. However, special precautions would have to be taken in those cases in which a utility in low memory (ie: I/O driver routine, etc) is called, or when memory-mapped I/O ports outside these address limits are used.

Resolving Allocation Conflicts

Allocating I/O devices has been a problem since the early days of computers. Devices like tape drives and card readers (ie: sequential devices) are nonshareable: only one program may use them at a time. However, disk drives are considered shareable, since the head may be positioned at random to gather data. The simplest method that can be applied to the system described in this article would be to have the initiator program check all communication control blocks to make sure that certain devices are not assigned more than once.

I/O Software Considerations

As mentioned earlier, I/O techniques in use on small systems leave all control up to the processor. If special timing is needed or if strobes or ready flags have to be checked, software is used instead of extra hardware, as in the case of larger systems. This in itself is good from the standpoint of economy, but requires that special care be taken when writing the driver and controller software.

For example, suppose a cassette read routine uses a universal asynchronous receiver transmitter (UART) implemented in software as an algorithm instead of hardware. In a nonmultitasking system, the program may simply loop and time down between bits, but in a multitask system the timer interrupt would surely halt the activity and execute other programs. It may be well over 30 ms before it can return to the cassette read routine. It is easy to see what can happen to critical timing loops on a system that uses any kind of interrupts.

The solution? If you must do the critical timing in software, it is necessary to turn off the interrupt timer while in the critical loop and reactivate it when in noncritical parts of the routine. If external hardware is used, and internal timing is reduced to noncritical loops, the intervention of the multitask interrupt timer will not normally affect the system. If the interrupt timer causes an interrupt just before a byte is received by the UART and returning in time for the next byte to be received, the easiest way to assure that the cassette read routine does not drop a byte is to set the timing of the interrupt oscillator to at least twice as fast as the transmission rate of the UART. This greatly reduces chances of losing a byte.

An alternate approach is to have even more hardware that forces the interrupt timer to timeout and return control to the program awaiting the data transfer operation when the incoming data is present. A third way involves the use of direct memory access (DMA) capability, in which the external controller reads the UART and deposits the data directly into memory. With this approach, the calling program need only initialize the external registers and go into a wait state until the transfer is complete, allowing the rest of the tasks to execute normally. This last approach is used on many large systems and constitutes what is called a *channel.*

Managing the System

As you can see, many levels of activity are required to control a multiprogramming system properly. It is also apparent that some minimal hardware is required to prevent one user from obtaining exclusive control of the processor or writing over someone else's program or data. The use of control tables and a standard interrupt routine are also important as a way of letting the interrupt routines and I/O drivers know which task had control of the processor last.

If the user plans to run BASIC software or some other kind of language interpreter, the safety features discussed earlier may be implemented as part of the interpreter. To run a lower-level operating system that allows the user to generate assembler-level code will generally require the hardware described in this article, thus safeguarding the system and its users from accidental loss of programs or data. In general, the use of timed interrupts allows for a fairly even distribution of processor activity, and depending on the cycle time of the host system, between four and twelve tasks may be handled without too noticeable a delay in response time.■

REFERENCES

1. Abrams, Marshall D, and Philip G Stein. *Computer Hardware and Software.* Addison-Wesley, Reading MA, 1973.
2. Davis, William S. *Operating Systems.* Addison-Wesley, Reading MA, 1977.
3. Martin, Donald P. *Microcomputer Design.* Martin Research Ltd, Northbrook IL, 1976.
4. *Signetics Data Manual.* Signetics Corporation, Sunnyvale CA, 1976.
5. Struble, George W. *Assembler Language Programming: The IBM System 360 370,* second edition. Addison-Wesley, Reading MA, 1975.
6. Tanenbaum, Andrew S. *Structured Computer Organization.* Prentice-Hall, Englewood Cliffs NJ, 1976.

Introduction to Multiprocessing

Mark Dahmke

My personal involvement with microprocessors began in 1975 when I constructed an 8008-based microcomputer. Over the years, I have added to a Martin Research 8080 board so that I now have 32 K bytes of memory, dual floppy disks, a modem, two serial ports, and 30A power supply— all with an assortment of S-100, Martin Research, and custom wirewrap boards. The system works as is, but it has fallen prey to the troubles of any system that has grown haphazardly to its limit.

The S-100 interface works properly with the existing boards, but I must be extremely careful when adding any new boards as they may not run on my bus. I also can't run interrupts, direct memory access, (DMA) or dynamic memory cards. Since I now have the money to expand, I could go out and buy a new mainframe and move all the S-100 cards over to it. However, then I lose the Martin Research boards which include both serial ports, the keyboard interface, 8 K bytes of memory, and a PROM board. I could sell them and convert to S-100, but why get rid of perfectly good hardware.

The answer to my dilemma is multiprocessing. Multiprocessing means running two or more processors in either a loosely or tightly coupled configuration. Loose coupling means that the machines are physically tied together via machine-to-machine input/output (I/O) ports, sharing the work load on a program-by-program basis. Figure 1 shows such a system, where each processor has its own main memory but shares the disk drives. On large machines programs are generally read in on cards (or from a terminal) and kept on disk in a queue (ie: waiting line) until the processor is able to work on them. Both processors can read jobs from the queue and begin executing them. As shown here, job A has requested to be run on processor 0, and so has job B. Job C wants to be run on processor 1, but job D has no preference. In the last case, job D will run on the processor that gets to it first.

Once in a given processor, the job remains there. From the user's standpoint, the system will appear to run twice as fast as a single machine. Note that the individual jobs are not running faster, but since two jobs may run at the same time, more work is done. A commonly used term for this arrangement is *shared spooling* or *shared queueing.* The primary advantage over two indepen-

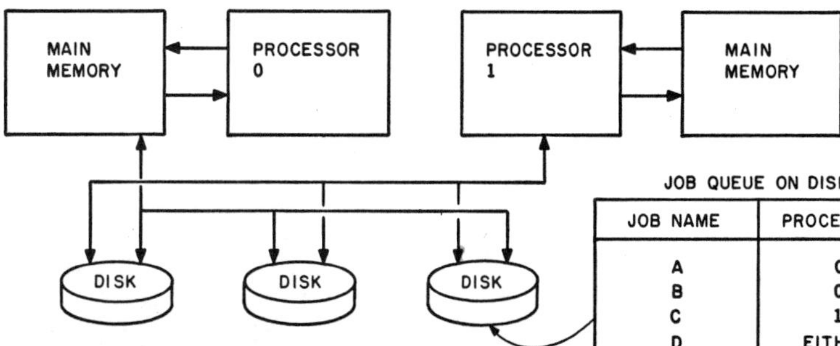

JOB NAME	PROCESSOR
A	0
B	0
C	1
D	EITHER

Figure 1: A loosely coupled multiprocessor. Each processor has its own non-shared main memory, but both processors share the disk drives.

dent processors is that both halves of the multiprocessor can access the same files on disk.

Tight Coupling

Tight coupling involves extra hardware that allows both processors to access the same main memory. Figure 2 shows a typical tightly coupled multiprocessor. The memory can be shared in a number of ways. First, the expensive and difficult-to-obtain multiport memory chips can be used. These memory chips have two sets of all address, data, and control lines. Both processors can access the same byte at the same time. In a large installation, multiprocessors are used to split the workload on a time-slice basis within a program. Hence a user's program may bounce back and forth between processors as the system attempts to run the two highest priority tasks (ie: programs) at all times.

The second approach involves direct memory access. Many microcomputers allow DMA, but very few people use it. Consider what happens on a typical microcomputer when two processors are on the bus and one begins a memory access. If it gains control of the bus, the other processor *must* be in a hold state, and vice versa. DMA may be useful for some I/O data transfers (ie: disk or tape at high speeds) where the microprocessor cannot keep up, or in graphics display hardware that accesses external memory, but DMA serves no useful purpose in a multiprocessor configuration. What good is it to have two processors when only one can perform at any instant?

On a 6800 microprocessor, one can complement the clocks and run two processors on the same bus without conflicts, however I have not seen it done commercially.

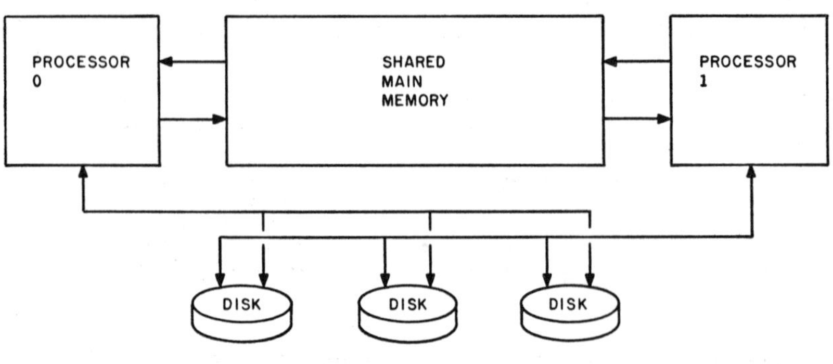

Figure 2: A tightly coupled multiprocessor. Both processors share the same main memory and also share disk storage.

Shared Memory Blocks — a Compromise

Perhaps direct memory access isn't the answer, but it would be convenient to have shared memory which both machines can access. Several minicomputers on the market already use this scheme. In figure 3, both processor 0 and processor 1 have 64 K address spaces, but each one has its own area from the 8 K boundary up to the top. The bottom 8 K of memory is either built with multiple-port access technology or resolves references by sending wait states out to the other processor while servicing a request. This way, the DMA access is cut to a minimum because a given processor will only be held up for a small percentage of the time.

Nonsymmetrical Machines

Until now, I have considered only those machines that are symmetrical; that is, capable of executing identical programs on either processor. Other possibilities do exist. Most hobbyists try to keep up with the latest technological advances by playing musical hardware —buying a Z80 to replace the 8080, which replaced the 8008, and so on. In my case, I have wanted to upgrade to a Z80 for some time, but am reluctant to change my existing system. I plan to leave the byte-oriented devices (ie: keyboard, video board, modem, etc) on the 8080 Martin Research system and move the ICOM floppy-disk controller and 24 K bytes of memory over to the Z80. The two systems will operate in a loosely coupled environment with shared I/O as a compromise between fully loose and tight coupling. This involves running two full handshaking parallel ports between the two processors. (See figure 4.) In this arrangement, the old processor acts more as a slave than as a second master. One of the advantages of this configuration is that the disk drives are on one system and the other slow I/O devices are on the other, giving the effect of overlapped processing. Most floppy-disk interfaces are processor intensive; they demand exclusive use of the processor until the input or output operation is complete. In some cases, the disk may be tied up for as much as a minute at a time, forcing the programmer to wait.

In the consulting business, personnel time is a far more valuable commodity than machine time. Having a slave I/O processor attached to the large machine is practical because the user can continue typing while waiting for the disk or any other time-consuming operation to finish.

When considering the loosely coupled master-master or master-slave arrangement, it becomes clear that the two processors must communicate with each other at a rather high rate. It is assumed that the majority of the interprocessor communication will be I/O related —that is, the master processor will load its I/O burden onto the slave processor. IBM calls the slave processors *channels*; some other manufacturers call them *peripheral processors*. Generally, a peripheral processor is somewhat more intelligent than a channel.

There is a great deal of ambiguity in the terminology. No clear-cut definitions have been made —or are likely to be made in the near future. Depending on the sophistication of the controlling software, an auxiliary processor might resemble a channel, a slave processor, or an attached processor (ie: a second master processor that is oblivious to the outside world) capable of executing the same instructions as the master processor.

Interrupts

In microcomputers, there are several ways of alerting the processor that a device needs to be serviced. The most common method is that of priority-based interrupts. In this case, hardware is built into the processor to halt activity on command and transfer control to a predesignated service subroutine. Later, control is returned to the original program.

Another method is to simply poll each device (ie: check a status bit to see if anything needs service). Polling requires processor time and implies that the program has the necessary machine code to handle the polling and that the code will be executed periodically.

It becomes obvious that interrupts are simpler to handle, but there are other complications. Most disk-drive controllers cannot tolerate interrupts. If you interrupt a disk data transfer, it may be impossible to recover properly. There are several other reasons for not running interrupts, but I will not pursue them here.

Hardware for a Loosely Coupled Multiprocessor

Loose coupling is relatively easy —all that is needed is a set of parallel or serial ports with handshaking, one going in each direction. (See figure 4.) This will allow a single path for byte or block transfers between machines. On my system, however, I would like to hook several devices to the slave. It would be wasteful to run a parallel port for each device, since the processor can only read or write to one at a time. So why not send along a device code or device

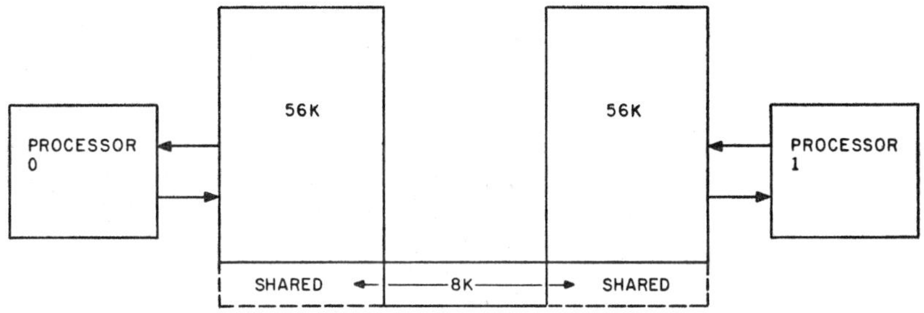

Figure 3: A tightly coupled multiprocessor with partially shared memory. Each processor has its own memory (up to 56 K in this example) but both share the bottom 8 K. Special hardware must be provided to resolve the conflicts in bus usage when accessing the bottom 8K block. Typically, if both processors try to access the 8 K block at the same time, the hardware will send out wait states to one processor while servicing the other.

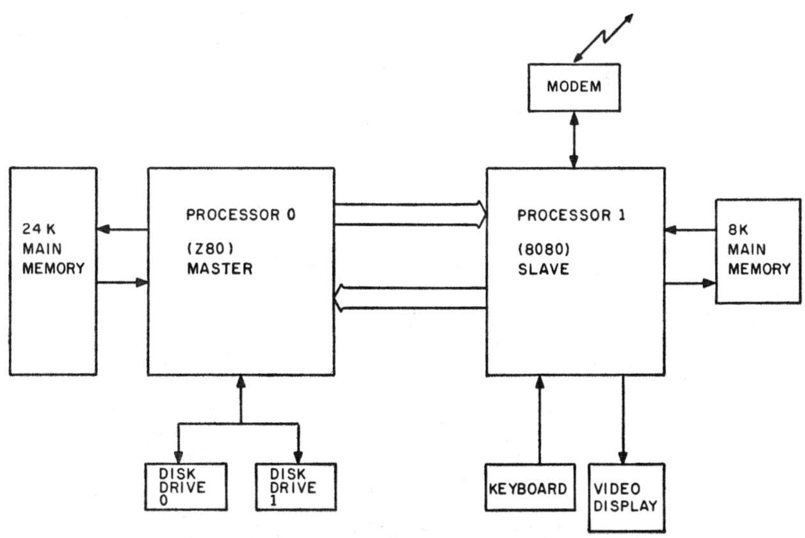

Figure 4: Master-slave configuration to be used in the author's system. Processor 0 owns the disk drives, and processor 1 owns all other I/O devices. The two parallel ports between processors 0 and 1 are for I/O communications. Processor 1 will be acting as a slave I/O processor, and will receive its commands and data from processor 0.

address in parallel with the byte being sent across? (See figure 5.) That way, the slave can poll the port and can use the device code to determine what to do with the byte of data. This approach is very similar to a common technique called *time-slice multiplexing,* where the processor's attention is divided equally among requesting devices. For example, device code 0 may be used for keyboard input, device 1 for console output, device 2 for a modem (ie: dial-up), and so on.

In order to run interrupts, the same bus structure can be used, but the data-ready line (in figure 5) will generate an interrupt. The interrupt routine will read the device code and determine which routine to go to for processing the incoming data.

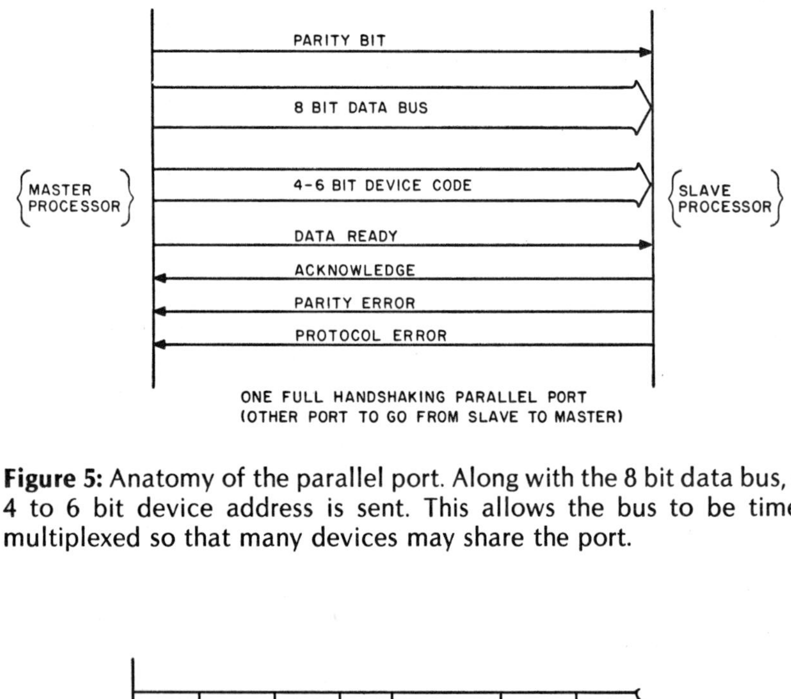

Figure 5: Anatomy of the parallel port. Along with the 8 bit data bus, a 4 to 6 bit device address is sent. This allows the bus to be time-multiplexed so that many devices may share the port.

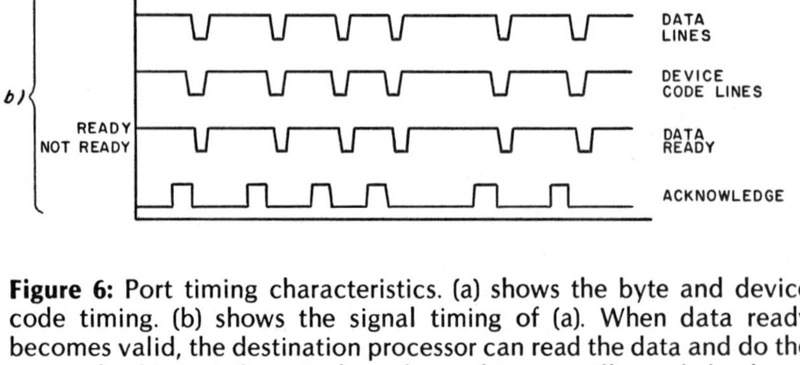

Figure 6: Port timing characteristics. (a) shows the byte and device code timing. (b) shows the signal timing of (a). When data ready becomes valid, the destination processor can read the data and do the error checking. When it has done this, it will send back an acknowledge, which will release the port for another transfer.

Software for a Loosely Coupled Multiprocessor

After years of software development, I have learned that there is both a quick and dirty way to do something, and a clean and organized way. It is always easier to write quick and dirty software because it is initially the least time-consuming. But in the long run, it is far more difficult to modify. Clean code requires some additional thought and planning but saves a lot of effort when making changes. For most purposes, it seems that elegance and flexibility go hand in hand. In this section, I will outline and discuss an elegant approach to the I/O slave multiprocessor configuration previously described.

First, I assume that the slave processor has many input and output devices attached to it and that the master will use the two parallel ports to communicate with all of these devices. The slave will have to have subroutines in order to work with each device. Another assumption I am going to make involves time multiplexing. Figure 6a shows how the port may be multiplexed, with the device code changing as successive bytes go to different devices. The unit time interval for a byte going out on the port is defined by the duration of the handshaking sequence. Figure 6b shows the timing of signals on the port. Note that the acknowledge line releases the port for another transmission. With this configuration, bytes destined for many different devices may be mixed on a byte-by-byte basis. How are they separated on the receiving side? Now programming and design philosophy become important. The simple solution would be to write a top-down modular structure. For most purposes this would be quite sufficient. But what would happen if we had a multiple byte protocol for one or more of the devices? Perhaps the console display routine has provisions for an addressable cursor and requires 2 bytes of data in succession after the command byte is sent (command, line number, column number). Can the next 2 bytes simply be read from the port? Remember that the port is being multiplexed; the next 2 bytes might have a different device code. The top-down technique may work well for a nonmultiplexed port, but runs into real problems when the port is multiplexed.

Coroutines

I would like to introduce a new concept before going on. Most people are familiar with subroutines —whether in FORTRAN, BASIC, Pascal, or assembly language, subroutines all do the same thing: they allow frequently used segments of a program to be referred to without duplicating the segment each time it is needed in the program.

In figure 7, subroutine A is called twice, but after the return instruction is executed in subroutine A, control is passed to the instruction immediately after the last instruction executed in the main program (namely, the call A instruction). No matter where subroutine A is called, the return instruction reloads the old address and continues where the main program left off.

Coroutines are similar to subroutines, but they do not return to the old address as in a subroutine. In figure 8, control appears to be oscillating (ie: flipping back and forth) between programs A and B. Whenever the coroutine is called, it returns to a point just after the last executed instruction of the other program. This in effect is a crude form of timesharing. A more general form of this mechanism is called *multitasking* or *multiprogramming*. A thorough discussion of multiprogramming can be found in "Introduction to Multiprogramming," also in this book. Multiprogramming gives us a clean mechanism for handling a time-multiplexed port. A main program or *task* is set up for each device. A generalized coroutine call is written that has a table of tasks and where each one left off when it encountered a coroutine call. The supervisor program, which includes the coroutine and task-switching routines, does the polling and, upon reception of a data-ready flag, will read the device code and look through the device assignment table. This table indicates which task should receive the byte of incoming data. The supervisor reactivates the specified task by loading up the task's old stack pointer and popping all registers (which are saved when the coroutine was called) off the stack. The reactivated task then reads the byte and performs whatever functions are required. This design is useful because it allows multiple threads of program logic without mixing them unnecessarily. Each task can be written independently of the others, without any register usage conflicts.

Control Blocks and Tables

Earlier I mentioned that several lookup tables are used to determine which task should be given control. The first control table is called the *channel-status table* or CHST. (See figure 9a.) Entries in the CHST have a byte for the device code, a task-assignment byte, and a status byte. If the device codes are put in ascending order, the device-code byte may be eliminated, saving a few bytes. The status byte includes a bit indicating whether the device code channel has been *opened* (ie: ready for service) or not. If it hasn't and someone tries to use it, a device error will be generated. Another bit in the status byte indicates whether the device code is defined or not. This is analogous to the open/close bit, but defines whether or not the device exists; if this bit is cleared, the

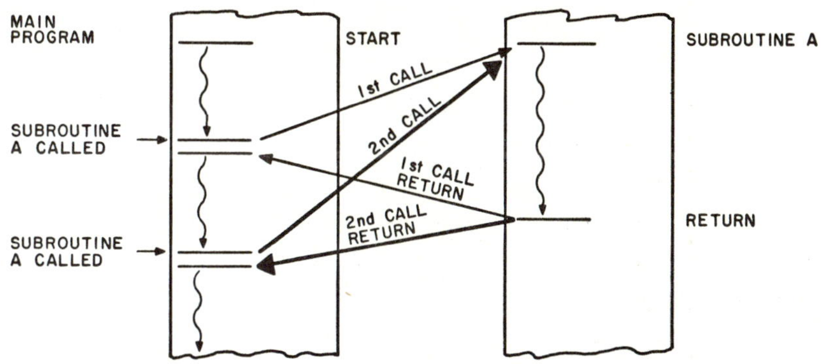

Figure 7: Flow of control when using subroutines. When subroutine A is called, the hardware in the processor must save the current value of the program counter so it can be restored when the subroutine finishes. Thus a subroutine can be called from any point in a program and will return to the instruction immediately after the subroutine call instruction.

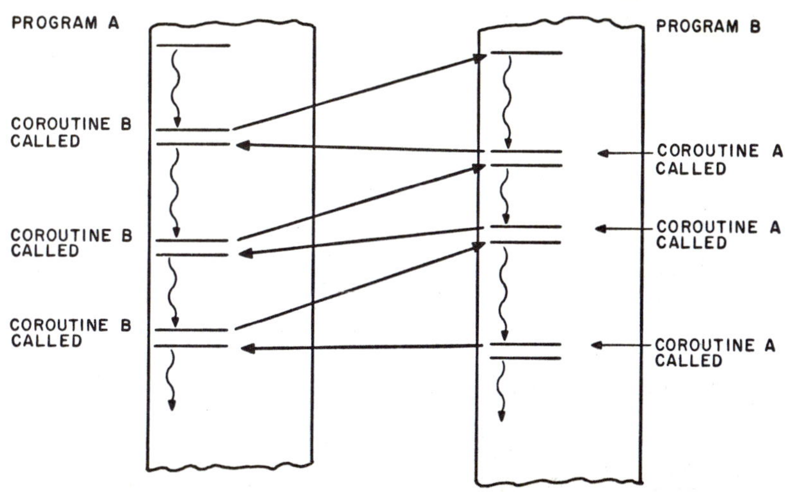

Figure 8: Flow of control when using coroutines. When coroutine B is called, control is passed to B. In B, when coroutine A is called, control is passed back to A to the instruction just after the first coroutine call instruction. Hence control appears to be flip-flopping between A and B. This is representative of a crude form of timesharing or multitasking.

device cannot be opened. Two other bits in the status byte define whether the device is to be used for input, output, or both.

The Task I/O Table

Another useful innovation is the *task I/O table* or TIOT. (See figure 9b.) Each task or program must have its own TIOT. The *task control table (TCT),* discussed in the previously referenced multiprogramming article, contains an entry for each task, which includes a pointer to the TIOT for that task. The subroutines that manage the port communications must check the TCT to determine which program called it and the location of the the task's I/O table. The TIOT has one entry for each device the program wishes to use. The first byte in a TIOT entry is the unit number that the program will use to refer to the device (ie: 0=console, 1=keyboard, 2=printer, etc). The second byte contains the actual device code. This allows the user program to reassign a device by changing the TIOT entry. For example, you may wish to have console output routed to the printer or have keyboard input come from a disk file. This also allows alternate consoles to be defined.

Shareable Devices

Some devices must be restricted so that no other task can send or receive data from them. The channel-status table (CHST) has a byte reserved for task assignment. When a channel (ie: device code) is opened by a task, the CHST must be updated to keep track of which task opened it. Later, when the task tries to read or write to a device, the CHST is checked to make sure it is legal. Without this checking process, unusual events may occur. For example, suppose two tasks tried to use the same printer? The printout would be a mixture of characters from each task. When the channel is closed, the task assignment byte of the CHST entry is set to hexadecimal FF to indicate that the device address is unassigned.

Opening and Closing Devices

Before any data can be transferred on a channel, it must be opened. This procedure is similar to opening a tape or disk file. The reason for doing this is to explicitly indicate that you wish to start reading or writing. The procedure also has a use when accessing tape or disk. When a device is opened that is assigned to a mass storage file device, the file name may be given instead of a device code. The supervisor should recognize this and establish a device-code link to the tape or disk I/O routine.

Slave-to-Master Interface

We now have a straightforward mechanism for handling the time-multiplexed port going from the master processor to the slave. Since there must also be slave to master communications, we could run multitasking on both processors. But in my system I only want to run one program on the master— either the operating system, the assembler, the editor, or an application program. The problem here is similar to the one discussed earlier: without multiple threads of program logic, how can one handle a multiplexed bus?

One approach would be to have one master channel (ie:port) I/O subroutine

a)

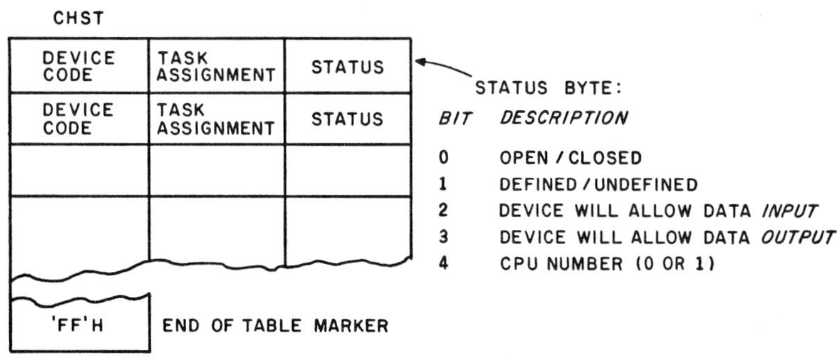

Figure 9a: The channel status table (CHST). Each table entry has a device code, a task assignment byte (hexadecimal FF, if unassigned), and a status byte. The table is terminated by an FFH in the first byte of the table entry after the last valid entry.

b)

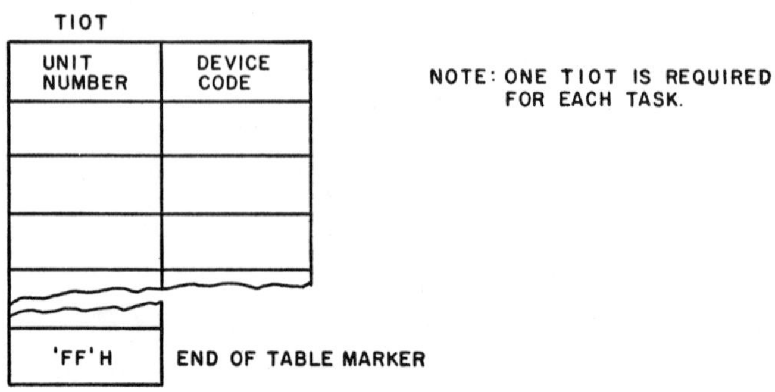

Figure 9b: Shows the task I/O table (TIOT). One TIOT must exist for each task in either processor. A TIOT entry consists of a unit number followed by the assigned device address. Using this scheme, device reassignments are easy to handle.

that is called for all input or output requests. The registers would have to be set up before calling the channel to indicate what function (eg: read, write, open, close) is to be performed. Another register would indicate the unit number to operate on, which is found in the task I/O table. Once the subroutine has been called, it will have to perform many things:

If the operation to be performed is an output-to-port:

(1) Check for an acknowledge.
(2) Check for errors.
(3) Output the device code.
(4) Output the data byte. (This should automatically set the data-ready line.)
(5) Wait for an acknowledge.
(6) Check for errors on the port.
(7) If an error has occurred less than five times, go to (1) to retry; otherwise, issue a write error.
(8) Return to calling program.

If the operation is an input, the problem becomes more complex:

(1) Check for data ready.
(2) Read in the device code.
(3) Read in the data and check for parity errors.
(4) If an error has occurred less than five times, issue a parity error, and go to (1) to retry; otherwise, issue a hard I/O error.
(5) Return to calling program.

At this point there may be difficulties. Suppose the device code of the byte is not the one desired? One alternative is

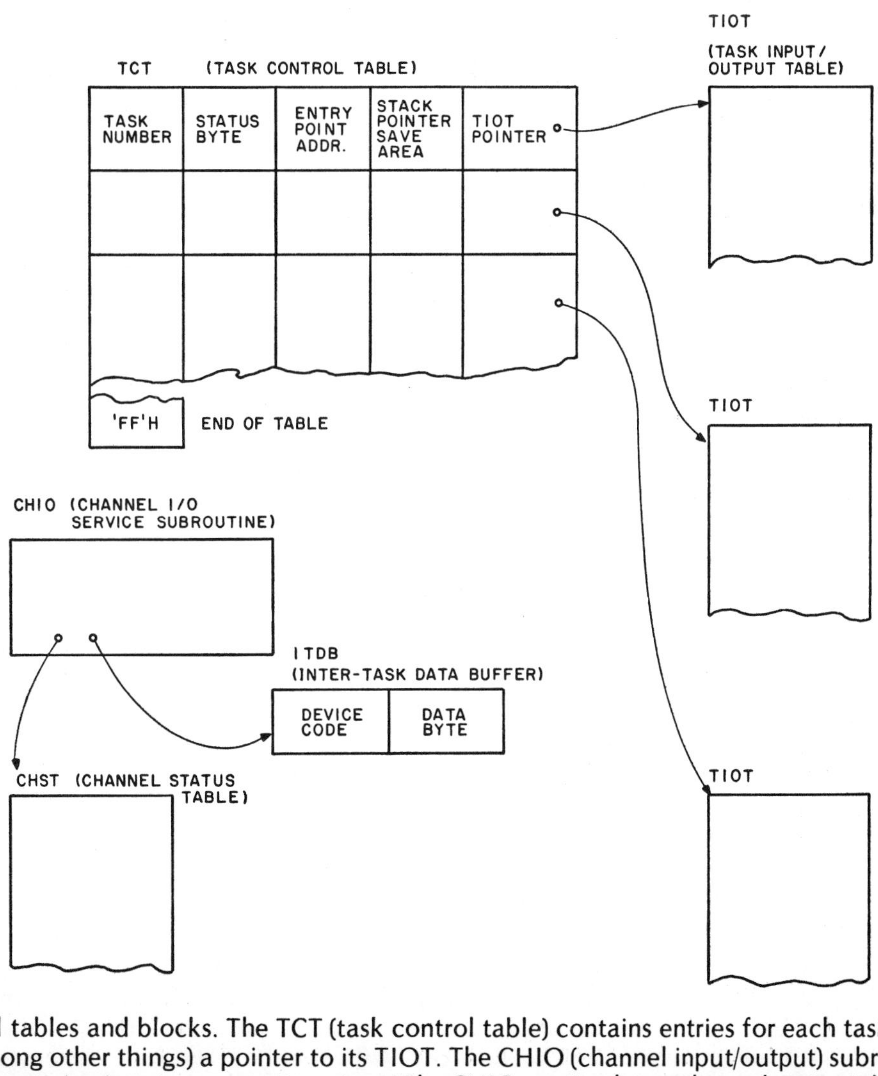

Figure 10: Control tables and blocks. The TCT (task control table) contains entries for each task in a given machine. Each task has (among other things) a pointer to its TIOT. The CHIO (channel input/output) subroutine may be called by any program to receive input or generate output. The CHIO routine has a channel status table which keeps track of each channel (device address) and its status. The ITDB (inter-task data buffer) is an internal buffer used for inter-task transfers of data.

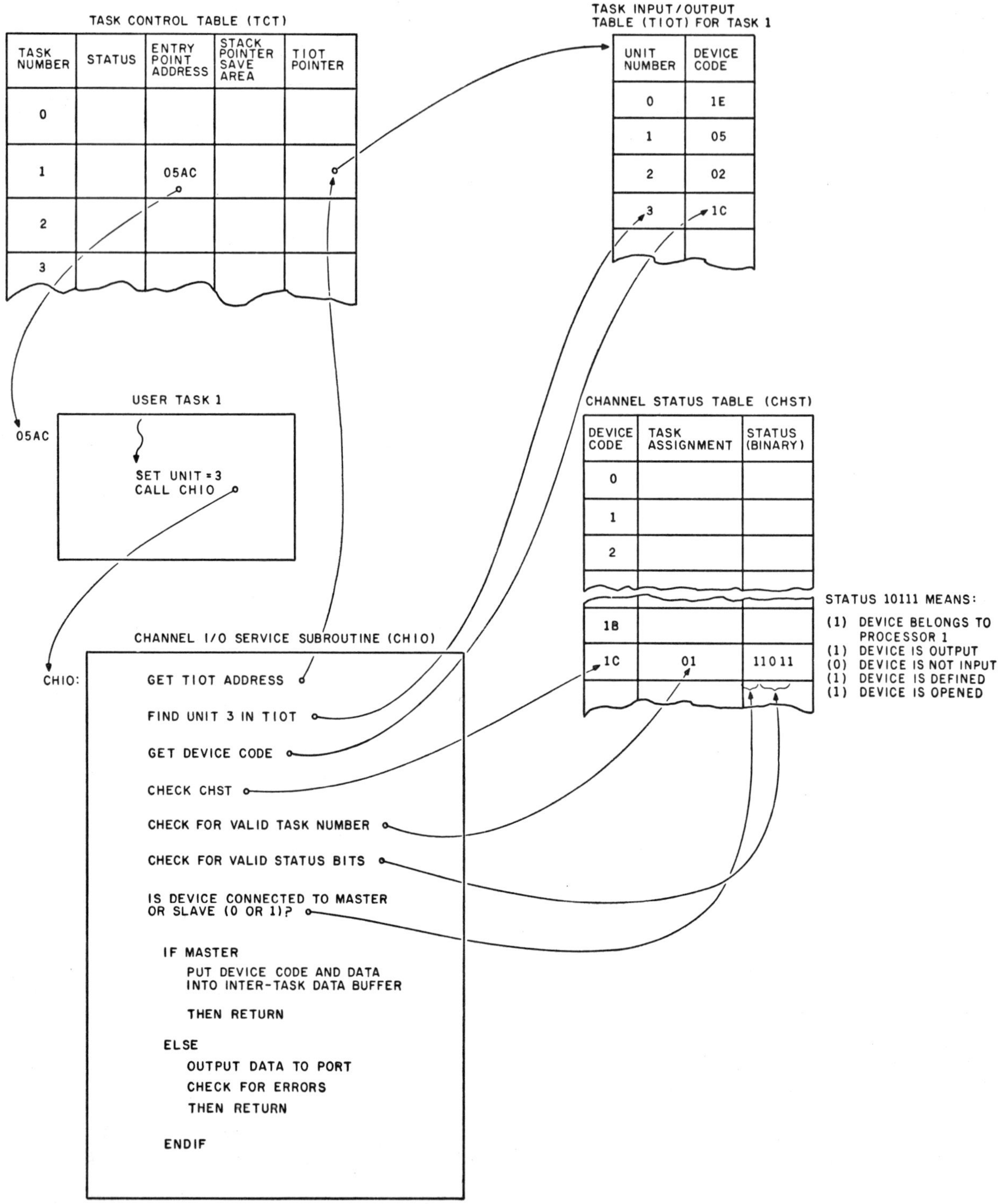

Figure 11: Shown here are the same tables described in figure 10, with the addition of user task 1. This task has loaded the registers and called the channel I/O routine, which will see that task 1 wishes to output a byte to unit 3. First, the routine gets the address of task 1's task I/O table by looking in the task control table (the task status byte will tell the channel I/O routines which task is active — in this case, task 1). Next, the routine scans the task I/O table to find the unit-device address assignment for unit 3. In this example, the device address for unit 3 is found to be hexadecimal 1C. The routine then scans the channel status table for device 1C. When found, the task assignment byte is checked and verified against the number found previously in the task control table. If they aren't the same, an invalid device code message is generated, and control is returned to the calling task. If they are the same, the channel I/O routine verifies that the device is defined and opened. Lastly, the routine must check the processor number bit to see which processor the device is on, if the device is on the other processor, the data and device code are sent to the port. If the data is to go to a device on this processor the data and device code are put in the inter-task data buffer for the destination task to read.

to set up a memory buffer as temporary storage for the bytes that come in but are not needed yet. The other is to force the slave to send only what is wanted and let it do the buffering. In the second case, an input operation, a device address would be reserved for processor-to-processor commands. Whenever the master wants something from the slave, it must issue a request for it on device 0. This makes the slave do the work, and drastically reduces the overhead of the master processor.

Distributing the Workload

As the word is defined, slaves are supposed to do the menial tasks. What else can we make it do? Parallel processing is a possibility. Perhaps it could be made to calculate equations that the master needs at a later time. This type of processing requires tricky programming, but can be done.

Loading and Starting a New Task

Assuming that there is a program to be run on the slave, there must be a manner in which to enter it into the slave and start it. First, either the slave must have sufficient unused memory (at a known address) in which to put the program, or the program must be in a relocatable format that can be loaded at any address and run correctly. Several assemblers and compilers are able to produce relocatable object code that can be translated into absolute addresses and loaded with a small loader program. Second, the master must have some way of adding the new task to the slave's task-control table (TCT) to initiate execution. The techniques involved are quite system dependent and will not be discussed here. Once the task is running, it may receive input from the master through an assigned input-device address defined in its task I/O table. Note that most of this discussion on distributing the work load also applies to a tightly-coupled multiprocessor.

Locating Devices on a Multiprocessor

Since both processors may have I/O devices, it is necessary to tell each one what it has and what the other processor has. An extra bit in the status byte of each channel-status table entry could be added to indicate what devices are where. For example, the slave may need to read bytes or blocks from the disk, which is located on the master-processor bus. Also, it is quite possible that a task may wish to communicate directly with another task on the same processor. The solution is to set up a small buffer that will be referred to as an *intertask data buffer (ITDB).* This buffer contains two bytes, a device code and a data byte. If the device code is set to hexadecimal FF, then the buffer is seen as being empty. When a valid device code is placed in the intertask data buffer and a data byte is loaded into the second location, the transfer request is said to be *posted.*

The standard channel I/O subroutine may be called to perform the post, because it will see that the desired device code is on the same machine. As with any other I/O operation, the post will be performed and the supervisor will again make a coroutine call to switch to another task. An I/O request is always seen as a top priority task, so the supervisor will look in the channel-status table (CHST) to find out which task must be activated, and will transfer control to it. When the task gains control, it will be able to call the channel I/O service routine and ask for the incoming byte. The service routine will again recognize that the byte came from an internal task, not the port, and will look in the inter-task data buffer (ITDB). The channel I/O service subroutine must of course have the necessary sequence of instructions to handle this extra buffer. Figure 10 shows the entire set of control blocks and service routines discussed in this section. Figure 11 shows an example, where user task 1 wants to output a byte to unit number 3.

Summary

It becomes apparent that even a simple master-slave interface may become quite complex if designed with flexibility in mind. Multiprocessing with shared memory blocks may be somewhat easier because the separation between the processors is greater. Each byte of the shared memory could be considered a separate device address, greatly simplifying the amount of buffering and checking that is needed in a tightly-coupled multiprocessor.

For the average hobbyist, multiprocessing has always been a curiosity, something that everyone dreams about but few people ever do. This discussion should be treated as a conceptual overview, not as the final word on the subject. I chose the approach described above because of my nonstandard hardware, and also because of my background knowledge and hardware experience. Others may choose totally different and possibly better configurations. ■

REFERENCES

1. Abrams, Marshal D, and Philip G. Stein. *Computer Hardware and Software.* Addison-Wesley Publishing Company, Reading MA, 1973.

2. Dahmke, Mark C. "Introduction to Multiprogramming" September 1979 BYTE. BYTE Publications, Inc, Peterborough NH.

3. Davis, William S. *Operating Systems.* Addison-Wesley Publishing Company, Reading MA, 1977.

4. Hasiao, David K. *Systems Programming.* Addison-Wesley Publishing Company, Reading MA, 1977.

5. Martin, Donald P, *Microcomputer Design.* Martin Research Ltd, Northbrook Ill, 1976.

6. Tanenbaum, Andrew S. *Structured Computer Organization.* Prentice-Hall, Inc, Englewood Cliffs NJ, 1976.

Microcomputer Time-Sharing

A Review of the Techniques, With Pointers to Further Reading

Kenneth J Johnson

Until I read Steve Ciarcia's article "Having a 'Private Affair' with your Computer" in April 1977 BYTE, page 18, I had not envisaged my 6800 or my 8080 as the basis of a time-sharing system. Then I asked myself, "Why not?" Why shouldn't a microprocessor be capable of supporting a time-sharing system?" I subsequently had the opportunity at the Online Conference held in London, England on May 14, 1977 to see Robert Uiterwyk's 6800-based multi-user system. This prompted me to search back through the early time-sharing literature to check on the problems their designers encountered and their solutions. This article is the outcome. It does not set out to specify in detail how a time-sharing system can be established, but it does deal with the main problems involved. Perhaps it will provide a starting point for readers' systems development.

Requirements

Time-sharing has been defined in many different ways. For our purpose it will be taken to mean the concurrent and effective utilization of computer resources by several users, possibly at remote terminals. It will imply multiprogramming, possibly multiprocessing and, in general, multiple access to system resources.

The key requirement in any multiprogramming of a time-sharing system is that programs and data should not be bound, that is, converted into a hardware-dependent form until the moment of execution. This requirement has many implications and may involve many problems, some of which have been solved in different ways with varying degrees of success. This article examines what is perhaps the main problem: relocating programs and data in a multiprogramming environment. The related problems of scheduling and priority systems, memory addressing algorithms and resource allocation are also discussed briefly.

The Problem

A time-sharing system should be designed to execute user programs to provide reasonable service and to satisfy each user's requirements. This means that each user should believe that he has all the benefits of a dedicated computer. It is the basic philosophy of time-sharing and leads directly to the concept of virtual machines linked to physical computer resources through address-mapping tables.

Typically, individual user programs are allowed exclusive use of the computer resources in some order of priority for short periods. They are stopped after a certain time, frequently before completion, to allow other user programs to be given their exclusive use of resources. They are continued at some future time from the point where they were stopped, in either the same memory area or a memory area different from the one they were allocated when first allowed to run.

To be able to continue a program in this way, the system must have facilities to preserve the status of a program when it is stopped and to restore it when it is resumed. That is to say, at the point in time when one user's program is stopped and another user's program is resumed, the instantaneous description of the former program must be saved and the description of the latter restored. These instantaneous descriptions are typically referred to as the current *state* of the user program. The state of a program typically contains such information as the contents of the accumulators, program counter, and condition code register. The state might also contain pointers to the address-mapping tables which determine the correspondence between virtual and physical addresses.

To explain this process in more detail, it is necessary to examine the factors which make multiprogramming possible and to study a typical system in operation.

Multiprogramming Requirements

Technically, there are a number of considerations which decide whether it is possible to run programs together. In the book *Computer Timesharing* (see reference 7), Popell specifies a minimum of five:

- a supervisory program referred to as executive, monitor, or supervisor
- an interrupt processing system
- memory protection facilities to prevent one program from destroying others
- dynamic program and data relocatability so that the same routine can be reentrant. That is, the routine can be used, unmodified, in different memory locations at different times
- direct access facilities, or at least the facility for the convenient addressing of peripheral equipment. (For personal computers the floppy disk is the typical example of a direct access device.)

Typically, user programs to be run are stored in auxiliary memory, usually disk, readily accessible so that the supervisory program can switch them into main memory when their times to operate arrive. Each program is allocated the required area in main memory and that area is protected by either hardware or software, from interference by other programs. Any instruction attempting to address an area outside the allocated memory block is trapped and prompts an error message.

A system of priorities is usually implemented. The supervisory program permits the execution of the program with the highest priority until such time as it is suspended for some reason. Priorities are usually determined by a scheduling algorithm which is used by the supervisory program to keep a record at the status of each user program. Table 1 lists all the possible states of a program at a particular point in time.

If, by bringing a program into its area in main memory, there is a storage conflict, the program with the lower-priority status must be restored to its place in auxiliary memory. This process is variously called swapping, switching, push-pull or roll-out, roll-in.

The most common cause of program suspension is a peripheral operation such as input/output (I/O). But there are others such as a machine or program error or the lowering of priorities. Until suspended, however, user programs run

state	condition
active	in a working state
wait	ready to run whenever brought into main memory.
user wait	waiting for the user to issue a command.
I/O wait	temporarily held up waiting to be serviced by I/O device.
file wait	temporarily delayed until another user program has finished using requested program of data file.
dormant	stopped running and has returned control to supervisory program, but its machine conditions have been preserved.
dead	terminated.

Table 1: All possible states that a program may exist in at a particular point in its execution cycle.

for periods of time determined by the scheduling algorithm. At the end of each program's appropriate time slice (or when it changes status) the supervisory program determines which user program is to be run next. The state of the program to be suspended (contents of accumulators, index registers, condition code register, etc) will then be saved either in a supervisor's stack or dumped to auxiliary memory.

The supervisory program then retrieves the next user program from auxiliary storage, together with that program's old state. It loads this program into main memory, processes it, restores it, proceeds to the next user program and so on, until it returns to the first user program to give it a second burst of processing if required. Then it continues the cycle. It can be seen that the quintessential function of the supervisory program in a time-sharing system is scheduling.

Scheduling

On early machines, programs were assembled into the part or parts of main memory they were to occupy during run time in much the same way as they are on microcomputers today. If a large program required too much memory, it was necessary to assemble the program in sections, transferring each section as it was completed to auxiliary storage and restoring it (if necessary in overlays) immediately prior to entry. For this purpose, a suitable portion of memory was reserved for the segment of the program being assembled, and for each instruction two separate addresses had to be recorded: one giving the address of the current instruction and the other indicating the address it would occupy at run time. With elaborations, this technique became the basis of early time-sharing systems.

Basic to the running of these early systems was the concept of independent peripheral operation. The processor, having initiated an I/O routine for one program, could then proceed to service the computational needs of other programs until the I/O routine signaled its completion by interrupting the processor operation. For various reasons, these time-sharing arrangements did not fully utilize even the relatively slow storage-access time on some computers. The multiprogramming concept was developed fully to realize this potential. The logic was incontrovertible: if the machine had spare memory and spare peripherals, these could have been utilized by a second program. If this still left unused capacity, why not load a third program to use the peripherals and access time not required by the first and second programs, and so on.

Tsujigado showed that it was theoretically possible to process simultaneously a large number of programs (eg: 256) in the conversational mode. (See reference 8.) Although theoretically possible, this would be impractical even now on large computers because of the large memory requirements. In consequence, it is necessary to resort to swapping techniques, and a suitable scheduling algorithm.

The swapping techniques adopted initially depended upon the hardware design; the control mechanisms varied widely between manufacturers and between models. Some hardware is still required for effective control of the process, but the software usually provides the necessary control procedures. In "Computer Software" Archibald et al specify the necessary software features. (See reference 1.) They include:

- a means of reserving memory and peripherals for exclusive use by individual programs for predetermined periods of time
- a means of switching from one program to another to optimize computer performance
- facilities to relocate programs dynamically during execution as the overall pattern of programs in the computer changes

The effect of these routines is to provide multiprogramming facilities which enable many users to initiate programs and to schedule them through the system according to their relative predetermined priorities.

The simplest system is based on a circular queue for *round-robin* scheduling. Each program accepted into the system is assigned a fixed time slice and processor operation is switched from one program to another in round-robin fashion until each program is completed. In this arrangement, only one active user program is in main memory at one time. Other active programs are held on disk.

In other systems several user programs may simultaneously reside in main memory. The operational switching between them is controlled by a clock which is used to generate an interrupt to signal the processor that a certain time period has elapsed. The scheduling algorithm is then entered every time a clock interrupt occurs. If it is found that the program in main memory has exhausted its time slice or has changed its status, that program is swapped for the next program in the queue.

Most sophisticated installations of any size find the need to operate a system of queues. The appropriate queue to be serviced by the processor at any particular time will be selected according to priority and program type by the scheduling algorithm. Programs are initiated, or released for processing by being selected from the tops of the various queues which are formed in accordance with the particular installation's design philosophy. In addition to systems of queues, the supervisory program normally has to deal with systems of priorities. Again, what determines these priorities will be a matter of design philosophy. Various criteria are used in practice. Usually it is possible for the system itself to cause priorities to be modified while programs are being queued. Such modifications are especially desirable in real-time systems because one program might be continually bypassed or because a deadline is approaching and the program concerned is not being serviced.

From time to time it may be that a program being queued will have to take precedence over a program being serviced. Downgrading of priorities happens often in scheduling systems. To facilitate this, some operating systems provide a roll-in roll-out facility which enables the supervisory program to make a request for processing time on behalf of a higher-priority program in the queue. This will result in a lower-priority program being rolled out to enable the new program to be processed. Programs rolled out in this way are written into temporary storage along with this current status. When changing circumstances permit the reloading of programs temporarily suspended, the supervisory program will automatically roll in these programs and they will restart from where they left off.

It may be that the exact locations in memory which such programs and their data were using are no longer available. To deal with this situation, operating systems provide the facility to relocate programs dynamically.

Scheduling Methods

To summarize the discussion so far, there are basically two methods of scheduling:

- simple swapping systems with only one program at a time residing in main memory for a fixed unit of time in accordance with a system of priorities
- elaborate systems which overcome the disadvantage of only one user program in main memory at a time with consequent waste of time due to switching

This necessity of switching programs into and out of main memory at speeds approaching the internal clock rate leads to further problems which can only be solved with additional hardware and software facilities. In particular, since a given user program does not always get loaded into the same place in memory, it leads to addressing problems.

Addressing Techniques

In most systems, individual programmers will have to write their programs without knowing which other programs, if any, will share main memory with theirs. The implication must be that they will need to use symbolic addresses that will be converted to absolute addresses at some time by the supervisory program when allocating memory space and peripherals to the various programs. This necessity has led to the present time-sharing philosophy which requires the conceptual separation of absolute storage addresses from the logical system addresses.

In a multiprogramming system, resources are not normally allocated to programs until execution time. Since the physical resources allocated may be different during each time slice, it is essential that the run time representation of programs should be in hardware-independent form. This means that the addresses in particular should be virtual addresses. Physical addresses will be represented by an address-mapping table which will be updated whenever programs are moved from main memory to temporary storage and vice versa.

As Wegner points out, the structure of the address-mapping table will depend not only on the relation between the virtual address space and the physical address space, but also upon the hardware facilities available for performing address mapping. For example, in "Addressing Structures" Gammage recalls that the need for dynamic program relocation was met on second generation machines by the provision of a single base register, the contents of which were added to a virtual address generated within the program to map it into an actual main storage address. (See reference 6.)

The major drawback here was that the program had to be moved between main storage and temporary storage as a single unit — a wasteful process where large programs are involved. It also meant that no program could be larger than the available main memory space.

To overcome these problems, more elaborate addressing structures were devised. These structures reflected the hierarchical organization of problem-oriented programs and the need in real-time systems to provide for the organization of sets of independent, multiprogrammed jobs. To give the facility of dynamic program relocation, for example, some machines were fitted with special hardware. IBM built upon the addressing system of the IBM 360, which allowed only two levels of addressing, and provided a third level. They did this by providing two sets of additional base registers, one set to act in the same way as the base registers of the IBM 360, being accessible to the programmer. The other set, sometimes known as segment registers, accessible only to the supervisory program, are used in allocating storage.

Gammage outlines three such schemes, but suggests that because these schemes use variable length segments as the basic unit for storage swapping, they are very inefficient in terms of storage utilization. Their inefficiencies cannot be overcome completely unless a full paging system is employed, using fixed length units for swapping.

Paging

Most modern machines provide some kind of virtual memory structure if they are to be used for multiprogramming. This addressing space may be provided by hardware or created interpretively by software. Most modern systems also interpose an address-mapping structure between virtual and physical addresses.

Typically, the virtual address of a word in memory consists of two parts. The first refers to a page number, a fixed size block of main memory. The second refers to a location within the block. In operation, secondary memory is connected to these blocks through high-speed I/O devices that permit programs to be swapped directly from disk into any one of the main memory blocks without interfering with processor operation. This process is known as direct memory access and allows execution of one user program in one block of memory while programs are being swapped to and from another block.

Main memory is similarly divided into physical pages, each capable of handling one page of a program or block of data. Program pages, although the same size as main memory pages, will not necessarily be contiguous in main memory and may well occupy different main memory pages at different times. One of the functions of the supervisory program in a paging environment is to form and keep up to date a page table which establishes a mapping of the program and data pages into physical pages. By this means, the address of a page within a program is transformed via the page table into an absolute memory location.

In practice, to achieve dynamic relocation, it is necessary to extend the instruction address to include a segment number as well as a page and location number and to leave the binding of address parameters until run time. The segment number is then used to access a segment table belonging to the user whose program is running at that instant. The reference in the segment table is to the page table which in turn maps onto the physical page and through this to the physical address.

This scheme can be very clumsy and take too long, unless the machine is fitted with additional registers which permit the development of an associative memory. The associative memory combines the segment and page numbers, so that only one interrogation is required to find the number of the physical page containing the appropriate address. Systems in which page registers are designed to be associatively accessed operate various page turning algorithms which determine:

- whether certain pages are in memory
- whether pages are to be preserved or overlaid
- how recently pages have been used so that, if need be, they can be disposed of when new pages are brought into memory

These systems are the basis of the virtual memory concept which in turn provides the means for dynamic relocation.

Dynamic Relocation

There is a clear need for dynamic relocation in a time-sharing system. In general, a program consists of instructions and data. While being executed it will contain references to intermediate results. These will need to be mapped or translated into references to specific parts of the machine (eg: machine addresses, device numbers, etc). This can be accomplished at three different times:

- During compilation, assembly, or translation into machine code. The result is an absolute program which will be assigned to the same memory locations and use the same peripherals each time it is run, assuming they are available. (This is the most common scheme for user programs in typical personal computers.)
- When the program is loaded. Most machines have a relocating loader which enables programs to be relocated statically.
- During execution, using dynamic relocation.

In multiprogramming it is difficult, if not impossible, to allocate memory concurrently to two or more independently written programs if they are absolute programs. The allocation method requires that the particular combination of programs to be run at any one time and their storage requirements are known in advance. This is information that is not always available when the programs are written.

If the absolute addresses are left untranslated by the assembler or compiler and translated by a relocating loader into actual addresses only when the program is loaded for execution, the particular combination of programs to be loaded together can be decided just prior to loading. This method is known as static relocation. Using static relocation it is possible, with a relocating loader, to allocate memory to a program each time it is executed, provided:

- The program can be separated into a data part and a procedure part.
- The procedure part is never modified during execution.
- The data part, including the contents of registers at the time of interrupt, contains no absolute memory addresses.
- When the program is interrupted, the data part is dumped onto auxiliary storage.

These four conditions are not difficult to achieve. Nevertheless, the relocation of an interrupted program by this method has a number of significant drawbacks, which are summarized by Denning in his article "Virtual Memory."

In dynamic relocation, the translation of virtual addresses to main memory addresses is delayed until the last possible moment (ie: until access to memory is required in running the program). Because the program contains no absolute addresses, it is independent of the actual memory allocation it receives. This means that it can be interrupted at any time and subsequently reloaded into a different part of memory without modification. This desirable facility can only be achieved at the expense of additional hardware and more complex instruction formats. This is desirable since instructions in general must now hold untranslated addresses in a form appropriate to the relocation technique adopted.

There is also the related problem of storage protection, that is, the need to prevent user programs from interfering with each other while being processed. The usual solution to this problem is to allow them to operate in well-defined areas of memory only, that is, unrestricted access to all parts of memory being reserved for the supervisory program only. Frequently the technique used to achieve dynamic relocation can also be used to effect storage protection.

Conclusion

Many programs running concurrently in a multiprogramming environment typically require far larger total memory space than is available in a particular system. The virtual memory concept and dynamic relocation techniques outlined here have solved many of the problems of managing and optimizing the use of large, hierarchical memories. These techniques are often seen in large computer systems and in principle can be adapted for use in microcomputer time-sharing systems.■

REFERENCES

1. Archibald, HIA, et al. "Computer Software." *Journal of the Institute of Administrative Management.* England, 1966.
2. Coffman, EG Jr, and L. Kleinrock. "Computer Scheduling Methods and their Countermeasures." *SJCC,* volume 32, AFIPS, 1968.
3. Denning, PJ. "Virtual Memory." *Computing Surveys,* volume 2, number 3, Sept. 1970.
4. Dennis, JB. "Segmentation and the Design of Multi-programmed Computer Systems." *IEEE International Convention Record,* part 3, 1965.
5. Dennis, JB, and EI. Glaser. "The Structure of On-line Information Processing Systems." Information System Sciences: *Proc of 2nd Congress,* edited by DW Walker, 1965.
6. Gammage, ND. "Addressing Structures." *Journal of British Computer Manufacturers,* 1966.
7. Popell, SD, editor. *Computer Timesharing.* Prentice-Hall, Englewood Cliffs NJ, 1966.
8. Tsujigado, M. "Multi-programming, Swapping and Program Residence Priority in the FACOM 230-60." *SJCC,* volume 32, AFIPS, 1968.
9. Wegner, P. "Machine Organization for Multiprogramming." *Proceedings of the ACM National Meeting,* 1967.

Time-Sharing: Squeezing the Most From Your Micro

Sheldon Linker

Although one normally thinks of time-sharing as only working on large computer systems, it is possible to run even on small systems. Many of the newer large-scale time-sharing systems use virtual memory and swapping, which is not possible or practical on smaller machines. Virtual memory requires mapping hardware (ie: a machine with interruptable instructions, such as an IBM 370). Swapping requires a reasonably fast disk, which could cost as much as $2000. What we are left with is an in-core system that keeps everything running in real memory at all times.

The first consideration is the assembler and loader. In your current system, a program's location can be assigned only at assembly time. On a time-sharing system, the programmer may not know where the program will be located in memory. The reason knowledge of this location is conditional is that a decision point in the design of the system has been reached. If the system is to be nonrelocatable, the programmer may define the location of the program. The problem that arises here is that if, at the time the program is to run, the place in memory that the program was supposed to run in is already occupied, it cannot be loaded. On the other hand, if the system is capable of relocating, the program can be put anywhere in memory. This produces the additional benefit that subroutines do not have to be assembled with the program. To perform this relocation the assembler leaves offset information in the object tape or file which the loader will interpret as it goes. One possible relocation code scheme is shown in table 1. Of course, all sorts of schemes are possible. Note that relocation alone will take some amount of coding and execution time.

The second consideration is the allocation of system resources. In most cases this should concern only input/output (I/O) devices, although there may be some systems with interrupts not associated with I/O devices. There are basically three types of I/O devices. The first and most common type of device is the single owner. This is a device which can only be used by one task at a time: a task is a program running in the time-sharing system. An example of a device which probably should be single owner is a cassette recorder. It would just not be particularly helpful to have someone else's data in the middle of your program.

The second type of I/O device is the shareable unit. The most common example of this is the floppy disk. For a disk to be correctly shared, the operating-system routine which is handling the disk must reposition the heads every time the disk is used. Most systems already use this method, but there are those that

Command to Run Time Loader	Explanation
Start absolute loading:	The header code is followed by the absolute start address. In this case, the loader behaves as any other loader. There is no relocation of the data and instructions that follow. Loading starts at the address given.
Start relative loading:	The header code is followed by an address. Loading begins at the first available address, as determined by the operating system. From this point on, a relocation factor will be added to all instructions and data flagged for relocation.
Skip bytes:	This code is followed by a number designating the number of bytes to be skipped. This is useful in defining uninitialized buffers and is more efficient than repeated uses of code to reserve 1 or 2 bytes (see below).
Define absolute start address:	The header code is followed by the absolute start address. If the routine is a subroutine, this code would not be used, as the module has no start address. When this code is used the program will be started at the specified address once loading is completed.
Define relative start address:	Similar to the preceding code; however, program execution will start in a position relative to the first location.
One byte:	The header code is followed by one byte. This code gets no relocation, because it is either an instruction without an address, or data which is too small to be an address.
Two bytes absolute:	The header code is followed by the 2 bytes. This code also receives no relocation because it is either an absolute address value, a 1-byte immediate instruction with its data byte, or it is a relative address instruction which is self-relocating.
Three bytes relative:	The header code is followed by the 3-byte instruction. This code will receive a relocation factor.
Three bytes absolute:	The header code is followed by a 3-byte instruction with an absolute address value which is unchanged in loading.
Two bytes relocatable address values:	The header code is followed by the address data. The address data is always relocatable.
End:	At this point, control returns to the program that called the loader if no starting address was given in the loading module. If the loading module contained a start address that address is called.

Table 1: An example of a quick relocation scheme designed with a 6800 processor in mind. This set of instructions would be stored along with the program on the auxiliary memory to direct the loader as to how to reinsert the data into main memory each time the program was run. The point of this scheme is to provide a minimal amount of computation when a program is loaded from a library into memory prior to execution. Similar schemes can be chosen for any particular computer's architecture.

have a call to position the head and another set of calls to read, write and verify. Separate calls cannot be used because a second task might reposition the heads before the first task had a chance to read or write.

The third type of I/O device is the device that is the system's alone. An example of this is the clock interrupt, a solitary interrupt device. It must be the system's job to keep track of time. It is also the charge of the system to keep track of which devices are owned by which tasks. The system must place all of the task's allocated devices back on the available list if a *cancel-the-program* function is executed.

When a task wants to perform input or output, it might use a considerable amount of system time monitoring status lines, thereby making time-sharing impossible, unless all, or at least some of the devices are interrupt driven. The best way to handle things is to have a routine which will cause a task to wait until an interrupt is received for that task, then let the task handle the interrupt, including polling. So far, the routines required are summarized in table 2. This is not to say that these are the only routines you will ever need; table 2 is probably the minimum set of functions you will ever need.

When handling disk interrupts, it is necessary to keep track of which task, if any, is using the disk. When a task requests the use of a disk or other shared device, it must get a return code stating whether or not the device is busy. Otherwise, the system must queue its request (ie: make the program wait and handle the request whenever it can).

A third consideration is scheduling. Each task has a status: ready to run, running, running with an interrupt pending, or waiting. At some point, the system must stop running one task and begin running another.

We will require the operating system to reschedule the tasks every time a task asks to wait. Since that task cannot proceed, we will perform a task that is not in a wait state. There are three other times when we may optionally reschedule the tasks: every interrupt, every clock interrupt, or every interrupt and system call. These methods are called demand scheduling, event scheduling, time slicing, and quick scheduling, respectively. The fastest method is to wait for WAIT calls. The other three methods are fairer, depending on how you look at things.

The actual method of scheduling leads to another decision point. The scheduler may be foreground-background, round-robin, or priority scheduling. Foreground-background is the fastest. In this type of scheduling, the system scans down the list of tasks and runs the first nonwaiting task. When this method is used, the position on the list is the important factor.

Round-robin scheduling starts the search for an executable task after the last task running. The search starts at the top of the list when it hits the bottom. This way gives every task its chance to run.

Priority scheduling requires a list of priorities. This scheduler runs the task with the highest priority which is not waiting. This is the fairest method because each task is given exactly what it deserves. When you run off the bottom of the list, using either the foreground-background or priority scheduling method, you have the option of starting over or executing a WAIT instruction. Although it will cost a byte of program memory, it will save considerable time on a 6800 or similar machine, since the interrupt vectoring will be half done by the time you get the interrupt.

- Attempt to allocate a particular device. This routine must give a return code stating whether or not the device is already being allocated.
- Free a device.
- Read a character from a particular device.
- Write a character to a particular device.
- Read a particular disk block.
- Write a particular disk block.
- Wait.
- End a task.

Table 2: Minimum routines that are required for handling a time-sharing system. The end task routine should return control to the supervisory program with information that the task is totally finished. The last thing you want to do is encounter a halt instruction in the program code and halt the machine.

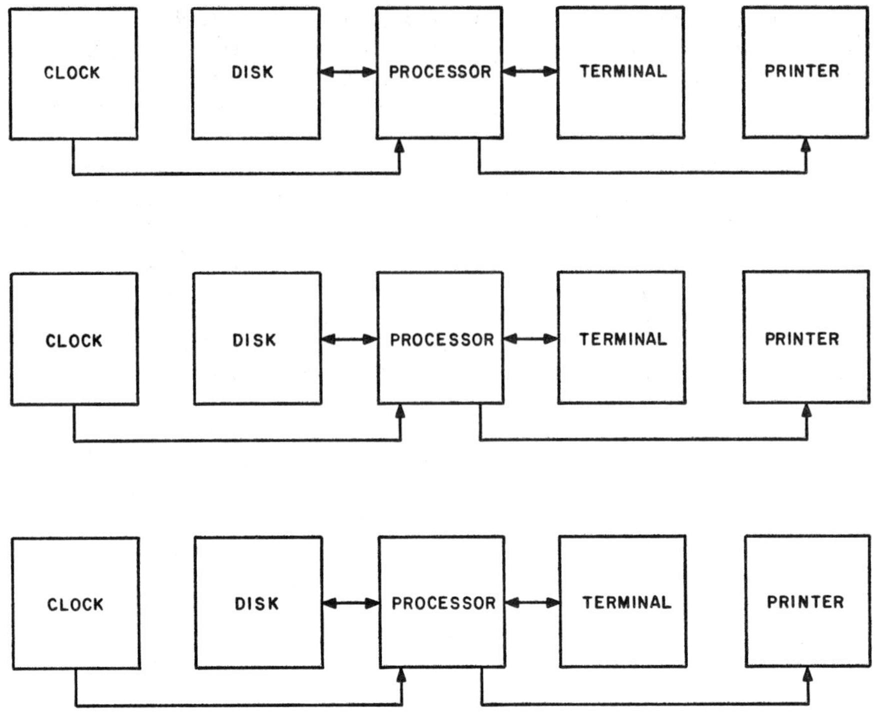

Figure 1: A system set up with each processor having its own mass storage device and I/O peripherals.

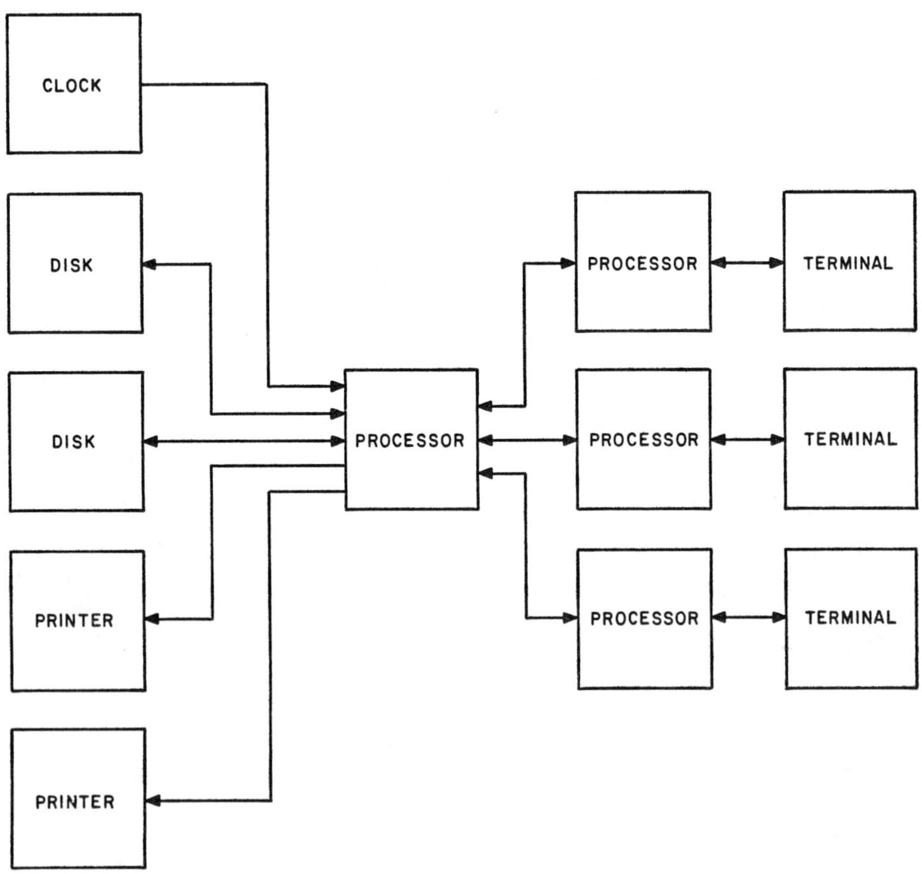

Figure 2: This arrangement uses resource sharing. To make this arrangement work, processor to processor data links must be added. Time-sharing and multiprogramming can be useful in the personal system. What happens when two children and two adults must share several terminals? What about the case when you want to do a listing or assembly on a slow printer while continuing an editing operation on a separate source file? The smallness of the scope of a computer does not rule out the use of resource sharing and multiprocessing.

This covers most of what you need, but there are a few more minor considerations to follow:

- A task has to get into the machine somehow. Two possible methods come to mind. One is the typical time-sharing method with each terminal getting its own task. The other is to add a system call which adds a new task.
- You can set things up so that each task has a fixed amount of memory, which may or may not be reset between tasks, or use some sort of a system where the tasks can acquire and free memory dynamically.
- Programs must be nice to one another, as very few of the machines around have any sort of memory protection or privileged instructions.
- When an interrupt occurs, or a task is otherwise stopped, the registers, including the program status word (PSW), and stack pointer must be saved and later restored. Depending on the type of programs you run and your type of machine you may have to save and restore all or part of page 0. If you have a 6502, you will also have to deal with the stack's page.
- Programs which can be run concurrently by more than one task are reentrant. You may wish to set up some way of effectively using reentrant programs, such as having a null task, which have reentrant subroutines; or by having various small reentrant routines always in the same place in memory, such as multiply and divide.

There are other methods of going about this completely. Many BASIC systems will have one BASIC interpreter in memory along with multiple programs, and will execute one line of BASIC code and then go on to the next pseudo-task. This will also work for APL, although long matrix operations will tend to extend the intervals between transitions from one process to another. It is a debatable point whether or not a time-sharing APL and two workspaces will ever fit into the same memory at one time.

Multiple-processor time-sharing systems are also possible. Assuming that you have a central processor with disks and printers, there is a method that can save a lot of money. This method is resource sharing. Figure 1 shows a typical group of three computers each working independently. Each processor handles everything with inefficient use of the printers and disks. Figure 2 depicts a resource sharing setup. This requires the addition of processor to processor data links. In this setup, each peripheral processor does the computing while the central processor handles queued I/O and interrupts much like the simple time-sharing systems above.■

Designing a Command Language

G A Van den Bout

Nearly every system, whether it is composed of ten lines of code or ten thousand lines of code, will perform three distinct functions. It will receive input from the user, it will process this input and it will output the results. Of these three functions, the one which undoubtedly receives the least attention from the system designer is the communication from the user of the system to the system itself.

Hours and hours may be spent perfecting a processing algorithm and computing field lengths so that the resulting output can be instantly understood, yet due to the lack of consideration put into the input stage of the system, the user may be forced to plow through a series of questions and answers directed to him by the system. This is a situation which would try the patience of even the most tolerant person. Sometimes a situation even worse than this series of questions may be caused by the designer who is very familiar with the system. In an effort to save time and memory space, the designer may decide to reduce or even entirely omit any prompting by the program. This leaves the decision of what information must be entered to the intuition of the user, or to a system manual which will probably not be around when it is needed.

A good solution to the problem would be a well-designed command language which would allow the user to supply all the information needed by the program at one time, in a single command. Then, if any of the required data has not been entered, the computer can prompt the user for the remaining items. This method allows for both the experienced user who knows exactly what data the program needs at every instant and for the first-time user who requires some help from the system now and then, but who will soon become familiar with the system and probably prefer to avoid the repetitious prompting.

Consider the following example which, although hypothetical and not necessarily typical of chess playing programs in general, illustrates problems which do exist in many systems. A superb chess playing program has been designed after months of hard work. Along with this program, a graphics output system has been devised to display the present formation of the board after each move is made. When the user sits down to test his skill against that of the machine, he becomes a partner to the following dialogue:

(C: COMPUTER; P: PLAYER)

C: DO YOU WISH TO MOVE(1), CAPTURE(2), OR CASTLE(3)?ENTER 1, 2, OR 3.

P: 1

C: ENTER NUMBER (1-8) OF ROW THAT PIECE IS ON.

P: 2

C: ENTER LETTER (A-Z) OF COLUMN THAT PIECE IS ON.

P: D

C: ENTER NUMBER (1-8) OF ROW TO WHICH YOU ARE MOVING.

P: ...

No matter how well the machine plays chess, it is doubtful whether it will be used by any particular person for more than a few games. Despite the thought that went into the rest of the

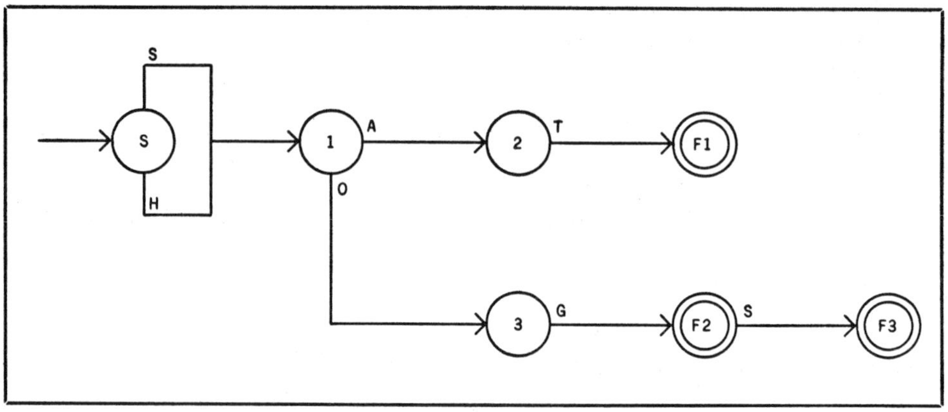

Figure 1: A finite-state machine with one initial state and three final states that is capable of recognizing the words: sat, sog, sogs, hat, hog and hogs.

program, no creative thought was put into the command language for the system.

Now, consider the following conversation between the computer and the player.

C: ENTER YOUR FIRST MOVE.
P: MOVE FROM D2 TO D4
C: I MOVE FROM H5 TO E2. CHECK.
P: CAPTURE E2
C: FROM WHERE?
P: H2
C: ...

This method not only reduces the unnecessary chatter that was encountered in the first case, but gives the player credit for possessing some knowledge of what is happening in the game. By taking time to design an easy-to-use command language, the designer can produce a game that will not only play well but will also be enjoyable to use.

The problem encountered when designing a program which handles a set of commands such as these is that often no organized approach is taken to assure that the allowable commands are processed correctly. Each input string may be scanned and rescanned for the information needed by the program. This type of haphazard approach will very likely produce unreadable code that is hard to debug and may contain hidden errors and ambiguities. To avoid these problems, the theory of finite-state machines (FSMs) may be used to produce a recognizer program which can parse the input commands and produce a structured command which can be interpreted by the system.

Finite-State Machines

Since the aim of this article is to show how to use finite-state machines to aid in programming a command language, not to thoroughly cover FSM theory, I will give a rather informal description of the machines. The representation used here has appeared in various places, and was chosen mainly because of its simplicity for this application.

Consider the finite-state machine shown in figure 1. Each circle represents a *state* of the finite state machine. In this example there are seven states: S, 1, 2, 3, F1, F2 and F3. The names chosen for the states are arbitrary. The directed lines between the states are called *state transition paths.* The state transition path, labeled with an H, located between state S and state 1, is named S-1(H). The parenthetical symbol will be omitted when there is no ambiguity, such as the path 1-3. The states which are circled twice are *final states.* The final states in figure 1 are F1, F2 and F3. The states which are pointed to by arrows which lead from no other state are called *initial states.* The only initial state in figure 1 is S.

This finite-state machine can be used to recognize several different strings, a string in this case being merely a sequence of letters. For a particular string to be recognized, an ordered path must exist between an intial state and a final state, such that every symbol in the recognized string exists in its original order along the path starting at the initial state. Using this finite-state machine the string HOG is recognized in the following manner. Starting at initial state S, the first symbol in the string, H, leads to state 1 along path S-1(H). The second symbol, the letter O, selects path 1-3 leading to state 3. Finally, the symbol G leads to the final state F2 via the path 3-F2. Since this path exists from the initial state S to the final state F2, the string has been recognized. The other strings which can be recognized by this FSM are SAT, HAT, SOG, SOGS and HOGS.

State transition paths need not proceed to a new state. A state transition path may return to a previous state or may even return to the state from which it started. Figure 2 is an example of a finite-state machine which will recognize any string which begins and ends with an A and which has zero or more Bs between the two As, such as the strings: AA, ABA, ABBA, etc.

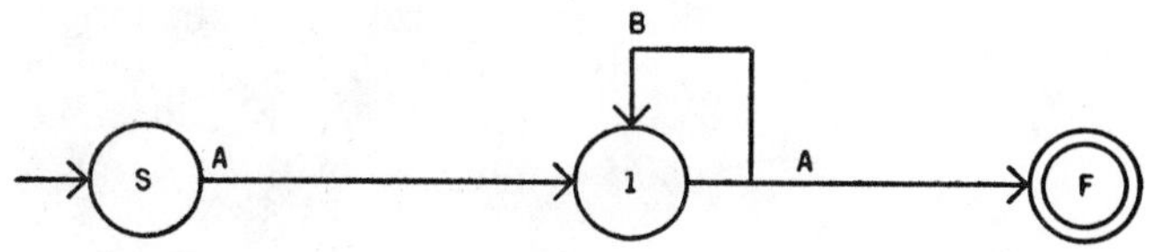

Figure 2: Finite-state machine that has a state transition path loop.

Sample Problem

Now that the basics of finite-state machines have been explained, a simple command language will be defined and implemented using them as a design tool. Using this example, a similar procedure can be followed to produce a recognizing program for nearly any command language that might be chosen.

Assume that there is a game played on a chess board. The columns of the board are labeled with the letters A thru H and the rows of the board are labeled with the numbers 1 thru 8. The three possible moves which may be made by any player consist of moving a piece from one square to another, MOVE, moving a piece to another square and capturing the piece on that square, CAP, or removing one of his own pieces from the board, TAKE. Some examples of commands which are to be accepted by the program are:

MOVE FROM A1 TO C3
CAP FROM 4H TO H1
TAKE FROM E5
MOVE TO F6 FROM 6G

It can be seen that the commands are made up of six basic entities that must be recognizable. Three of these entities are the commands, MOVE, CAP and TAKE. TO and FROM are keywords which must be identified in order to interpret a command. The final type is a position which may consist of a letter followed by a number or a number followed by a letter and will exist one or more times in each command.

Command Recognizers

When a command is entered to be interpreted by the computer, it consists merely of a sequence of *symbols* (letters, numbers and spaces) having no syntactic meaning of their own. The meaning only starts to become clear when the symbols are grouped together to form *tokens*. The tokens existing in this game are the six entities described above. These tokens will be referred to as <MOVE>,<CAP>,<TAKE>,<TO>, <FROM>,<POS>. A finite-state machine which will recognize each of these tokens is shown in figure 3. Blanks are shown on this diagram and in the following diagrams as small squares. Note that one new token has been added to the six types listed above. This new token is <END> recognized when an end of line (EOL) delimiter is found.

Most of this finite-state machine is self-explanatory. Note, however, the two states L15 and L23 which are entered after matching an initial C or F, respectively. These states represent a point in the matching process where the token being recognized may be either a command (<CAP>or<FROM>) or a position (<POS>). When the next symbol in the input stream is examined, the recognition of the token as a position (paths L15-L20 and L23-L20) or as a command (paths L15-L16 and L23-L24) can be made.

The finite-state machine described performs the process known as *lexical analysis*, the process of grouping together input symbols to determine the input tokens. The next process to be performed is the process of *syntactic analysis*, checking the order of the tokens to see if they form a valid command. For example, the two "commands":

MOVE FROM A1 TO C3
A1 C3 FROM TO MOVE

are both composed of valid tokens for the example language, but only the first command is syntactically correct. To determine the syntactic correctness of a command another finite-state machine must be designed. This machine, rather than having paths labeled with symbols from a character set, will have labels that are valid tokens of the language being processed. Figure 4 shows a finite-state machine which will accept the valid commands of the language.

Semantic Routines

At this point two finite-state machines have been produced to be used to recognize valid commands for the game. Before these machines are used to help produce code to process actual commands, the results of processing each command must be defined. After a decision has been made regarding these results, *semantic routines,* routines to carry out the processing of the various commands, should be associated with each state transition path of the finite-state machines. In our system, each command will be converted to a set of codes and placed in an array called COMMAND which will have five elements. COMMAND(1) will be set to a code describing the command operation (1=MOVE, 2=CAP, 3=TAKE), COMMAND(2) and COMMAND(3) will hold, respectively, the column and the row position associated with the FROM keyword. COMMAND(4) and COMMAND(5) will hold the column and row position associated with the TO keyword. Figure 5 shows the expected results of processing following two commands:

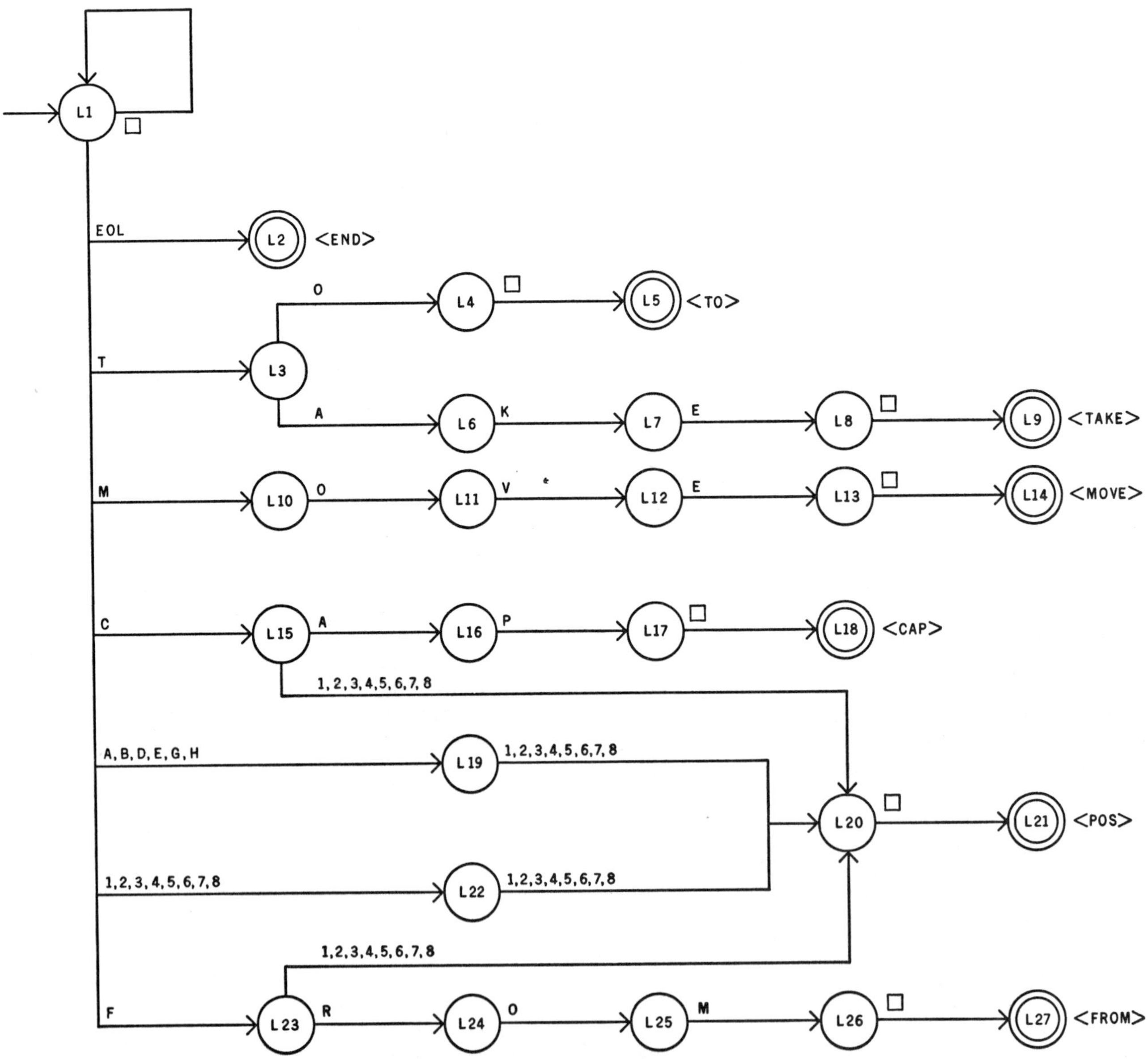

Figure 3: A lexical finite-state machine for recognizing the entities that will be accepted by the <TO>,<TAKE>, <MOVE>,<CAP>,<FROM>,<END>,<POS>.

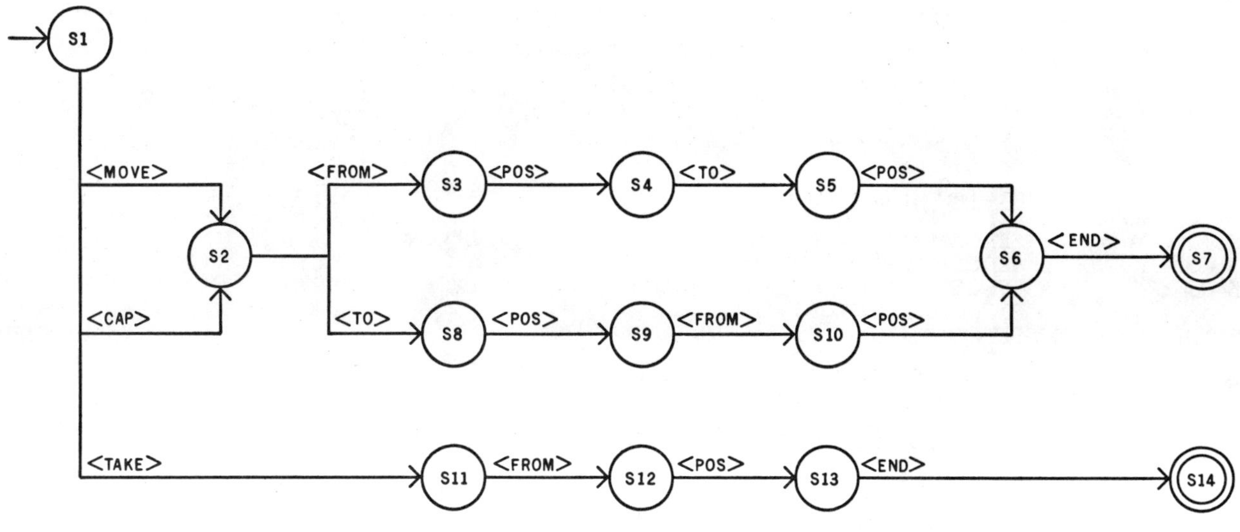

Figure 4: A syntactic finite-state machine for accepting valid commands.

MOVE TO C1 FROM H6
TAKE FROM A7

For the FSM that is shown in figure 4, table 1 shows the semantics which will produce the desired results. Routines for paths such as S1-S2(<MOVE>) set the first element of the COMMAND array to indicate which command was recognized. Path S2-S3 is an implicit recognition of the word FROM and has no semantics associated with it since nothing must be done until the path S3-S4 is traversed. When this action occurs, the row and column are stored in the COMMAND array to indicate the FROM position. When a final state is reached, an entire command has been parsed and the COMMAND array contains all of the necessary information to fully describe the command.

The lexical finite-state machine shown in figure 3 will be used by the syntactic finite-state machine just described to obtain tokens from the input stream when they are needed. The output from the lexical finite state machine will be a two-element array named TOKEN which will contain the following codes. If the token is <POS>, then the first element of TOKEN will be the row number and the second element will be the column letter. If the token is not <POS>, then the first element of TOKEN array will be set to 0 and the second element will be a code indicating which type of token was recognized (1 for <MOVE>, 2 for <CAP>, 3 for <TAKE>, 4 for <TO>, 5 for <FROM>, 6 for <END>). The semantic routines associated with the lexical finite state machine to set TOKEN correctly are shown in table 2.

Implementation

The first step in implementing the command language is the conversion of the lexical FSM into a subroutine which locates the next token in the input stream and places the necessary codes into TOKEN as described above. If at any time, an error is detected while attempting to recognize a new token from the input stream, then TOKEN(1) is set to 0, TOKEN(2) is set to 7 and this routine returns to its calling routine.

A program named LEX, written in a BASIC-like language, which accomplishes these results is shown in listing 1. Prior to the invocation of this routine, the input command must be ob-

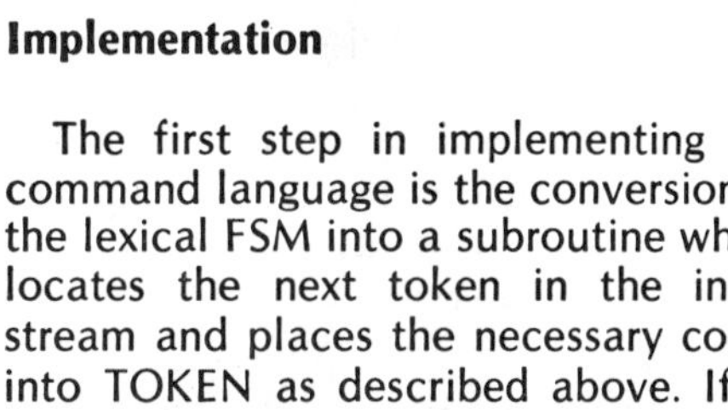

Figure 5: Two example COMMAND arrays. COMMAND array A results after processing the command MOVE TO C1 FROM H6. COMMAND array B is the result of processing TAKE FROM A7.

S1-S2(<MOVE>)	:	SET COMMAND (1)	TO 1
S1-S2(<CAP>)	:	SET COMMAND(1)	TO 2
S1-S3	:	SET COMMAND(1)	TO 3
S4-S7	:	SET COMMAND(2)	TO COLUMN (A-H)
		SET COMMAND(3)	TO ROW (1-8)
S10-S13	:	SET COMMAND(4)	TO COLUMN (A-H)
		SET COMMAND(5)	TO ROW (1-8)
S8-S9	:	SET COMMAND(4)	TO COLUMN (A-H)
		SET COMMAND(5)	TO ROW (1-8)
S10-S6	:	SET COMMAND(2)	TO COLUMN (A-H)
		SET COMMAND(3)	TO ROW (1-8)
S12-S13	:	SET COMMAND(2)	TO COLUMN (A-H)
		SET COMMAND(3)	TO ROW (1-8)
OTHERS	:	(NO SEMANTICS)	

Table 1: Semantics for the syntactic finite-state machine.

L1-L2	:	SET TOKEN(1)	TO 0
		SET TOKEN(2)	TO 6
L4-L5	:	SET TOKEN(1)	TO 0
		SET TOKEN(2)	TO 4
L8-L9	:	SET TOKEN(1)	TO 0
		SET TOKEN(2)	TO 3
L13-L14	:	SET TOKEN(1)	TO 0
		SET TOKEN(2)	TO 1
L17-L18	:	SET TOKEN(1)	TO 0
		SET TOKEN(2)	TO 2
L26-L27	:	SET TOKEN(1)	TO 0
		SET TOKEN(2)	TO 5
L1-L19	:	SET TOKEN(2)	TO INPUT CHARACTER
L1-L22	:	SET TOKEN(1)	TO INPUT CHARACTER
L19-L20	:	SET TOKEN(1)	TO INPUT CHARACTER
L22-L20	:	SET TOKEN(2)	TO INPUT CHARACTER
L15-L20	:	SET TOKEN(1)	TO INPUT CHARACTER
		SET TOKEN(2)	TO "C"
L23-L20	:	SET TOKEN(1)	TO INPUT CHARACTER
		SET TOKEN(2)	TO "F"
OTHERS	:	(NO SEMANTICS)	

Table 2: Semantics for the lexical finite-state machine. These routines are used to set up the array TOKEN.

tained from the user and stored in a buffer followed by a blank and the end of line character. A routine RCHAR is assumed to exist. This reads the next character from the input buffer and places it into the variable CHAR. Because of the way that the program has been designed, the flow of the program is easy to understand and modifications are easy to make if necessary, especially if the corresponding finite-state machine diagram is available. The program is divided into sections corresponding to the states in the finite-state machine. Each section determines which state-transition pointer should be followed from the character which is being scanned. It then performs the semantics associated with this state-transition pointer and moves along the path by means of the appropriate GO-TO statement. If during the processing of any state, the input character being examined does not correspond with any valid state transition pointer, the routine sets TOKEN to the error code described above and returns to its caller.

Listing 2 shows the routine constructed from the syntactic finite-state machine. The structure of this program is almost identical to the structure of the previous routine. This time each section of the program examines the next token which has been obtained by a call to LEX, performs the appropriate semantics for the path to be traversed, and then moves to the next defined state. Again, if either an invalid token is encountered or if the routine LEX returns an error code, this routine returns to its caller after leaving an error code of 0 in COMMAND.

Due to the way these routines were constructed, a single-error code is returned if any error occurs in a command. But, because the exact location in the state diagram is known whenever an error occurs, more descriptive error messages can be generated, or fix up action may be performed. If the command:

```
MOVE TO A8
```

is entered, then the syntactic routine would encounter the <END> token while processing state S8. Based on the present form of the program, the error message printed would most likely be "INVALID COMMAND SYNTAX — ENTER NEW COMMAND" since no attempt is made to analyze the syntax error.

However, instead of merely returning the zero-error code to its caller, the syntactic routine could return a unique code to indicate that the FROM section of the command is missing. The calling routine could then prompt the user for the coordinates of the piece which is to be moved. Depending on the extent to which this error checking is carried out, a very elaborate and easy to use command system can be created.

Other Representations

The FSM diagrams in figure 3 and 4

Listing 1: Routine constructed for the lexical finite-state machine.

```
*
*       LEX IS A SUBROUTINE WHICH EXAMINES INPUT
*       CHARACTERS UNTIL IT FINDS A VALID TOKEN OR
*       AN INPUT ERROR, SUBROUTINE RCHAR READS THE
*       NEXT CHARACTER FROM THE INPUT BUFFER INTO
*       CHAR.'#' IS THE END-OF-BUFFER CHARACTER.
*       LEX SETS TOKEN (THE TWO ELEMENT ARRAY) TO
*       THE FOLLOWING CODES:
*
*                          TOKEN(1)           TOKEN(2)
*
*       <MOVE>     -         0                  1
*       <CAP>      -         0                  2
*       <TAKE>     -         0                  3
*       <TO>       -         0                  4
*       <FROM>     -         0                  5
*       <END>      -         0                  6
*       ERROR                0                  7
*       <POS>      -      ROW: 1-8           COL: A-Z
*
LEX:    SUBROUTINE;
        TOKEN(1) = 0
*
*       STATE 1 - BEGINNING STATE
L1:     CALL RCHAR( );
        IF CHAR = ' ' THEN GO TO L1;
        IF CHAR = 'T' THEN GO TO L3;
        IF CHAR = 'M' THEN GO TO L10;
        IF CHAR = 'C' THEN GO TO L15;
        IF CHAR = 'F' THEN GO TO L23;
        IF CHAR = '#' THEN DO;
            TOKEN(2) =6;
            RETURN;
            END;
        IF CHAR = 'A' | 'B' | 'D' | 'E' | 'G' |
                     'H' THEN DO;
            TOKEN(2) = CHAR;
            GO TO L19;
            END;
        IF CHAR = '1' | '2' | '3' | '4' | '5' |
                   '6' | '7' | '8' THEN DO;
            TOKEN(1) = CHAR;
            GO TO L22;
            END;
        GO TO LEXERR;
*
*       STATE 3 — HAVE FOUND 'T'
L3:     CALL RCHAR( );
        IF CHAR = 'O' THEN GO TO L4;
        IF CHAR = 'A' THEN GO TO L6;
        GO TO LEXERR;
*
*       STATE 4 — HAVE FOUND <TO>
L4:     CALL RCHAR( );
        IF CHAR = ' ' THEN DO;
            TOKEN(2) = 4;
            RETURN;
            END;
        GO TO LEXERR;
*
*       STATE 6 — HAVE FOUND 'TA'
L6:     CALL RCHAR( );
        IF CHAR = 'K' THEN GO TO L7;
        GO TO LEXERR;
*
*       STATE 7 — HAVE FOUND 'TAK'
L7:     CALL RCHAR ( );
        IF CHAR = 'E' THEN GO TO L8;
        GO TO LEXERR;
*
*       STATE 8 — HAVE FOUND <TAKE>
L8:     CALL RCHAR( );
        IF CHAR = ' ' THEN DO;
            TOKEN(2) = 3;
            RETURN;
            END;
        GO TO LEXERR;
*
*       STATES 10 THRU 13 ARE VERY SIMILAR
*       TO STATES 3 THRU 8 ABOVE AND ARE
*       NOT SHOWN.
*
*       STATE 15 — HAVE FOUND 'C'
L15:    CALL RCHAR( );
        IF CHAR = '1' | '2' | '3' | '4' | '5' |
                   '6' | '7' | '8' THEN DO;
            TOKEN(1) = CHAR;
            TOKEN(2) = 'C';
            GO TO L20;
            END;
        IF CHAR = 'A' THEN GO TO L16;
        GO TO LEXERR;
*
*       STATES 16 AND 17 RECOGNIZE THE REST OF
*       <CAP> AND ARE NOT SHOWN.
*
*       STATE 19 — HAVE FOUND COLUMN LETTER (A-Z)
L19:    IF CHAR = '1' | '2' | '3' | '4' | '5' |
                   '6' | '7' | '8' THEN DO;
            TOKEN(1) = CHAR;
            GO TO L20;
            END;
        GO TO LEXERR;
*
*       STATE 20 — HAVE FOUND <POS>
L20:    IF CHAR = ' ' THEN RETURN;
        GO TO LEXERR;
*
*       STATE 22 — HAVE FOUND ROW NUMBER (1-8)
L22:    IF CHAR = 'A' | 'B' | 'C' | 'D' | 'E' |
                   'F' | 'G' | 'H' THEN DO;
            TOKEN(2) = CHAR;
            GO TO L20;
            END;
        GO TO LEXERR;
*
        STATE 23 — HAVE FOUND 'F'
L23:    IF CHAR = '1' | '2' | '3' | '4' | '5' |
                   '6' | '7' | '8' THEN DO;
            TOKEN(1) = CHAR;
            TOKEN(2) = 'F';
            GO TO L20;
            END:
        IF CHAR = 'R' THEN GO TO L24;
        GO TO LEXERR;
*
        STATES 24 THRU 26 ARE SIMILAR TO OTHER
*       STATES WHICH RECOGNIZE KEYWORDS AND ARE
*       NOT SHOWN.

        LEXERR — AN ERROR HAS BEEN ENCOUNTERED
*                IN THE INPUT STRING.
LEXERR: TOKEN(1) = 0;
        TOKEN(2) = 7;
        RETURN;
END LEX;
```

Listing 2: Routine constructed for the syntactical finite-state machine.

```
*
*        SYN IS A SUBROUTINE WHICH EXAMINES INPUT
*        TOKENS TO DETERMINE IF A COMMAND IS OR IS
*        NOT VALID. SYN USES SUBROUTINE LEX TO
*        OBTAIN THE TOKENS FROM THE INPUT STREAM.
*        A FIVE ELEMENT ARRAY NAMED COMMAND IS
*        SET USING THE FOLLOWING CODES:
*
*        COMMAND(1) : 0=ERROR,1=MOVE,2=CAP,3=TAKE.
*        COMMAND(2) : COLUMN (A-H) OF "FROM".
*        COMMAND(3) : ROW (1-8) OF "FROM".
*        COMMAND(4) : COLUMN (A-H) OF "TO".
*        COMMAND(5) : ROW (1-8) of "TO".
*
SYN:     SUBROUTINE;
*
*        STATE 1 — BEGINNING STATE
S1:      CALL LEX( );
         IF TOKEN(1)=0 & TOKEN(2)=1 THEN DO;
             COMMAND(1) = 1;
             GO TO S2;
             END;
         IF TOKEN(1)=0 & TOKEN (2)=2 THEN DO;
             COMMAND(1) = 2;
             GO TO S2;
             END;
         IF TOKEN(1)=0 & TOKEN(2)=3 THEN DO;
             COMMAND(1) = 3;
             GO TO S3;
             END;
         GO TO SYNERR;
*
*        STATE 2-<MOVE>OR<CAP>FOUND
S2:      CALL LEX( );
         IF TOKEN(1)=0 & TOKEN(2)=5 THEN GO TO S3;
         IF TOKEN(1)=0 & TOKEN(2)=4 THEN GO TO S4;
         GO TO SYNERR;
*
*        STATE 3-<MOVE><FROM>FOUND
S3:      CALL LEX( );
         IF TOKEN(1)>0 THEN DO;
             COMMAND(2) = TOKEN(2);
             COMMAND(3) = TOKEN(1);
             GO TO S4;
             END;
         GO TO SYNERR;
*
*        STATE 4-<MOVE><FROM><POS>FOUND
S4:      CALL LEX( );
         IF TOKEN(1)=0 & TOKEN(2)=4 THEN GO TO S5;
         GO TO SYNERR;
*
*        STATE 5-<MOVE><FROM<>POS><TO>FOUND
S5:      CALL LEX( );
         IF TOEKN(1)>0 THEN DO;
             COMMAND(4) = TOKEN(2);
             COMMAND(5) = TOKEN(1);
             GO TO S6;
             END;
         GO TO SYNERR;
*
*        STATE 6 - ENTIRE COMMAND FOUND
S6:      CALL LEX( );
         IF TOKEN(1)=0 & TOKEN(2)=6 THEN RETURN;
         GO TO SYNERR;
*
*        STATES 8 THRU 13 ARE VERY SIMILAR TO STATES
*        2 THRU 6 AND ARE NOT SHOWN.
*
*        SYNERR—INVALID COMMAND SYNTAX.
SYNERR:  COMMAND(1) = 0;
         RETURN;
END SYN;
```

have been chosen to illustrate the techniques of using finite-state machines for designing command languages and do not represent the only way to implement this sample command language. An alternate machine that performs lexical analysis for the example game is shown in figure 6. In this machine all of the commands and keywords (MOVE, CAP, TAKE, TO and FROM) map into the single token <KEYWORD>. Semantic routines associated with the paths L1-L6, L1-L7, L6-L7, and L7-L7 would be used to save the symbols which have already been matched. Then when path L7-L8 is traversed, the semantics associated with this path would include a table-lookup routine to identify the command or keyword and correctly fill in the TOKEN array.

To illustrate this technique, observe how the finite-state machine in figure 6 would recognize the capture command. Starting with state L1, the C would cause the traversal of path L1-L6 and would be saved to later help identify the token being parsed. The A and the P would similarly cause the program to move along the paths L6-L7 and L7-L7, respectively, and again these letters would be saved by the semantics associated with these paths. Finally, the ending blank would cause the traversal of path L7-L8. At this time, the semantics associated with path L7-L8 would examine the saved letters, identify the parsed word as either a valid token or an invalid word, and correctly fill in the TOKEN array with the code for the token or the error code.

Certain advantages exist for both the method used in the finite-state machine in figure 3 and for this method but as the number of keywords increases, this method becomes much more efficient in terms of memory used.

Conclusion

Now you have been shown how finite-state machine theory may be applied to produce correct and well-structured code for command recognizers. I have used finite-state machines to produce both an information retrieval command language and a FORTRAN free-format input processor of character strings and numbers; and methods similar to these shown here have significantly speeded up the implementations. The efficiency of this method will vary depending on the language used to program the pro-

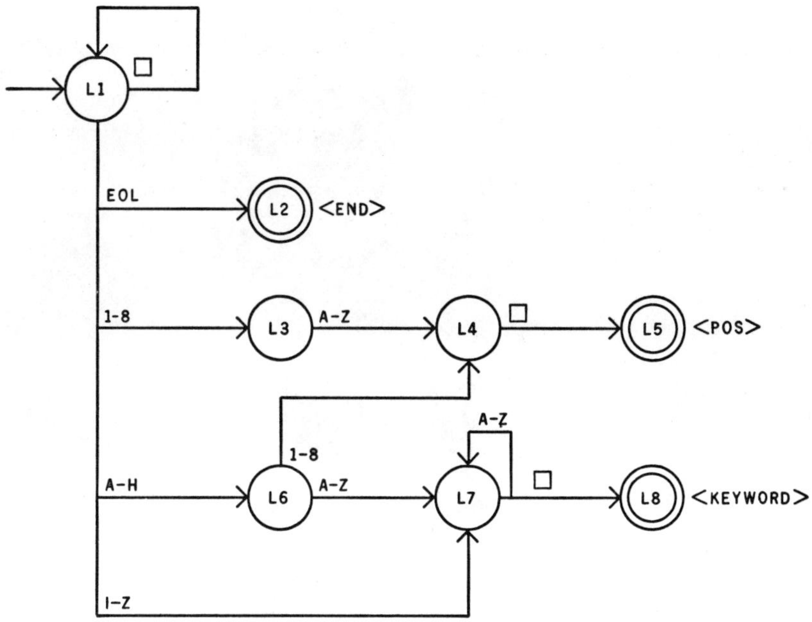

Figure 6: An alternate solution for the lexical analysis of the game program.

cedures and on the programming techniques. The sample programs previously shown were designed with clarity in mind and are not the most efficient routines which could have been written. I would recommend that the lexical FMS be coded in assembly language if possible since many techniques exist to improve the performance of character-by-character scanning and comparison. Of course, both of the routines may be written in any language desired, but because of the memory space limitations of most small computers, assembly language would probably be an asset. As memory size increases, however, the advantages of assembler tend to decrease. Whichever language is chosen, the finite-state machine method of designing a command language should produce a system that runs correctly after less programming effort, can be more readily understood and changed as necessary, and can provide a series of error and prompting messages that help to make the system easier and more enjoyable to use.■

REFERENCES

For examples of the use of finite-state machines to identify tokens of a programming language read:

Gries, David. "The Scanner." *Compiler Construction for Digital Computers*. John Wiley and Sons, New York, 1971, pages 64 thru 71.

More information on FSM theory can be found in many books, including:

Gill, A. *Introduction to the Theory of Finite State Machines.* McGraw-Hill, New York 1962.

Linking and Loading

Harry Tennant

There are two processes that add enormously to the flexibility of computing systems. They are linking and loading. Loading is the process of bringing a piece of code in from secondary memory (ie: tape, disk, bubble memory) and placing it in primary memory, ready to run. The most basic type of loader is the absolute loader, which can place a program in only one location in primary memory—the place it was written to reside in. In that location, the address references in the jumps, calls, moves, etc, all refer to the appropriate locations in memory. A more flexible and much more useful type of loader is the relocating loader. A relocating loader places a piece of code anywhere in memory that there is space available to accommodate it. Addresses in the jumps, calls, moves, etc, that depend upon the placement of the code in memory are then adjusted by the relocating loader so that they match the current placement of code.

The linking process is used to combine several pieces of code that have been written separately into one piece. For example, these pieces could be a main procedure and a number of subroutines. The main function of linking is to examine each piece of code for references to variables and procedures that are defined in other pieces, and translate these references into absolute addresses that must be used in the address fields of instructions.

Linkers and loaders have existed for years on large computers, and are now beginning to be seen on microcomputers. The construction, operation, and benefits of linkers and loaders will be discussed in this article.

The Use of Linkers and Loaders

The following situations will help to illustrate the benefits of linkers and loaders. After the situations, there will be a description of ways to implement the benefits. The situations described demand linkers and loaders of varying degrees of complexity. As with other programs, the complexity of linking and loading routines that are chosen for a computer should agree with the requirements put on the system and the available resources, such as memory space and type of secondary memory.

Nearly all computers that are to be used for purposes other than simple control functions will require storing programs and data on some form of secondary storage. A loader is required to accept information from secondary storage and place it in primary memory (eg: from tape to main memory). The simplest kind of loader moves the bytes from the tape to memory, making only minor changes to the information. In particular, no address fields are changed. This is an absolute loader. The highest degree of intelligence exhibited by an absolute loader would probably be to receive information in a blocked format with a checksum. The absolute loader would verify the checksum, flag errors, and unblock the data. Absolute loaders are present on large computers for taking *snapshots* and reloading. A snapshot is a copy of the entire program and data space sent to secondary memory. Snapshots are taken during the course of a long computation for safety purposes. If some calamity occurs preventing completion of the job, such as a hardware malfunction, the user can call upon the absolute loader to load the last snapshot completed before the problem occurred. The job is continued from that point, minimizing the amount of computing that needs to be duplicated.

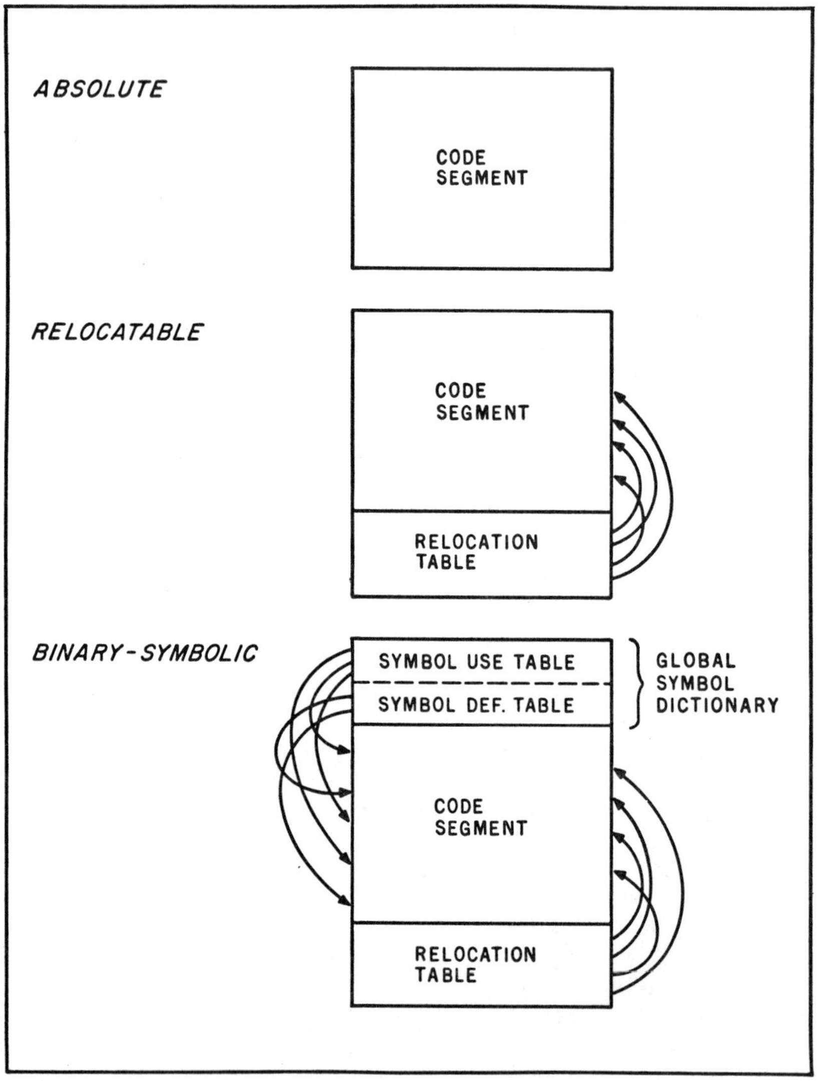

Figure 1: Forms of machine code. The segments of code used as input to linkers and loaders, called object modules are of three varieties. Absolute code has no unresolved external references and no added information necessary for relocation. Notice that if absolute code is written with relative or absolute addressing only, the segment can still be relocated. If some addresses will need changing for relocation, they must be marked with bit flags or pointers. (Pointers should always be made to addresses relative to the origin of the code rather than to absolute locations.) The binary-symbolic form of object module contains information necessary for resolving references to symbols made in one segment. All the tables shown here appear to occupy memory adjacent to the code segment. Of course, there is no reason for this to be so.

Often code that has been written for one computer will not run on a second because the code was originally written in an area of memory of the first computer that does not exist in the second. One would like to be able to translate the program to an area of memory that does exist in the second computer. To do this, the address fields of jumps, calls, and other instructions will have to be altered. This is called *relocation.* Relocating loaders examine a table associated with the code to find the addresses that need changing. The addresses are changed, then the code is executed.

It can be useful to defer relocation of code until it is actually used. For example, say one wanted to run a program that took 40 K bytes of memory to run, but it must be run on a computer that has only 20 K bytes of memory. It can be done, and is done all the time on larger machines. The program is broken into segments of convenient size. Some of the segments are loaded into primary memory and the rest are left out on some relatively fast secondary storage medium such as a disk or bubble memory. A table is made where each of the segments can be found. Each segment is relocated so that its addresses correspond to its current location. As the program is executed the addresses are observed (through hardware) for references to segments that are not currently in primary memory. When one is detected, an interrupt occurs that exchanges one of the segments that is in primary memory with the desired segment from secondary memory. The segment just loaded must now be relocated to its current position in primary memory. Waiting until a segment is needed before adjusting its address fields is called *dynamic relocation.* The concept of running a program in a primary memory space smaller than that addressed by the program is called *virtual memory.*

So far, all the situations described have been handled by loaders. When several subroutines are brought from secondary memory into primary memory to be connected into a single program, each may be relocated just as above. In addition, however, references to subroutine names and names of variables made in one piece of code that are defined in one of the other pieces of code must be resolved. That is, they must be changed from symbolic references to actual memory-location references. This is linking. As with relocation, linking can be performed before execution begins (ie: statically) or when the reference is actually encountered during execution (ie: dynamically).

Forms of Machine Code

Before describing implementation details, it is in order to point out that three types of machine code were alluded to above. See figure 1. The simplest and most familiar is absolute code which will not be discussed further. Next is relocatable code. This type of code includes information to tell the relocating loader which address references are supposed to be adjusted if the code is moved. It generally has the block of code, written as though it were to begin at memory location 0, and a table of pointers to the location-dependent addresses. If the code is relocated to begin at location 137 instead of at 0, 137 is added to each memory location pointed to from the relocation table.

The third kind of code is binary-symbolic code. This is like relocatable code with two more tables added on. The first table contains memory locations associated with all the symbols defined in this piece of code which other pieces of code can refer to. These primarily include subroutine names, labeled addresses, and variable names. The second table holds the symbolic names referred to in this piece of code which are defined in other pieces. Associated with the names are the locations where the references are made.

Relocating Loaders

There are several methods of telling the relocating loader which memory references need relocation. The first method is to set a particular bit in the address field, tagging a relocatable address. This can be used in a microcomputer by using the most significant bit of addresses. A 1 would indicate a relocatable address. Addresses that are absolute are left unchanged by the relocating loader and given a 0 in the most significant address bit. The relocator would scan the code for instructions with address-field operands, then check the relocation bit.

This presents a few problems. First, each byte needs to be examined, and every instruction type must be held in a table to record whether it is a 1-, 2-, or 3-byte instruction. Second, this method

Hexadecimal Address	Contents	
0000	CALL	Call the input routine at location 0020
0001	20	
0002	00	
0003	LDA	Load the AC with the byte at 0060
0004	60	
0005	00	
0006	LXI	Load H-L with the address 0061
0007	61	
0008	00	
0009	ADC	Add AC to the byte at the location in H-L
000A	CALL	Call the output routine at 0030
000B	30	
000C	00	
000D	CPI	Compare AC to 0
000E	00	
000F	JNZ	If not 0, continue
0010	00	
0011	00	
0012	JMP	If zero, jump to absolute location 00DD
0013	DD	
0014	00	
.		
0020		INPUT routine defined here
.		
0030		OUTPUT routine defined here
.		
0060		Data byte 1
0061		Data byte 2

Figure 2: Absolute version of a sample program. In the absolute version, the main procedure and the two subroutines are written in a block. This code is not relocatable.

Relocation Table

Hexadecimal Address	Contents	
F000	0A	number of bytes
F001	01	→ 0001
F002	00	
F003	04	→ 0004
F004	00	
F005	07	→ 0007
F006	00	
F007	0B	→ 000B
F008	00	
F009	10	→ 0010
F00A	00	

Relocatable Code

Hexadecimal Address	Contents
0000	CALL
0001	20
0002	00
0003	LDA
0004	60
0005	00
0006	LXI
0007	61
0008	00
0009	ADC
000A	CALL
000B	30
000C	00
000D	CPI
000E	00
000F	JNZ
0010	00
0011	00
0012	JMP
0013	DD
0014	00

Figure 3: Relocatable code. The sample program has been written with the origin at 0000. The relocation table is located in a distant area of memory. It is composed of a byte describing the number of bytes in the table and double byte address pointers. If the code is to be relocated to location 0137, then the addresses are selected one at a time from the relocation table. 0137 is added to the address to find the new absolute address that needs relocation. The double byte address pointed to by this sum is now added to the relocation base, 0137, and this sum is substituted into the program. This process is repeated for every address in the relocation table.

cannot be used if the code is to be moved at anytime during its execution because the relocation information, the marker bit, has been destroyed. This makes dynamic relocation impossible.

Dedicating an address bit to relocation does not necessarily cut the potential address space (eg: 16 bits or 64 K bytes) in half (eg:to 15 bits or 32 K bytes). It only implies that all absolute references must be to locations in the lower 32 K memory locations of primary memory. The code can still be placed anywhere in the 64 K address space, adjusting the relocatable addresses as necessary. (The absolute addresses could all be contained in the *upper* 32 K instead of the *lower* 32 K by switching the marking convention to 0 for a relocatable address and 1 for an absolute address. This convention may be more appealing in systems where monitor subroutines and input/output (I/O) devices are located in the high addresses of memory.)

A second and more common method for relocation is to make a table of the addresses that need to be relocated, and append the table to the code (see figure 3). The code would be written as though it started at location 0. All the memory addressed for internal jumps and calls, etc, would be relative to this origin. A minimal relocation table would consist of a list of pointers that are relative to the origin of the code to the addresses needing relocation. If the code is placed in memory so that its origin is at location 137, then the relocation table is used to add 137 to every address field pointed to from the relocation table. If the relocation table and the address of the origin are saved, the segment of code can be relocated during execution by dynamic relocation. This is necessary for virtual-memory systems. If dynamic relocation is not desired, the relocation table can be eliminated after the first loading. Notice also that absolute memory references in the code are unaffected by this relocation method. They simply are not pointed to from the relocation table. Relocation tables have the advantage of requiring the relocating loader to deal only with those address fields that actually require relocation.

In some circumstances it is desirable to relocate relative to more than one base. For example, when developing software for a microcomputer system, programs can be located in the read-only memory area of memory while data is placed in programmable memory. A separate relocation base can be used for the two areas. In the relocation-table method, multiple relocation bases can be accommodated by adding another field to each table entry, as in figure 4. This field designates the relocation base to be used.

The information held in the relocation table can also be expressed by storing the code in variable sized blocks. Information associated with each block specifies whether the instructions in the block need relocation, and if so, by what relocation base.

Two observations have been made concerning memory references in machine code. First, the majority of references are the kind that require relocation. There are usually many more relocatable references than absolute references. Second, many of the relocatable addresses refer to locations that are relatively close to where the jump or call is. Hardware features have been built into many larger computers and some microcomputers to take advantage of these observations.

Because there are more relocatable references than absolute references in a piece of code, it would be more efficient if the relocating loader could manipulate the absolute addresses and leave the relocatable addresses alone. This is accomplished on many computers by having a relocation register that is always added to address references. Consider again the code that was written to start at location 0, but is being relocated to start at location 137. Instead of changing the relocatable addresses, 137 is put into the relocation register, which is always added to address references. In this way, all relocatable addresses are displaced to the appropriate memory location 137 locations higher in memory than the code was originally written for. If there is a reference in the program to, say, absolute location 70, it is relocated 137 locations. To make this reference refer properly to absolute memory location 70, in spite of the fact that it will be added to the relocation register (containing the value 137), the relocating loader adds −137 to the address field. This cancels the effect of the relocation register, thereby allowing the reference to indicate absolute location 70 as it should. Relocation on a computer with relocation registers is much simpler than on other computers. The relocation table need only point to the absolute memory references, making it a much smaller table than it would be otherwise; an example of this is in figure 5. An instruction is generated, perhaps in the segment of code or perhaps in the operating system, to set the relocation register before entering the code segment.

When relocation registers are used, they must be altered or disabled when leaving the code segment. (See figure 6 for a block diagram of a relocation register.) For instance, if an interrupt occurs, and an RST instruction is generated, the relocation register must not be added to the address field of the generated call. This can be done by disabling the relocation-register circuit with the interrupt-acknowledge signal. The contents of the relocation register could be pushed onto the stack and changed while the interrupt is processed. It must then be recovered before the interrupt routine is returned from. An instruction to reactivate use of the relocation register would have to be included in the interrupt subroutine, but not take effect until the return instruction has been read. Otherwise, the fetch for the return instruction would be displaced by the relocation base. If the return is preceded by an interrupt enable, reactivation of the automatic indexing circuit could be dependent upon interrupts being enabled. This way, indexing is not resumed until after the return has been processed. It would also be necessary to disable the relocation register on input/output (I/O) instructions.

In addition to relocation registers, the relocation table can be greatly reduced by using relative addressing. Relative addressing allows references to memory locations that are a specified distance from the current location. On the 6800 microcomputer, locations up to 125 bytes before or 129 bytes after the current contents of the program counter can be referenced. On the 2650, locations up to 64 bytes before and 63 bytes after the current contents of the program counter can be referenced. (This accounts for 7 bits, one sign and six for the number of bytes. The eighth bit is used for indirect referencing, which is useful for linking discussed below.) If code can be written using only these relative memory reference and absolute references, it can be relocated without relocation registers and without a relocation table of any kind. This is called position-independent code. Relative addressing works regardless of its position in memory. This is useful for dynamic relocation as well.

The concept of relocation registers

Relocation Table
Hexadecimal

Address	Contents	
F000	0F	
F001	01	→ 0001
F002	00	
F003	00	refers to address base
F004	04	→ 0004
F005	00	
F006	01	refers to address base
F007	07	→ 0007
F008	00	
F009	01	refers to address base
F00A	0B	→ 000B
F00B	00	
F00C	00	refers to address base
F00D	10	→ 0010
F00E	00	
F00F	00	refers to address base
.		
.		
.		

Relocatable Code
Hexadecimal

Address	Contents
0000	CALL
0001	20
0002	00
0003	LDA
0004	00
0005	00
0006	LXI
0007	00
0008	00
0009	ADC
000A	CALL
000B	30
000C	00
000D	CPI
000E	00
000F	JNZ
0010	00
0011	00
0012	JMP
0013	DD
0014	00
.	
.	
.	

Figure 4: Relocatable code with multiple relocation bases. The use of more than one relocation base enables the loader to put different parts of the code into different areas of memory. Two bases are used in this figure, one for data and the other for the program. The third byte in each relocation table entry specifies which relocation base to use. Notice that the code would not run at location 0000 without relocation. The references to the data bytes at 0004 and 0007 need to be relocated out of the program area prior to execution.

Relocation Table
Hexadecimal

Address	Contents	
F000	02	
F001	13	→ 0012
F002	00	

Relocatable Code
Hexademical

Address	Contents
0000	CALL
0001	20
0002	00
0003	LDA
0004	60
0005	00
0006	LXI
0007	61
0008	00
0009	ADC
000A	CALL
000B	30
000C	00
000D	CPI
000E	00
000F	JNZ
0010	00
0011	00
0012	JMP
0013	DD
0014	00
.	
.	
.	

Figure 5: Relocation table required with automatic indexing by a relocation register. Automatic indexing through a relocation register dramatically reduces the size of the relocation table. The contents of the relocation register are automatically added to all addresses. The table only references absolute addresses and is used to subtract the contents of the relocation register from the altered address, giving the absolute address.

can be extended to implement virtual-memory systems. Recall that virtual memory allows the user to address more memory space than there is primary memory in the computer. The entire program is stored in secondary memory, divided into regular-sized chunks of between, say, 512 bytes to 4 K bytes each. The chunks, called pages, that are currently in use are placed in primary memory. For example, the page size of a particular computer is 1024 bytes. The 6 most significant bits of an address would refer to the page of the memory reference, and the 10 least significant bits refer to the address within the page. As with automatic indexing, a circuit is built to operate on the addresses as they are generated by the processor. Instead of adding a register value, however, the most significant 6 bits of the address are used to address a small special memory, as in figures 7 and 8. The actual current locations for all the pages in the program are stored in the special memory called page memory. If the page addressed is currently in primary memory, the 6 bits specifying the actual location of the 1024-byte page come out of the page memory onto the address bus. If the page addressed is not currently in primary memory, this reference causes an interrupt (perhaps by a 1 in the seventh bit of the page-memory output). An interrupt routine is called to locate the desired page in secondary memory, to select a relatively unused page that is in primary memory and send it out to secondary memory, to read in the desired page and to update the contents of the page memory to reflect the change. The memory reference that caused the interrupt (called a page fault) is then allowed to proceed.

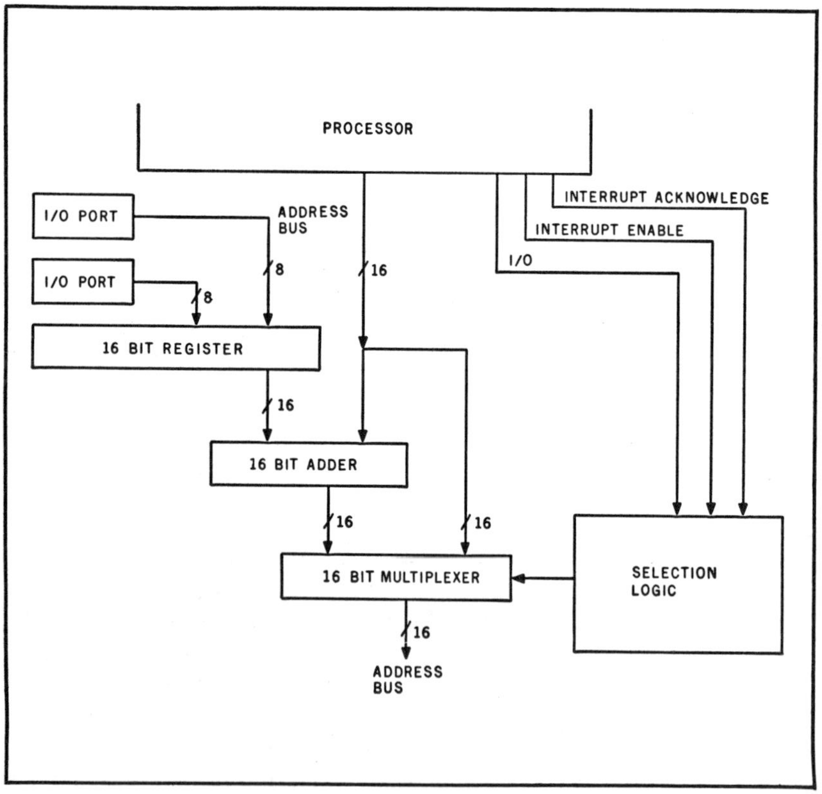

Figure 6: Relocation register block diagram. In automatic indexing, a 16-bit relocation base is almost always added to the address lines before going onto the address bus. The only exception is when an interrupt occurs. The interrupt-acknowledge signal selects the non-relocated address to be passed through the multiplexer onto the bus. When the interrupt service routine has been completed and interrupts have been reenabled, the input to the address bus reverts back to the relocated addresses. Automatic relocation is also disabled for use of I/O instructions.

Linking

The preceding section has dealt with loading code from secondary storage into primary storage, and loading with relocation. The process of linking pieces of code together is invariably discussed whenever loading is discussed, and vice versa. The two processes are often combined into one program called a linking loader. A linking loader takes several procedures, resolves the references of each procedure that is defined in one of the other procedures (linking), and loads and relocates all the pieces into primary memory.

The process can be executed in two passes like a two-pass assembler. In the first pass a segment of code is loaded and relocated. A global symbol table is compiled from all the symbols used or defined in the current segment of code but which are defined or used in the other segments. Then the next segment is loaded and the global symbol table is added to. This is continued until all segments are loaded. In the second pass, the global symbols that are referenced in each segment, but defined elsewhere, are resolved using the global symbol table. This consists of substituting appropriate locations into the address fields of calls, jumps, and data-area references.

Linking loaders are quite common, but there is no reason that linking must be done while loading. Linking can be done as early as prior to assembly or as late as at execution time (ie: dynamic linking). A linkage editor is a program that only performs linking. A loader must be used to load link-edited code at a later time.

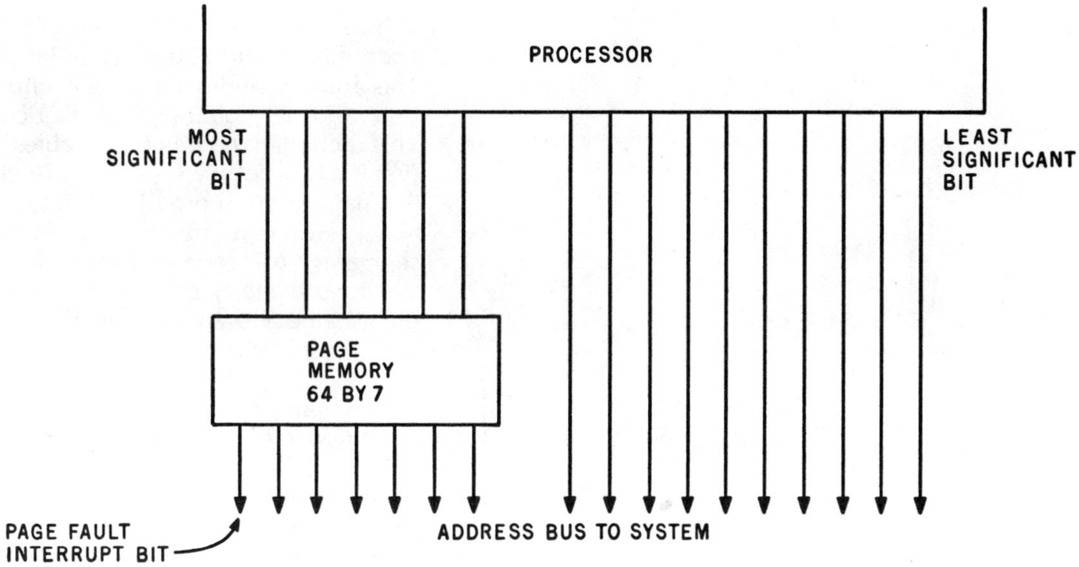

Figure 7: Page memory. In this figure, the page memory is shown as a 64 by 7 bit memory. The six address bits to the memory are ties to the six most significant bits of the CPU address bus outputs. Six of the seven output bits of the page memory become the most significant bits of the address sent out on the address bus. The seventh output bit designates whether or not the page specified by the CPU is currently loaded in primary memory. If not, an interrupt is generated to bring the desired page in from secondary memory.

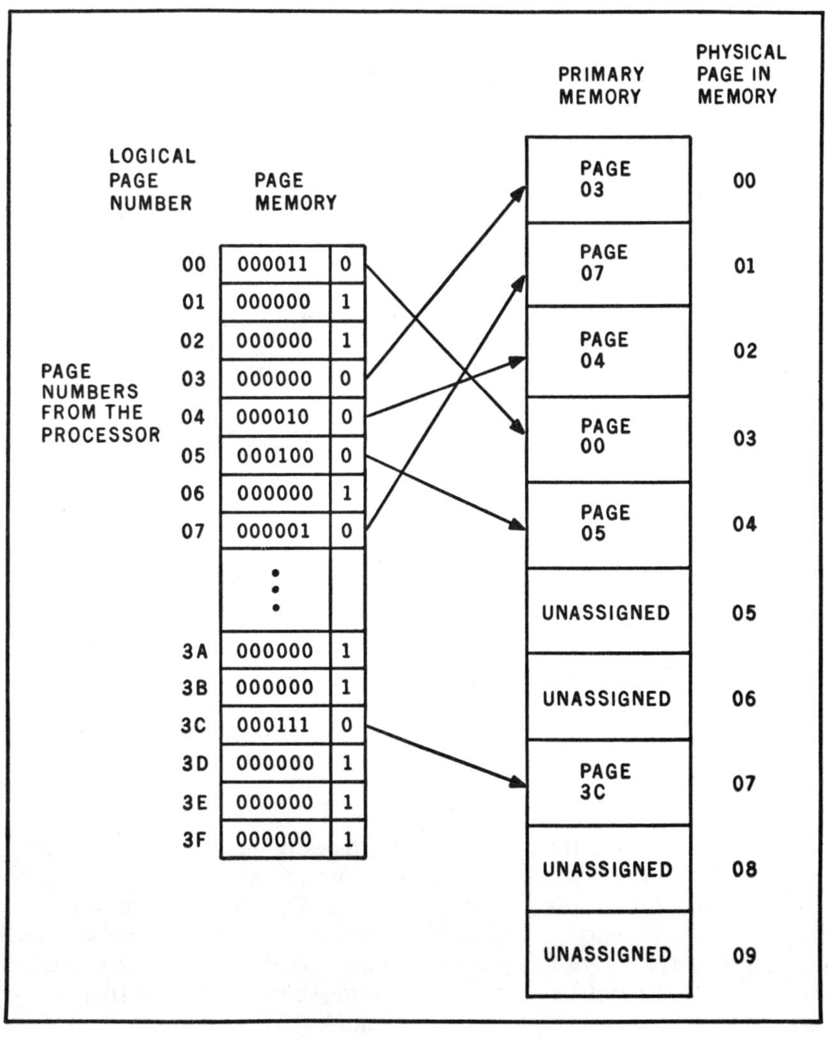

Figure 8: Physical and logical pages. This more detailed look at the sample contents of page memory illustrates the difference between physical and logical addresses. The processor outputs a page number, say page 07. This is the logical page number. To the processor it appears as though it is addressing the 1024 bytes starting at location 0001110000000000. The page memory converts the logical page address to a physical page address. The physical page corresponding to logical page 07 is the 1024 bytes starting at location 0000010000000000 (physical page 01). The logical pages that are physically in secondary memory, such as logical pages 01,02,06,7A,7B, etc , will cause an interrupt if addressed.

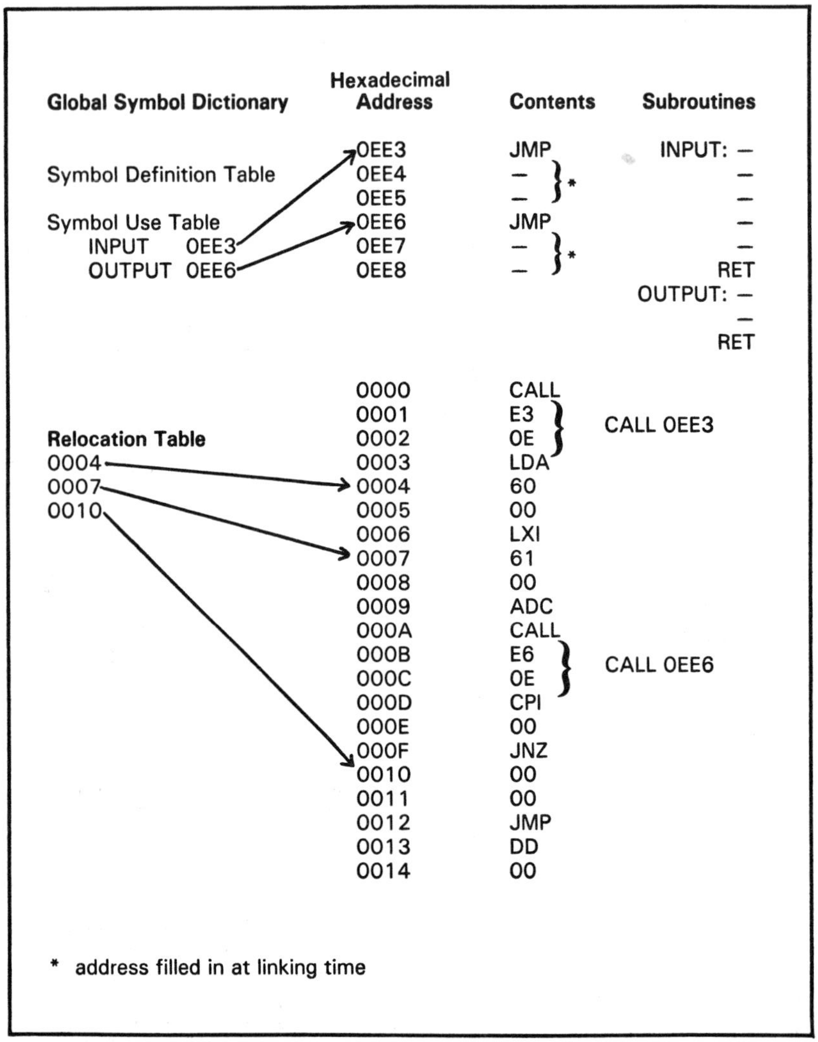

Figure 9: Transfer vector linking. In the sample program the two subroutines called have been assumed to be internal to the code segment. From this point on, they are assigned the symbolic names INPUT and OUTPUT, and are assumed to have been defined externally (in another object module). The sample code segment defines no symbols for use by other object modules, so the symbol definition table is empty. Here we see preparations made for linking calls to the routines INPUT and OUTPUT. Jump instructions have been generated by the linker and placed in memory. All the calls to INPUT, as well as to OUTPUT,call the same jump instruction. The linker will combine the symbol definition tables from all object modules to form one master table. When this has been done, the address of the first location of the INPUT routine is placed in the address field of the INPUT jump instruction (hexadecimal 0EE4 and 0EE5). Similarly for OUTPUT (hexadecimal 0EE7, 0EE8). Notice that the address fields of the call instructions need to be relocated only if the jumps are relocated.

In order to link code segments, the code must be in binary-symbolic form. This form includes relocation information and a global-symbol dictionary. This dictionary contains two tables. The first is a table of the symbolic references (ie: names) to subroutines, data locations, etc, that are defined in other segments of code. This table, the *symbol-use table,* consists of the symbolic name and an identification of the location in the code where the symbol is referenced (eg: the address field of a call instruction). The other table, the *symbol-definition table,* is a listing of all the global symbols that are defined in each code segment and the pointers to the locations where the symbols are defined (eg: pointers to the beginning of subroutines, data areas, other blocks of code). Four methods of building symbol-use tables will be discussed.

The first method of symbol-use table building to resolve references to symbols defined outside of the code segment is the transfer-vector technique. (See figure 9.) A jump instruction is appended to the code for each external symbol. All calls in the code segment to, say, the function SQRT, defined in a different segment, are calls to the location of the appended jump to the SQRT function starting address. (The SQRT routine ends with a return-from-subroutine instruction, which returns program control to the code following the call.) Until the segments are linked, the address field of the jump instruction is undefined. The linking process places the starting address of the SQRT subroutine in the jump address field. If there are many calls to SQRT in the segment they all call the same jump instruction. Notice that the address field of the call is an address requiring relocation unless it is a relative address. The 6800 and 2650 both can accommodate relative addressing, but the 2650 has the additional advantage of indirection. Instead of calling a jump instruction, the 2650 can use an indirect call. The indirect call references a memory location that contains the address of the subroutine. This saves entering the jump command. The transfer-vector technique works well for calls and jumps, but it cannot work for references to data.

A second technique of resolving references to symbols external to a code segment is chaining. (See figure 6.) The symbol-use table consists of the symbol name and a pointer to the first occurrence in the segment where the reference is made. If there is more than one reference to the same external symbol in the segment, the address field of the table entry points to the first reference, the address field of the first reference points to the second reference, and so on. The address field of the last reference contains a special address, such as hexadecimal FFFF, signifying the end of the chain. When the segment is linked to other segments, the linker starts at the symbol-use table and goes from address field to address field. At each address field the actual location of the external memory reference is inserted. Chaining can be used for all types of memory references: calls, data, or others. Chaining is therefore more general than transfer vectors, but it is still limited to static linking. Notice that in both technqiues, the links to the jump instruction (for the transfer vector) or to the next address field (for the chain) are lost after linking. There is no way to relink the segment dynamically if this were required.

The third technique combines the flexibility of chaining with the capability for dynamic linking. This method has a list of address fields in the external reference table associated with each symbol. (See figure 11.) Each address field in the list associated with a symbol points to a location in the code segment where that symbol is referred to. When the linker operates on this table, it finds the current location that the symbol refers to, then goes down the address list of the symbol substituting the proper address for each reference to the symbol in the code segment. The advantage of keeping a list in the symbol-use table is, of course, that it need not be destroyed after linking. A code segment can then be relinked if there is a need to do so.

The last technique is similiar to symbol and list construction. Instead of having a list of pointers for each time a symbol is used, a different symbol and pointer entry is made for each use. (See figure 12.) Therefore, if the segment contains four calls to SQRT, the use table will include four SQRT entries, each with one pointer.

Dynamic linking makes the linker more complex. It also requires that the symbolic form of global-symbols must be retained in the global symbol dictionary. Dynamic linking is required for providing maximum flexibility for memory allocations.

The virtual-memory description given earlier in the article assumed a program that had already been linked. However, virtual memory can benefit from

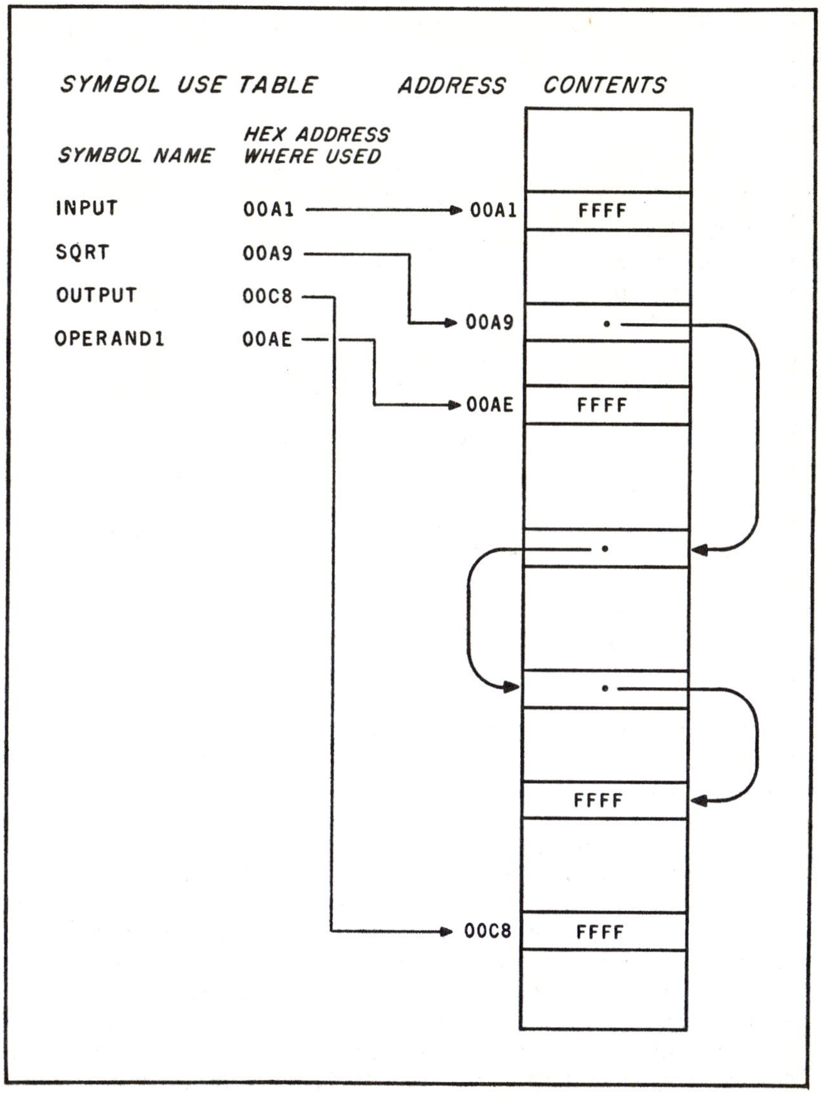

Figure 10: Chained references to global (external) symbols. The four references to SQRT are chained together. The last reference in the chain is signified by hexadecimal FFFF in the address field. Unlike vector linking, chaining may refer to more than jumps and subroutine calls. The symbol OPERAND1 refers to a data byte address. This is the advantage of chaining over vector transfer.

dynamic relocation, with dynamic linking at execution time. Execution is begun before any linking is done. The address fields of instructions with unresolved references are tagged so that they will cause an interrupt. For example, assume that all the unresolved address fields are filled with all ones. When a reference is made during execution to hexadecimal FFFF, an interrupt is generated. The interrupt service routine then performs the linking for the referenced symbol, bringing in pages from secondary memory, if necessary. This way, linking to a symbolic reference is put off until the first actual reference is made during execution. When the first reference is made, all references to the symbol are linked.

At the other extreme from dynamic linking is linkage editing. A *linkage editor,* as mentioned earlier, is not concerned with relocation and loading prior to the execution of code. The linkage editor takes several code segments in binary-symbolic form, and relocates and links them into one large module (ie: a load module). The addresses of the entire load module are written with an origin at location 0. All references to global symbols are resolved. The relocation information is retained within the load module. The entire load module can now be relocated to be executed, or it can be sent to secondary storage for use at a later time. The word *editor* in linkage editor points out the fact that after linking has been completed, the user has an opportunity to make changes in the load module prior to execution, if desired.

Linking symbolic references between code segments has been described as if all code segments are presented to the linker at every linking operation. This is not always the case. A collection of segments may always be assumed available to the linker. This collection is the system subroutine library. If the linker cannot resolve a symbolic reference using the global symbols defined in the code segments that are currently being linked, it searches for the symbol in the global-symbol table of the system library.

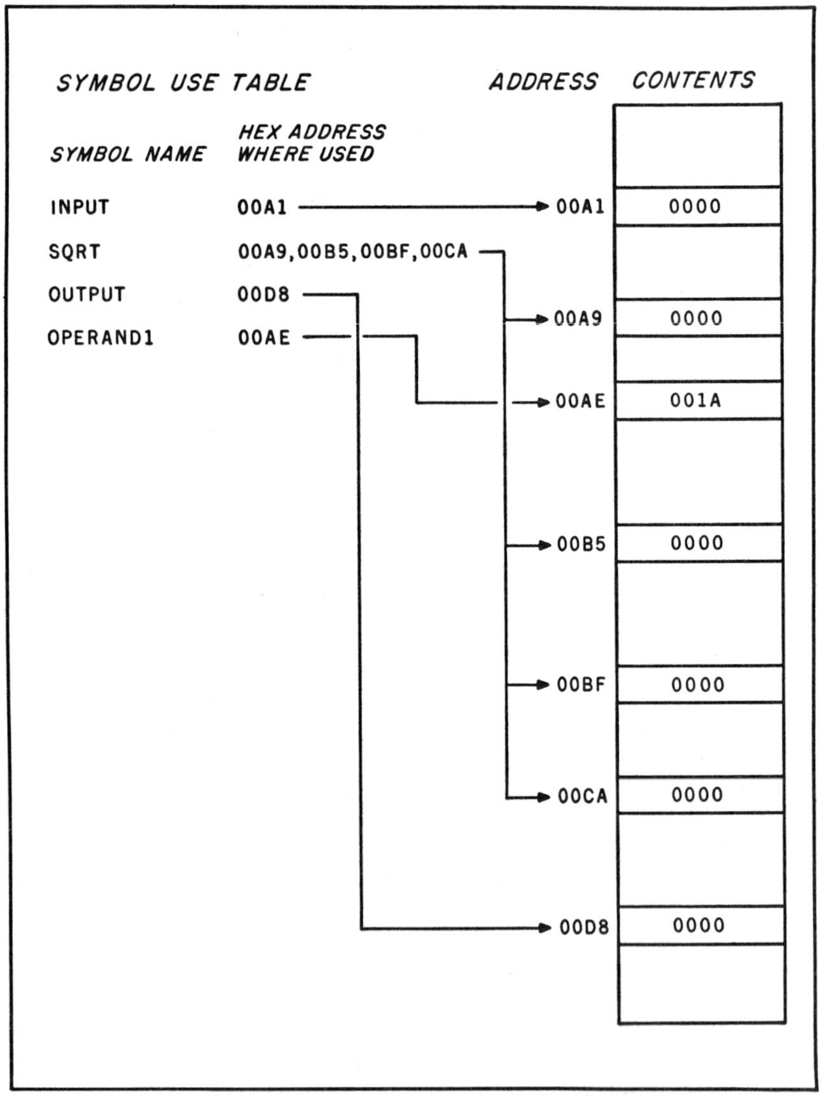

Figure 11: Multiple references listed. This method has the advantage of chaining, but is nondestructive. This allows relinking if desired. Also, a reference can be made to an address relative to a defined symbol by adding the relocation constant to the contents of the address pointed to. Here, the address at hexadecimal 00AF refers to a location 1B bytes beyond the location of OPERAND1.

Conclusion

Linking and relocatable loading provide a computer system with considerable flexibility. Relocatable loading permits a segment of code to be executed in any area in primary memory that is available at load time. This gives much more freedom than insisting that code be executed in the locations it was written in. Linking of code segments encourages the development of modular software and the reuse of code segments in different contexts.■

BIBLIOGRAPHY

1. Barron, D. W. *Assemblers and Loaders.* New York: American Elsevier, 1969.

2. Gear, C. W. *Computer Organization and Programming.* New York: McGraw-Hill, 1974.

3. Organick, E. I. *The Multics System: An Examination of its Structure.* Cambridge, Mass: MIT Press, 1972.

4. Presser, L. and J. R. White. "Linkers and Loaders" in *Computing Surveys,* vol. 4, September, 1972, pp. 149-167.

5. Shaw, A. C. *The Logical Design of Operating Systems.* Englewood Cliffs, N.J.: Prentice-Hall, 1974.

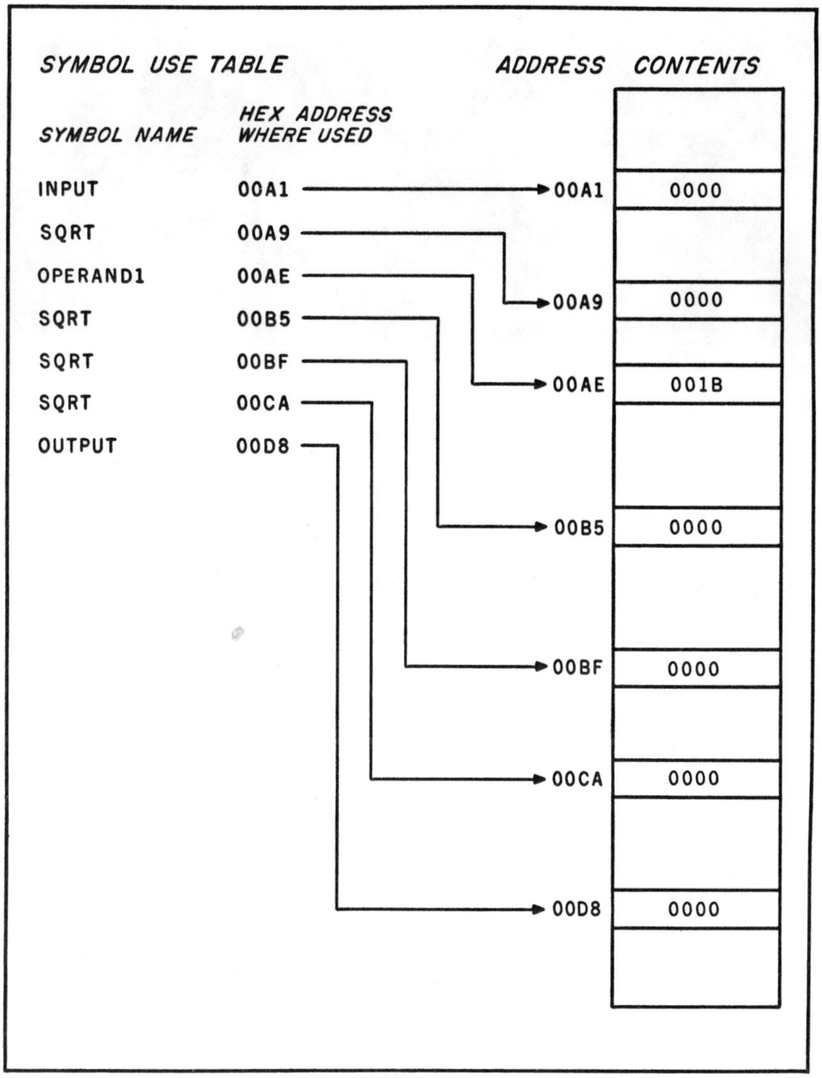

Figure 12: Multiple entries in symbol use table for multiple references. An alternative way of making entries in the symbol use table is to make a separate entry for each external reference. The code in this figure makes four references to SQRT.

Data Handling

About This Section

One of the main elements of any program is the data being operated on by the program. Data can take many forms, and can change form depending on many factors. The data can represent pure numbers, alphabetic characters, or even both simultaneously. It all depends on how you look at what is encoded in memory, on tape, on disk, and so forth. And that is entirely the point of this section — how the programmer can use his or her perception of data as an advantage to simplify the programming task.

The topics covered in this section make both the task of manipulating the data and storing the data easier and more efficient. This includes articles on hashing functions, tables, and sorting. One article will even help you avoid serious errors while passing data back and forth to subroutines.

The arrangement of data on tape or disk is always important, leading to decreased access speed or an increase in the efficiency of the use of space if done well. When unlimited time or space is available, these topics are moot; but in most microcomputer systems, they must be dealt with on a daily basis.

Sorting It Out

Brian D Murphy

Have you ever noticed that as you get further into programming you have use for a basic group of routines fairly frequently? Some examples are: input/output (I/O), table searching, and American Standard Code for Information Interchange (ASCII) digit-to-binary conversion. You can think of these routines as primitive software functions since they are used by many different types of software. An analogy would be the relationship between the compiler (be it FORTRAN or Pascal) and the machine instructions in your computer. The machine instructions are used by any compiler, so in this sense they are primitives. This article talks about another type of software primitive, sorting. Rearranging a card hand, entering names in a black book, and putting club members' names in alphabetical order are all examples of sorting. The basic idea is to use some information associated with the items you are sorting to arrange the items by increasing or decreasing value. In general, each item you sort has two elements associated with it, a key and data. The key is the part of the item that is used for comparison to see which item gets placed before another, while the data associated with the key tags along with it. Often the key and the data are the same, such as cards in a bridge hand. Other times they are two distinct creatures, such as the list of entries in a telephone directory. In the case of the directory, the name is the key while the address and number are the data.

The idea of this article is not to give you a thorough understanding of the workings of the various sorting techniques, but to provide an easy-to-use source to go to if you have a program to write that requires sorting. There are dozens of sorting schemes, each having their own points of interest and usage, and if you really want to get down to the details, I have listed three excellent sources at the end of this article for that purpose.

Included are four techniques to choose from when trying to decide which method is best suited to your particular application. Consult table 1 for the characteristics you desire, and locate those software characteristics most important to you.

Methods \ Parameter	Speed for Table Size <20	Speed for Table Size >20	Memory Usage
Binary Insertion Sort	Fastest	Medium	Medium
Heap Sort	Medium	Fastest	Most used
Selection Sort	Slowest	Slowest	Least used
Counting	*	*	Medium

Table 1: *Comparison of four different sorting techniques. To find the optimal sort for your purpose, it is sometimes necessary to have a trade-off between execution speed and the amount of memory used. *The counting method is best for speed if less than sixty items are involved and the object of the sort is a ranking of entries.*

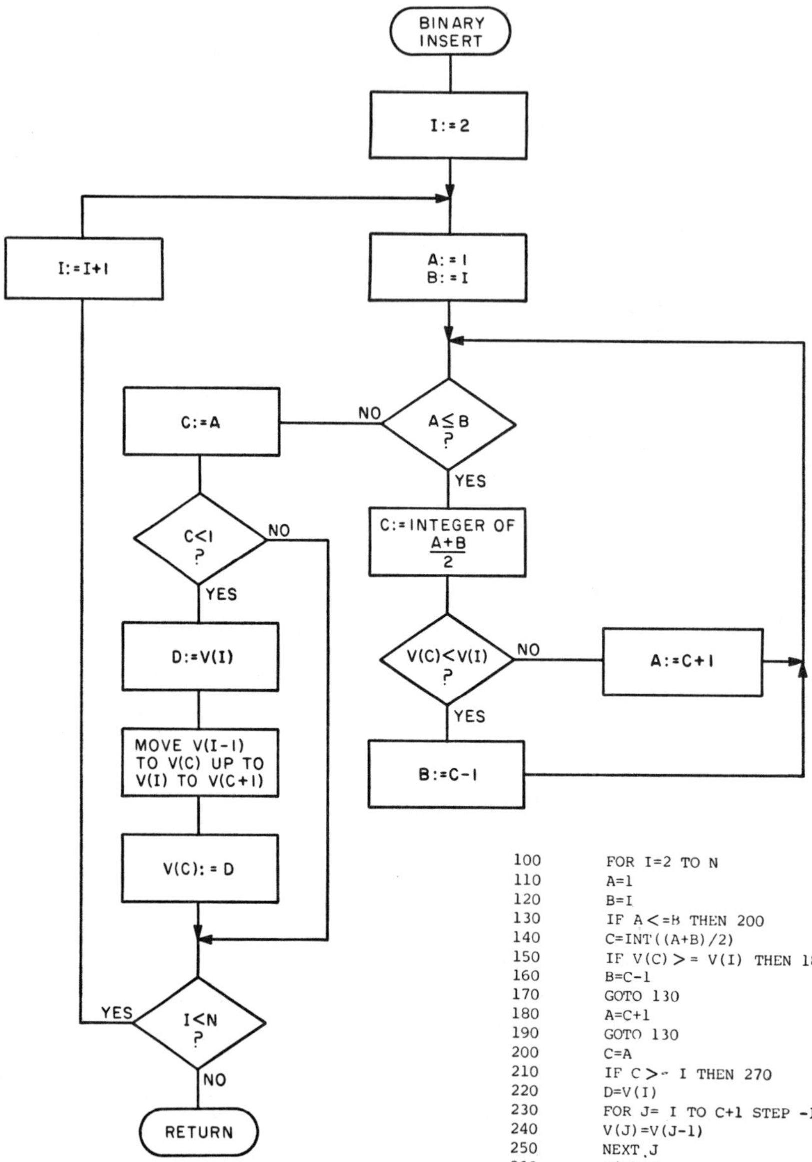


```
100     FOR I=2 TO N
110     A=1
120     B=I
130     IF A<=B THEN 200
140     C=INT((A+B)/2)
150     IF V(C)>= V(I) THEN 180
160     B=C-1
170     GOTO 130
180     A=C+1
190     GOTO 130
200     C=A
210     IF C>= I THEN 270
220     D=V(I)
230     FOR J= I TO C+1 STEP -1
240     V(J)=V(J-1)
250     NEXT J
260     V(C)=D
270     NEXT I
280     RETURN
```

If the items to be sorted are viewed as a row of N cards laid out on the table, binary insertion is used to sort them in the following manner. Moving from left to right, each card is compared to the ones preceding it to see which two it fits between. When the correct position is found, all cards to the right of the position are moved right one position, and the card is placed in the proper location.

Figure 1: *Flowchart of Binary Insertion with a BASIC program.*

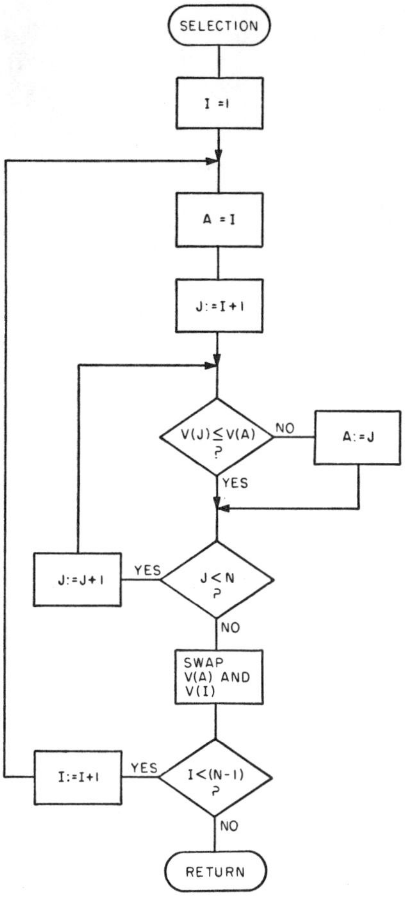

Using the idea of the table as a row of N cards, selection sorting works as follows. Moving from left to right, each card is compared to all those to the right of it and is swapped with the card that is largest of those cards found to be larger than it.

```
100        For I=1 TO N-1
110        A=I
120        FOR J=I+1 TO N
130        IF V(J)<= V(A) THEN 150
140        A=J
150        NEXT J
160        T=V(A)
170        V(A)=V(I)
180        V(I)=T
190        NEXT I
200        RETURN
```

Figure 2: *Flowchart of selection sort with a BASIC program.*

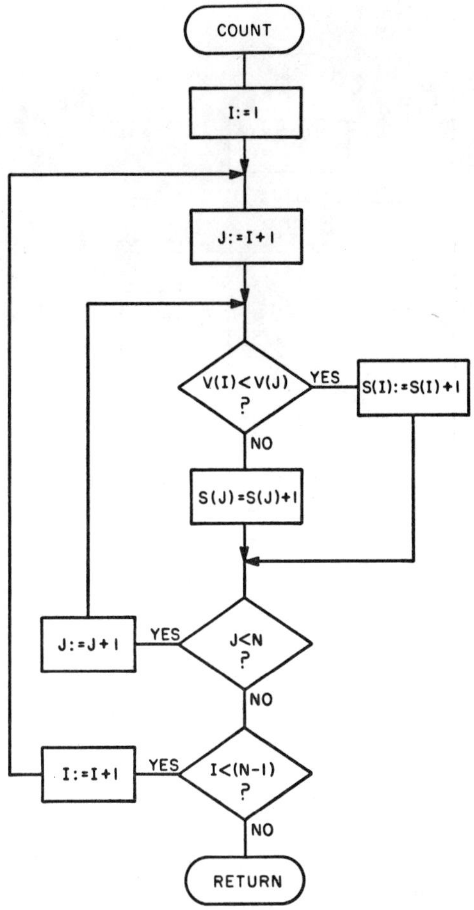

As mentioned in the introduction, counting does not rearrange a table of items, but generates a corresponding table that gives, for each item, its relative standing in its table (ie: how many items are greater or less than it). Suppose you have a list of participants and their scores from a golf tournament and you wish to find the standing of each player. The counting method would be used as follows. Going down the list from top to bottom, each player's score is compared to all those below his on the list. If his score is greater than someone else's score, a tally mark is entered next to the other player's name on the list. If his score was the same or less, he gets the tally mark. After you have moved all the way down the paper, you count each player's tally marks. A player with fewer marks next to his or her name has a higher standing than another who has more.

```
100        FOR I=1 TO N-1
110        FOR J=I+1 TO N
113REM
114REMMMMMMMMMMMMMMMMMMMMMMMMMMMMMMMMMMMMMMMMMM
115REMMMMM  IF THE LOWEST KEY IS TO RECEIVE THE STANDING OF 1
116REMMMMM                USE A > TEST NEXT RATHER THAN A <
117REMMMMMMMMMMMMMMMMMMMMMMMMMMMMMMMMMMMMMMMMMM
118REM
120        IF V(1) < V(J) THEN 150
130        S(J)=S(J)+1
140        GOTO 160
150        S(I)=S(I)+1
160        NEXT J
170        NEXT I
180        RETURN
```

Figure 3: *Flowchart of counting with a BASIC program.*

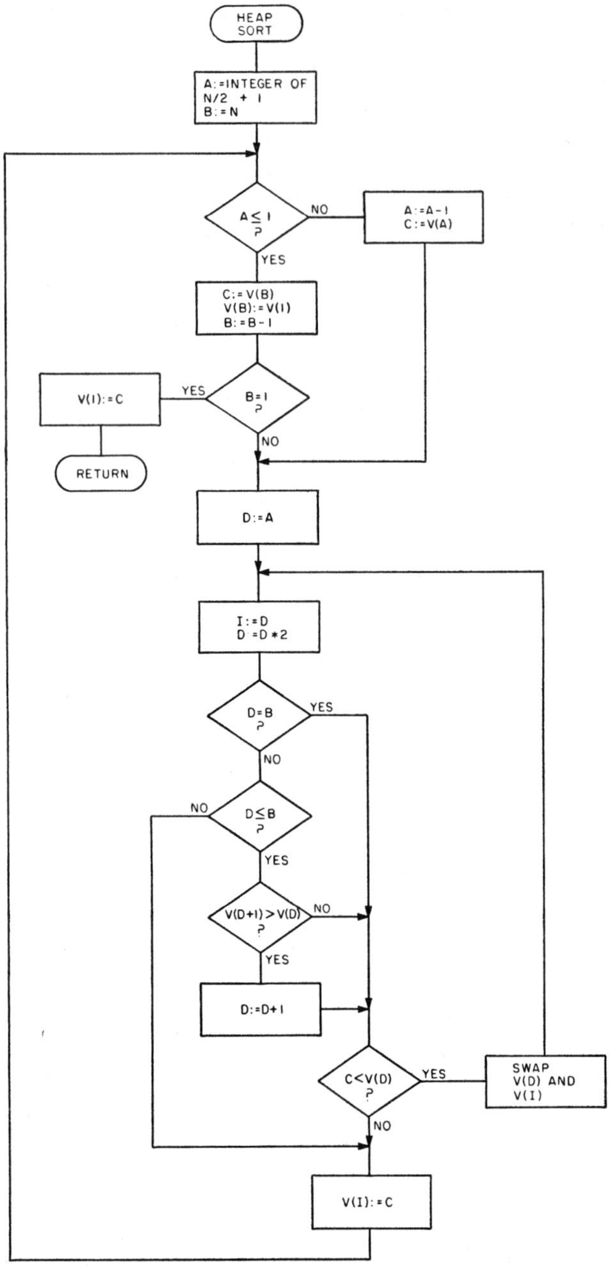


```
100    A=INT(N/2)+1
110    B=N
120    IF A<=1 THEN 160
130    A=A-1
140    C=V(A)
150    GOTO 220
160    C=V(B)
170    V(B)=V(1)
180    B=B-1
190    IF B<>1 THEN 220
200    V(1)=C
210    RETURN
220    D=A
230    I=D
240    D=2*D
250    IF D=B THEN 290
260    IF D>B THEN 320
270    IF V(D)>=V(D+1) THEN 290
280    D=D+1
290    IF C>=V(D) THEN 320
291    T=V(D)
300    V(D)=V(I)
301    V(I)=T
310    GOTO 230
320    V(I)=C
330    GOTO 120
```

Deviating from the policy of trying to give an idea of what is happening, I will not try to explain how the Heap Sort works. It is similar to the process of eliminating players in a tournament: playing the winners of matches against each other. If you really want to see how it works, read the description of it in the book by Mark Elson listed in the references. It is not that difficult to understand, but it takes a fair amount of room to explain. This method is one of the fastest for larger lists of items.

Figure 4: *Flowchart of Heap Sort with a BASIC program.*

Two categories of methods are listed. The first category, represented by binary insertion (figure 1), selection (figure 2), and heap sorting (figure 4), actually rearrange a list or table of items. The other category, represented by counting (figure 3), generates a second list or table containing the standings of each item in the original table. An example of counting is a professor checking an alphabetical list of exam grades to determine the class standing of each student. As shown in table 1, if relative standing is the goal of the sorting, and if there are fewer than sixty items to be examined, counting is the fastest technique. If a table must be rearranged to print out a membership list for example, then the first category of techniques must be used.

Before getting into the methods of sorting, you should note that each method is defined by a flowchart and a BASIC program. BASIC was chosen because it is the most prevalent high-level language in personal computers at this time. The flowcharts and programs assume that the key and data for each item are the same (as in the card hand). If they are separate, as in the case of the telephone directory, a second table containing the data must be kept. In this case the two tables (ie: key and data) must be thought of as tied together. If keys swap position during sorting in the key table, the corresponding operation must be performed on the data table. To use a method chosen from table 1, you can either code in assembly language from the flowchart or the BASIC listing, or, if you have BASIC on your system, you can use the program as it stands. The sorting programs are presented as subroutines that sort the keys stored in the array V(I). If you relate to assembly language rather than BASIC, V(I) refers to a table of keys stored in consecutive memory locations. The associated data, if any, is stored in a corresponding table. When sorting occurs the keys are often swapped. If this happens, the corresponding data entries must also be swapped. In binary insertion, movement of entries, rather than swapping, occurs, in which case the data entires must be moved to correspond to the key movement.■

REFERENCES

Donovan, J J. *Systems Programming.* McGraw-Hill, 1972.

Elson, Mark. *Data Structures.* Science Research Associates, 1975.

Knuth, Donald E. *The Art of Computer Programming, Volume 3: Sorting and Searching.* Addison Wesley, 1973.

Computer Information Arrangement

David Holladay

An examination of the small-system computer field might lead the observer to take a limited view of the potential uses of small systems. This is unfortunate, because a computer, even a small one, can do more than play games or make lights blink.

One general application of computers is the information retrieval system. A classic goal of information retrieval is the construction of a system that absorbs the contents of books and can answer questions concerning the information contained in them. This goal has been unapproachable in even the largest of computer systems. The best approach is to put the burden of intelligence on the user's shoulders and make use of the computer's bookkeeping ability. This reduces the program to a large-scale sorting system tailored to a microcomputer's capabilities.

Small systems have limitations in memory size, data transfer rates and throughput. To cope with these limitations, I propose a mass information handling system called the Computer Information Arrangement, or CIA. The basic hardware required for this system includes a processor, 8 to 16 K bytes of programmable memory, keyboard, video interface and several cassette interfaces with a data rate of at least 300 bps. One cassette drive has to be controllable by the computer in a manner beyond that of simple motor control.

The main storage memory for the huge data base is magnetic tape. Tape is slow and serial, meaning that only the information physically located near the tape head can be dealt with — however, it is inexpensive. For the moment, our data base will be a dictionary (ie: a list of definitions sorted alphabetically by keyword). If the dictionary is closely packed on the tape, it will be difficult to add to it without shifting half of the data base. It would be more logical to spread out the entries on the whole tape to avoid future space problems. Unless the tape is getting full, the proper position of an entry is solely a keyword function.

If entries are to be added in an efficient manner, close attention must be paid to differing data rates. A human can type 2 to 5 characters (ie: bytes) per second, while a computer can take things on or off tape much faster. The typical personal computer can internally manipulate at least 250,000 bytes per second when programmed with an assembler. A video display can depict about 1,000 characters at a time, and can refresh itself 30 or 60 times per second, depending on the way the display handles the interface. It will be the objective of the CIA system to put information onto the cassette tape in sorted order as fast as the user can type in the unsorted data. The user can therefore type the definition of words like *best* and *machine* into our imagainary dic-

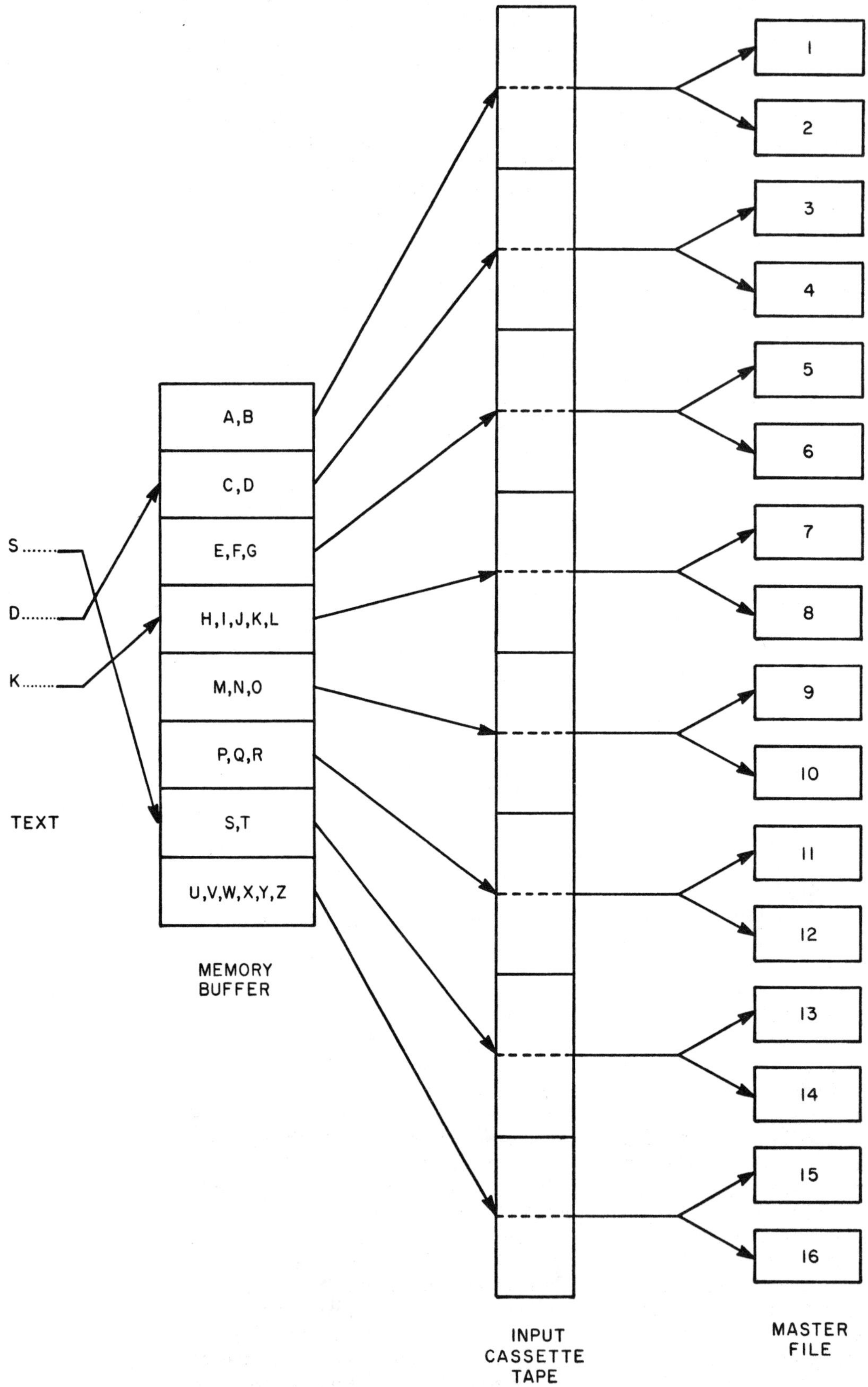

Figure 1: This is a basic diagram showing the input arrangement for the information retrieval system. The text is entered from a keyboard into a buffer area, and sorted alphabetically. In the example, the three text strings start with S, D and K. When a certain buffer area is filled the information it contains is dumped to an input cassette tape. The information on the tape is sorted in alphabetical order. When any one tape is filled, or an updated master file is desired, the input tape is added to the master file.

tionary, and the computer will place both in their proper places on the tape.

A large part of main memory, at least 4 K bytes, is used as a buffer. As new data is typed in, it is added to the buffer and sorted on keyword. This sorting can be done by rearranging the data in the buffer in sequential order. An alternative is to keep items in unsorted order and maintain two pointers for each item, one pointing to the location of the item which is next in sorted order, the other pointing to the previous item in sorted order. The second system eliminates unnecessary searching in memory, but involves longer and trickier programming.

As the memory buffer accumulates data, it is important to keep track of how it is filling up. The alphabet is divided into eight sections for accounting purposes. The first section may be for words starting with A or B, etc. Eight counters keep track of how many bytes are taken up in the buffer by different ranges of the alphabet. When one counter exceeds certain limits, the cassette is moved to the region of tape that corresponds to that range of the alphabet. Next, the data held in the buffer is transferred onto the tape in the proper location. Obviously the data would then be erased from the memory buffer to make room for more data. The end result is a cassette tape containing sorted information which generated at the same rate that the user is typing in the unsorted data. (See figure 1). If the data is sorted as fast as it can be input, what would be the advantage of greater throughput? The system works as fast as is necessary.

The system is generalized: it can be used to make huge mailing lists, keep track of books in a library, and so on. It has two principal limitations in addition to speed, size and the simple nature of the data that it can handle.

What can you do when you fill up a cassette? It may take a while, since it is possible to fit as many as 500,000 characters on a digital cassette tape. You could maintain a master set of twenty-six tapes, one for each letter of the alphabet. Once your tape is full, it would be merged with the master file, an unwieldy process at best. This procedure would mean putting master tape #1 in one cassette machine, your input cassette in another, and starting the merging program. After a while, the computer could signal that it had put all of the A entries onto master tape #1. Then you would take out tape #1, replace it with tape #2, and so on, up to tape #26. This process would happen rarely, or as often as you would require an up-to-date master file. But imagine how much data your system could hold. A friend of mine humorously pointed out that if you were mechanically inclined, you could automate cassette manipulation. It would be a hybrid of a jukebox and large-scale automated mass memory with media manipulation mechanisms. An automatic, multimegabyte memory system for a few thousand dollars would be very impressive.

The question of data bases is a bit tricky. Data can be abstract, highly interrelated, and difficult to categorize. Your data will be interrelated in ways that the data base cannot show or represent. There are two approaches to follow. One way is to design very abstract data structures that show relationships inherently. The other is to maintain the simple dictionary alphabetic system and add several cross-reference pointers. An example would be "Kennedy, Jackie: see Onassis, Jackie." By pursuing all the pointers listed under a keyword, and checking out all the pointers listed there, a tree structure is developed. A multicassette data system implies a significant amount of tape manipulation, unless you have built the jukebox system.

Although a pointer system is a bit crude, it can be handled automatically. The following example illustrates a typical entry. The original data entry: "Beethoven, Ludwig van, Symphony Number 3 (The Eroica)" would be filed under "Beethoven, Ludwig van." If the user wants to generate the cross-reference pointer "Eroica Symphony, see Beethoven, Ludwig van," a special character could be typed before "Beethoven, Ludwig van" which the program would recognize. The program could then add "Eroica Symphony, see Beethoven, Ludwig van" to the text buffer. This would insure that the pointer and the data match, eliminating a problem with typographical errors.

Later, if it is necessary to eliminate the entry, you would know that the cross-reference pointer is also in memory because of the existence of the special character. Other special functions can be implemented by special characters, such as labeling the data source of facilitating tabular data. This is left as an exercise for the reader. The power of this information handling system is limited mainly by the size of programs that can be sorted in memory, and by the speed of the tape recorder.

The Computer Information Arrangement needs five separate programs to work properly. Note that it is not necessary for more than one to be in memory at any time. Program 1, the input program, is the biggest and most difficult. It accepts characters from the keyboard, edits them, adds the cross-reference, puts them in the buffer, recognizes when the tape machine is idle or part of the alphabet range is getting full in the buffer, and spreads the data on the input cassette by means of a linear hashing formula. It may be necessary for the tape recorder to be controlled by a separate microprocessor and 1 K bytes of programmable memory shared by both processors, because of timing considerations. The second one is the merge program, which merges the input tape with the master set of cassettes. The third program, called the clean up, goes through tapes, "unbunches" data, and straightens out any local area that gets "out of sort." The fourth program is the display program. The user can tell it to display the Richard Nixon file, whereupon it will display all the references and pointers that are filed under the keyword "Nixon, Richard." The last program does a crucial, but easily forgotten job: altering or deleting outdated or incorrect data from the input tape or from a master tape.

The CIA is a general computer-information arrangement, an answer machine, or a list maker. Put in randomly ordered data and it comes out neat and organized. The arrangement has many applications: small business, journalism, research, or help for folks who have trouble organizing things. This is the type of program that will sell small systems to the world.■

GLOSSARY

Alphabet range: a part of the contiguous alphabet used to decide where to store alphabetically sorted data.

Buffer: a section of random access memory used to temporarily store data until enough is collected to pass on.

Cross-reference: a notation to look elsewhere in the data base for more information.

Data base: a collection of information and the system used to organize it for use by a computer program.

Entry: a block of data that stays together during the sorting routine. The end of an entry is recognized by a special termination character.

File: a set of entries with the same keyword.

Input tape: a cassette that accepts the sorted data. For larger data bases, it must be merged with the master tapes.

Keyword: a word in an entry used to sort the entire entry into the data base.

Master tapes: a set of cassettes that make up the entire data base. Each cassette covers a portion of the alphabet range.

Computer Information Arrangement (Upgrade #1)

Bill Roch

Mr Holladay's article "Computer Information Arrangement," in the October 1977 issue of BYTE, describes a method of creating and maintaining data for a data-retrieval system. Obviously, the approach to do the job right is with a large disk system, an expensive proposition. Even using floppy disks, there is a substantial investment involved.

The system described in this article has the advantage of handling large amounts of sequential data with only one cassette interface and only two or three recorders. The heart of the system is a multiple-cassette controller that operates under program control and handles up to four cassette recorders with one Tarbell cassette interface board. There is no question that tape cassettes are slower than disks and that they are sequential, but by using the speed of the Tarbell board (ie: 540 bytes per second, 2200 bits per inch) and compressing out the blanks, large amounts of data can be handled rapidly.

Only two programs including a third optional sort program are necessary to operate the system:

- an input program that builds input records in sequential order and writes them to tape
- an update program that reads the input tape and updates the old master tape to a new master tape
- an optional sort program that sorts the input tape so inputs may be made in random order

Actually, one program will do the job if updating is done sequentially from the keyboard. A single file maintenance program is more complicated than the multiple-programs system, and will be described later.

Input Program

This program displays or prints out the field name, then accepts keyboard input. When all the fields are full, the program allows the user to correct the record if necessary; otherwise, it writes the record to tape. Refer to the input program in figure 1 for step numbers.

In step 1, the maximum number of records to be input is entered. This is important if the records are to be sorted, since memory limitations dictate the quantity of records a sort program can handle. The RO-CHE Systems Cassette Operating System (RCSCOS) software that comes with the multiple-cassette controller opens and closes files and allows files to be named. In step 2, the file is named and opened. (The ability to name files is included in a section of the basic program that turns the control of program from BASIC to the input/output (I/O) driver.) At this time, a beginning file mark is written on the tape and the file name is written.

The input aspect of the program (steps 3 thru 7) consists of a loop that displays the field names and asks for the appropriate field value for the current record. The first field should be used as a code to later inform the update program of the type of record it must handle (ie: add, delete, or replace). This field should also be used to enter an end-of-program indicator. After each field is filled with information, the next field comes up until all fields are filled. Step 7 provides the option of correcting the records. With some extra coding, it is possible to only redo a particular field or to jump back to the previous field.

Now that we have several valid fields, we can do the following:

- Write each field separately with RCSCOS placing delimiters between fields.
- Concatenate the fields together with a delimiter between each field.
- Pad each field with blanks to its full size, then concatenate the fields together.

The RCSCOS software uses a buffer, and each write merely moves data to the buffer. Only when the buffer is full

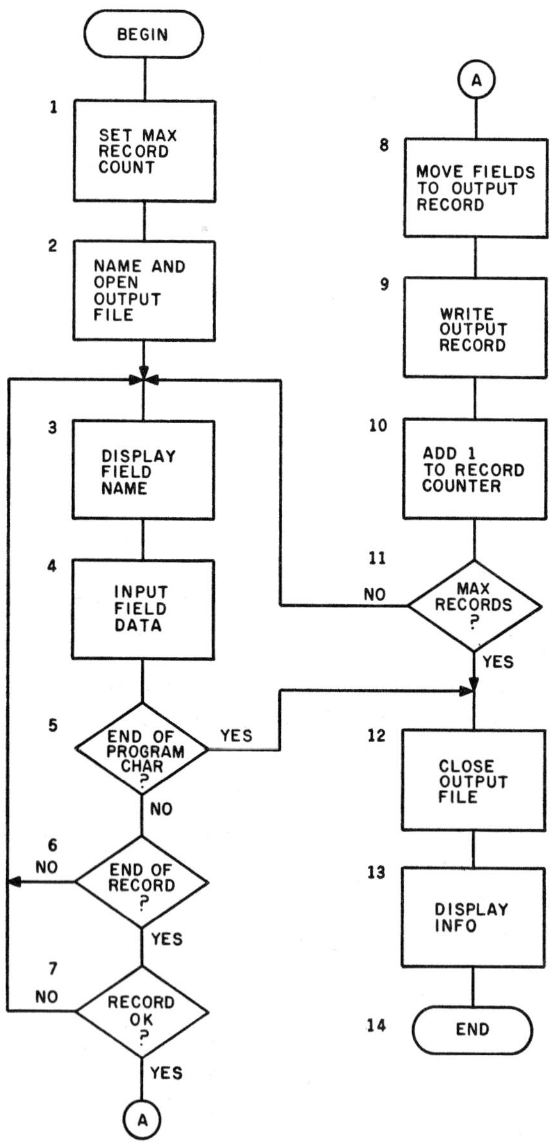

Figure 1: Flowchart for data entry (input) routine. In this routine, user entry is prompted on a field by field basis. The incomplete record can be inspected before it is written to the output tape file.

(ie: 256 bytes) does the software turn on the cassette recorder and write to the cassette tape. The greatest advantage of long records in the sort and update programs is that the data is moved to and from tape as only one record rather than as a number of fields that make up a record.

Do not be concerned about padding a field with blanks because blanks are compressed out by the RSCCOS software. For example, a twenty-character field containing only five data characters left-justified uses only 7 bytes on tape: 5 bytes for the data, a blank count indicator, and 1 byte for the blank count. Step 10 monitors the number of valid records written. When this count matches the count entered in step 1 or when an end-program indicator is entered in field 1, the file is closed, as in step 12. When a file is closed, the remainder of the data in the buffer is written, followed by an end-of-file mark. Step 13 may be omitted, or it may be used to print out a record of what has been accomplished.

Another variation to this program would be to use two or more cassette recorders and presort the data within the input program, such as letters A thru D to recorder #0, E thru I to recorder #1, etc, and have the counter keep track of the records being written to each tape. To this variation there could be added a routine to close a full-tape file. After the cassette is repositioned, a new file would be opened and processing could continue to all recorders.

Sort Program

If the input data is always in sequential order, there is no need for sorting and this program is unnecessary; but this is often not the case. Refer to the numbered steps in figure 2.

Step 1 of the sort program requests the number of records to be sorted so that arrays can be dynamically diminished. In steps 2 and 3, the input and output files are named and opened. In the case of the input file, RCSCOS software turns on the recorder and reads until it finds a beginning file mark, then reads the first physical record. The program then checks the file name keyed in with the file name of the input file. The file name may be overridden is desired. For the output file, only the file mark and file name are written to tape.

The input file is read into memory in steps 4 thru 7. As each record is read into its array, two additional arrays are created. One contains the record ID which uniquely identifies that record. The other is a number array which carries the subscript number of the record read (ie: the record count number).

Use whatever sort routine you prefer (step 8) to sort the two new arrays (record ID and record number) in order by record ID. Then write out the data records in memory in the new sorted-subscript order from the sorted-record-number field (step 9 and 10).

To clarify this sorting technique, refer to table 1.

The example file contains six names and address records with the ID made up of the first three characters of the name and the first character of the state. The index may be constructed of any characters in a record —your option. After sorting the index and record number only, the record-number array contains the record numbers in sorted order. That is RECNO (1) = 3, RECNO (2) = 4, etc. Write the records (stored in an array) in RECNO (ie: subscript) order and you will have the input data written to tape in sorted order. Now that the data has been sorted and written, the files are closed and some type of a completion message may be printed (step 12).

Update Program

While the flowchart in figure 3 has more boxes, it is still a relatively short program. The first thing the program wants is the names of the three files —Old Master, Update, and New Master. The program then opens the three files and initializes their flags. The flags have the following properties:

- The Old Master file flag is set at end-of-file (EOF).
- The Update file flag is set at EOF.

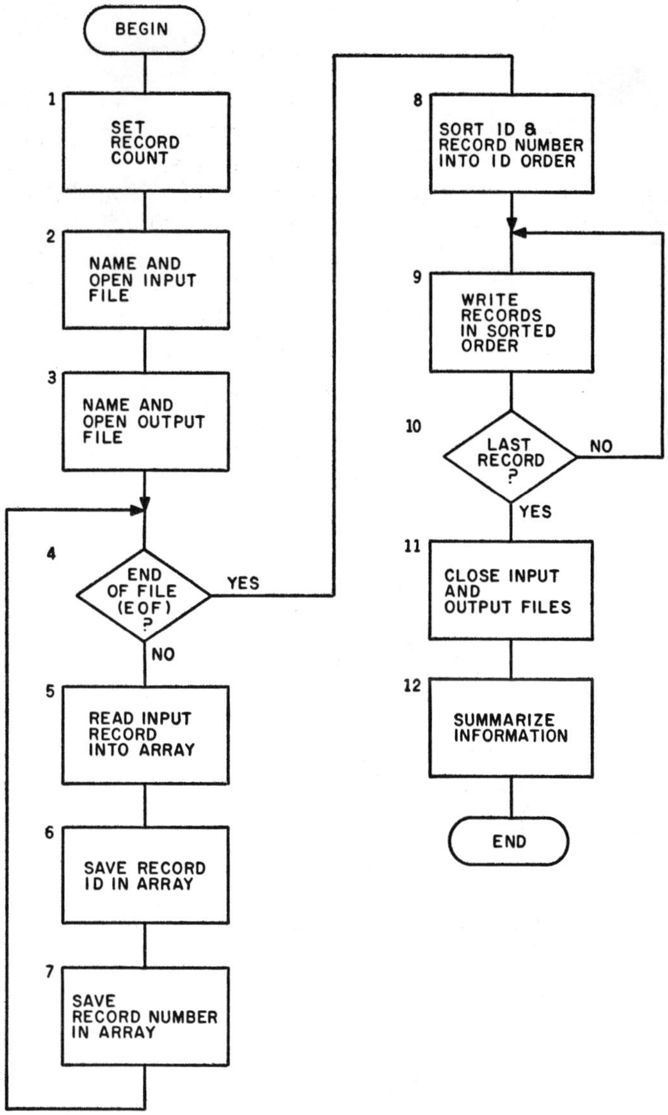

Figure 2: Flowchart for in-memory sort routine. Although the entire file of records to be sorted must be in memory, the entire record is not manipulated during the sort. Instead, the record key and relative record number are sorted together, and the sequence of relative record numbers is used to index the array containing the body of each record.

		BEFORE SORT		AFTER SORT	
ARRAY INDEX	DATA RECORDS IN ARRAY	SORT INDEX	RCRD NO	SORT INDEX	RCRD NO
1	J O N E S . . . . CA	J O N C	1	B E N M	3
2	S M I T H . . . . OH	S M I O	2	B R O T	4
3	B E N S O N . . . MA	B E N M	3	J O H C	1
4	B R O W N . . . . . . TX	B R O T	4	J O H F	5
5	J O H N S O N . FL	J O H F	5	J O N C	6
6	J O H N S O N CA	J O H C	6	S M I O	2

Table 1: A simple sort example. The input data is encoded as the first three letters of the last name, and the first letter of the state. The data is sorted by rearranging the indexes in the record number array.

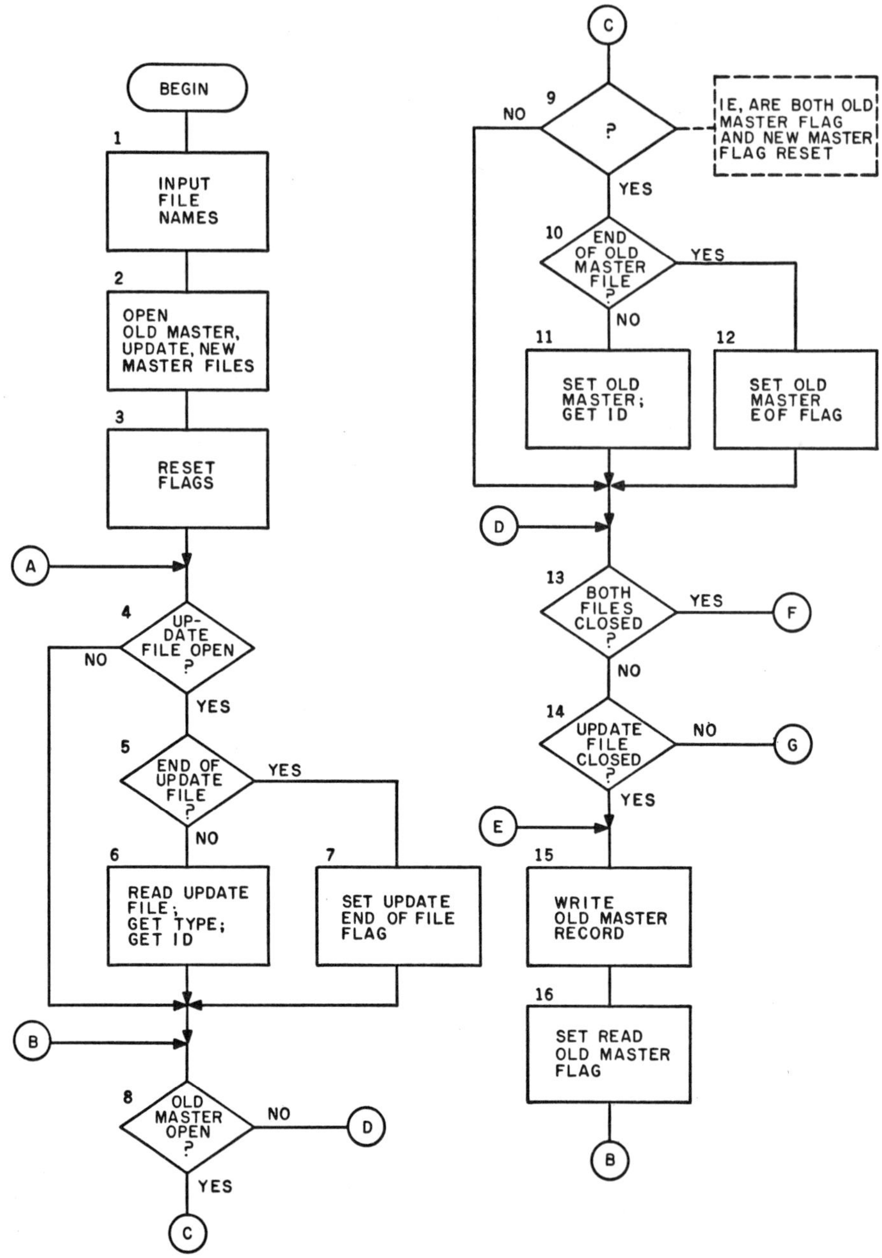

- The New Master file flag is set when the Old Master file is to be read, and reset when the Old Master file is to be skipped.

In step 4, the Update EOF flag is tested. If the Update file is at EOF, no further attempt is made to read the Update file; otherwise, an update read takes place. If the data read is an EOF mark, the Update EOF flag is set; otherwise, the first character, which indicates the type of record (ie: add, delete, or replace) is saved as well as the Update record ID.

In steps 8 thru 11, the same process is carried out for the Old Master file except that the ID is saved. Step 9 checks to determine if the Old Master should be read completely through this time. Step 12 tests to see if both files are closed; if they are, the file updating is complete.

If either file has not reached EOF, a test is made in step 13 to see which is still active. If the Update file is at EOF, the last Old Master record read is written to the New Master file and the program loops until the Old Master EOF is reached. If the Update file is still active and the Old Master file is at EOF then the Update record is written if it is an add record.

If both files are active then an ID comparison is made in steps 18 and 19. If the Upgrade ID is less than Old Master ID, the updated data is written —that is,

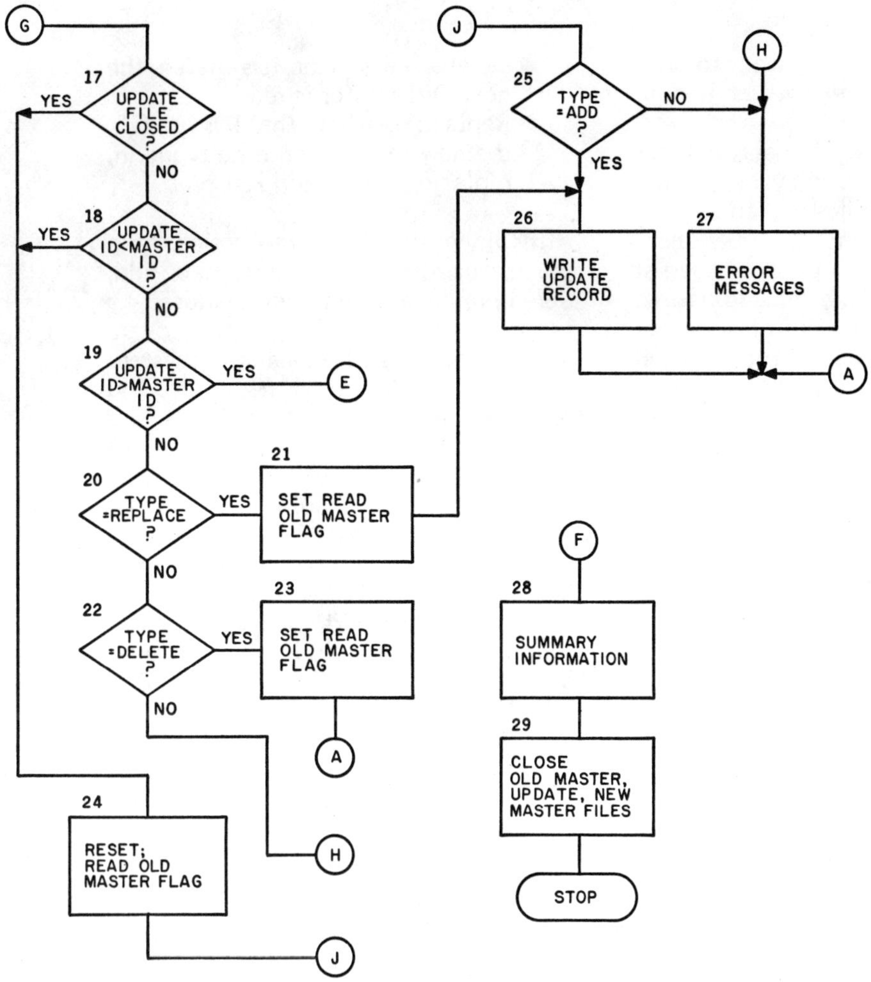

Figure 3: Flowchart for file update routine. This routine assumes the existence of the file to be updated (Old Master file) and a file containing the updates to be made (Update file). Each Update record contains the record type (add, replace, or delete) and a record ID (used as a key for sorting).

if it is an add record (steps 25 and 26). Step 24 tells the program not to read another Old Master file record next time through the read loop.

If the Update file record ID is greater than the Old Master file record ID, then write the Old Master record, set the flag to read the Old Master file, and then read it (steps 19 back to 15).

If both IDs match, then the Update record must be a replace or delete record. If it is a replace record, write it and set the flag to read the Old Master, then loop back and read in the next Update and Old Master records. If the record is a delete record, set the flag to read the Old Master, then read a second Update and Old Master record without writing the first Old Master record —this deletes a record.

There should be an edit step in the input program to prevent any invalid record type codes being used for add, delete, and replace. Error messages can be printed out (step 27) that indicate an attempt was made to do one of the following:

- add a record to an existing record
- delete a nonexisting record; or
- replace a nonexisting record

The use of error messages of this type help insure that invalid transactions do not happen. This will also help insure the integrity of the New Master file. For ease of identification, you may want to print out the ID of the erroneous update record.

A count of transactions and number of records in the file may be printed prior to closing the files in step 29.

The three programs described here should use less than six pages of code at one statement per line. In addition to this, it uses one half page of code per program for the BASIC I/O routine used with the BASIC I/O driver that comes with the multiple-cassette controller. This driver acts as software interface between the BASIC program and the cassette operating system.

Let us turn to the single program that updates the Old Master file to a New Master file. This program would be a combination of the input program and the update program.

One version would be to build the update data in an array in sequential order to sort the array as you build it, then have the program read the update data from the array as it would from the update tape. Another version would be for the user to enter the record type and the record ID at the point where the update program normally reads the Update file. The program would then read the Old Master file and write the New Master file until an ID match was found or the Old Master ID was greater than the ID typed from the keyboard. The following action would take place:

- Add —when the Old Master ID is greater than the ID typed in, the program would stop and the new record could be typed in, and then written to the New Master file.
- Delete —when the IDs match, the next Old Master is read.
- Replace —when the IDs match, the new record would be typed in, replacing the record last read.

After any of the above transactions take place, the program accepts new add, delete, replace, or end commands.

One of the most important advantages of this type of file-handling system is the cost for the work it can do. $40 recorders become your tape drives. The Tarbell cassete interface kit from Tarbell Electronics, 950 Dovlen Place, Suite B, Carson CA 90746, costs $120, and the Multi-Cassette Controller kit from Elliam Associates, 24000 Bessemer St, Woodland Hills CA 91367, sells for $55 for the two-port, and $70 for the four-port model, including software to operate with MITS BASIC versions 8 K 3.1, 8 K 4.0 and extended 4.0. Elliam Associates also offers a table-driven, file-maintenance system written in BASIC, similar to the one described, on cassette (Tarbell format) for $20.

Summary

The programs described in this article provide the means for building and maintaining sequential files that can contain any type of data desired. Only string records have been described here, but records containing numbers can also be handled. This means that in addition to the mailing list-type files, accounting type information can also be maintained. The fact is, this system allows the user to have big computer power on a hobby budget. ■

Table Manners: An Introduction and Guide to Table Handling Techniques

Timothy L Gauslin

Did you ever have that sinking sensation when you ran a new program for the first time and the output appeared so slowly that you felt you could have performed the calculations and plotted the results just as well by hand? Most programmers encounter this problem entirely too often. A debugging effort usually leads to the discovery of some form of array manipulation as the culprit behind the performance problem.

In this article I will examine some common and not so common techniques for handling the loading and searching of arrays. The methods being used are usually applied to handling string data in single-dimensioned arrays which are often called tables. The methods I will employ in building and searching tables are quite straightforward. There are many techniques other than those included in this article for arranging and finding data within tables. The obscure program code and complex math often associated with these other techniques prompts me to leave them to the programming and math gurus.

Let us look, then, at what remains that is straightforward, efficient, and programmable on a microcomputer. In progressive steps we will start with the way most programmers build and search tables, and work our way toward the exotic.

The following techniques will be examined:

- serial table loads and searches
- binary table searches
- bubble sorts
- percolated table searches
- hashed table loads and searches
- indexed tables

Each of these techniques is presented in its simplest form. It is left to the reader to research and develop further improvements to each technique.

Definitions

To aid in understanding the varied approaches to array handling which will be examined, some common understanding of the terms used is in order. First to clarify the definition of an array, or table, as it is used in this discussion:

> An array is a programming-language description of a series of data elements having common attributes.

The elements of an array (or table) consist of a *key field* and one or more related *data fields.* The key field is examined during table loads and searches to place or locate the related data fields within the table.

Some programming languages provide a facility to define the key and data fields of a table through a single definition. A COBOL example of such a definition is provided herein.

```
01 ZIP-CODE-TABLE.
    05 ZIP-TABLE-ENTRY OCCURS
       1000 TIMES.
     10 ZIP-CODE                        PIC 9(5).
     10 CITY                            PIC X(20).
```

Other programming languages, such as BASIC, require that each element of the table be defined using a separate definition. For purposes of this article such multiple definitions will be considered to be a single table. A BASIC definition similar to the COBOL example given previously is presented below:

```
10 DIMENSION ZIP(1000)
20 DIMENSION CITY$(20,1000)
```

Figure 1: Array definition examples.

Table 1: *Definitions used in the text and figures.*

Table load: A programming language routine that accepts one or multiple elements of data and places these elements within selected occurrences of a table.

Table Search: A routine that locates data within a table based on an argument passed to the routine.

Table sort: A routine that accepts one or multiple elements of data and places these elements into a table in an ordered sequence; a table sort is a specialized form of table load.

Table key: A data element contained within a table that is compared to an argument presented to a search, sort, or load routine to locate a corresponding data entry within the table.

Argument: A data element presented to a table search routine for location of a similar value in the table, or load routine for inclusion in the table.

Subscript: A numeric integer element of data used to identify a specific occurrence of data within a table. For example, a table might contain 500 elements of data, all of which are named A$. One way to reference, for example, the fiftieth occurrence of A$ is A$(50).

Table 2: *Legend for variable names used in flowcharts.*

a. KEY — A key data element contained within a table.

b. DATA — A non-key data element contained within a table or presented to a table load routine for inclusion in a table.

c. M — The maximum number of entries to be contained by a table, or the number of entries under consideration by a binary search routine; the notation INT((M1+1)/2) refers to M/2, rounded up to the nearest integer.

d. T — The maximum number of tries to be attempted at accessing a table key value.

e. F — The current number of filled table entries.

f. S1 — A data element used as a subscript.

g. S2 — A data element used as a subscript.

h. PREFIX — The portion of an argument used to address an index table.

i. PFX — A short form of PREFIX.

j. SPREFIX — A prefix save area used by the Indexed Table Load routine.

k. SAVE — A temporary area used for storage of argument, key, and other data elements.

An array often eliminates the need for separate entries for repeated data, since it can indicate the number of times data with identical format is repeated. Reference to single elements within an array is accomplished through the use of a subscript following the data-element name.

This definition is not all inclusive, but will suffice for the purposes of this article. Let it be further understood that a single array, as defined above, may require multiple descriptions to define all of the elements of data to be housed by the array. Figure 1 serves to illustrate this fact.

Some other terms used throughout this article are subscript, table load, table search, argument, and key. Table 1 provides these definitions. A glossary of symbol definitions used in flowcharting examples presented throughout this article is provided in table 2.

Serial Table Handling

For most, logic patterns occur as a series of events leading to a conclusion. Therefore, programming the serial table load is the easiest way of placing information into a table for later access. A flowchart for this procedure is illustrated in figure 2.

The process involved here consists of acquiring an entry for the table and placing the entry in the next available slot in the table. This technique is as efficient as any that will be discussed for placing data into a table, but it may cause problems in later accessing the table data if the table is loaded in an unordered sequence.

Assume, for example, that the table just created is loaded with the key values:

(W, Z, X, B, Y, D, C, A)

Each and every key value in the table must be examined until the key A is located. This table-search technique is known as the serial table search. Figure 3 presents one implementation of this type of table lookup.

In our example, eight iterations of the search logic are required to locate key field A. In this case the search time is not excessive. If, however, key field A were the 1000th occurrence in the table, it is obvious that considerable time would be spent in searching for this table entry.

Binary Table Searches

If the table described above is ordered (ie: sequenced by key) as shown below, certain assumptions can be made about the relative location of any key element within the table:

(A, B, C, D, W, X, Y, Z)

First, it may be assumed that the key being searched for is located higher in the table if the key we are presently looking at has a value less than that of the desired key, and vice versa.

If the search of an ordered table is begun in the middle, logically the size of the table can be halved each time we fail to locate the desired key. For instance, if a table contains one hundred entries, and the fiftieth entry is greater than the key being searched for, we know that the desired key is somewhere within entries 1 thru 49. The maximum number of tries it should take to locate a key within a certain size table can be computed. Since the table is halved each time it is examined, in essence we are converting the number of entries in the table to a binary value. The number of digits in this binary number, plus 1, gives the maximum number of attempts necessary to locate a key within the table.

When converted to binary, the one hundred occurrences in our sample table produce the number 1100100. The seven digits in this number, plus 1, reveal that a maximum of eight attempts would be made to locate a key value within this table. The information available may now be combined to produce the binary-search algorithm illustrated by figure 4. Note that the average number of attempts at locating data in a table of one hundred entries has been reduced from fifty for the serial search to seven for the binary search. (The average number of attempts required to locate a key using the binary search is approximately one less than the maximum number of attempts, or 8 − 1 = 7 in this case.) The larger the table, the more significant is the saving realized in using binary-search techniques. Due to the additional overhead of the binary-search algorithm, however, it should be limited to use in searching tables of twenty-five entries or more.

Bubble Sorts

As you may have already noticed, the primary limitation to the use of binary searches is the requirement that the table being searched must be sequentially ordered. If this is not the case,

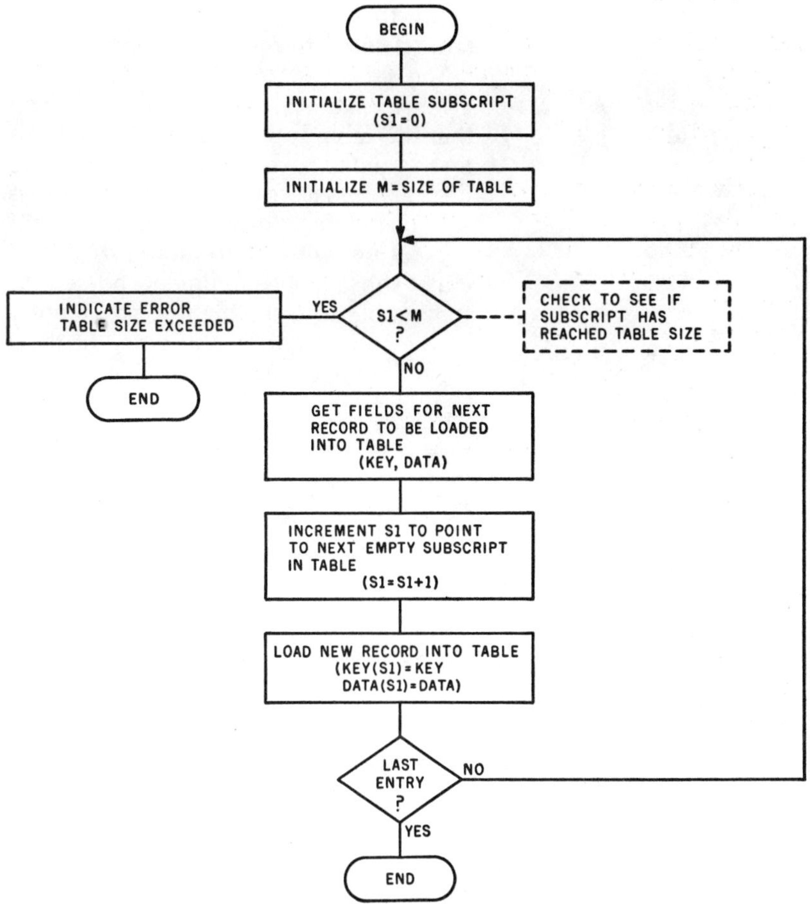

Figure 2: Flowchart for serial table load. In this load, data is placed in the table in the order in which it is presented to the table loading algorithm.

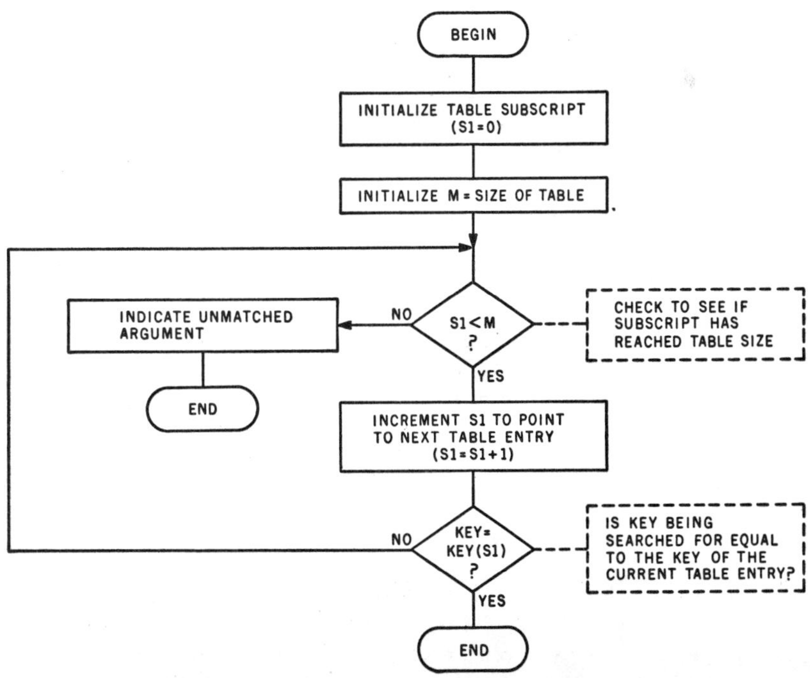

Figure 3: Flowchart for a serial table search. In this search, each table entry is examined in turn until the key value matching the argument is found.

apply the bubble sort during entry of table data to overcome this obstacle.

The flowchart for the bubble sort is given in figure 5, where it can be seen that the table to be loaded with data is first assumed to be empty (F = 0). The first argument to the bubble sort is stored at table entry 1, and subscripts for future entries are initialized. For each subsequent argument passed to the bubble sort, the highest active entry in the table (that is, the entry furthest from the beginning of the table) is compared to the argument. Each time the argument compares lower than the key value in the table, the key is shifted upward (opening a "hole" in the table), the subscript pointing to the active entry in the table being looked at is decremented, and the comparison is repeated. When the proper (ie: ordered) location for the argument is discovered, the hole left by the prior pass through the bubble sort is filled with the argument value. The end result of this table manipulation is an ordered table produced from unordered input data. We may now apply the binary search in referencing our table.

One other item: since the bubble sort is invoked only once per table entry, it is considered far more efficient than the use of the serial search, which examines each table entry an untold number of times based on the number of arguments presented to the search.

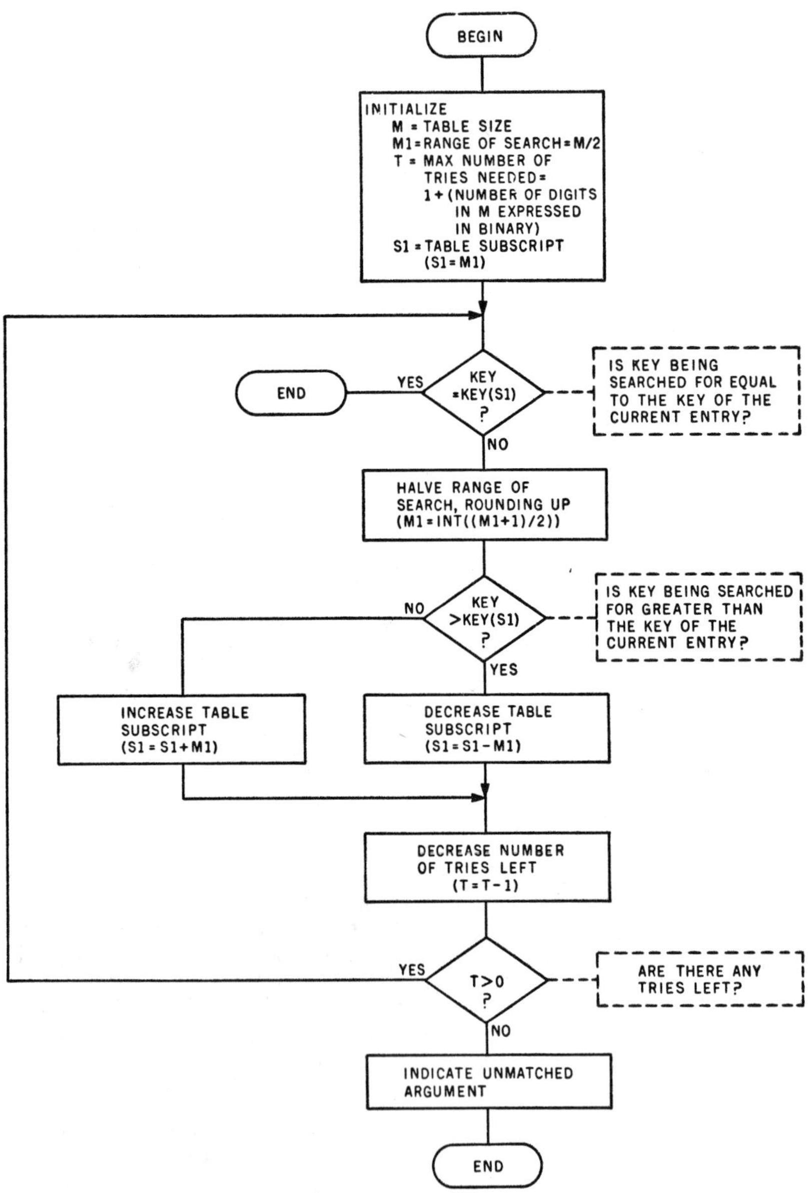

Figure 4: Flowchart for a binary search. In this search, the number of table entries under consideration is halved with each search iteration until a key that matches the argument is found; the table is assumed to be sorted by ascending key. In the example in the text, the table size is 100, giving the number of tries needed in the search as T=8.

Percolated Table Searches

The table-handling techniques discussed so far assume that the key values being searched for are uniformly distributed throughout the table. In many applications, a few entries within the table receive the bulk of attention during processing. A prime example of this type of processing is a mailing list, where zip codes from a common area are used to retrieve city names from a table.

Assume that a computer club is located within a moderately sized town, with membership centered within the town. A mailing list maintained by this club would certainly reference zip codes within the town more frequently than those representing outlying areas. One is able to cause these high-activity table entries to be located more rapidly by applying the percolated table search. The flowchart for the percolated search is illustrated by figure 6.

In the illustration, the table to be searched has previously been loaded using the serial table load. A comparison of figures 3 and 6 will show that the percolated search is nothing more than a serial search with additional logic appended to flip a key satisfying an argument with the key immediately below it (ie: closer to the beginning of the table). In a high-volume processing environment, the net result of this logic moves high-activity table keys downward in the table and low-activity keys upward in the table. Thus high-activity keys are located by the serial search with a smaller number of tries, even though the table is unordered. In effect, what we have is a table ordered by activity rather than by key value.

A major advantage of the percolated table search is the load sensitive nature of the technique. As demands against the table vary, the organization of the table changes in compliance. To take full advantage of this dynamic attribute, the table should be loaded from external media at the beginning of each program run, and stored back to external media at the end of each run. This insures that the order of the table elements reflects the relative activity of the cumulative use of the table.

Hashed Table Loads and Searches

The fastest technique for loading and retrieving data from tables is the use of randomized, or *hashed*, values to determine starting locations for table loads and seaches. This technique is commonly employed in managing the symbol tables of compilers and assemblers. A major drawback to this technique is the requirement for oversized tables to avoid the generation of an inefficient number of table synonyms. Synonyms are separate key values that attempt to occupy the same location within a table. To avoid synonyms, tables that utilize hashed techniques are usually established at least 20% oversize.

In considering the use of hashed tables, two items must be given priority:

1) Every possible argument presented must randomize within the number of entries set aside for the table.
2) Hashed values derived from arguments should be distributed evenly within the range of the table to avoid synonyms.

A simple technique for hashing the content of a table argument is to strip the left half of each byte in the argument, packing the right halves together to form a binary numeric value. This value is then divided by the prime number which is closest to, yet still less than, the number of entries in the table. The remainder from this division is employed as the value of a subscript to load or retrieve the desired table entry. An example of this hashing algorithm, applied to a table of 1000 entries, is presented in figure 7.

In figure 7, an argument value of ABYZ is hashed to a subscript value of 518. A synonym argument for ABYZ is ABYJ. That is, argument ABYJ will also hash to a subscript value of 518. There is a total, in this example, of three synonyms possible for each position in the argument. That is, three equivalent characters in each position of the argu-

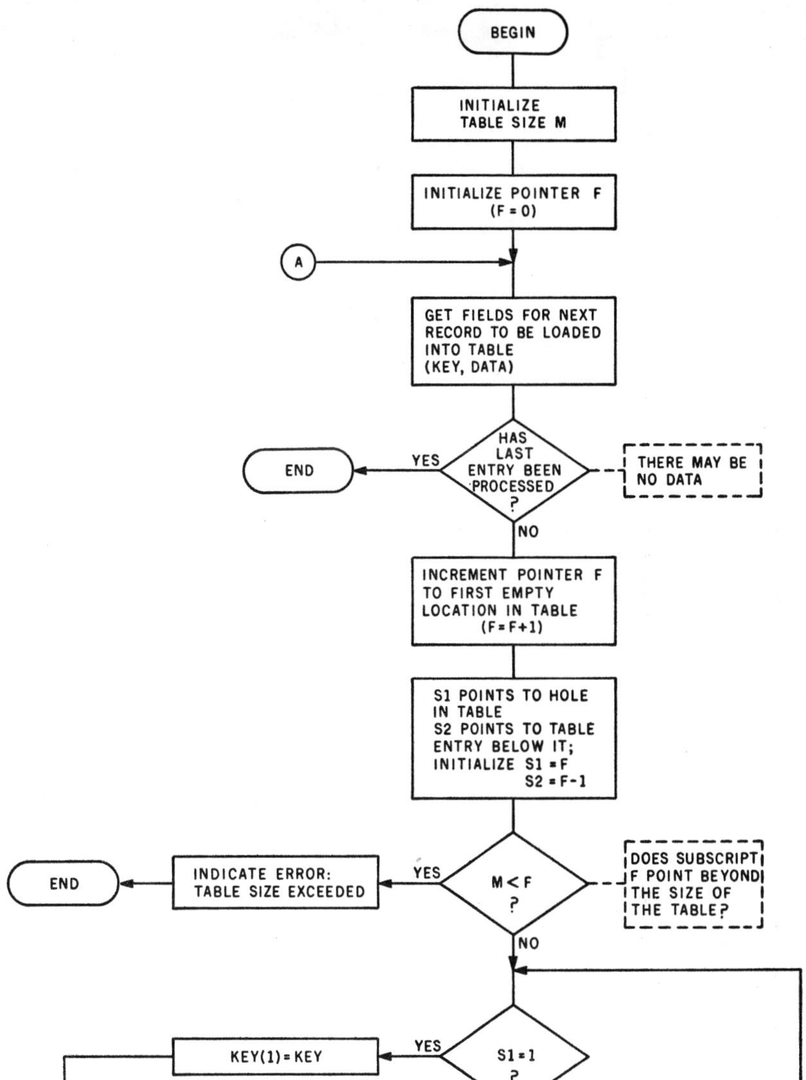

Figure 5: Flowchart for a bubble sort. In this sort, data is entered in an unordered sequence and "bubbles" from the end of the present table to its beginning, stopping when it is in ascending key sequence in relation to the rest of the entries in the table.

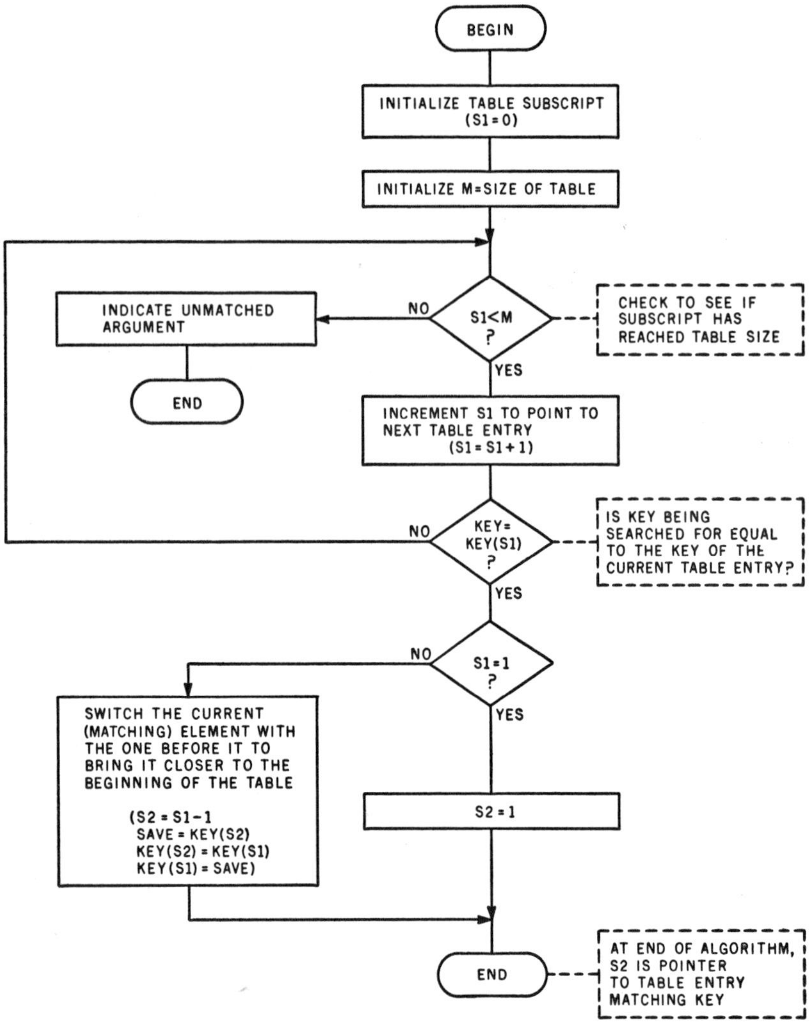

Figure 6: Flowchart for a percolated table search. In this search, a serial search is conducted, but when a match is found, the desired entry is switched with the entry before it. This has the effect of moving frequently used entries toward the beginning of the table, where they can be found in fewer tries.

Maximum number of table entries = 1000
Prime number less than 1000 = 997
(Note that arguments are four alphabetic characters.)

For a sample argument of ABYZ:
Hexadecimal (ASCII) representation = 41 42 59 5A
With high order nybble stripped = $129A_{16}$
$129A_{16} = 4096_{10} + 256_{10} + 144_{10} + 10_{10} = 4506_{10}$
$4506 \div 997 = 4$, remainder 518
The 518th table entry will be used for storage of key value ABYZ.

Figure 7: The hashed table addressing algorithm. This is perhaps the most efficient method of storing and retrieving entries from a table. In this example, a four character alphabetic argument produces a (usually) unique subscript value in the range of 1 to 1000.

ment will produce the same hashed subscript value. Therefore, there are 3^4 possible synonyms for each table location, or 81 possible synonyms. There is also a possibility of 26^4 key values, or 456,976 keys. Since our table will hold only 1000 of these possible keys, or about 0.2%, our synonym rate should be about 0.2% of 81, or approximately 0.16 synonyms per table entry. To be safe, place any synonyms encountered in loading the table in the first vacant table position following the location selected by hashing. Assume also, based on our computed average synonym rate of 0.16 synonyms per entry, that any synonyms will be located within five entries of the original hashed table location. This number should provide for any deviation from a normal distribution. The flowcharts for loading and searching hashed tables are presented in figures 8a and 8b.

Indexed Tables

The final area of discussion centers around the use of multiple tables to optimize the use of a cumbersome single table.

Let us make an extension to the earlier zip code example. The normal approach to a mailing list would require that each record contain the member's name, his street address, city, state, and zip code. But since the members all come from the same area, a better way to form the mailing list is as follows: remove the city and state fields from the mailing list file and, instead, build a table with zip code as key and city and state as data fields. When a label is printed, use the zip code, which is in the mailing list record, to find the appropriate city and state in the table.

When the (sorted) zip code table records are loaded into their own table, an index table that points to the beginning of a zip code group can be used to narrow down the range of a particular search method. (See figure 9a.) In this example, the indexed table lookup with a binary search will be followed.

Since the computer club's membership represents only a single geographic area, only the last four digits of the zip code may be used (assuming a constant value for the first digit). We may now segment the four-digit zip codes into a zip code prefix (ie: the second and third digits) and suffix (ie: the fourth and fifth digits). As the zip code table is loaded, I will track the first occurrence of each zip code prefix and record its location in the zip code table through an entry in the index table. The index table will contain one hundred entries representing zip code prefixes 00 thru 99. Thus the first entry in the index table will represent zip prefix 00 and will contain a value of 01, indicating that the first entry in the zip code table is zip code 00xx. The second entry in the index table will represent zip code prefix 01 and contain a value identifying the first occurrence of zip code 01xx in the zip code table, etc. An example of the tables generated by this method is given in figure 9a.

When both tables have been built, there is an index table which may be accessed without a search (using the zip code prefix +1 as a subscript) to identify the first location to be searched in the zip code table. From the point in the zip code identified by the index table, a serial, binary, percolated, or other form of search may be initiated. Figures 9b and 9c illustrate the logic of an indexed table load and indexed binary search.

Summary

I have now examined, at a glance, a variety of techniques that allow us to rapidly access data stored in single-dimensioned tables. In the case of small

Text cont. on page 118

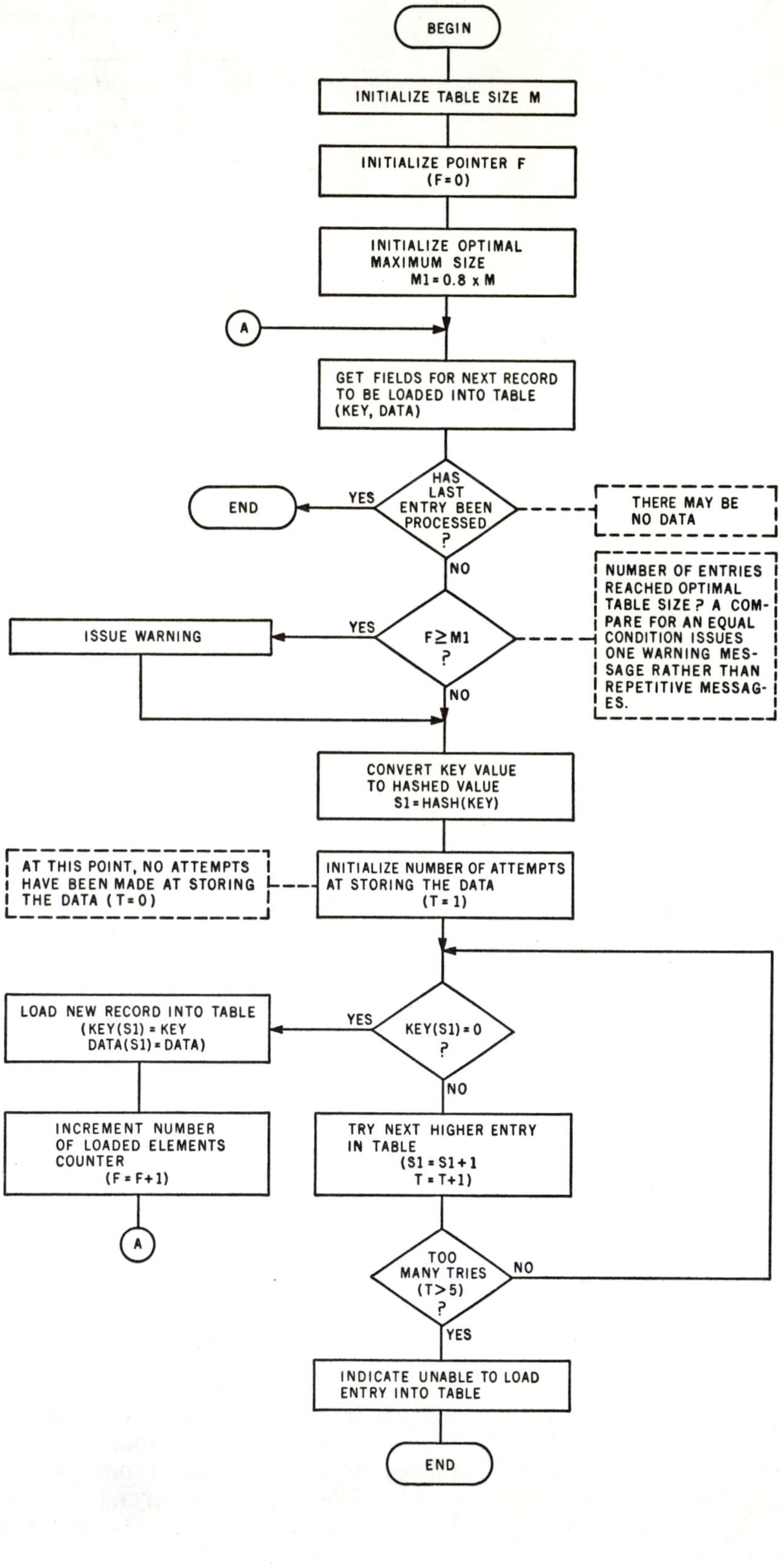

Figure 8a: Flowchart for a hashed table load. Here, the hashed value of the key is used as a subscript for storing the current entry in the table. If the current entry is already filled (this is known as a collision), the next higher table entry is tried, up to a total of five attempts. A hashed table cannot be entirely filled, so the table size must be somewhat larger than the expected maximum number of entries to be loaded into the table.

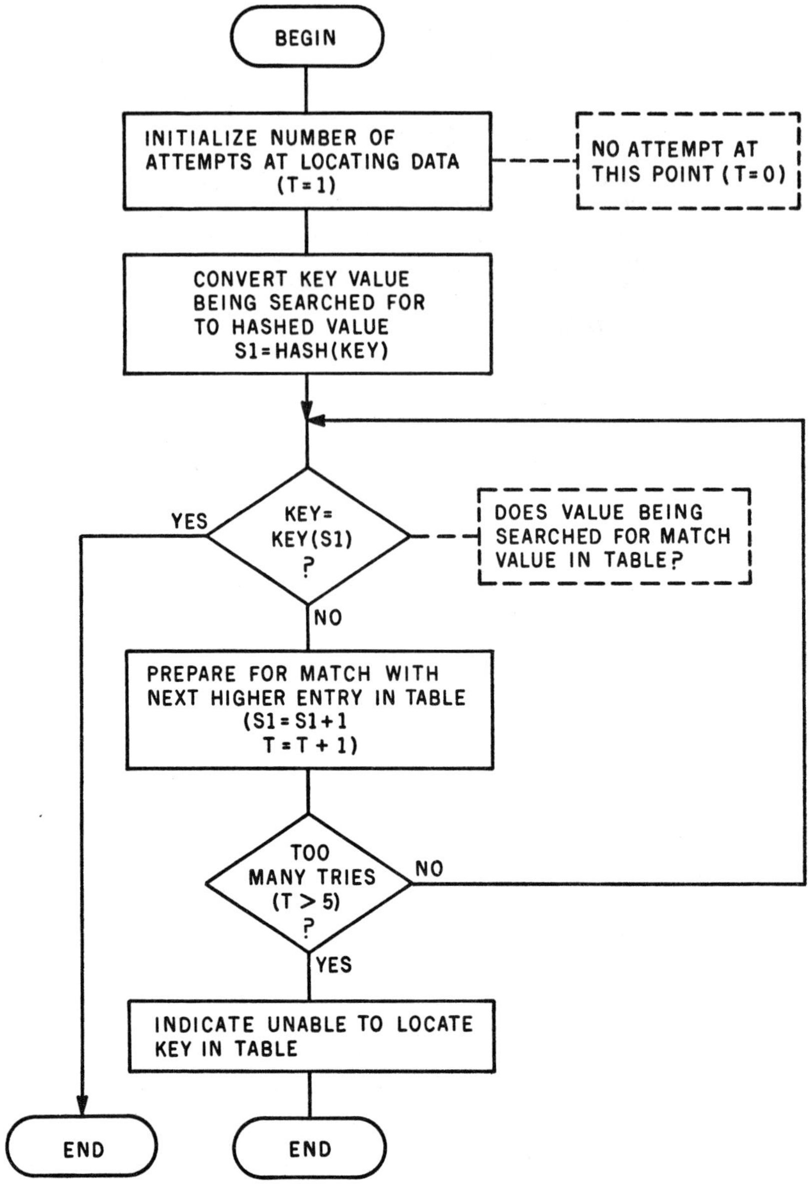

Figure 8b: Flowchart for a hashed table search. In this search, the hashed value of the key being searched for is used as a subscript to the expected location of the record in the table. If the desired record is not in that location, the next four table entires are checked for a match.

30012	IND(1)=zip code 300xx=01	KEY(1)=30012
30015	IND(2)=zip code 301xx=04	KEY(2)=30015
30017	IND(3)=zip code 302xx=00	KEY(3)=30017
30121	IND(4)=zip code 303xx=05	KEY(4)=30121
.	.	KEY (5)=30130
.	.	.
.	.	.
.	.	.

Figure 9a: Indexed table lookup example. In this mailing label example, the zip code table to be loaded, left, must be ordered in ascending key sequence. (The data associated with each key is not shown here.) Each key is loaded into the KEY table with a pointer from the IND table indicating the first occurrence of a new prefix (ie: digits 2 and 3 of the zip code). The associated data is loaded similarly into a data table.

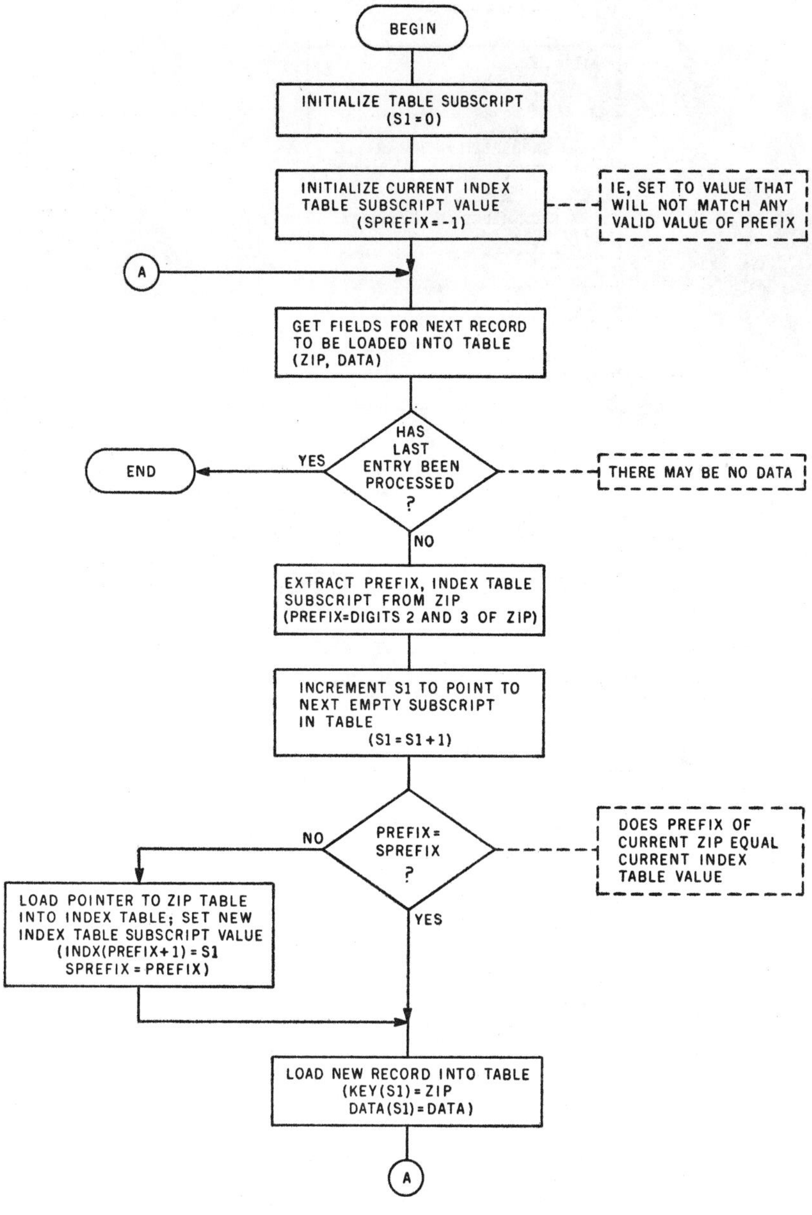

Figure 9b: Flowchart for an indexed table load. This load concurrently builds two tables, the first of which identifies major areas within the second. It is assumed that records are available in ascending key sequence. In this flowchart, the zip field is being used as the key of a record that contains city-state pairs as data.

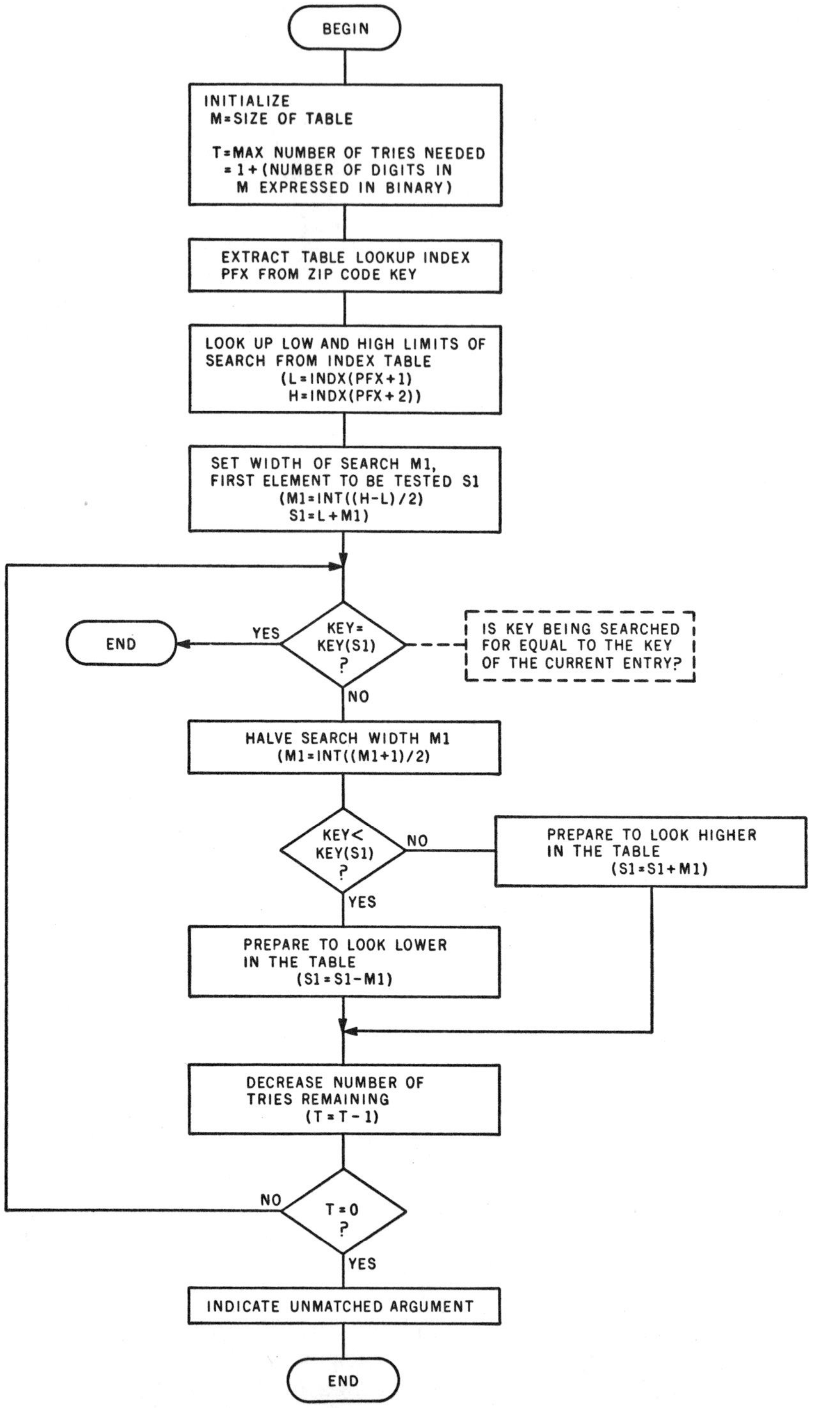

Figure 9c: Flowchart for an indexed binary table search. Here, the index table INDX is used to set the upper and lower limits of search. The index table method can be used in conjunction with any search method. Here, it precedes a binary search.

Text cont. from page 115

arrays (ie: under twenty-five entries), serial searches prove to be most effective most of the time. For larger arrays, binary load and search techniques tend to be most efficient. For very large arrays, or where access to array data is biased, the use of percolated, hashed, or indexed table-handling techniques may prove beneficial.

None of the techniques described in this article should be applied in conscientious programming without thoroughly reviewing the overall effect of the technique on the application. There is no greater frustration than to optimize yourself out of the most effective way to accomplish your programming goal. ■

Variables Whose Values Are Strings

W D Maurer

Almost every programmer has wanted to write a program in which there were one or more variables with strings as their values. Many programmers, however, are discouraged by the programming difficulties that arise in this connection, in all but the simplest cases. This is particularly true when space is at a premium and assembly language is used as it is in many microcomputer applications. I will describe here two alternative ways of solving these problems. Stylistically, these are quite different from each other. Each is fascinating in its own way, and each has certain difficulties which have to be surmounted, but either one of them will solve the basic problem with which we are concerned.

Many versions of FORTRAN allow variables to have strings as their values, but these strings cannot have lengths which are greater than some maximum, and this maximum is usually much too small for practical purposes. The maximum is, in fact, the number of characters in a word, which is usually two, four or six; sometimes it is five (as on the PDP-10) and sometimes eight (as on the IBM 370, using double words), but in practice the strings we are concerned with are often twenty, forty, or even sixty characters long. In many COBOL programs, this problem is taken care of by assigning some large number of characters to every such variable. This is particularly common when the value of the variable is somebody's name and address, to be printed on an envelope by the computer. Often twenty-five characters are reserved for the name, twenty-five for the address, and twenty-five for the city, state and zip code. This gives rise to two kinds of problems. In the first place, twenty-five characters is not enough for an address like 1527 San Jose-Los Gatos Rd., even if we leave the period off the end. More important, however, is the fact that if we reserve that many characters for *every* name and every address, there are going to be quite a lot of wasted characters. That doesn't matter too much in a COBOL program, where space, particularly on a disk, is usually quite abundant; but on a microcomputer we would like to make optimum use of all the space we have.

The first solution to this problem to consider involves the use of a large array, called SPACE, for the storage of strings. Let us consider each element of this array to be one character long. Then the first string (whose length is L1, say) is stored in the characters SPACE (1), SPACE(2) and so on up through SPACE(L1). The next character, SPACE(L1+1), contains an illegal character code (0, for example) to denote the fact that this is the end of the first string. The second string starts at SPACE(L1+2) and continues from there.

Every string ends with a 0-character code, and all the strings are stored in the array called SPACE, in sequential order.

Suppose now that these strings are supposed to be the values of variables K1, K2 and so on in the program. The actual value of each of these variables will be an integer that indicates where the corresponding string starts. Thus, for example, if 17 is the value of K2, then SPACE(17) is the first character of the given string; SPACE(18) is the next character, and so on. This is the basic concept of a *pointer*: a quantity which indicates where another quantity is in memory. The pointers we have set up have been *index pointers,* but it would have been just as easy to set up *address pointers*. That is, instead of the integer 17, we could have used the address, in memory, of the character SPACE(17).

The basic problem that arises when this method is used can be seen if we consider the process of setting a variable to a new value. Suppose that the value of K1 is 'SMITH' and we want to change it to 'JOHNSON'. Unfortunately, 'JOHNSON' has more letters in it than 'SMITH', so we cannot simply store the new characters in the same places as we stored the old ones. We can, however, take advantage of the fact that not all of our array SPACE has been used. Suppose that we have used the characters from SPACE(1) up through SPACE(LSPACE); then 'JOHNSON' can start at SPACE(LSPACE+1), and we can set the pointer in K1 to be LSPACE+1. Of course, we also have to update LSPACE at this point, by adding to it the length which contains a pointer to a third group. The last three characters appear in the third group, followed by three 0 characters.

If a string is exactly six characters long, it appears in a single group, but the pointer itself contains 0. If a string is twelve, eighteen, twenty-four, etc, characters long, it appears in more than one group, but the pointer in the last group will contain 0. In general, the pointer in the last group always contains 0, and it is this, rather than the presence of 0 characters, that determines the fact that it is the last group.

We thus have one or more *chains* (sometimes called *simple lists*) which involve various eight-character groups in FREE. We are now in a position to make use of a basic idea in advanced programming techniques: the *list of available space*. In this case, the list of available space is a chain which contains all those eight-character groups, and only those groups, which are *not* on any other chain. That is, we think of all these groups as being in some order: the order is of no consequence. Then the first group, in this order, contains a pointer to the second group; the second group contains a pointer to the third, and so on, up to the last group, which contains a 0 pointer.

We use a list of available space because it is now no longer necessary to use a collapsing process, as described in connection with the previous string storage method. In particular, we are no longer "abandoning" anything, as we were before. All we have to do is to make sure that, at all times, *every* group into which FREE is divided is on some chain, either the list of available space, or a chain which represents the string value of some variable.

There are also programs which use a list of available space, but in which some groups are abandoned, and a process somewhat like collapsing, known as *garbage collection*, is used to collect all these abandoned groups into a new list of available space. This, however, is necessary only when the various chains contain pointers to each other, which is not the case in the present application.

By a pointer to a group, we mean a pointer to the first character in the group. Thus if K is such a pointer, then the group consists of FREE(K), FREE(K+1) and so on up through FREE(K+7). We will assume that FREE(K) through FREE(K+5) are the six characters in the group, and that FREE(K+6) and FREE(K+7), taken together, are the pointer to the next group. A variable called LAVS (for "list of available space") contains, at all times, a pointer to the *first group* in the list of available space. The basic operations on the list of available space are taking one group off of JOHNSON, or 7 (plus 1, for the 0 character).

The trouble with this method is that now SMITH is still in memory, together with its 0 character. We are not really using *all* the space from SPACE(1) up through SPACE(LSPACE); there are five characters, plus a 0 character, that we are not using. By itself this causes no problems; but now consider what happens as our program continues to run. Every time we have a variable with a string as its value, and this variable gets a new string as its value, we are going to "abandon" some of our string storage area, just as we did with SMITH in this case. Eventually, we are going to run out of space; the whole SPACE array will be used up, except for "abandoned" areas as above. What do we do next?

Let us agree that, whenever we abandon a string, we write a 0 character over the first character of that string. This character will immediately follow the 0 character at the end of the preceding string, so that two 0 characters in a row will denote the start of an abandoned area. We can now consider the possibility of moving all the strings backwards by just enough so that the abandoned areas disappear, as shown in figure 1. This is known as *collapsing* (or sometimes *compactifying*). If we think of the left side of figure 1 as a row of bricks, with spaces between them to represent the abandoned areas, then putting our hands on the two ends of the row and collapsing it would produce the situation shown in the right side of the figure.

An algorithm to do this involves two pointers, I and J. As we move each character in SPACE, we set SPACE(J) = SPACE(1) and then add 1 to both I and J. When we have to skip over an abandoned areas, we increase I, but not J. Thus I always indicates the current character we are moving, and J always indicates the place we are moving it. At the start of the algorithm, both I and J are initialized to 1.

There is still one difficulty. All our variables with string values involve pointers, and after the collapsing process has taken place, the pointers will be wrong. We must have some way of adjusting these pointer values. There are at least two reasonable ways of doing this. One of these involves what may be called *back pointers*. The first character (or possibly the first two characters) of each string, as given in the array SPACE, is now some indication of which variable has this particular string as its value (such as, for example, the address of that variable). Whenever a back pointer is moved, by the operation SPACE(J) = SPACE(I), we look in that position (which should contain I) and change it to J.

The other method involves a sorting operation. All the pointers that are contained in all the variables with string values are placed in an array and sorted in ascending order, together with back pointers to the given variables. As we are going through the SPACE array and setting SPACE(J) = SPACE(I), we are also going through this new array, from the beginning to the end. At each stage, the currently considered pointer in this array points to the place in the SPACE array that we will have to treat next, as the start of a string to be moved. When we get to this point in SPACE, we reference the associated back pointer and proceed as before; then we continue through the SPACE array, but also move forward by one position in the new array, so that we will be ready to treat that pointer when we come to it.

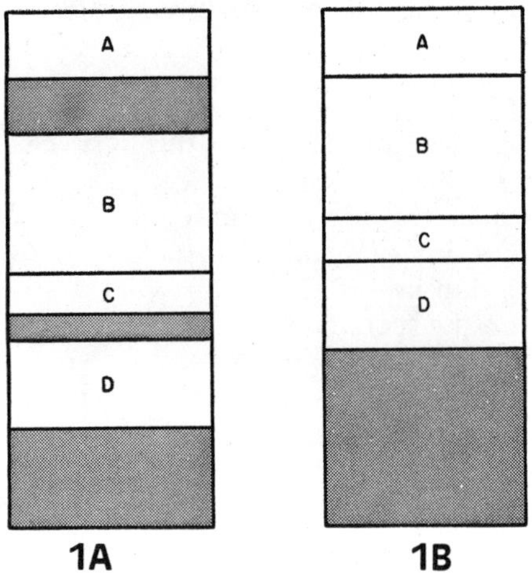

Figure 1: Collapsing or "compactifying" an array. In figure 1a A, B, C and D are separated by empty space (shaded area). In figure 1b this empty, available space is consolidated by moving B, C and D up so that they are contiguous with A.

Let us now pass to the second method of handling string values of variables. Again we use a large array, which we will call FREE this time, rather than SPACE. FREE is organized into groups of characters. To make our example concrete, we will assume that each group is eight characters long. The first six of these characters are actually characters of the given string; the remaining two character positions, taken together, contain a pointer to another group of eight characters.

Any string which is less than six characters long is stored in a single group. If a string is four characters long, for example, the last two characters are 0 characters; this tells us that these are not actually to be counted as part of the string. A string which is more than six characters long is stored as a chain. Thus, for example, if a string is fifteen characters long, the first six of these characters appear in one group, which contains a pointer to another group. The next six characters appear in the front of this second group and add a new group to it. The first of these operations, removing a group from the list of available space, is performed as follows:

- Set K = LAVS; the new group will consist of FREE(K) through FREE (K+7).
- Since this group is no longer to be on the list of available space, the first group in this list is now what used to be the *second* group. But a pointer to this second group is currently in FREE(K+6) and FREE(K+7). This pointer now has to be taken and put into LAVS, because LAVS must contain, at all times, a pointer to the first group in the list of available space.

The second of our two operation, adding a group to the list of available space, is performed as follows:

- Suppose that FREE(K) through FREE (K+7) is the new group. This will become the first group in the list of available space, and it must contain a pointer to the second group. But the second group is the old first group, and a pointer to that group was contained in LAVS. This means that LAVS must be moved into the pointer position FREE(K+6) and FREE(K+7).
- Since LAVS must contain, at all times, a pointer to the first group in the list of available space, we must now set LAVS equal to K.

The first operation above can be modified to check for overflow. If it is performed when the list of available space contains exactly one group, it is not hard to see that LAVS will be set equal to 0. This is not in itself an error; it merely means that all available space is being used. The next time we do this, though, there will be an error unless we check for it. Therefore, when we set K = LAVS, we should check to see if K is now 0; if so, there is an overflow condition. We are, of course, using the word "overflow" in a generalized sense to denote the fact that there is too much space being used for the available memory in the FREE array.

Using these two basic operations, we can now make sure that our available space list is always kept up to date. Suppose that we have a variable J with a string value, and suppose that this string value is kept in *m* 8-bit groups. A pointer to the first of these groups will be kept in J itself. Suppose that we are now going to set J to a new string value, which is kept in *n* 8-bit groups. First we apply the second algorithm above to the first group in the chain that represents the old value of J. This process puts this group on the list of available space. If $m \neq 1$, that is, if the pointer in this first group was not originally 0, we apply the same process to the second group in the chain representing the old value of J, and so on through the rest of these groups. (It is not necessary to know *m*, of course; we merely test for the pointer being 0, which indicates the last group.) Now we take *n* groups, or, in general, as many groups as we need, off the front of the list of available space by using the first algorithm above, and use these groups to store the new string value of J.

This system is quite workable as it stands; the only real problems with it come when we try to extend it. Suppose, for example, that we want to set the string value of J equal to the current string value of I. In that case we might want to save quite a bit of time by setting the pointer in J to be the same as the pointer in I. Thus we would have two pointers to the same group, or to the first group of the same chain, in the FREE area. This scheme, however, will not work unless we change our setup a bit. The problem comes when the value of I is later changed to something else. In this case the old value of I is put back on the list of available space, and this is improper because it is still the current value of J.

Now look at this case in more detail. Suppose that the value of I is 'SMITH', and we set J equal to 'SMITH' by setting J to point to the same place that I does. Suppose that we later set I equal to 'JOHNSON'. In this case, according to the algorithms we have discussed, the group [there is only one in this case; let us call it FREE(K) through FREE(K+7)] which contains 'SMITH' is put back on the list of available space, even though K is still the integer value of J. Now we need two groups to represent 'JOHNSON'. One of these will be this same group, that is, FREE(K) through FREE(K+7), because it was just put back on the beginning of the list of available space. This group will therefore contain JOHNSO, with the final N in the next group. This means that if at some later time we want to print out the value of J, we will print out JOHNSON rather than SMITH.

One solution to this problem which is sometimes adopted is to reserve the first character of any string for a special integer telling us how many variables have this particular string as their value. This integer is known as a *reference count*. It is usually 1, but in the case above, where J and I point to the same string, it would be 2. Every time a variable is set to a new value, the reference count in the *old* value is decreased by 1. Only if its value is then 0 do we return the space it uses back to the list of available space, because otherwise there are all variables which have that string as their value. The trouble with this scheme is that it may very easily not be worth the effort. Do we really want to add an extra character to every string, not to mention the extra testing that goes on whenever we set a string to a new value, just to be able to save a little time and space in an operation (eg: setting one string to be the same as another) that might not be that commonly used in our program? It is certainly a debatable point.

It should also be clear that there is nothing special about the number of characters in a group — eight, in this case. The fewer characters we have in a group, the more pointers we will have, and the more space these will take up. The more characters we have in a group, the more wasted or 0 characters we will have in strings, because the length of a string is not always evenly divisible by the number of characters in a group. This is a space trade-off which should be tuned by the user to fit the requirements of a particular program.■

Subroutine Parameters

W D Maurer

If you have written computer programs in any language, you must be aware by now what a subroutine is, although you might not have written any. The basic concept of a subroutine is present in all computer languages, although every language implements it a bit differently from the others. In systems based on the 8080, the 8085, or the Z-80, you write CALL SUB to call the subroutine called SUB. On the 6800 and the 6502, it's JSR SUB, while in BASIC it's GOSUB α where the first statement of the subroutine SUB is on line number α. But regardless of the language, the concept is the same: you have something in your program that you want to do more than once. It may be looking up an element in a table; it may be printing out a list; it may be making an access to a data structure; but whatever it is, you need it at various times in your program. You don't want to have to write out the same instructions over again every time you need that particular job to be done, because this is wasteful of memory space. So, therefore, you group together the instructions that do this job into a subroutine, and then at any point that you want the job to be done, you put in an instruction to *call* the subroutine. When the subroutine is finished, it *returns* to the point immediately following the place where it was called. This is also done differently in different programming languages — you write RETURN in BASIC, RET for the 8080 and Z-80, and RTS (ie: return from subroutine) for the 6800 and 6502.

All this is fine if the job you want to do repeatedly is exactly the same every time you want to do it. But, in practice, this is usually not the case. For example, if you are looking up an element in a table, you are probably looking up a different element each time. If you are multiplying two 16-bit quantities — a very common subject for a small-system subroutine — the quantities you are multiplying are probably not the same from one multiplication to the next, and the result is also probably not the same variable. This is true even though the logic of multiplication does stay the same. It is this that has led to the idea of subroutine parameters, the subject of this article.

Parameters

In applied mathematics, there is a concept of parameter which will be familiar to those small-system users who have backgrounds in engineering or physical science. Consider, for example, the graph of a function. You are usually expressing y in terms of x, but if you are constructing the graph of a circle, it is sometimes more useful to introduce another variable θ to represent the angle, and then to express both x and y in terms of θ. The variable θ, in this context, is called a parameter. In computer programming, however, whether on large or small systems, the word "parameter" has a more general meaning, and one which does not require any knowledge of applied mathematics; it is simply any variable which is used by a subroutine, and which is supplied to that subroutine by the program that calls it.

Parameters of subroutines are related to *arguments* (sometimes called parameters or formal parameters) of functions. If you have a function *f(t)* or *g(a, b)* or *h(x, y, z)*, then *t, a, b, x, y,* and *z* are the arguments. On a computer, the value of a function is computed by a subroutine, and this must be considered as one special kind of subroutine. Some languages allow you to use functional notation for functions; thus *h(x, y, z)* might be FNH(X, Y, Z) in BASIC, provided that the definition of *h* was simple enough. In assembly language, however, one generally uses the same instructions (eg: Call, JSR, or whatever), whether one is calling a subroutine to calculate the value of a function or a more general subroutine.

Those who work with big computers have laid out a considerable amount of terminology dealing with parameters and how they are supplied, or *passed*, to a subroutine by the program that calls it (and sometimes vice versa). One of the purposes of this article is to lay out this terminology for the small-system user so that he or she will not have to "reinvent the wheel." It should be emphasized that for a long time mathematicians believed that there ought to be a single concept of parameter that would work well in all situations. Gradually we have come to realize that there are at least four, and probably a good deal more, reasonable implementations of parameter passing. These will be detailed in what follows.

Two Examples

To illustrate why the concept of parameter differs from one situation to another, let us consider two simple subroutines: an output subroutine and a multiplication subroutine. The output subroutine will be called OUTPUT(X), and its job will be to output the character X. The multiplication subroutine will be called MULT16(I, J, N), and its job will be to multiply the two 16-bit quantities I and J, producing the result N. The problem we are to solve is how to call OUTPUT(Z), OUTPUT(Q), and so on, for various characters we wish to output, and similarly MULT16(A, B, C), MULT16(U, V, W), and so on, for various multiplications we wish to perform.

Consider first the case of the output subroutine. Suppose that in this subroutine there is a variable called X. In order to output Z, for example, we move Z to X just before calling OUTPUT. The same sort of thing will work for Q, or any other character we wish to output. This method of passing parameters is known as call by value. It may be defined more formally as follows. Suppose we have a subroutine such as OUTPUT(X), where X stands for *any* parameter, such as Z or Q, that might actually be supplied. Here Z and Q are called the *actual* parameters, and X is called the *formal* parameter. Then call by value consists of:

1. Moving the value of the actual parameter to the formal parameter. (If there is more than one formal parameter, as in the case of a function *h(x, y, z)*, then they must all be moved.)
2. Calling the subroutine.

In assembly language it is very common for X, in a situation such as the above, to be a register. Then all we have to do is to load the register before we call the subroutine; the subroutine assumes that Z, or Q, or whatever stands for X, is in that register. (On the 8080, the Z-80, the 6800, and the 6502, the most common register used for this purpose is the A register, although ISIS, the operating system for the Intellec, which is an 8080-based system, uses the C register.)

If we now look at MULT16, however, we can see without too much trouble that call by value does not work. Let us see why not by laying out a specific example. Suppose we are calling MULT16(U, V, W), where MULT16 has been defined as a subroutine with parameters I, J, and N. That is, I, J, and N are the formal parameters. To use call by value, we would first have to move the values of U, V, and W into I, J, and N. That is, U would be moved to I; V would be moved to J; and W would be moved to N. Now we would call the subroutine; and the subroutine, we are assuming, multiplies the 16-bit quantities I and J and sets N equal to the result.

What is wrong with this? Since we were calling MULT16(U, V, W), what we presumably wanted was to multiply the two 16-bit numbers U and V, and set W equal to the result. It is not too hard to see that we did, actually, multiply U by V, because we set I equal to U, and J equal to V, and then we multiplied I by J. But what happens to W? We set N equal to the result of multiplying U by

V; but we did not set W equal to anything. (Earlier, we also set N equal to W, a useless operation.) The general situation here is that whenever we have a *formal* parameter that is *set* to some new value by a subroutine, call by value will not work; the formal parameter will not be set to the new value or to any other new value.

Because of this, people who work with big computers came up with three alternative methods of passing parameters. The first of these is known as call by value and result or, sometimes, informally as "copy-restore." The second is known as call by reference or sometimes as "call by address' or "call by location." The third is known as call by name. We shall take up each of these in turn.

Call by Value and Result

Call by value and result is a rather straightforward way of fixing the bug in call by value that should be evident from the preceding discussion. In fact, what we wanted to do in our MULT16 subroutine was as follows:

1. Set I equal to U and J equal to V.
2. Call the subroutine (which multiplies I by J, giving N).
3. Set W equal to N.

In other words, there are two parameter-passing operations — one just before the subroutine starts, the second one after it ends — and one is the reverse of the other. In the first operation, we move *actual* parameters to *formal* parameters. In the second operation, we move *formal* parameters to *actual* parameters. The parameters we move the first time are the ones that are *used* by the subroutine; the parameters we move the second time are the ones that are *set* by the subroutine.

But how can we tell which parameters are used and which ones are set? It won't always be the case that the first two are used and the last one is set (if there are three altogether). They might all be used, or two of them might be set, or any number of possible combinations. Again, there is more than one reasonable solution to this problem.

The solution chosen by the designers of a number of computer languages in wide-spread use by the American military establishment (NELIAC, JOVIAL, CMS-2) was to build the distinction between used and returned parameters into the syntax of the language. In other words, when you call a subroutine in any one of these languages, you would have to specify, in some way, which of these you intended to be used and which you intended to be returned. (JOVIAL, for example, uses a semicolon; we would speak of MULT16(U, V; W), for example, where the semicolon separates the used parameters U and V from the returned parameter W.) This certainly solves the problem, although only if you are going to use call by value and result, at the cost of making life a trifle more complicated for those who do not want to have to worry about how parameters are passed.

The other solution, chosen by IBM, is to regard *all* parameters as *both* used and returned at all times. This may seem a bit wasteful, but in fact, compared to call by reference (to be described below), it is more efficient, most of the time. It does, however, lead to some strange and unusual results, the most famous of which may be illustrated as follows. Suppose we have a subroutine D(X, Y), where X and Y are the formal parameters, and suppose that this sets X to 0 and does not change Y. Now suppose that we call D(L,L). Of course, we would like this to set L equal to 0. But see what happens:

1. Since X and Y are treated as both used and returned, our first step is to set X equal to L, and Y equal to L.
2. Now we call the subroutine, which sets X equal to 0 and does not change Y.
3. Finally, we return the actual parameters. First we return X by setting L equal to X. Since X is now 0, this will set L equal to 0, which is exactly what we wanted. But now we return Y by setting L equal to Y. Since Y is still the original value of L, this will undo the previous result, and the final outcome will be that L is the same after calling D as it was beforehand!

The behavior illustrated above can be avoided simply by setting L1 equal to L and then calling (DL, L1), rather than D(L, L). In general, when using call by value and result, with all parameters used and returned, one should never use two actual parameters which are the same. The problem above actually happened to one of my students, who wrote a big FORTRAN program that ran on the CDC 6400, a computer using call by reference, but mysteriously failed to run on the IBM 360, a computer using call by value and result. Many hours of analysis traced the bug to a subroutine call like D(L, L) above.

Call by Reference

Call by reference, historically, preceded call by value and result, although it was not known by that name at that time. The idea of call by reference is to give the subroutine the *addresses* of its parameters, rather than their values. Then, when the subroutine either uses or sets one of its formal parameters, it does so by making a *reference* to that address. Let us see how this would work on a small system.

1. On the 8080, you can load the HL register pair with the address of the parameter α with the instruction LXI H, α just before calling the subroutine. Then, in the subroutine, if you need to load this parameter into any register *r*, you can use MOV *r*,M; if you need to operate on it arithmetically, you can use ADD M, SUB M, ANA M, and the like; if you need to set it to a new value which is now in register *r*, you can use MOV M,*r*. If you need the HL register pair for other purposes in your routine, you can do an XCHG if you don't need the DE register pair, or you can PUSH H while you use HL and POP H afterward. If there are two parameters, you can load one into HL with LXI H, α as before, and load the other one into BC or DE. If there are several parameters, you can push their addresses onto the stack before calling the subroutine, and pop them back within the subroutine.

2. On the 6800, you can load the X register with the address of the parameter α with the instruction LDX # α (where the # specifies an immediate addressing instruction) just before calling the subroutine. You can now use indexed addressing instructions to manipulate the parameter by loading it (LDAA 0,X or LDAB 0,X), storing it (STAA 0,X or STAB 0,X), or performing arithmetic operations such as ADDA 0,X or ANDB 0,X. If there is more than one parameter, you can move the addresses of all the actual parameters to fixed locations within the subroutine before calling it. The subroutine can then load each of these into the X register when needed, after which any of the indexed instructions discussed above may be used.

3. On the 6502, there is a general method involving loading the X register, just before calling the subroutine, with the address of a table of addresses of actual parameters. That is, we execute JDX #α where we have written (in page 0):

```
α    DFB    U MOD 256
     DFB    U/256
     DFB    V MOD 256
     DFB    V/256
     DFB    W MOD 256
     DFB    W/256
```

for exmple, defining a byte for the low-order address and then for the high-order address of each of the parameters U, V, and W. One can then make reference to the actual parameters by indexed indirected addressing: LDA (0,X) for the U, LDA (2,X) for V, and LDA (4,x) for W. This is perfectly general, since LDA (load) can be replaced by STA (store), ADC (add with carry), CMP (compare), AND, and so on.

4. On the Z-80, you can (as always) mimic the 8080, or you can use registers IX and IY to contain the addresses of parameters.

An additional advantage of call by reference is that it allows you to have, as a parameter, the name of an array. For example, you might be writing a subroutine to compare two character strings to see if they are the same. There would be two parameters, namely the two character strings. If you used call by value, you would have to move these entire strings into new locations just before calling the subroutine. This would be wasteful of both time and space, and is, in fact, never done; even systems that use call by value or call by value and result, if they allow array names as parameters, use call by reference (or call by name, to be discussed below) for these. Thus you would only be passing, from the program to the subroutine, the two string starting addresses; that is, for each string, the address of its first byte.

One important source of confusion, when call by reference is used, has to do with how to return a parameter. A large number of programmers try, when they are writing a subroutine, to have it put its answer *somewhere* and then furnish the main program with the address of where that *somewhere* is. This never works, because the main program has no way of using that information. It is not up to the *subroutine* to tell the main program where the information is to be returned; it is up to the main program to tell the subroutine *where to return* the information, and then the subroutine *must* return the information to that point. In particular, the subroutine will never be right if it returns a subroutine. If call by reference is used, it should be remembered that this subroutine can be called more than once, with different actual parameters each time, and therefore, when it changes the value of one of its actual parameters, that change must be made by storing this new value in an *indexed* location — where the index is normally the HL register pair on the 8080, the X register on the 6800 and 6502, and possibly the IX or IY register on the Z-80.

Call by reference is, in general, more inefficient than call by value and result, particularly if we make reference to a parameter inside a loop. One technique that has been tried on big computers, and works rather well for subroutines that take large amounts of time, is address modification. This involves storing the addresses which are passed as parameters directly into the instructions that use them. Unfortunately, this technique is inappropriate in most microcomputer systems, where the instructions are in read-only memory and thus cannot be modified as the program is running. It should also be mentioned that on some systems which use both call by reference and call by value and result, the second of these is implemented as a special case of the first. That is, it is always the addresses, or references, that are passed, so that there is only one kind of standard subroutine protocol rather than two. But whenever call by value and result is to be used, the subroutine, rather than the main program, performs the setting of formal parameters to actual parameter values and vice versa.

Call by Name

This finally brings us to call by name — the easiest to define, yet the hardest to understand, of the better known parameter passing methods. For years, call by name was a *pons asinorum* among big computer software people; that is, the way of distinguishing the bright from the dumb, or the "with-it" from the "not-with-it," was whether you understood call by name. Lately there has been a bit less interest in call by name among practical computer people, since, although it was used in ALGOL 60, one of the first big computer languages (in both senses — big [computer languages] and [big computer] languages), it has not been used in most languages developed since then. But an understanding of it, and of some of the problems that arise with it, is still essential to the amateur as well as the professional computer scientist.

Call by name is defined as follows. Suppose I have a subroutine with a formal parameter X. Suppose I call this subroutine, with actual parameter Y. Then call by name implies that the subroutine is executed as if we had gone through it and substituted Y for every occurrence of X.

There is one important proviso to the above, which may be illustrated as follows. Suppose that in the subroutine we have A=B+X. Suppose now that the actual parameter is not Y, but rather U+V. (It is quite permissible to call SUB(U+V), for example, where SUB is the name of a subroutine.) Now we would like to proceed as if A=B•X really means A=B•(U+V); but if we substitute U+V for X, as in the above definition, we obtain A=B•U+V, which is not quite the same. Therefore we need to change the definition so as to specify the insertion of parentheses. On the other hand, it should also be clear that we do not want to insert parentheses all the time. For example, the variable A could have been the formal parameter, rather than X. In this case, the actual parameter could not be U+V, because then A=B•X would be interpreted as (U+V)=B•X, which makes no sense. But suppose the actual parameter is Y, just as before; we still do not want to write (Y)=B•X (with parentheses) in BASIC or any other algebraic language. Therefore the rule is that the actual parameter is substituted for the formal parameter, *inserting parentheses wherever syntactically possible;* this is the phrase used in the definition of ALGOL 60.

So long as the actual parameters are not expressions like U+V (or like A(I), which could be either a subscripted variable or a reference to a function), call by name is almost identical to call by reference. Therefore, in studying the differences between the two, we have to look at the general rules for handling actual parameters which are expressions. These are that an actual parameter cannot be an expression (other than a single variable, either subscripted or not) when the corresponding formal parameter is *returned*, as we have illustrated above with the formal parameter A and the actual parameter U+V; and, of course, a *formal* parameter can never be an expression.

Suppose that in our subroutine we have S=S+X, where X is a formal parameter, and the corresponding actual parameter is A(I). (This is a simplification of an actual example given with the definition of ALGOL 60.) Therefore S=S+X becomes S=S+A(I). But now suppose that we want to do this for I=1 to 10. That would be, presumably, a way of adding the numbers A(1) through A(10), if S were originally set to 0. If we use call by reference, however, this will not work. In call by reference, the address of the actual parameter, in this case, the address of A(I), would be given to the subroutine. When the subroutine does S=S+X, it would get X from the location which has that address. But that location is a *constant* location — the location, in fact, of A(I) where the variable I has whatever value it had before the subroutine was called. This means that we add X ten times, whatever X is, and in this case we add the *same* value of A(I) ten times, rather than adding A(1) through A(10).

How would we implement call by name? In the above case, when the subroutine does S=S+X, it has to have a way of finding out whether X will stand for a different variable each time. Therefore it loads S and then calls a subroutine to find the value of X, which it then adds and stores the result in S. This means that it is *the address of the start of this subroutine* that is passed, rather than the address of X itself as in call by reference. (This is known as Jensen's device, after a programmer at Regnecentralen, or the National Computer Center of Denmark, who used it in implementing ALGOL 60.) We should remark that there is another entirely different way of implementing call by name, which is to replace each *call* to a subroutine, separately, by the subroutine with the substitutions performed as discussed above. This will not work for ALGOL 60, because it will not work, in general, for recursive subroutines, and it also takes up quite a bit of space if the subroutines are long.

Call by name is considerably less efficient than the other methods we have discussed, which is a big reason for its general decline. Nevertheless, it has its own unexpected advantages. Let us consider a subroutine like D(X, Y), which we discussed earlier, but this time suppose that it simply *uses* X and does not use Y, and let us call D(A, F(B)), where F(B) is a reference to a function. Suppose further than that calculation of F(B) (for some reason) gets the computer into an endless loop. If we use call by name, then, since we never use Y, we have no occasion to call the subroutine that calculates Y — that is, we never call F(B). If we use call by value, however, the first thing we do is to set X equal to A and Y equal to F(B). The result is that we get into the endless loop, in this case, if we use call by value, but not if we use call by name.■

Easy-to-Use Hashing Function

Don Kinzer

Hashing, or scatter storage, is a well-known and widely used technique for handling lists. Perhaps the most common usage is in assemblers and compilers where it greatly speeds the handling of symbols. This article briefly discusses the merits and drawbacks of hashing relative to other sorting and searching techniques and presents an easy-to-use hashing function implemented on a 6800 microprocessor.

The concept of hash tables first appeared in the literature around 1953, but it is generally accepted that hashing was used prior to that. Other names given to the same process are scatter storage, randomized storage and key transformation table. These names will be seen to be equally applicable shortly.

Using the hashing technique, a symbol (ie: collection of alphanumeric characters) to be put in the table is processed through a hashing function to obtain an index into a storage table. This index is then used for the address of a potential storage space for that symbol. We say potential because it is possible that some other symbol could have previously hashed to the same location. Such an occurrence is called a collision and the current symbol must be reprocessed to generate a new table address which is again checked for being empty and so on until an opening is found.

When it is necessary to look up the value of a symbol a process similar to that above is performed. The symbol is processed through the same hashing function as before. Next the address is checked to make sure that it is not empty. If it is empty, the symbol is undefined. Now that we know a symbol is stored there, we must check if it matches the symbol we are looking for because this may be a collision. If the symbols do not match, we have to rehash just as before until we find the symbol or an empty location.

With a given set of symbols, a given hashing function and a specified table length, it is possible that trying to insert a particular symbol into the table will result in an infinite number of collisions indicating no empty spaces even though the table is not full. Likewise, another symbol may take many attempts before being finally inserted.

It should be quite obvious that the ideal case would be an infinitely long table space. However, a real-world compromise dictates that we waste a percentage of the table to keep the number of rehashes low. The trade-off is very evident. The lower the percentage of table utilization, the lower will be the number of collisions. As the percentage of table utilization increases, so will the number of collisions. Furthermore, the number of collisions, and therefore the number of rehashes, directly affects execution time. We encounter the memory size versus speed trade-off once again. In practice, a reasonable compromise is to try for 50% to 80% table utilization and to determine empirically the hash count (ie: number of rehashes allowed). If the hash count is exceeded on a symbol in-

Listing 1: The assembly listing of the hash function and random-number generator. If the first hash of a label does not work, the routine is entered a second time through the REHASH function. The random-number generator generates a 24-bit random number which is used to determine the table location of the label.

```
                 *
                 *
                 * STORAGE
                 *
0020                    ORG   $20
0020             RNDM   RMB   3
0023             TBLADR RMB   2
                 *
                 *
1000             SYMTBL EQU   $1000
                 *
                 *
0100                    ORG   $100
                 *
                 *
                 ** HASH
                 * THIS ROUTINE PROCESSES THE SYMBOL POINTED TO BY X
                 * AND RETURNS THE ADDRESS OF A SYMBOL LOCATION OF
                 * THE 4K SYMBOL TABLE IN THE X REGISTER.
                 * IT IS UP TO THE CALLING ROUTINE TO CHECK THE
                 * VALIDITY OF THE SYMBOL LOCATION.
                 *
                 * REHASH IS THE ENTRY POINT IF A RETRY IS NECESSARY
                 *
                 * THE B REGISTER CONTAINS THE HASH COUNT (THE
                 * NUMBER OF TIMES HASH + REHASH HAVE BEEN CALLED).
                 *
0100 5F          HASH     CLR B                  SET HASH COUNT TO 0
0101 A6 00                LDA A  0,X             GET FIRST CHAR
0103 AB 05                ADD A  5,X             FOLD THE SYMBOL TO 3 BYTES
0105 97 22                STA A  RNDM+2
0107 A6 01                LDA A  1,X
0109 A9 04                ADC A  4,X
010B 97 21                STA A  RNDM+1
010D A6 02                LDA A  2,X
010F A9 03                ADC A  3,X
0111 97 20                STA A  RNDM            FOLD DONE
                 *
                 *
0113 5C          REHASH   INC B                  UP THE HASH COUNT
0114 BD 01 2C             JSR    RANDOM          GENERATE RANDOM BITS
0117 96 22                LDA A  RNDM+2          GET A BYTE OF RANDOM
0119 94 0F                AND A  $0F             MASK OFF 4
011B 36                   PSH A                  SAVE TILL LATER
011C 96 21                LDA A  RNDM+1          GET ANOTHER BYTE
011E 94 F8                AND A  $F8             MASK OFF 5 (9 BITS TOTAL)
0120 8B 00                ADD A  #SYMTBL         ADD TO LS HALF
                 *                               OF SYMBOL TABLE ADDRESS
0122 97 24                STA A  TBLADR+1        SAVE
0124 32                   PUL A                  GET FIRST BYTE BACK
0125 89 10                ADC A  #SYMTBL/256     ADD TO MS HALF OF
                 *                               SYMBOL TABLE ADDRESS
0127 97 23                STA A  TBLADR          SAVE
0129 DE 23                LDX    TBLADR          GET ENTRY ADDRESS
012B 39                   RTS                    DONE
                 *
                 *
                 ** RANDOM
                 * THIS ROUTINE RETURNS A 24 BIT RANDOM
                 * NUMBER IN RNDM THROUGH RNDM+2 WHICH MUST BE
                 * NON-ZERO UPON ENTRY.  THE ROUTINE MAKES 24
                 * PASSES TO INVOLVE ALL BITS OF THE SEED IN
                 * THE RESULT.
012C 36          RANDOM   PSH A
012D 37                   PSH B                  SAVE REGS
012E C6 18                LDA B  #24             GET LOOP COUNT
0130 96 20       RNDLP    LDA A  RNDM            GET MS BYTE
0132 49                   ROL A
0133 49                   ROL A
0134 49                   ROL A
0135 49                   ROL A
0136 49                   ROL A
0137 98 20                EOR A  RNDM            XOR BIT 18 WITH 23
0139 49                   ROL A                  PUT RESULT IN CARRY
013A 79 00 22             ROL    RNDM+2          SHIFT IT IN
013D 79 00 21             ROL    RNDM+1          PROPAGATE ACROSS
0140 79 00 20             ROL    RNDM            ALL THE WAY
0143 5A                   DEC B                  PASS DONE
0144 26 EA                BNE    RNDLP           LOOP TILL DONE
0146 33                   PUL B
0147 32                   PUL A                  RESTORF REGS
0148 39                   RTS                    DONE
                 *
                 *
                 *
                          END
     NO ERROR(S) DETECTED


  SYMBOL TABLE:
HASH    0100      RANDOM  012C      REHASH  0113      RNDLP   0130
RNDM    0020      SYMTBL  1000      TBLADR  0023
```

sertion operation, the table is declared full, but on a symbol retrieval operation the symbol is declared undefined.

When the table size and hashing function are selected appropriately, the average number of hashes is generally less than $log_2 n$, where n is the number of symbols in the table. Compare this to a linear search which averages $n/2$ comparisons. An average assembly-language program will contain about 100 labels and symbols. Hashing would average about seven collisions while a linear list would require about fifty comparisons on the average.

The crux of the hashing matter is finding a good hashing function which will minimize collisions. The procedure for this usually involves some complex mathematical analysis based on the characters expected in the symbols and their relative frequency of occurrence. The optimum hash function generally ends up being division by certain prime numbers or some other equally awkward scheme for a microprocessor.

As an alternative to this, I offer an empirically determined hashing function that works well within the confines of an assembler. The reason for using it, however, was logically derived and is something like this: it is the purpose of hashing to randomly distribute symbols about a table, so why not use a random-number generator to generate the table index?

The random-number generator, RANDOM, and the HASH routine used are shown in listing 1. The random-number generator uses the maximal length sequence generator technique to generate a 24-bit random number. With a nonzero initial state in the 3 bytes, each call to RANDOM will leave them in a specific final state. Different initial states produce randomly different final states.

The HASH routine merely loads the 3 bytes with the symbol and calls RANDOM to generate a random bit sequence. The assembler for which HASH was written allowed six character symbols. In order to utilize every bit of symbol information to hash to an address, the six-character symbol is crammed into 3 bytes by "folding" it in half. This is done by adding the outermost bytes (ie: characters) together for 1 byte of the random-number generator followed by adding together the next outermost two characters and lastly the innermost two. This can be done without losing information because the ASCII characters of the symbols have a hexadecimal value less than 7F. Two of these added together have a value less than hexadecimal FE which fits in eight bits.

The HASH routine in listing 1 assumes a 4 K-byte symbol table limitation. With 6 bytes for the symbol name and 2 bytes for its value this allows 512 symbol spaces. This being the case, only 9 bits are needed for a table index. Since the result of the call to RANDOM is 24 random bits, we are perfectly free to choose any 9 of those bits for the index. HASH does this by taking out the most significant 9 bits of the least significant 12 bits of the generator.

Recall that HASH only returns a *potentially* useful table address. In the case of a label insertion operation it is up to the calling routine to check that the returned address is empty. If not, REHASH is called which utilizes the last contents of the random-number generator as a seed for the next random number. Calling HASH again will produce exactly the same address. Alternate means of handling collisions such as linear of quadratic distribution will not be discussed here.

In the case of a label-retrieve operation the calling routine needs to check if the symbol matches that at the table address. If they do not match and the location is not empty, REHASH until the hash count limit is exceeded or an empty location is found whereupon the symbol is declared to be undefined. Note that it will take exactly the same number of attempts to find a symbol as it did to put it in the table to begin with.

This has by no means been a thorough treatment of the subject of hashing but only an attempt to pass on something which works rather well in my experience. The interested reader is encouraged to do further research into the topics mentioned here.■

References

1. Grappel R. *Randomize Your Programming.* BYTE, volume 1, number 13, September 1976.
2. Hopgood, F R A. *Compiling Techniques.* American Elsevier, 1970.
3. Knuth, Donald E. *The Art of Computer Programming, Volume 3, Sorting and Searching.* Addison Wesley, 1973.
4. Lancaster, D. "Understanding Pseudo-Random Circuits." *Radio Electronics,* April 1975.

Text Compression

James L Peterson

A continuing problem on any computer system is storage. There is never enough computer memory for all the information we wish to store. This is true both for programs in main memory and for the information which resides on peripheral devices.

One solution to this problem is simply to buy more memory. Particularly in the case of storage devices with removable media, such as cassettes, floppy disks, magnetic tape and even paper tape, additional media can be purchased and used as necessary. But even here economics will eventually limit the amount of storage available.

An alternative approach is to try to make better use of existing storage media. This is where *text compression* can be of great use. The idea of text compression is to reduce the amount of space needed to store a file by compressing it, making it smaller. Compression is accomplished by changing the way in which the file is represented. The *encoding* procedure is performed in such a way that it is reversible; that is, it can later be *decoded* to produce the original uncompressed file. This is illustrated in figure 1. The hope is that the encoded version of the file will be smaller than the original file, hence space will be saved.

The cost of this space saving is processor time. Additional processor time will be needed to encode and decode the compressed files as they are processed. However, it should be noted that microprocessors are seldom processor bound, but more commonly have extra processor cycles available. In fact, the total execute time of many programs will be less on a compressed file despite its encoded form. This is because the input/output (I/O) transfer time for a compressed file is less than the transfer time for an uncompressed file, since there are fewer bits to read or write. Therefore, I/O bound programs, like assemblers and loaders, may execute faster on compressed files.

The basic idea of text compression is to find an encoding method that takes up minimal space. Many algorithms for text compression have been invented, and we present some of them here. In general, these algorithms will work for any type of data, such as numeric, character string, and so on; but for purposes of this article we limit ourselves to text (ie: strings of characters). This will include programs, documentation, mailing lists, data, and many other files stored in computers. In fact, object programs, if considered as simply strings of bytes, can also be compressed, although this must be done carefully.

Text compression is accomplished by careful selection of the *representation* of the information in the compressed file. For many small computer systems, the ASCII code is generally used to represent characters. The main advantage of the ASCII code is that the representation is standard and easy to define. A major

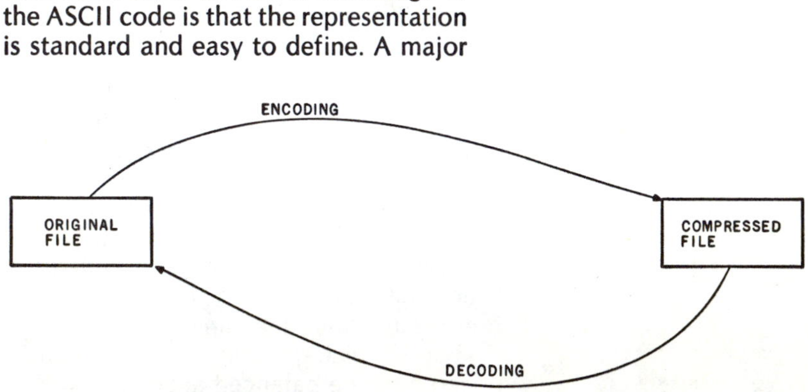

Figure 1: The text compression process.

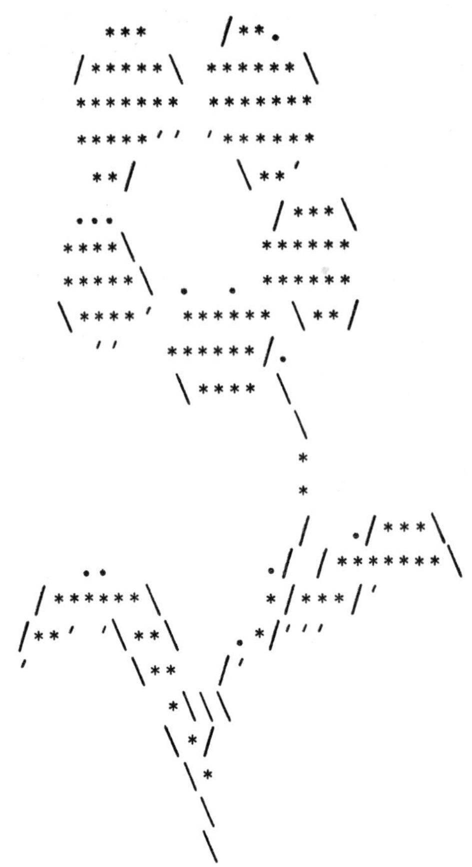

Figure 2: A file which can benefit from simple text compression techniques. The original file is a 24 by 80 character video display image consisting of 1920 characters. Deleting trailing blanks and using tabs set for every eight columns will reduce the size of this file to 412 characters — a savings of 78.6%

disadvantage is its poor space utilization. ASCII is a 7-bit code, while most processors handle 8-bit bytes. Thus, 1 bit out of 8 (ie: 12.5%) is wasted simply because a 7-bit character code is used in an 8-bit byte. Further, most control codes are seldom used, and many applications do not need both uppercase and lowercase characters. Thus, another bit can generally be reclaimed with ease, providing at least 25% savings in storage space. Many of the algorithms presented here can turn these extra bits into even greater savings of space.

Notice, however, that this approach requires a description of how the compressed file is to be represented. This description commonly consists of the encoding and decoding routines. The savings which result from text compression must be balanced against both the additional processor time for encoding and decoding, and the storage space necessary for the encoding and decoding routines. Also, different types of files may be best encoded by different methods, so several different encoding and decoding routines may be necessary.

Trailing Blanks and Tabs

A simple approach to compression for text files, but not for object code files, is eliminating blanks which come at the ends of lines before the carriage return and line feed characters. These are known as trailing blanks. For systems which store large amounts of assembly language, BASIC or FORTRAN programs, much of each line will be blank. Any trailing blanks can be deleted without changing the meaning of the file.

Tabs can be used to reduce the number of blanks elsewhere in a line. Particularly with block structured programs, such as ALGOL, Pascal, or PL/I, or with column-oriented languages such as FORTRAN or assembly language, tabs can be quite effective in text compression. Two varieties of tabbing mechanisms can be used. One is called *fixed tab stops*. In this case, tab stops occur every n columns, where n is a system-wide constant. Typically $n=8$, although some studies have shown that $n=4$ or $n=5$ will produce additional savings.

The other possibility is to use *variable tab stops*. In this case, tab stop positions are selected for each file separately. This requires a decision to select which tab stops would produce the best compression. In addition, it would be necessary to indicate with each file what tab settings are to be used. This can be done easily by appending a tab stop dictionary at the head of each file. Such a dictionary would be used to initialize tables for the decoding routine which would replace each tab with an appropriate number of blanks. This approach allows different tab settings to be used for different programming languages or data sets.

Multiple Characters

Trailing blanks and tab mechanisms are used for compressing strings of multiple blank characters. Some applications may result in strings of identical nonblank characters occurring frequently. For example, picture processing by computer often requires storing long sequences of identical characters, such as the characters which produce figure 2. The approach here is to replace a string of *n* identical characters by the number *n* and 1 character, thus saving *n*-2 characters. The count can be represented as a byte. If the count exceeds 256, it can be output as a count of 256 followed by the character, and then another count and character for the remainder.

Encoding consists of simply counting identical characters until a different one is found, and then outputting the count and character. Decoding simply expands each count and character to the appropriate number of characters.

Obviously, *n* should be greater than 2 most of the time for this approach to succeed. If *n* were generally 1, this approach would actually double the size of the file. Since this is commonly the case for text files, a more sophisticated approach is generally used.

We wish to replace sequences of identical characters by a count and character, but leave single or double characters alone. The problem is representing the multiple characters in such a way that the count is not misinterpreted as a character. A common solution is to use an *escape* sequence, which is a means of indicating that a special interpretation should be applied to the characters which follow. To create an escape sequence, choose any character which is seldom' and preferably never used. For example, in ASCII one of the control codes or special characters might be used. ASCII even provides an escape character, but if it is already being used for another purpose, any other character code can be used. Now a sequence of *n* identical characters would be represented by the escape character, the value *n*, and the character to be repeated. Figure 3 shows the text of figure 2 compressed by this method.

This allows normal text to be represented normally, except for the escape character. The problem we must now solve is how to represent the escape character if it occurs in the input (ie: uncompressed) text. If we simply copy it to the compressed file, the decoder will incorrectly think it is the start of an escape sequence and interpret the following two characters as indicating a sequence of identical characters. This is essentially the same problem that language designers face in trying to represent a quoted string consisting of a quote. Several approaches to this problem can be used: outlaw all occurrences of the escape character; replace all escape characters by a special escape sequence such as one with a 0 count; replace all escape characters by an escape character, a count of 1, and an escape character, treating it as a sequence of length 1. Any of these approaches will allow a file to be encoded and decoded easily and correctly.

Note that in choosing an escape character, we can always use the same one (ie: a system-wide constant) or we can select a different one for every file. If we choose a different one for every file, we must make a preliminary pass through the file to look at all characters used and find one which is not used. We should then append the escape character at the beginning of the file to allow the decoding algorithm to know what character is used as the escape character.

Keyword Replacement

A very common type of file stored in computer systems is a program file. Programs offer great possibilities for text compression because of their stylized form and syntax. The techniques of deleting trailing blanks and using tabs to replace leading blanks can reduce storage requirements considerably. But an even larger gain can be made from keyword replacement.

Most programming languages use a number of *keywords* or *reserved words*: in FORTRAN, such words as INTEGER, FORMAT, CALL and so on; in BASIC, such words as LET, READ, PRINT, REM and so on. These words are used throughout these programs and are prime candidates for text compression.

Two techniques are commonly used. First, one can replace each keyword by

```
$32 $3*$4 /**.@$30 /$5*\  $6*\@$30 $7*  $7*@$30 $5*'' '$6*@$31
**/$6 \**'@$30 $3.$9 /$3*\@$29 $4*\$7 $6*@$29 $5*\.  .$6*@$29
\$4*' $6* \**/@$31 '' $6*/.@$36 \$4* \@$43 \@$43 *@$43 *@$43/
./$3*\@$30  ..$9  ./  /$7*\@$27  /$6*\$6  */$3*/'@$26  /**'  '\**\$3
.*/$3'@$26 '$6 \** /'@$35 *$3\@$35 \*/@$36 \*@$37 \@$37 \@
```

Figure 3: Further compression of the file shown in figure 2 done by replacing multiple identical characters with an escape sequence. The escape sequence in this case is the escape character ($) followed by the number of repetitions and the character to be repeated. This scheme is useful only when the repeat count is greater than 2. The count would normally fit into 1 byte, but is here shown in decimal. The character @ represents the carriage return and line feed. Only 287 characters are needed to represent the file in figure 2 using this representation. This reduces the file to 14.9% of its original size.

10 READ A	10 $5 A
20 IF A=0 THEN 110	20 $2 A=0 $6 110
30 IF A>0 THEN 80	30 $2 A>0 $6 80
40 LET B=-A	40 $3 B=-A
50 LET R=SQR(B)	50 $3 R=SQR(B)
60 PRINT A,R," $ "	60 $4 A,R," $$ "
70 GO TO 10	70 $1 10
80 LET R=SQR(A)	80 $3 R=SQR(A)
90 PRINT A,R	90 $4 A,R
100 GO TO 10	100 $1 10
110 END	110 $7

Figure 4: Compressing a BASIC program by using keyword replacement. The keywords (1) GO TO, (2) IF, (3) LET, (4) PRINT, (5) READ, (6) THEN and (7) END have been replaced by an escape sequence consisting of an escape character ($) followed by a keyword number. Note that the escape character occurred within the original program and was replaced by a special escape sequence ($$). In actual use, all delimiting blanks around keywords would be subsumed into the keyword. Thus line 10 would be 10$5A, and $5 would mean "READ".

an escape sequence. The escape sequence might consist of the escape code, followed by a number, indicating which keyword is being used. This has the advantage of allowing a large number of reserved words up to the number which can be held in 1 byte, and can be particularly useful for assembly language symbolic op codes.

An alternative approach is to look through the existing character code for unused character codes. For example, if ASCII is being used, many of the control codes, some of the special characters, and perhaps the lowercase characters are not normally used. If 7-bit ASCII is being used with 8-bit bytes, then the extra bit can be used to define 128 new unused codes. These unused codes are paired up with the most frequently occurring reserved words. One code should be reserved for use as an escape or quote character, in case any of the codes assumed to be unused should happen to be used in an input file.

For encoding, the input file is scanned for reserved words and each reserved word is replaced by the appropriate special code as illustrated by figure 4. If any of the special codes should show up in the input stream, they are replaced by the two-character sequence of the escape code followed by the input character. For decoding, all special codes are replaced by their equivalent keyword, except that any character preceded by an escape code is copied directly to the output, with no replacement.

At this point, a problem may become apparent. Note that the keywords for any particular language are fixed and relatively small in number, but that the keywords vary from language to language. Hence, the appropriate correspondence between special codes and reserved words may vary greatly. In single language systems, such as those which offer only BASIC, this is not a problem, but more general systems need to consider this problem.

Several solutions are available. First, one can simply use separate encoding and decoding routines for each language, leaving it to the programmer to use the appropriate one. Second, one can tag each compressed file with a byte which indicates if this is a BASIC compressed file, a FORTRAN compressed file, or a type X compressed file. Then the encoder must either be told how to encode the file or be able to guess or compute whether it is a FORTRAN, BASIC, or type X file and apply the appropriate compression algorithm. The compressed file is tagged as it is encoded. The decoder looks at the tag and uses the appropriate decoding scheme.

A third approach is more general, but potentially more expensive. The difference between the encoding and decoding algorithms for the different types of files is simply the table of pairings between keywords and character codes. Therefore, another approach is to prefix each compressed file with a dictionary of character codes and reserved word pairs. The dictionary explains the meanings of the special character codes by indicating the reserved words for which they stand.

Substring Abbreviation

The idea of appending an abbreviation dictionary to the front of a compressed file opens the way to using the keyword replacement scheme for more general files. The idea is quite simple. Pick out those sequences of characters which occur most frequently in a file and replace them with a special character code. To allow decoding, we append a dictionary at the beginning of each file to show which special character codes correspond to each replaced character strings. This approach can yield very good text compression, especially for programs or natural language text, since keywords, variable names and some words, like *the, and,* and so on, are used very frequently.

But there are some problems with this approach also. The major problem is selecting the character strings to be abbreviated. With programs written in particular languages, keywords occur frequently and so are a safe bet for substitution, but what constitutes appropriate character strings for general replacement? These can be determined only by examining the file, since the appropriate strings will vary from file to file.

The objective, of course, is to realize the greatest savings in space. Here we are limited mainly by the number of codes available for substitution. If we use unused codes in the existing character set, we are limited from ten to fifty abbreviation codes, typically. If we extend the character set (eg: by using 8-bit codes with 7-bit ASCII), then we may have as many as 128 codes available. Using an escape sequence may provide up to 256, but at a cost of at least 2 characters per abbreviation. In all cases, the number of codes available will always be limited to, say, *m*. Thus we need to pick those *m* strings for abbreviation, which will result in the greatest space savings.

We do not always want to pick merely the most frequently occurring *m* strings. Consider the two strings, *to* and *text compression*. If *to* occurs one hundred times and *text compression* only fifteen times, which should we replace? Replacing the two-character sequence *to* by a single abbreviation code saves only one character (assuming 1-byte abbreviation code) per occurrence, or a total of one hundred characters. Replacing the sixteen-character sequence *text compression* saves fifteen characters per occurrence, or 225 characters total. Thus, in general we wish to replace that character sequence whose product of length and frequency is greatest. An example of substring replacement is shown in figure 5.

```
Dictionary:        $A  "the"
                   $B  "text compression"
                   $C  "computer"
                   ...

Text:
    This paper is concerned with $A use of $B in $C systems, where $A amount of
    $C storage is limited.
    ...
```

Figure 5: Text compression by substring replacement. Substrings are replaced by abbreviation codes: here we use escape sequences. A dictionary is placed at the beginning of the file to define the meanings of the abbreviations.

The encoding problem then becomes that of finding the *m* sequences whose length-frequency product is greatest, replacing all occurrences of them with the *m* abbreviation codes, and appending the abbreviation dictionary at the front of the compressed file. The decoding problem reduces to merely reading in the abbreviation dictionary and replacing all abbreviation codes with the appropriate character sequence.

The only real difficulty is finding the *m* sequences to be abbreviated. No really good solution to this problem is known. The best solution I have seen works as follows: first, make one pass through the file to compute the most frequently occurring pairs. There should be no more than 2500 of these, and probably many fewer. Compute the frequency of these pairs and keep only the *m* or 2*m* most frequent. Now consider that any sequence of length 3 both begins and ends with a subsequence of length 2, and that these 2 subsequences of length 2 must be at least as frequent as the length 3 sequence. That is, if there are twenty-three occurrences of *abc*, then there must be at least twenty-three *ab* and at least twenty-three *bc*. Thus we can make another pass through the file, counting the frequency of subsequences of length 3, but limiting ourselves to those sequences which begin and end with subsequences of length 2, which are also frequent. Next we can make another pass for length 4 (limiting the sequences to those with frequent length 3 subsequences), another pass for length 5, and so on until we decide to stop. We can stop either when our last pass has produced no new sequences whose frequency-length product exceeds the previous set, or after a fixed number of passes.

Huffman Coding

All of the schemes for text compression discussed so far are similar in the sense that they confine themselves to working within the given character code and byte structure. Even more savings can result from recoding the character code representation itself. Almost all character code representations use a fixed code size: 6 bits for binary coded decimal(BCD), 7 bits for ASCII and 8 bits for EBCDIC. This can be very wasteful of space.

Consider the simple problem of encoding the four characters: *A, B, C,* and *D*. If we use a fixed code size, then we could encode each character with 2 bits, as follows:

A 00
B 01

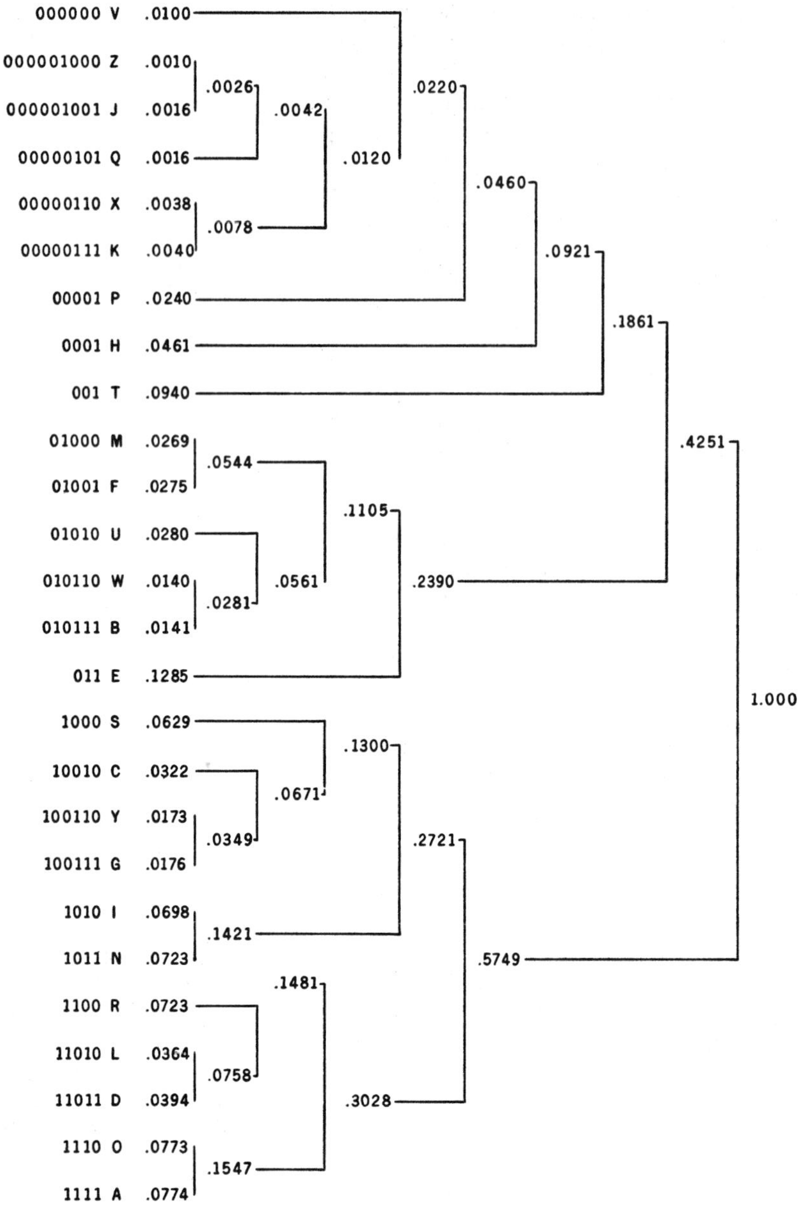

Figure 6: Huffman code for the letters of the English language, based on the probabilities (ie: frequency of occurrence) of the letters in English. The code length is inversely proportional to the frequency of occurrence of a given letter in much the same manner as Morse code. Code lengths vary from 9 bits (for z and j) to 3 bits (for e and t). The average length is 4.1885 bits per letter. Five bits would be necessary for a fixed length code, a space saving of 16%.

C 10
D 11

But suppose that the letter *A* occurs 50% of the time in the text, *B* occurs 25% and *C* and *D* split the remaining 25% equally. Then the following *variable* length character code will produce a shorter *average* text length:

A 0
B 10
C 110
D 111

To compute the average text length, consider that out of *n* characters, *n*/2 will be *A* which requires only 1 bit, n/4 will be *B* for 2 bits each and the remaining *n*/4 will be *C* or *D* for 3 bits each. Thus the total number of bits to represent *n* characters is:

$$1(n/2) + 2\,(n/4) + 3\,(n/4) = 1.75n$$

Comparing this with the 2*n* bits needed for the fixed length code, we see that we have saved 12.5% of the total file size.

Variable length coding and decoding is somewhat more complex than fixed length coding, but not really difficult. It involves much more bit manipulation. To encode a string like *ABAABCDAB*, we simply concatenate the bit representations of each character, packing across byte boundaries as necessary:

A	B	A	A	B	C	D	A	B
0	10	0	0	10	110	111	0	10

To decode, we must scan from left to right, looking at each bit. For the string 01001100, we notice that the first bit is a 0. Only *A* starts with 0, so our first character is an *A*. The next bit is a 1, so it could be a *B, C* or *D,* but looking at the next bit we see that the next character must be a *B*. We remove the 2 bits for the *B* and continue. The next bit is 0, so the next character is an *A*. The following bit is a 1, signifying either a *B, C,* or *D*. The next bit is a 1, signifying a *C* or *D*. Finally the next bit indicates a *C*. The last character is an *A*. So our decoded text is *ABACA*.

Computer-stored text files can benefit greatly from Huffman coding. Huffman coding can be used anytime that the probabilities of the character codes are not equal. In fact, the more unequal the probabilities, the better the compression with a Huffman coding. Looking at a table of frequencies of the letters in English, we can see that they are quite unequal, and hence can be compressed nicely with Huffman coding.

To construct a Huffman code, a very simple algorithm is used. Refer to figure 6. First, it is necessary to compute the probabilities of the characters to be encoded. This requires one pass through some sample text, a part of a file, the whole file or several files, as desired, counting the occurrences of different characters. Then we need to sort the characters according to their frequency. Take the two least frequently occurring characters, and combine them into a *super character* whose frequency is the sum of the two individual characters. The code for each of the two characters will be the code for the *super character* followed by a 0 for one character and 1 for the other. Now delete the two least frequently used characters from the list and insert the new *super character* into the list at the appropriate place for its frequency. Continue this process until all characters and *super characters* are combined into one *super character*. The result is a Huffman code of minimal average code length. The Huffman code may best be seen as a binary tree with the terminal nodes (ie: the leaves) being the characters which are encoded.

Huffman coding can be quite successful in text compression, in extreme cases reducing the size of a file more than half. The basic technique can be improved upon in a number of ways. For example, pairs of characters, rather than single characters, can be used as the basis of encoding. This requires a much larger table of character frequencies, since now we need to compute the frequencies of character pairs, and larger tables of character pair and Huffman code associations, but can result in greater savings.

Another possibility is to use conditional Huffman coding. The objective here is to utilize the fact that the probability (ie: frequency) of a character will vary depending upon what character proceeds it. For example, compare the probability of a *U* following a *Q* (nearly 1) to the probability of a *U* following a *U* (nearly 0). So an optimal encoding should use a very short code for a *U* which follows *Q* and can use a very long code for a *U* which follows a *U*. The encoding algorithm involves computing the frequency with which each character follows every other character. A separate Huffman code is then computed for the characters which follow each character. The encoding scheme remembers the last character encoded and uses that to select the code to be used for the next character. The decoding algorithm must also remember the last character decoded in order to be able to select the correct decoding algorithm.

Huffman codes are really quite simple, but they can be made more sophisticated to achieve increased text compression. However, even with simple Huffman codes, some problems can arise. First, notice that Huffman encoding and decoding both involve a great deal of bit manipulation, which can be very slow to program. Second, the best compression is achieved if a Huffman code can take advantage of the unequal frequencies of characters in a file, but these will differ from file to file. Thus a separate encoding may be best for each file. This can be done by appending the code at the front of a file, as with the dictionaries used for abbreviations, but this increases the size of the file significantly for small files.

Third, the variable length code nature of Huffman coding can make them extremely vulnerable to transmission or storage errors. In a fixed length code, if one bit is changed, only that one character is affected, while with Huffman codes, both that character and all succeeding characters may be decoded incorrectly because of a mistake in the assumed length of the incorrect character. A similar problem would happen to a fixed length code if a bit were dropped or added. Thus, for safety, it is necessary to add error detection and correction redundancy back into the file, increasing its size.

Still there are environments in which Huffman coding can be quite useful. Consider a word-processing system storing files on a low-speed serial device such as a cassette. Since the system is special purpose, one can compute the expected frequencies of English characters and use one Huffman code for all files. Encoding and decoding would be done automatically by the tape driver routines. Alternatively the encoding and decoding could be built into the tape drive hardware as special purpose logic or into a small processor with a read-only memory encoding/decoding table. This encoding/decoding approach would be totally transparent to the user. The only effect on the user would be the ability to store a larger, but variable number of "characters" on a fixed amount of tape.

Conclusions

The amount of storage space needed to store information can be greatly reduced by simple text compression techniques like the ones we have presented here. Each of the techniques presented can save some space in many files. And many of the techniques can be used one after another to achieve more and more compression. Text compression can be a simple and effective method of increasing the amount of storage available in exchange for some processor cycles.■

REFERENCES

1. deMaine, P A D. *The Integral Family of Reversible Compressors.* Computer Science Department, Pennsylvania State University, 1971.
2. Dishon, Y. "Data Compaction in Computer Systems." *Computer Design,* volume 16, number 4, April 1977, pages 85 thru 90.
3. Huffman, D A. "Method for Construction of Minimum-Redundancy Codes." *Proceedings of the IRE,* September 1952, pages 1098 thru 1101.
4. Knuth, D E. *The Art of Computer Programming: Volume 1, Fundamental Algorithms,* second edition. Addison-Wesley, Reading MA, 1973.
5. Peterson, J J, Bitner, and J Howard, *On the Selection of Optimal Tab Settings.* Department of Computer Sciences, University of Texas, December 1977.
6. Rubin, F. "Experiments in Text File Compression." *Communications of the ACM,* volume 19, number 11, November 1976, pages 617 thru 623.

Advanced Techniques

About This Section

This is perhaps one of the more advanced sections of the entire **Programming Techniques** series. It covers topics of interest to advanced programmers who want to tackle some of the more fundamental subjects of computer science. Some of the topics can only be briefly introduced here, and the reader is encouraged to seek out the appropriate course of textbook in computer science to continue the study.

Stacks and interrupts are only one step removed from the actual microcomputer hardware, but advanced applications often require dealing with them. You might find these topics useful, for instance, when dealing with language processors (ie: compilers, interpreters, assemblers, etc), real-time processing, or high-level operating systems.

Another topic of interest to advanced programmers is program optimization. Under certain circumstances, the execution speed of a routine can be critical to the successful completion of the assigned task. This is especially true when dealing with real-time occurrences, but can be just as important when dealing with a more-or-less trivial programming problem. No one wants to wait 2 hours for a program to update a master file with only a few transaction records!

One of those seemingly never-ending subjects is queuing theory. It has become an area of specialization within computer science in recent years, but don't let its depth keep you from applying some of the simple techniques of using queues in your own programs. Again, queues are useful in operating systems, communication networks, and real-time processing.

The other subjects covered in this section (eg: BNF grammar, hand assembling, Polish postfix notation, the Exclusive OR, etc) will help you make the most of your programming efforts. Remember, even if you are only a beginning programmer, don't be afraid to tackle some of the more formidable topics in programming. The only way to sharpen your skills is to experiment with new techniques, even if you don't have a ready use for them. And after all, isn't that one of the main reasons for having a microcomputer — the opportunity to experiment?

The Algebra for the Boolean Exclusive OR:

With an Application to Hamming Codes

Webb Simmons

Many of us have been repeatedly drilled in the Boolean algebra operations AND and OR. Less well-known is the full set of operations that can be performed using XOR (exclusive OR). In order to eliminate any possibility of confusion with other operations, I will use the notation XOR(list), where (list) denotes a list of variables separated by commas. Within one sentence, the repeated use of the list notation means the same list in each place is used. The truth table for the exclusive OR is:

A	B	XOR(A,B)
0	0	0
0	1	1
1	0	1
1	1	0

The first theorem is:

XOR(A,true) = $\overline{A}$

or:

XOR(A,1) = $\overline{A}$

Conversely:

XOR(A,false) = A

or:

XOR(A,0) = A.

Whenever the string of arguments to the exclusive OR contains repetitions of the same variable, an even number of such repetitions can be removed; thus:

XOR(A,A,B,C,C,C) = XOR(B,C).

More generally:

XOR(A,A,list) = XOR(list).

We prove the above from facts that:

XOR(list1,list2) = XOR(XOR(list1), XOR(list2))

or, by replacing list1 by A,A and list2 by list:

XOR(A,A,list) = XOR(XOR(A,A), XOR(list))
= XOR(false,XOR(list))
= XOR(list)

remembering that XOR(A,flase) = A.

The fact that:

XOR(list1,list2) = XOR(XOR(list1), XOR(list2))

must be proven by a truth table for various replacements for list1 and list2. In table 1, I show the proof for:

XOR(A,B,C,D) = XOR(XOR(A,B), XOR(C,D)).

My acceptance of "XOR(list1,list2) = XOR(XOR(list1),XOR(list2))" before it was proven in table 1 was the use of a lemma. After it is proven, it is no longer a lemma, but a theorem.

Two included cases of our new theorem are:

XOR(A,list)=XOR(A,XOR(list))

and

$\overline{XOR(A,list)} = XOR(\overline{A},list)$.

The term list can be replaced by XOR(list) and will finally evaluate to either true or false (1 or 0). Consider the cases:

$\overline{XOR(A,0)} = XOR(\overline{A},0)$

and

$\overline{XOR(A,1)} = XOR(\overline{A},1)$.

Each of the above can be shown to be true for A=1 and for A=0.

We will finish this discussion with three sets of "if,then" clauses.

ifXOR(A,B,C)=false,
then A=XOR(B,C).

The proof of this lemma is shown in table 2. Obviously, cyclic rotation gives us, for the same condition:

B=XOR(A,C)
C=XOR(A,B).

A	B	C	D	E	F	G	H
0	0	0	0	0	0	0	0
0	0	0	1	1	0	1	1
0	0	1	0	1	0	1	1
0	0	1	1	0	0	0	0
0	1	0	0	1	1	0	1
0	1	0	1	0	1	1	0
0	1	1	0	0	1	1	0
0	1	1	1	1	1	0	1
1	0	0	0	1	1	0	1
1	0	0	1	0	1	1	0
1	0	1	0	0	1	1	0
1	0	1	1	1	1	0	1
1	1	0	0	0	0	0	0
1	1	0	1	1	0	1	1
1	1	1	0	1	0	1	1
1	1	1	1	0	0	0	0

Table 1: *Theorem: XOR(A,B,C,D)=XOR(XOR(A,B),XOR(C,D)).*
Proof: let E = XOR(A,B,C,D)
let F = XOR(A,B)
let G = XOR(C,D)
let H = XOR(F,G)
= XOR(XOR(A,B),XOR(C,D))
Allowing all possible combinations for A, B, C, and D, and solving for E, F, G, and H, we find that E always equals H. The theorem is proven to be true.

You may also prove that:

if XOR(A,B,C)=true,
then $\overline{A}$ = XOR(B,C).

For our second, "if,then" clause we have:

if A=XOR(B,list),
then B=X(A,list).

The proof of this lemma is left as an exercise for the reader, as is our final lemma:

if XOR(A,list) =XOR(B,list),
then A=B.

Hamming Codes

Exclusive OR algebra is used in conjunction with an error correcting code called the Hamming code which, in 4 bits, is able to encode the values 0 and 1 such that any error of 1 bit can be corrected and any error of 2 bits can be detected but not corrected. The values of 0 or 1 are encoded by evaluating the exclusive OR of three arguments, where the arguments are:

- the value itself
- the value rotated left by 1 bit position
- the value rotated left by 3 bit positions

This produces 0000 for *zero* and 1101 for *one*. These are decoded by performing the exclusive OR of three other functions:

- the encoded value
- the encoded value rotated right 1 bit position
- the encoded value rotated right 3 bit positions

The desired value, *zero* or *one*, will be in the upper (ie: most significant) bit position if there has been no error, and the 3 low bits will all be *zero*.

It is an interesting fact that any one or two errors will cause the low 3 bits to be other than all *zeroes*. In fact, the particular value will tell you the position of any 1 bit error and will blow the whistle for two errors. Hamming codes cannot be covered here, but I will show that an error in the first causes the low 3 bits to be 101. The entire value will be either 0101 or 1101. Bits received without error will be the logical variables A,B,C, and D. When received correctly, we have:

ABCD	(the encoded value)
DABC	(right rotated by 1 bit)
BCDA	(right rotated by 3 bits)

---

x000 (the x is either *zero* or *one*).

which gives us the four Boolean equations:

XOR(A,D,B)=don't know
XOR(B,A,C)=0
XOR(C,B,D)=0
XOR(D,B,A)=0.

If the first received bit is in error, we get $\overline{A}$ rather than A to produce:

$\overline{A}$BCD
D$\overline{A}$BC
BCD$\overline{A}$

????

If XOR(B,A,C) =0, then XOR(B$\overline{A}$,C)=1.
If XOR(C,B,D)=0, then there is no change.
If XOR(D,C,A)=0, then X(D,C,$\overline{A}$)=1.
This gives us:

$\overline{A}$BCD
D$\overline{A}$BC
BCD$\overline{A}$

?101 =XOR(three arguments)

— the predicted result.

A	B	C	D	E
0	0	0	0	0
0	0	1	1	1
0	1	0	1	1
0	1	1	0	0
1	0	0	1	0
1	0	1	0	1
1	1	0	0	1
1	1	1	1	0

(a)

A	B	C	D	E
0	0	0	0	0
0	1	1	0	0
1	0	1	0	1
1	1	0	0	1

(b)

Table 2: *Method used to prove that, if XOR(A,B,C)=0, then A=XOR(BC). If D=XOR(A,B,C)=0, then we delete all rows in table 2a for which D=1. This produces table 2b. We now let E=XOR(B,C). It is evident that column E equals column A. Therefore: if XOR(A,B,C)=0, then A=XOR(B,C). Similar exercises will show that, under the same initial assumption, B=XOR(A,C) and C=XOR(A,B).*

Actually, the first question mark can be shown to be $\overline{x}$ as follows:

if XOR(A,D,B)=x
the XOR($\overline{A}$,D,B)=$\overline{x}$.

As an exercise, you may wish to prove that $\overline{B}$ alone causes a decoded result of x110, that $\overline{C}$ alone causes x111, and that $\overline{D}$ causes x011. Then work out the results of any two errors. As expected, three or four errors should lead you to the wrong value.■

Stacks in Microprocessors

T Radhakrishan, MV Bhat

The stack or the *last-in first-out* (LIFO) data structure has become an essential tool in computer systems. There are two major operations associated with this data structure:

- PUSH: which places a new data item on top of the existing ones in the stack.
- POP: which removes the topmost element of the stack for succeeding operations.

A spring-loaded plate holder in a cafeteria is a good example of a stack, since addition and removal of items occur at the same end in a last in, first out sequence. (See figure 1.) When the capacity of a stack is "n" items, then n+1 consecutive PUSH operations will cause the stack to overflow. Similarly, popping an empty stack creates an underflow. Even though stack underflow may not occur intentionally, programmers should account for this condition. Stack overflow is more probable when the stack capacity is not large enough to accommodate all the occurring conditions simultaneously.

Stack size is one of the major design parameters in processor architecture. For instance, the earlier Intel 8008 processor had a built-in seven-level subroutine control stack which was later increased to a more general stack pointer which could range throughout memory in 8080.

In the software realization of stacks, a programmable memory location is used along with an address pointer, called the stack pointer (SP). The SP points to the memory location that holds the top element of the stack; the pointer is updated (ie: incremented or decremented) after

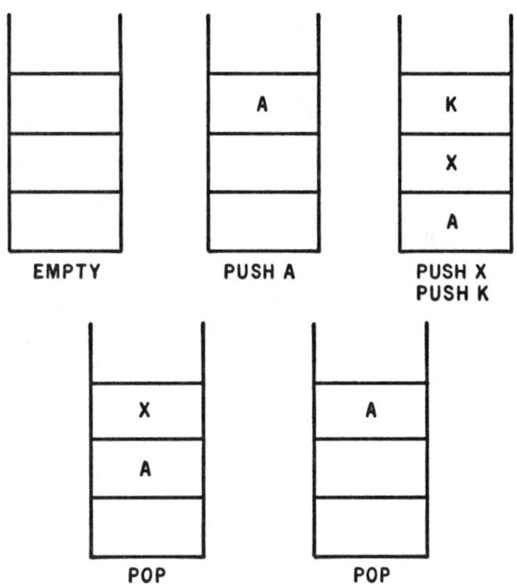

Figure 1: A sample three-word stack. A PUSH command causes one piece of data to be PUSHed onto the stack; the resident data is pushed downward to make room. Similarly, a POP command removes the topmost piece of data and shifts the rest of the stack upward.

every push or pop operation as shown in figure 2. In this case, the programmer must set aside a portion of the main memory to accommodate the stack. Consequently, the stack capacity is determined by the free space in the main memory and is more flexible. In figure 2, the occupied portion of the stack grows from low to high memory addresses. Hence, the PUSH operation increments the stack pointer and the POP operation decrements it. It is not difficult to introduce the stack overflow and underflow conditions in the above simulation.

In another realization of stacks, a set of n registers constitutes a stack. Every POP operation takes the data item from the topmost register; the data in each stack location is then shifted upward. The PUSH operation shifts the stack contents down one place and adds the new data item. In this approach, reading from and writing to the data structure occur only with the topmost register. Inter register transfers can be achieved in parallel during the same clock period. The stack facility available with IMP-8C microprocessor, an example of this type, has a capacity of sixteen words. This method of realization is known as the *fixed top*, as in figure 1, in contrast to the *moving top* approach explained earlier, as in figure 2. The flexibility associated with the latter can be combined with the speed advantage of the former as is done with PACE microprocessors. (See table 1.)

Most modern processors provide one or more registers to hold stack pointers. For example, there is one stack pointer register in the Intel 8080 and there can be as many as sixteen stack pointers in the RCA 1802 processor. The pop and push instructions update the SP registers automatically. The architecture and the stack-oriented instructions differ widely among the various processors, and table 1 gives details of some of the common ones.

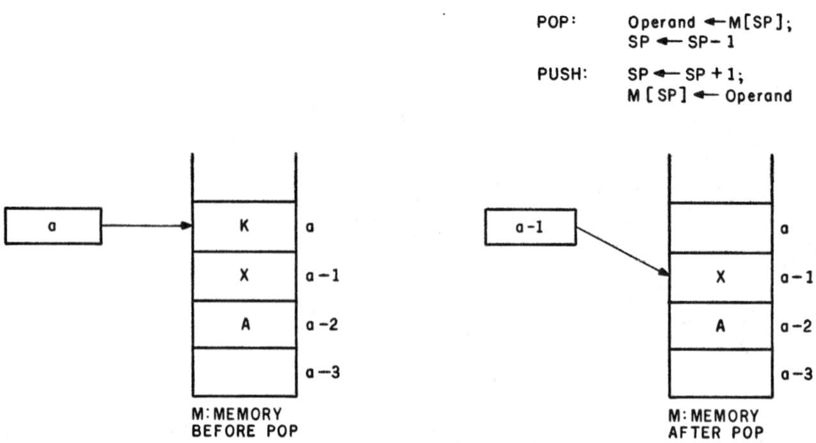

Figure 2: A software simulation of the pushdown stack. Operation of the stack is identical to the hardware stack in figure 1, except that there is no dedicated hardware involved. Instead, a program creates a stack pointer in memory which points to the current location at the top of the stack.

Typical Applications of Stacks

Suppose a routine A calls another routine B at some point a in A. Similarly, let B call C at point b. The addresses a+1 and b+1 are the return addresses where execution control will return from the called routine. It is evident from figure 3 that the return addresses are used in the reverse order of their sequence of occurrence. The labels c1, c2, c3 in figure 3 stand for the first, second and third calling of routines, and r1, r2, r3 stand for the first, second and third returns from the called routines. This last-in first-out (LIFO) nature of the use of return addresses in multilevel calling is commonly implemented with stacks. Simple extensions have been devised to pass the parameters along with these return addresses using the stack structure.

The calls shown in figure 3 could also be considered as calls to service routines due to asynchronous interrupt signals. In the latter case, the return addresses are not predetermined address points, but are the contents of the program counter. However, the last-in first-out nature of the return addresses remains valid. The call due to an interrupt creates a new process, and hence the status of the current process (ie: process status word, flags, etc) has to be additionally saved. Some processors, like the IMP-8C, have instructions to push and pop status flags onto stacks. In other processors, this is done automatically when an interrupt occurs. Stacks in microprocessors, starting from the early Intel designs, have traditionally been used primarily for subroutine control and interrupt handling.

Another use of stacks, though one not much used in the hardware of processors, is in the compiling arithmetic expressions. Consider the following arithmetic expression:

$$A+B\times C-D/E$$

In this form, the operator is between the two operands. This is known as *infix* notation. The form in which the operator follows the operands is called *postfix* or *reverse Polish* after the Polish logician J Luckasiewicz, who investigated the properties of this notation. The postfix equivalent of the above expression, which does not require any parentheses, is as follows:

$$AB+C\times DE/-$$

Algorithms exist which use the stacks to

convert arithmetic expressions from infix to postfix notation. (See reference 2.) Figure 4 shows a sample code for the above postifx expression; it is meant for a computer with stacks, and is used to evaluate arithmetic expressions. Operations such as ADD and SUB take the top two elements of the stack, perform the operation, and then push the result back onto the stack. Such a system is called a *stack computer*. Using the postfix notation, it is not hard to generate code for machines with single accumulators or for machines with multiple registers.

Stack Machines

Among the architectures with two stacks, two broad categories are evident. The first kind of machine provides stack features along with conventional architecture. This stack feature might be implemented through a hardware-realized stack, a stack-pointer register with a set of associated hardware instructions, or a complete software simulation using a memory location as the stack and its pointer. Some combinations of these three approaches are also

Processor	Hardware Stack or Stack Pointer	Stack-Oriented Instructions	Remarks
1. 8080	16 bit stack pointer	a) Push register pair into stack b) Pop register pair from stack c) Push/Pop processor status word d) Exchange stack top with register pair (H,L) e) Load SP from register pair (H,L)	
2. Z-80	16 bit stack pointer	a) All the instructions of Intel 8080 b) Push/Pop the (two) index registers	
3. M6800	16 bit stack pointer	a) Push/Pop the (A or B) accumulator b) Load SP from memory c) Store SP into memory d) Transfer index register contents to SP e) Transfer SP into index register f) Increment/Decrement SP	
4. RCA 1802	16 bit stack pointer	a) Increment/Decrement the selected register (SP) b) Push/Pop the working (D) register c) Load the D register into left or right half of SP	Any of the 16 registers can be used as a SP
5. PACE	Hardware stack 8 16 bit words	a) Push/Pop program counter b) Push/Pop the specified register c) Exchange the contents of the register with SP d) Push/Pop the flag register	Stack overflow Underflow Interrupts are provided
6. IMP-8C	Hardware stack 16 8 bit words	a) Push/Pop the selected accumulator into stack b) Exchange the stack top with the selected accumulator c) Push/Pop the status flags into the stack	No overflow Underflow Interrupts

Table 1: Stack features of some common microprocessors. The stack is a storage place in a computer designed to hold pieces of data in serial order. PUSHing an element onto the stack causes the existing elements in the stack to be moved downward, in much the same manner as a spring loaded plate holder found in restaurants. POPing an element from the stack removes the most recent addition to the stack for use. Because of these two features, the stack operation is often referred to as last-in first-out (LIFO).

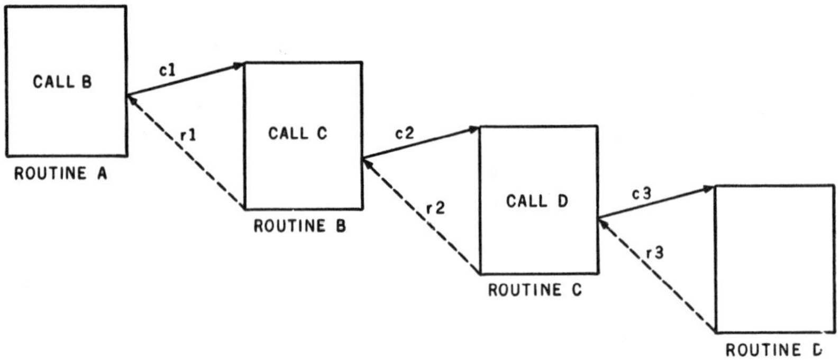

Figure 3: Diagrammatic representation of multilevel, or nested, subroutines. The return address of each subroutine call must be remembered so that the program can return to the right place after the subroutine is completed. The last-in first-out nature of nested subroutines is such that the stack is a logical way to keep track of the return addresses.

Op Code	Contents of Stack (read left to right)
PUSH A	A
PUSH B	B,A
ADD	(A+B)
PUSH C	C(A+B)
MPY	(A+B)*C
PUSH D	D(A+B)*C
PUSH E	E,D,(A+B)*C
DIV	(D/E),A+B)*C
SUB	(A+B)*C−(D/E)

Figure 4: Op code designed for use with Polish postfix notation on stack oriented computers. Polish notation is a method for rewriting expressions unambiguously by systematically segregating operators and operands. For instance, the expression used in this example appears as $(A+B)\times C-D/E$ in normal, or infix notation; the Polish postfix equivalent is $AB+C\times DE/$. The latter can be directly used by a stack oriented computer, which automatically performs stack operations. (For example, a stack ADD instruction takes the top two elements of the stack, adds them together, and pushes them back onto the stack. The MULT, DIV and SUB operators work in the same manner.) The algorithm for evaluating the expression then reduces to examining each element in the Polish notation string from left to right, pushing it onto the stack if it is an operand and performing the operation if it is an operator.

present in some recent processor architectures. Most processors have some sort of stack facility and instructions to manipulate data with stacks or stack pointers.

The second kind of machine with stack facility can be called a *stack machine.* Its architecture is completely centered on stacks. The Burroughs B5500 and B6700, HP3000 and ICL2900 are examples of this category. In these machines, the three basic functions of process management, memory management, and data management of jobs, are all stack oriented. Most of these architectures support block-structured languages similar to ALGOL or PL/I. A program written in a block-structured language can be visualized as a tree structure; execution of the program traces some paths in this tree structure. The relationship between tree structures and stack data structures is well known. (See reference 4.) An example is shown in figure 5 along with various points of stacks holding the program variables. Because of the limited-access points with stacks, certain extensions are required in stack machines to implement the array data structures. These extensions are of a different kind, such as the use of index registers for addressing. Similarly, to facilitate process and memory management, special software tools are used.

Computer systems and architectures can be appraised from three points of view: the languages available to users such as application and system programmers, the operating system, and the hardware. These three areas are highly interrelated, and it is difficult to separate their capabilities. A few stack-machine architectures are commercially available with facilities for multiprogramming and timesharing. The architecture of the Burroughs systems is such that the system software can be effectively written in a high-level language. Stack machines have good and bad points. Their advantages are noticeable in block structured programming, which is becoming popular. As Doran points out, stack machines have proven to be successful. (See reference 1.) The increasing cost of software and the flexibility available through microprogramming indicates a trend towards stack machines or, at least, toward a greater use of stack features in computer architectures.

Conclusions

Developments in software and programming techniques during the past decade have proven the advantages of stack data structures. Microprocessors of recent origin provide adequate facilities to support this data structure. The provision of stack pointers is a compromise between the expensive and inflexible hardware stacks at one end and the inexpensive and flexible software simulation at the other end. Most microprocessors have stack pointers and a set of associated machine instructions.

Stack machines have certain advantages in higher-level, block-structured programming and the implementation of operating systems. At present, programming with microprocessors is done mostly in machine- or assembly-language level. Large in-house software systems for microprocessors are not yet a reality. As a result, stack-machine architectures are still in the realm of large machines.■

REFERENCES

1. Doran, R W. "Architecture of Stack Machines" in *High Level Language Computer Architecture.* Edited by Y Chu, Academic Press 1975.
2. Gries, D. *Compiler Construction for Digital Computers.* John Wiley & Sons, NY 1971.
3. Knuth, D E. *The Art of Programming, vol 1, Fundamental Algorithms.* Addison Wesley, Reading MA 1968.
4. McKeeman, W. "Stack Computers." *Introduction to Computer Architecture,* edited by H S Stone SRA Inc 1975.
5. Organick, E I. *Computer System Organization: The B5700/B6700 Series.* Academic Press 1973.

Acknowledgement

We gratefully acknowledge the help of K Vekatesh, research assistant, Computer Science Department of Concordia University, in the preparation of this manuscript.

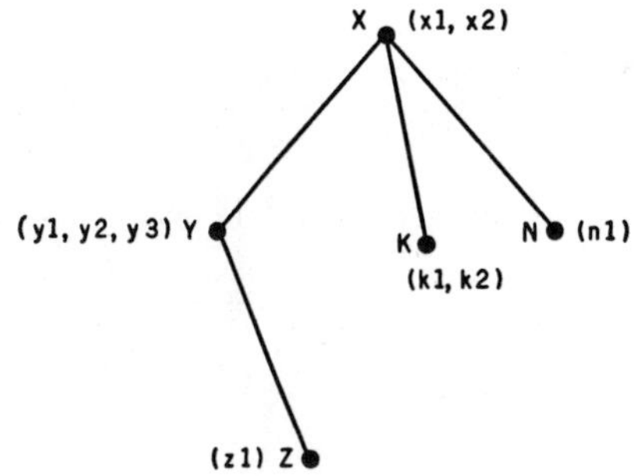

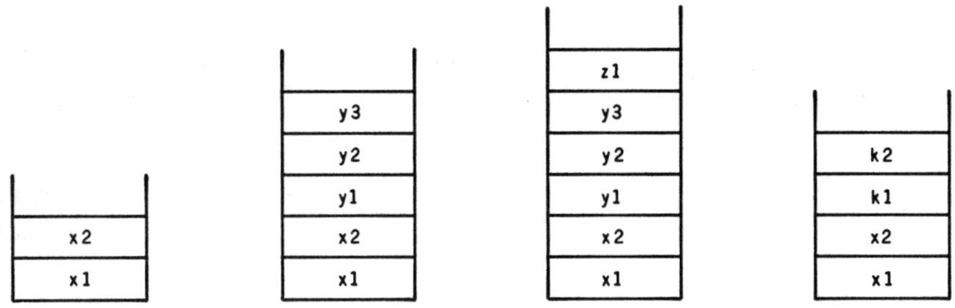


```
X: Begin
   Integer x1, x2;
      .
      .
      .
   Y: Begin
      Integer y1,y2,y3;
         .
         .
         .
      Z: Begin
         Integer z1;
            .
            .
            .
         End;        (Z)
            .
            .
      End;     (Y)
   .
   .
   K:  Begin
       Integer k1,k2;
          .
          .
          .
       End;   (K)
   .
   .
   .
   .
   N:  Begin
       Integer n1;
          .
          .
          .
          .
       End;     (N)
   .
   .
End;     (X)
```

Figure 5: A block-structured program. Programs written in block-structured languages can be visualized as tree structures (figure 5a). ALGOL and PL/I are examples of this type of language. The tree in this illustration shows how the program is structured. Figure 5b shows how the stacks in a stack-oriented machine would look at various points of the program. Figure 5c shows the block layout of the program.

Stack It Up

Charlton H Allen

Most microprocessors currently available employ a stack of some sort. This stack is either a scratch memory in the processor itself or an addressable, programmable memory characterized by retrieval of information in the reverse order of storage using a pointer. In the common parlance, a stack is a last-in first-out (LIFO) mechanism. It is a very useful feature for preserving the proper order of subroutine call and return points with minimal hassle. Experienced programmers using 8080-type machines, quickly discover its other uses. For example, a direct register store instruction is 3 bytes long on the 8080, whereas a register stack instruction is only 1 byte. As a result, saving registers used by subroutines and restoring them later is cheaper if the stack is used in preference to some directly addressed memory area. More importantly, perhaps, the availability of such a mechanism greatly simplifies the writing of reentrant routines (ie: ones which do not modify themselves in the process of execution). Note, however, that all the mechanisms provided in microprocessors to date for stack operations are explicitly fixed mode and singular. There is only one stack, and it operates on entities of the same width, in number of bits, as the accumulator(s). Moreover, these entities have no attribute other than their fixed width, in bits.

In contrast, several large-scale computers, such as the Burroughs 5500 processor with which I am familiar, employ a more generalized stack mechanism in which:

- The storage area for the stack(s) is independent of the central processor's memory (ie: not directly addressable).
- The entities being stored and retrieved have attributes of type (ie: integer, logical, real, string, array) and of length (ie: array size).
- Multiple stacks may be processed simultaneously and independently.

To achieve the latter, the stack controller requires a *stack-control block* in central-processor addressable memory to be uniquely associated with each active stack. Otherwise, such stack controllers bear approximately the same relation to the central processor and its addressable memory as a high-speed data channel. Since the data transfers are generally affected through cycle-stealing direct-memory addressing, and an unmaskable interrupt to the central

Listing 1: PARSE, a translation procedure written in an informal ALGOL

```
STRING PROCEDURE PARSE(Exp):
STRING Exp;
BEGIN
  EXTERNAL  INTEGER  PROCEDURE       Intoken  ;
  LOGICAL            Endinput,        Errflag  ;
  INTEGER            Position,     I,    J,    T;
  INTEGER ARRAY S=   (   1   -1   -2    2   -9,
                        -3    3    4   -4   -9,
                         5   -5   -6    6   -9,
                        -7    7    8   -8   -9,
                        -9   -9   -9   -9   -9);
  STACK Q;

  Errflag  := Endinput  := false;
  PARSE  := null; Position  := 0
  I  := Intoken(Exp, Position, Endinput);
  J  := Intoken(Exp, Position, Endinput);
  COMMENT I is last token, J is current  ;
  IF Endinput THEN Errflat  := true
  ELSE WHILE NOT Endinput DO BEGIN
    T  := S(I,J); IF T<0 THEN Errflag  := true
    ELSE CASE T OF BEGIN
      COMMENT valid sequence of tokens  ;
      CASE1: BEGIN
               Q := PARSE; PARSE := null;
             END;
      CASE2: null;
      CASE3: PARSE := PARSE . Q;
      CASE4: PARSE := PARSE . Exp(Position) . '$';
      CASE5: BEGIN
               Q := PARSE . '$'; PARSE := null;
             END;
      CASE6: PARSE := PARSE . Exp(Position);
      CASE7: PARSE := PARSE . Q;
      CASE8: PARSE := PARSE . Exp(Position) . Exp(Position - 1);
  END;
  I := J;
  J := Intoken(Exp, Position, Endinput);
  END;
  WHILE NOT Q = empty DO PARSE := PARSE .Q;
  IF Errflag THEN PARSE := null;
END.
```

processor occurs only when an error condition, in this case stack overflow or underflow is detected.

I don't seriously propose such a stack controller for the representative homebrew computer system. I do propose, however, to show by example that incremental programming development in that direction can provide correspondingly simpler solutions to a large class of computing problems.

A Problem

One of the curious properties of calculators using Polish notation techniques is that any expression using the operators provided on the keyboard can be evaluated in an absolute minimum of keystrokes. Moreover, the required number of temporary storage areas (ie: depth of stack) is at most the number of operands for the most complex operator. In an exactly analogous way, a stack of depth two or a second accumulator is sufficient in digital computers for evaluating any size expression using operators corresponding to native instructions, provided that the terms are calculated in the correct order. The price to pay for this admittedly pleasing property is learning to think things from the inside out. We mentally seek the interior of the expression, innermost term in parentheses, and works outward in calculation left to right. The pity is that it does not come easily to lots of folks, since most people use the algebraic method of solving expressions which is the way they were taught in school. *[If a larger stack is used, the expression can be evaluated from the left to right with the intermediate answers pushed onto the stack....* **RGAC]**

A Solution

The main problem with Polish notation is really one of representation. We favor entering an expression in the same way it appears in, for example, a statistics handbook. If that could be done, if a way could be found to rearrange expressions from algebraic form to Polish notation, a mathematical calculator or computer could be constructed having the computational efficiency of Polish notation without sacrificing ease of use. In fact, this process of rearrangement has been intrinsic to most higher-level programming-language compilers and interpreters for many years. The manner of rearrangement is most easily explained in terms of its program that uses a stack only slightly more general than the native stack in microprocessors.

Explanation

Listing 1 is a procedure for parsing, computer jargon for rearranging generalized binary operator expressions. In somewhat less prosaic language: PARSE is a program which takes an algebraic form expression and rearranges it to produce a sub-Polish notation form expression containing references, where needed, to the run-time stack. Its output presumes that the result of each calculation is immediately placed on the stack.

Note that PARSE does not count parentheses. In fact, it does not even use them directly. Instead, it uses an external procedure called INTOKEN to scan the input expression, EXP, and produce encoded tokens depending on the current input:

Input string: 1+(((A+B)/C)−(D*(E−F)/G))/H

Position	i	j	t	PARSE	Q
1	4			null	empty
2	4	3	8	+1	
3	3		5	null	+1$
4	1	1	1	null	null, +1$
5	1	1	1	null	null, null, +1$
6	1	4	2		
7	4	3	8	+A	
8	3	4	6	+AB	
9	4	2	7		null, +1$
10	2	3	4	+AB/$	
11	3	4	6	+AB/$C	
12	4	2	7		+1$
13	2	3	4	+AB/$C−$	
14	3	1	5	null	+AB/$C−$$, +1$
15	1	4	2		
16	4	3	8	*D	
17	3	1	5	null	*D$, +AB/$C−$$, +1$
18	1	4	2		
19	4	3	8	−E	
20	3	4	6	−EF	
21	4	2	7	−EFD$	+AB/$C−$$, +1$
22	2	3	4	−EF*D$/$	
23	3	4	6	−EF*D$/$G	
24	4	2	7	−EF*D$/$G+AB/$C−$$	+1$
25	2	2	3	−EF*D$/$G+AB/$C−$$+1$	empty
26	2	3	4	−EF*D$/$G+AB/$C−$$+1$/$	
27	3	4	6	−EF*D$/$G+AB/$C−$$+1$/$H	

Figure 1: Sample parsing process resulting from use of program PARSE.

1 for a left parenthesis.
2 for a right parenthesis.
3 for an operator.
4 for a constant or symbol.
5 if none of these.

Another peculiar property of PARSE, presuming you have not figured out how it works yet, is that only one complete INTOKEN scan of the input expression is required because the use of a stack, Q, for retaining the symbols for intermediate expressions. INTOKEN recognition of parentheses (output codes 1 and 2) effectively controls stacking and popping up symbols for intermediate expressions in the required order.

The operation of PARSE depends critically on the array S. In use, its row subscript is presumed the value of the last INTOKEN output, its column subscript the value of the current INTOKEN output. Specifically, if the last input token was a left parenthesis and the current input token was a symbol or constant, then INTOKEN's last and current outputs would be 1 and 4; the matching element in S (row 1 column 4) has value 2, so that the statement CASE2 would be performed. Subsequently, J replaces 1 and INTOKEN is again invoked to evaluate J anew; a new element of S is fetched using the new values of I and J as subscripts; and the element of the CASE statement list matching the new value taken from S is performed. This process is repeated until INTOKEN sets Endinput true, indicating the end of the input string Exp has been detected. Since the last two tokens might be right parentheses, and PARSE does not in fact process the last token since tokens are used only in pairs, the stack Q is always flushed before PARSE finishes.

PARSE is presented in informal ALGOL only in the hope the process per se of suitably rearranging algebraic form expressions can be made more easily understood than via an equivalent 8080 assembly-language program which might prove to be a transliteration nightmare for the novice LSI-11 or PPS-8 programmer. Contrarily, the step by step listing of PARSE and the associated control indices in figure 1 should aid in understanding what PARSE is really doing, with respect to the hypothetical expression. The function of INTOKEN, recognizing and encoding the elements of an expression, is sufficiently straightforward that an explicit statement of it is hardly necessary, but listing 2 is includ-

Listing 2: INTOKEN encodes the current character in the input expression, Exp. As before, an informal ALGOL type notation is used.

```
INTEGER PROCEDURE INTOKEN (Exp, Position, Endinput):
LOGICAL Endinput;
INTEGER Position  ;
STRING        Exp;
BEGIN INTOKEN :=0;
  If Position = SIZE(Exp) THEN Endinput := true
  ELSE BEGIN
    Position := Position + 1;
    WHILE Exp(Position = ' ' DO Position := Position + 1;
    IF Exp(Position) = '('THEN INTOKEN := 1
    ELSE IF Exp(Position) = ')'THEN INTOKEN :=2
    ELSE IF Exp(Position) = ANY('+','-','*','/') THEN INTOKEN := 3
    ELSE BEGIN
      INTOKEN := 5;
      COMMENT Presume error first, determine otherwise later;
      IF NOT (0>Exp(Position) OR '9' <Exp(Position))
      THEN BEGIN
        INTOKEN := 4;
        WHILE NOT (0>Exp(Position) OR '9'<Exp(Position))
        DO Position :=Position+1; Position := Position -1;
      END ELSE
      IF NOT ('A'>Exp(Position) OR 'Z'<Exp(Position))
      THEN BEGIN
        INTOKEN := 4;
        WHILE NOT('A'>Exp(Position) OR 'Z'<Exp(Position))
        DO Position := Position+1; Position := Position - 1;
      END;
    END;
  END;
END.
```

Listing 3: Single stack-control routines written for the 8080 processor. STACK places a string of characters on a LIFO list, followed by the length of the string. POPSD removes the length of the last entered string, if any, from the list. POPUP removes the last entered string, if any, from the list. (Note: These routines are not debugged; in fact, the symbol STACK is multiply defined, so that it will not assemble correctly. They are included here only to suggest an appropriate technique.)

```
STACK: PUSH   PSW     ; COMMENT The following presumes
       PUSH   B       ; external procedures ABUF and
       PUSH   D       ; RBUF whose functions are
       PUSH   H       ; respectively
       XCHG           ;   acquire a buffer of byte size
       LHLD   STACK   ;     specified by A, returning
       PUSH   H       ;     address in H,L or zero if
       POP    B       ;     none available
       ADI    3       ;   release a buffer addressed by
       CALL   ABUF    ;     H,L to the buffer pool     ;
       MOV    A,H     ;
       ORA    L       ; STACK:  SAVE(H,L);
       JZ     STKOF   ; ABUF(A+3); IF 0
       SHLD   STACK   ; THEN SET(Carry)
       MOV    A,C     ; ELSE BEGIN
       STAX   H       ;   COMMENT Stack entry contents;
       INX    H       ;   +0     address of previous entry
       MOV    A,B     ;   +2     size of current item
       STAX   H       ;   +3     current item
       INX    H       ;
       POP    PSW     ;     caller provides size in A,
       MOV    B,A     ;     item data address in H,L;
       STAX   H       ;     RESET(carry);
       ORA    A       ;     MEMORY(H,L) :=Stack;
       JZ     STKCX   ;     s size in A,
       MOV    B,A     ;     item data address in H,L;
       STAX   H       ;     RESET(carry);
       ORA    A       ;     MEMORY(H,L) :=Stack;
       JZ     STKCX   ;     Stack :=(H,L);
       INX    H       ;     (H,L) :=(H,L)     + 2;
STKCY: LDAX   D       ;     memory(H,L) := A;
```

Listing 3, continued:

```
        STAX   H        ;   (H,L) := (H,L)     +1;
        INX    H        ;   RESTORE(D,E);SAVE(D,E);
        INX    D        ;   WHILE NOT A=0 DO
        DCR    B        ;   BEGIN
        JNZ    STKCY    ;     MEMORY (H,L) := MEMORY (D,E);
STKCX:  POP    H        ;     (H,L):=(H,L)+1;
        POP    D        ;     (D,E):=(D,E)+1;
        POP    B        ;     A : A -1;
STC                     ;   END;
CMC                     ; END;
RET                     ; RESTORE(H,L);
STKOG:  POP    H        ;
POPUF:  POP    D        ;
        POP    B        ;
        POP    PSW      ;
        STC             ;
        RET             ;
;
;
POPSD:  PUSH   H        ; POPSD: IF Stack = 0
        STC             ; THEN SET(Carry)
        LHLD   STACK    ; ELSE BEGIN
        MOV    A,H      ;   COMMENT Give caller size
        ORA    L        ;   of next entry to pop, for
        JZ     POPZD    ;   buffering as needed  ;
        INX    H        ;   RESET(Carry);
        INX    H        ;   SAVE(H,L);
        CMC             ;   (H,L):=Stack+2;
        LDAX   H        ;   A:=MEMORY(H,L);
        JMP    POPXD    ;   RESTORE(H,L);
POPZD:  SUB    A        ; END;
POPXD:  POP    H        ;
        RET             ;
;
;
;       The following must be in R/W
;       memory, since Stack is the
;       list-origin address, and LHLI
;       is externally modified to
;       effect an indirect LHLD.
LHLI;   LHLD   0  ;
        RET       ;
STACK:  0         ;
POPUP:  PUSH   PSW      ; POOPUP: IF Stack=0
        PUSH   B        ; THEN SET(Carry)
        PUSH   D        ; ELSE BEGIN
        PUSH   H        ;   COMMENT Target area is
        LHLD   STACK    ;   specified by caller H,L;
        XCHG            ;   RESET(Carry);
        POP    H        ;   SAVE(D,E,H,L);
        MOV    A,D      ;   (D,E):=Stack;
        ORA    E        ;   B:=MEMORY(D,E+2);
        JZ     POPUF    ;   SAVE(D,E,H,L);
        PUSH   H        ;   (D,E)  :=(D,E)+3;
        PUSH   D        ;   WHILE NOT B=0 DO
        INX    D        ;   BEGIN
        INX    D        ;     COMMENT Zero-length entries
        LDAX   D        ;     are removed but not copies  ;
        ORA    A        ;     MEMORY(H,L)  :=MEMORY(D,E);
        JZ     POPCX    ;     (D,E):=(D,E)+1;
        INX    D        ;     (H,L):=(H,L)+1;
        MOV    B,A      ;     B:=B-1;
POPCY:  LDAX   D        ; END;
        STAX   H        ; RESTORE(D,E,H,L);
        INX    HZ       : Stack  :=MEMORY(D,E);
        INX    D        ; RBUF(D,E);
        DR     B        ; RESTOR(D,E,H,L);
        JNZ    POPCY    ; END;
POPCX:  POP    D        ;
        XCHG            ;
        SHLD   LHLI+1   ;
        CALL   LHLI     ;
        SHLD   STACK    ;
        LHLD   LHLI+1   ;
        CALL   RBUF     ;
        POP    H        ;
```

ed nonetheless in informal ALGOL. The remaining question, perhaps, is one of making the stack Q of PARSE operable on a microcomputer. To that end, listing 3 shows a hypothetical implementation of single stack control routines STACK, POPUP, and POPSD using 8080 assembler format.

Now what? Well, for a start let's observe that PARSE will work only with binary operator expressions. Right? Well, not quite. Note that PARSE passes the buck for recognition. If INTOKEN can recognize unary operators, it can also stuff in a dummy operand on the fly, since PARSE initializes Position, and thereafter leaves it alone. That is, the common unary operators are special cases of a binary and either 0s or 1s: NOT FRED is equivalent to ones exclusive-OR FRED; NEGATIVE VIBES is equivalent to 0 — VIBES; and INVERSE HYPOTHESIS is equivalent to 1/HYPOTHESIS.

How about the results? PARSE can easily be modified to directly generate machine-language code if INTOKEN is modified to create or at least have access to a symbol table; or its output can be used, as is, by an interpretive calculator program. Obviously, 8080 machines and, for that matter, most microprocessors lack multiply and divide instructions, but nonnative operations can easily be interpreted as operator subprogram calls. PARSE makes no presumption about the computer on which it is run except the availability of a stack to use with its output referenced by '$'. The operators, for example, for which PARSE was developed in the form shown were character string operators of combination and proximity. The PARSE output was interpreted by a program for searching large textual files on an IBM System 360 disk unit. The point is that the results are what you make of them, PARSE being no more than a procedure for rearrangement of expressions.

A final apology before getting under way. FORTRAN programmers may by now have noticed an "error" in that although the tokens 1 and H in the example of figure 1 are at the same parenthesis level, the add-1 parse precedes the divide-H in the final step. Why? I prefer to ask why one bothers with operator priorities so long as the desired order of computation can be explicitly specified by using parentheses. The example of figure 1, in fact, was contrived in part to illustrate that PARSE as shown here presumes a strict left to right evaluation at any parentheses level. Operators are not "ranked" as in FORTRAN and several other higher-level programming languages.

One More Time

If the available stack mechanism is only once more generalized, to provide multiple stacks simultaneously, some conceptual simplification of a large class of problems occurs. As a near trivial example, we illustrate in listing 4 a two-stack sorting procedure. In essence, it removes records (ie: strings) from a file one at a time and manipulates the two stacks, Highside and Lowside, back and forth until the new record fits in the inclusive interval of values bounded by the top elements of the two stacks. The procedure has two virtues:

- It is easy to describe and understand.
- It requires an absolute minimum of workspace.

The price we pay is speed. It is probably one of the two or three slowest sorting algorithms around.■

Listing 3 continued

```
POP   D     ;
POP   B     ;
POP   PSW   ;
STC         ;
CMC         ;
RET         ;
```

Listing 4: A SORT procedure expressed in informal ALGOL type notation demonstrates use of two stacks.

```
STRING ARRAY PROCEDURE SORT(File):
STRING ARRAY File;
BEGIN
  INTEGER              K;
  STRING               This;
  STACK Highside, Lowside;
  Lowside: = File(1);
  Highside: = File(2);
  COMMENT top function references item
  on the top of some stack;
  IF TOP(Lowside) > TOP(Highside)
  THEN BEGIN
    This      : = Highside;
    Highside: = Lowside;
    Lowside  : = This;
  END;
  COMMENT size function produces the
  current number of elements in array;
  K: = 3;
  WHILE K ≤ SIZE(File) DO
  BEGIN
    This      : = File(K);
    K         : = K + 1;
    WHILE This < TOP(Lowside) DO Highside : = Lowside;
    WHILE This > TOP(Highside) DO Lowside : = Highside;
    Highside : = This;
  END;
  WHILE NOT(Lowside = entry) DO Highside : = Lowside;
  K: = 1;
  WHILE K ≤ SIZE(File) DO
  BEGIN
    SORT(K): = Highside;
    K         : = K + 1;
  END;
END.
```

The program examples which appear in this article are written in an informal ALGOL type notation. The basic unit of ALGOL is the statement. It can be either a simple statement such as:

```
Position: = 0;
```

which is read "position is evaluated as 0," or a compound statement defined by BEGIN . . . END such as:

```
BEGIN
  Q: = PARSE;PARSE: = null;
END
```

which is read "Q is evaluated parse, PARSE is evaluated null."

The statements defined between the BEGIN and END statements are not restricted to type. A preceding conditional such as (IF . . . THEN . . . ELSE) will affect the entire command statement. One of the constituents of the statement may well be another compound statement. For example, to add an array of samples having subscripts 1 through Limit which is specified elsewhere we could write:

```
BEGIN
  Subscript: = 1; Sum: = 0;
  WHILE Subscript < Limit DO
  BEGIN
    Sum: = Sum + Sample(Subscript);
    Subscript: = Subscript + 1;
  END;
END;
```

The WHILE statement's operand (the statements after the DO) rather intuitively is in execution so long as the conditional part (Subscript < Limit) is true.

The CASE statement is simpler in effect. It acts approximately like an indexed jump. It has two operands. The first of these (T in the PARSE procedure) is an integer, and the second is a list of statements bracketed by BEGIN and END. The first list whose position matches the value of the index specifier.

Following are the informal extensions that have been made to ALGOL and used in the programs:

- The period indicates concatenation of character strings. Presuming values of 'WHAT' and 'STUFF' for symbols A and B, A . B will have a value of 'WHATSTUFF.'
- Q is declared to be of type STACK which, however implicit in most implementations of ALGOL-60, was not construed to be explicitly available. It is, in effect, a LIFO indexed character-string array.
- Null and empty are used for assigning values, respectively, of a character string of length 0 and a stack having 0 entries.

What Is an Interrupt?

R Travis Atkins

Busy work! It's a terrible thing to inflict on people or computers. Wait loops in input or output operations are busy work for computers, and unless you learn how to tap your computer on the shoulder when you need it, it will probably spend most of its time doing busy work.

As hobbyists, we are always concerned about squeezing the greatest value out of our investments. We want our computers to run as efficiently as possible. Since it is likely that we will be involved in designing and building some of our own input/output (I/O) devices, we should develop an understanding of the concept of interrupts. To efficiently program peripherals for I/O purposes it is often necessary to use interrupts.

This article introduces the basic concepts of interrupts, defines the terminology that applies to interrupt mechanisms, and describes the processing events that must occur during the time from the receipt of an interrupt to the return from that interrupt.

Concepts

An excellent example of interrupt processing is the system used in telephones. Let's see why.

We know when someone is trying to call us because the telephone rings. But consider how much time would be wasted if we had to periodically pick up the receiver to see if anyone was on the telephone if the phone had no bell. This periodic method is called *polling*; it works well for telethons and radio talk shows. However, it's not the best method for normal home telephone installations. Assume you receive an average of one or two phone calls a day at home. Imagine yourself as a processor and the callers as the I/O requests from a keyboard. The order of magnitude differences in this example are about the same as with your processor and its I/O. The bell on your telephone is, of course, an *interrupt*. It is an excellent way to resolve the asynchronism and speed differentials of the telephone communications system. Interrupts can resolve the same fundamental mismatches for computers as well.

Terminology

Let's carry this analogy a little further to introduce the terminology that refers to variations of the basic interrupt concept.

If your phone is ringing, and you are about to process an interrupt, what are your reactions? How does your interrupt processing work?

More than likely, you will perform a sequence of actions precisely analogous to those your microprocessor performs when it receives an interrupt. Figure 1 is a flowchart of the typical procedure we would run through for a telephone interruption. It consists of both the *housekeeping* chores of switching from the background task you were doing, reading, to the interrupt task, answering the phone, and back again in an orderly and complete fashion, as well as the interrupt handler itself.

In the computer an interrupt is a special control signal that is sent to your microprocessor when a given asynchronous event, such as a switch closure, or an I/O ready signal, is detected by your system. It is the mechanism that forces the processor to take note of that exceptional event.

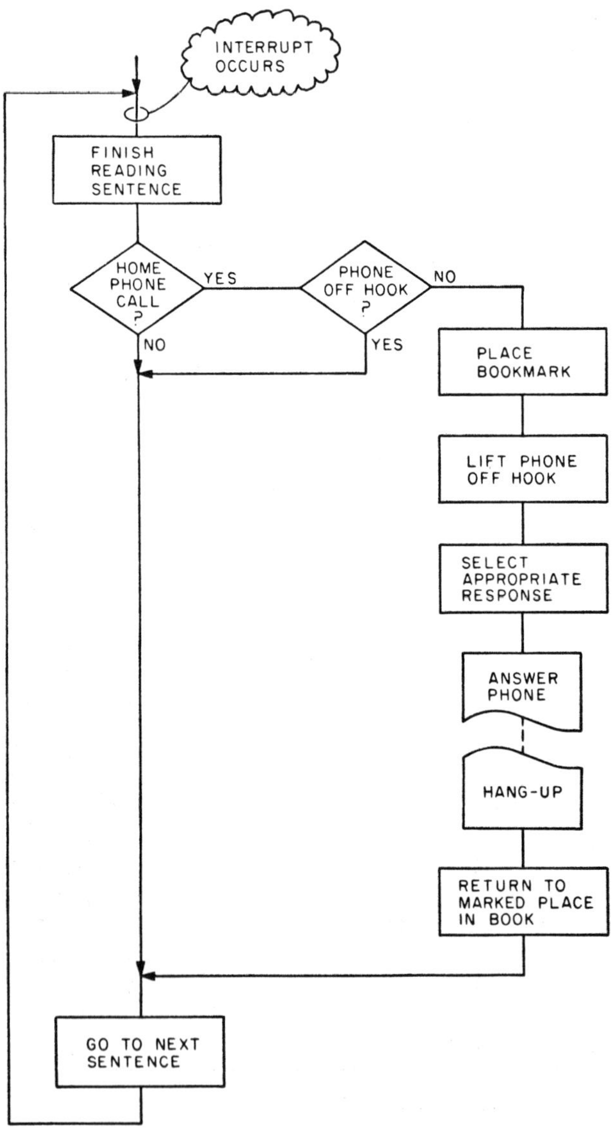

Figure 1: One example of a way to handle a human being's interrupt processing in response to a ringing bell. The ringing bell is like a signal on a multiple source interrupt line of a computer. The first object is to identify the source of the interrupt. If processing is done, the state of the interrupted process (eg: reading a book) is saved (eg: with a bookmark) while the phone is answered. After the phone call, the reading of the book may be resumed at the place of the bookmark, restoring the original process.

The interrupt causes your processor to transfer control to a set of instructions known as the *interrupt handler*. The interrupt handler is nothing more than a precoded contingency plan in the form of a subroutine that may be called at any time in response to an interrupt signal. What you do in this subroutine is limited only by the software capabilities of your processor.

In microprocessors, interrupt processing is basically a software technique with varying degrees of hardware support depending on your particular processor and system. The term *vectored interrupt* refers to a simple method of reacting to an interrupt. The processor is sent to the interrupt handler which will lead the processor through steps to determine the source of the interrupt, initiate appropriate actions and return to the point of interruption. The *vector* is simply the starting address of the interrupt handler and is supplied either externally or internally, depending upon your particular processor's hardware.

Microprocessor integrated-circuit designers who seek to minimize the hardware requirements in their processors often assign a fixed location or set of locations in the processor's address space to hold the vector(s). The 6800 processor uses this approach, as does the Texas Instruments TMS-9900. Other processors such as the 8080 receive their vectors directly from external sources, a method which usually involves more system hardware.

The built-in process that occurs in your microprocessor integrated circuit is usually limited to saving the program counter and the processor's status register, masking subsequent interrupts, and then *transferring control* to your interrupt handler (ie: loading the program counter with the interrupt handler's starting address). The task of determining where the interrupt came from is left to the interrupt handler itself. In the simplest case, where you have only one device tied to an interrupt line, the origin of the interrupt is implied. Since we may at some time have more devices than we have separate interrupt lines, we should also know how to make a more sophisticated system capable of handling many devices.

To see how multiple interrupts are handled, consider another analogy.

Assume you had just settled back into your easy chair after finishing with the telephone interruption, when suddenly a pair of hands covers your eyes and a voice says, "Guess who?" You've been interrupted again, and you don't know which of your twelve children it is, so you will have to save your place again, and begin by saying, "Is that you Olen?"... "No."..."Is it you Travis?"... "No."..."Is it you Mary Ellen?" ... etc, until you get a positive response. In much the same way, several devices can use a single, common interrupt line to your processor so that, once the interrupt handler is initiated, it can interrogate all the devices to see which one sent the interrupt signal. To accomplish this, it is customary to have a *device status register* in the microprocessor's address space for each individual device. The data in this location indicates the device's current status: busy or ready.

Now suppose this game of guess-who is very popular with your children, and they are all playing it on you, some much more often than others. Your best strategy would probably be to adopt an ordering scheme *to optimize* the handling of these many interruptions. This simply means that you would guess the names of the children who were the most frequent players first and check the least likely ones last. Similarly, in interrupt processing you should arrange the order of checking the device status registers of your I/O units from the most frequent source of interrupts to the least frequent. By ordering your interrupt servicing this way, you can add significantly to the efficiency of your system.

By now you've probably realized that the idea of letting multiple devices share one interrupt line is problematical: two devices may want to interrupt the processor at the same time. In terms of our analogy, all twelve of your children may want to play the guess-who game with you at the same time. The way to handle this situation is to say, "Hold it! I will play the game with each of you ... but only one at a time." By doing this you act on one interrupt while you *mask* out the rest.

The concept of *maskable interrupts* is incorporated in many of today's processors. There is usually a mask bit or bits used to block or *mask* the interrupt signal from the processor. This masking is frequently part of the built-in process on your microprocessor chip to protect the function of saving critical information, such as the program counter and status register, from subsequent interrupts. Once masked out, your system's design will determine if a subsequent interrupt will be held pending or lost. Interrupts that are kept pending are often referred to as *queued interrupts*. Sometimes circuitry external to the processor chip itself is used to give the pending interrupts an order of priority in much the same way as you might tell your children to line up in the order of

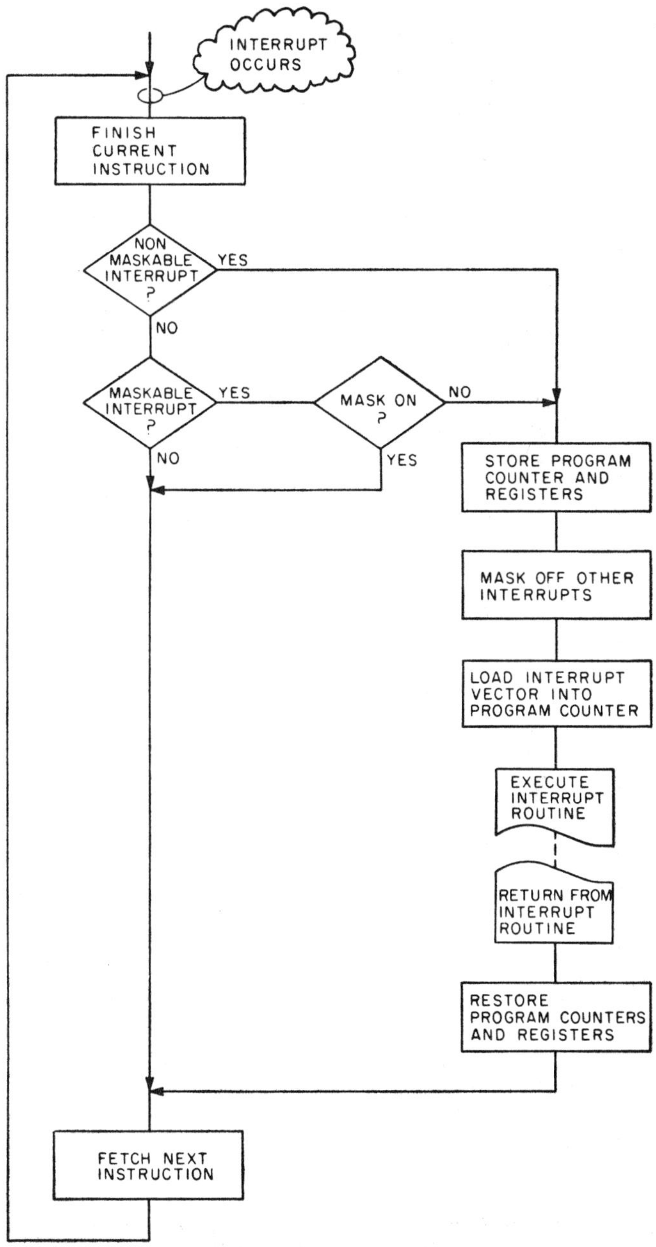

Figure 2: Analogous to the human interrupt processing of figure 1, the typical computer's interrupt processing activities are shown by this chart. The difference between figures 1 and 2 are largely in the activities described in each box; the form of the processing logic in this particular set of examples is nearly identical.

Table 1: The following list of responsibilities must be jointly met by both the programmer and the system programmed, if interrupts are to be properly handled. The key item to remember is that when the interrupt occurs, the critical data values determining the state of the machine must be saved so that at the end of the interrupt process, the original process can be resumed as if the interrupt never happened.

- Sensing an interrupt signal and determining appropriate response.
- Setting the mask to protect the processor from subsequent interrupts.
- Note where you are by saving the program counter and status register.
- Transferring processor control by loading the program counter with the interrupt vector address.
- Executing the interrupt handler which may:

  save accumulator(s).
  save index register(s).
  save pointer(s).
  search for interrupt source.
  satisfy device request.
  restore pointer(s).
  restore index register(s).
  restore accumulator(s).
  clear the interrupt mask.

- Resume normal processing by restoring the program counter and the processor status register.

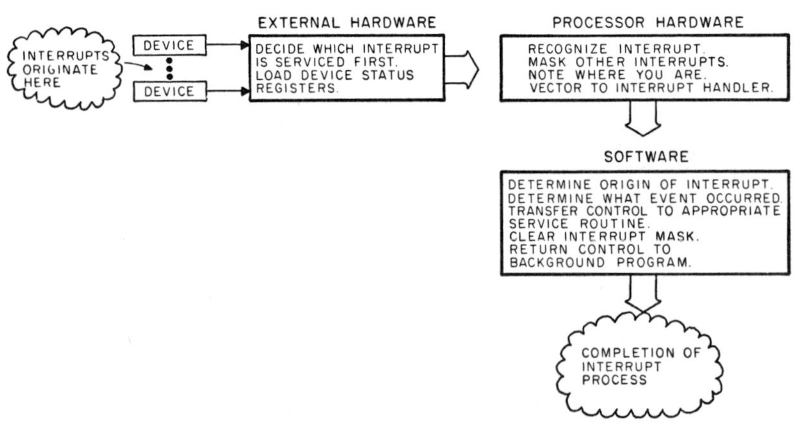

Figure 3: A division of the functions at an interrupt between hardware and software is detailed in this diagram. The exact boundaries are often set by the system's hardware and software design details.

youngest to oldest to play the guess-who game. The *N-level priority* interrupt capabilities that are mentioned as features of microprocessor systems refer to this type of interrupt queuing. A higher-priority interrupt that arrives after several low-priority ones will usually bump the lower-priority interrupts down in the queue.

For those cases where an interrupt must get the processor's attention right away, a *nonmaskable interrupt* is usually also provided in the integrated circuit's structure. This control line is for a very high-priority function of your choice, which can override the maskable interrupts even if they are in progress. This is valuable for very high-speed I/O, such as a floppy-disk unit, and for hardware emergencies such as fire or power-loss routines. Your system reset is usually a nonmaskable interrupt.

Mechanisms

Now that you have a feel for the terminology, let's take a look at the mechanisms and processing that are common to all interrupt routines. Figure 2 is a typical flowchart of the functions necessary to accomplish the transfer of control from the background processing to the interrupt handler and return. You may think of this as putting the background process *on hold* while the interrupt is processed and recommencing the background process when it returns. The background process is not affected by what has happened; thus the interrupt processing is completely transparent to the background process and may be executed at any time without fear of disturbing it. The only definite change is that the background processing will slow down somewhat because the processor has to take extra time to service the interrupt(s). As a result, any real-time clocking in the system will be offset by that interrupt processing time.

The joint responsibility of the processor and you, the interrupt routine programmer, is to insure that the background process is not disturbed. These responsibilities are simply stated in table 1.

Within the interrupt handler it is not always necessary to save all of the working registers for every interrupt, but you must at least save and restore every register used in your routine.

Deciding when to remove the interrupt protection (ie: clear the mask) is your responsibility. The key is to pick a point which comes after the saving of the critical registers. The mask shouldn't be removed in the middle of your interrupt routine unless the routine is *reenterable.* Reenterancy is a term that refers to software routines that find new memory locations to store their working data each time that they are reentered before they have been exited. The significance of this is that if you clear the mask and a subsequent interrupt arrives, stops your current interrupt processing, and begins to use the same interrupt routine you were just using, you must ensure that it does not destroy your current working data. The safest procedure is to stay masked throughout the interrupt processing until you become experienced with the reentry software techniques. Figure 3 shows the division of these interrupt processing duties for a typical microcomputer system.

If your processor's monitor was supplied by the manufacturer, there is much to be learned from studying its interrupt handler section. Look for the methods used to accomplish the basic steps we have outlined above, then write your own simple interrupt handler, modify the interrupt vector to point to your routine instead of theirs, and execute your interrupt handler.

Once you have done this successfully, you will have developed an appreciation of how the modern digital computer, large or small, appears to simultaneously service the requests of so many peripheral devices. Understanding interrupt driven processing, which is the central concept of computer operating systems, will help you to grasp the awesome power that lies within your own personal computing system.■

A Little Bit on Interrupts

Robert R Wier

While talking with fellow enthusiasts attending meetings of computer clubs, there seem to be several aspects of small computer systems which are particularly confusing to newcomers to the hobby. One of these is interrupts. This article explains how the mechanisms of interrupts work, and what can be done with them in a personal computer system.

History

When computers first came into widespread use, they ran primarily on card or tape batch principles. The operator had long lists of instructions telling him which card decks to use to run the specific jobs. Each job had to be set up independently, which was acceptable as long as this setup time was short in relation to the amount of time each job ran.

A desired goal was to keep the machine running as much as possible. As technology advanced and job run times became shorter, setup time became a significant fraction of the total job run time. It was clear that if the machine could take over some of the chores of the operator, but at machine speed, the utilization of the system could be increased.

Accounting and setup procedures could be accomplished by programs stored inside the machine, and then the computer could request the operator to perform only those duties that actually required human intervention (eg: mounting a disk pack). Thus programs called *operating systems* came into use.

About this same time, it was realized that if such a machine were going to run jobs under an operating system, there had to be some way to return control to the operating system should the program encounter difficulties. That is, the operator should be able to jerk control of the machine away from the program currently running and give it to the operating system without having to go through the process of clearing the machine and reloading the operating system manually each time.

Another problem emerged at this time with the fact that as the central processing unit improved in efficiency due to the faster technology, the devices used for input and output, called peripherals, remained at about the same speed. Therefore, if the central processing unit had to wait for the completion of an input or output operation, it would just sit there testing and retesting to see if the program could proceed. This was frequently called a busy wait loop, or spin lock. It is a technique which is still frequently used in microprocessor systems.

Clearly, since input/output (I/O) operations were so slow, it would be nice if the processor could simply request the I/O hardware to input to or output from memory directly without processor intervention. Then the processor could go on and perform useful computations while the I/O operation was in progress. Of course this required considerably more sophisticated input/output hardware than was in use previously, when the processor orchestrated every data transfer. But since the I/O hardware didn't need to be able to perform complicated arithmetic functions, it could be regarded as a minicentral processing unit or microprocessor. Indeed, the original purpose of the microprocessor chip which has made our hobby possible was to produce reasonably smart peripheral systems at low cost. That is, each I/O channel would have its own smaller processor to handle only data transfers between an I/O device and memory. A little thought will reveal a problem, however. If the processor simply starts an I/O operation and then pursues other matters, how does it know when the operation is finished, so that it may use the data input or refill the buffer just output? What if the drive mangles the tape and the data has to be output or input again? What was needed was the ability for the I/O processor to be able to tap the central processor on the shoulder and say, "I'm finished," or "I fouled it up."

There was also the problem of real-time applications which, depending on the system, needed the computer to be able to detect some condition, make a decision, and act on it quickly. If you had a big busy wait loop, where several instructions were executed in the loop between each checking of the status of each separate input signal, your refinery's catalytic converter might go critical before the computer even

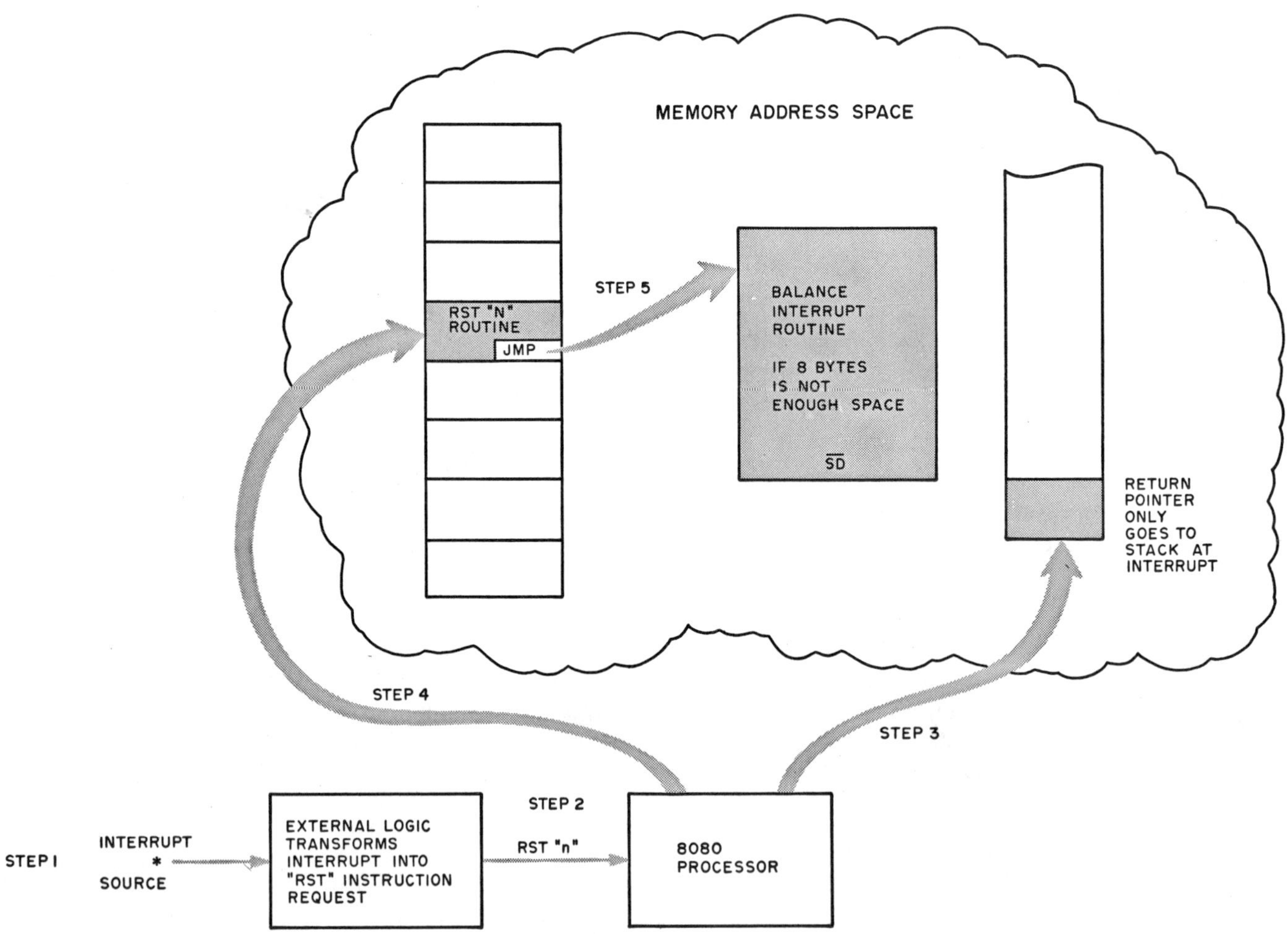

Figure 1: What happens when an 8080 interrupt occurs? The interrupt signal occurs first at some external device. Then, external circuitry creates an interrupt signal and sends a restart (RST) instruction to the processor as the second step. As a third step the old program counter information is saved on the stack to allow later return. Then the fourth step, part of executing the RST instruction, is to jump to one of eight possible restart locations in the first 64 bytes of memory address space; if the 8 bytes are not sufficient, step 5, shown here, is a jump to an extension of the interrupt routine. Responsibility for saving the state of the processor (beyond the return from subroutine pointer pushed automatically into the stack by RST n) is up to the programmer coding the interrupt response routine.

checked to see if something was wrong, a disquieting development.

What Interrupts Do

So, interrupts were devised. Indeed, some computer scientists feel that the major difference between the second and third generation machine was not only the transition to integrated circuitry, but the advent of the interruptible machine as well. But exactly what happens when something from the outside world or a condition internal to the processing wants attention?

Suppose the processor is hardwired with at least one interrupt line, and probably more. When an interrupt occurs, the desired effect is to:

- Store *all* the information regarding the presently running program which is necessary to resume execution at the same point some time in the future, to prevent having to start it again from the beginning. This includes the program counter, any status information, and, optionally, the processor registers. This state-saving activity must be complete or unpredictable behavior can ensue upon return to the interrupted process.
- Insert into the program counter the address of the first instruction in the interrupt program which will handle the condition causing the interrupt. When the interrupt routine is finished, the status register(s), program counter, and processor registers of the interrupted program may be restored and the interrupted program resumes running without being aware that it was temporarily not in control of the processor. This process of restoring the machine state is the inverse of the state-saving activity.

Interrupt Hardware

The actual hardware included to effect interrupts varies somewhat from

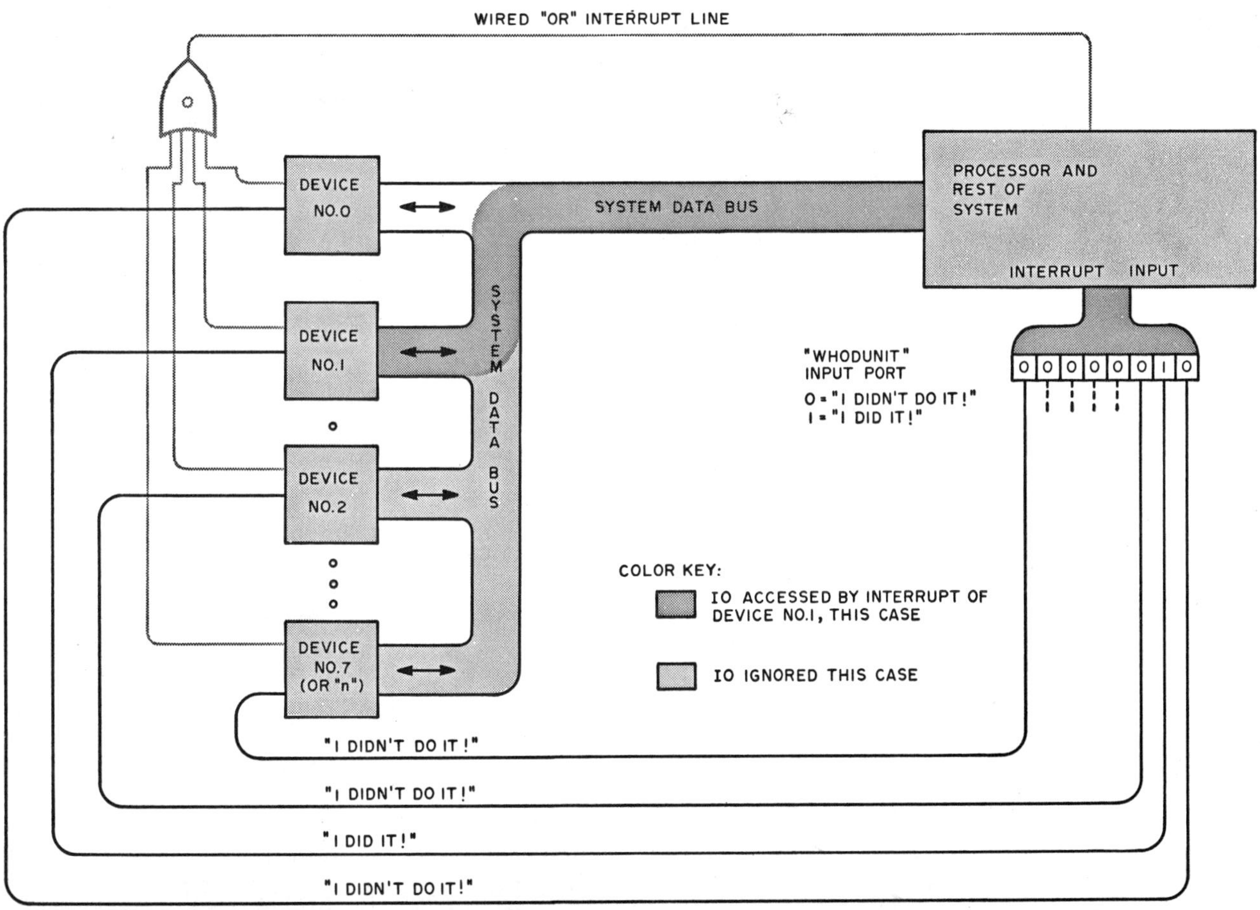

Figure 2: The "Who Done It" problem on interrupts. Some means must be provided to determine which I/O device requested service when more than one device shares an interrupt line on any processor. Here is one way of determining "who done it": The input port "WHO-DUNIT" looks at 8 single-bit status flags corresponding to up to eight devices; if the flag is on, then that device "did it."

one processor to the next. Virtually all of them save the old program counter in some specified location and insert the address of the interrupt handler's first instruction into the program counter. This is an unconditional branch to a subroutine with linkage for return after interrupt processing. Each machine is different, though, in the actions taken beyond these two basic functions. In the IBM 370 series, the hardware does practically everything for the programmer. In microprocessors, the software interrupt program must do some of the things that the hardware does in the larger machines. Let's look at the most popular microprocessors and see what they do.

Interrupts on the Intel 8080

When an interrupt request is received, the 8080 completes the current instruction before taking any action on the interrupt. Virtually all miniprocessors and microprocessors do this, since there would be all sorts of problems encountered if an interrupt were recognized in the middle of the execution of an instruction. A little thought will show why. The 8080 does not increment the program counter. The program counter for the old program is pushed (ie: saved) onto the stack. The next instruction to be executed is *jammed* onto the data bus by external interrupt circuitry and is called the restart instruction. Depending on the restart instruction operand, the next instruction executed (ie: the address placed into the program counter) may be one of eight possible decimal memory locations: 0, 8, 16, 24, 32, 40, 48, or 56. 8080 programmers will note that there are just enough memory locations, eight, between these addresses to save the registers of the old program, disable further interrupts, and execute a jump to another location, which in this case will be the interrupt service routine. This entire operation is explained in figure 1.

Obviously, if you ever contemplate using all eight classes of interrupts, you should be sure not to program using the first sixty-four memory locations since those are reserved by the hardware for interrupt handling. But what if you want to have only one class of interrupt? For example, you have a panel switch that you can push to get the attention of the machine. Then just program the particular location that you, or the computer hardware designer, hardwired in. Suppose for a minute that you need more than eight interrupts. It is possible, within a few restrictions as shown in figure 2. Just OR the interrupt request lines from the outside world together and feed them to the same interrupt line going into the processor. But then how do you know which device has caused the interrupt? Obviously there will have to be another signal somewhere to indicate which device needs attention. This could be implemented in a variety of ways:

- The device could place an identifying number on the data bus which would identify the device.
- An input port could be wired so that the device would signal that it needed attention.
- The processor could send an interrogation to each device connected to that interrupt line asking if it was the one that sent the request.

The first and second methods are faster since the device number or input data could be used as an index to go to the appropriate interrupt handler program. The third method is called polling and may be somewhat time consuming if many devices use the same interrupt line. Because so much of the interrupt logic of the 8080 is external to the chip, there can be considerable variation. Most 8080 systems use a simple restart (RST) operation code, but any instruction including jump (JMP) or call (CALL) can be used with appropriate external logic.

Motorola 6800 Interrupts

This chip has the capability of decoding and servicing a smaller number of interrupts, but in a more automatic way than the 8080. The 6800 uses an indirect, vectored interrupt situation in which each source of an interrupt looks up a unique vector location for the address of its service routine. When an interrupt is indicated to the 6800 by one of three possible sources, the processor automatically saves the two accumulators, index register, status register, and program counter on the stack, and in the process of doing so changes the stack pointer. Thus, the 6800 has the advantage of never requiring program code to achieve state saving functions. It simultaneously has the disadvantage of always performing a complete state save so there is no way to "cut corners" and save time by ignoring the saving and restoring of data which is not changed by the interrupt routine. This vectoring method also has

PUBLIC LIBRARY REQUEST TO OREGON STATE LIBRARY

Keep green and pink copies. Send yellow and white copies to OSL.

State Library call number	Book author (last name first) OR ☐ Periodical vol., number, and date
	Book title OR periodical article author, title, pages
	Book edition
	Publisher
	Date of publication
If material is not listed in OSL catalog, please supply the following information if available:	This space for notes of further information
ISBN	
LC #	Verified in ☐ OSL MFC ☐ OSL MFCS ☐ OSL MBC ☐ Monthly Cat. ☐ ORULS ☐ NUC ☐ CBI ☐ BIP ☐ FCB ☐ Other
Price	Name of patron or branch
Source of Review	Library Name and Address

O.S.C.I. LIBRARY
3405 DEER PARK DR., S.E.
SALEM, OR 97310

Library Phone ____ Library contact person ____

Date of request

Not needed after

If material is not available, may OSL

☐ Reserve for you?

OR for a faster response,

☐ Substitute by author?

☐ Substitute by subject? (explain subject)

Vol., date, page OR fiche number for above verification

Please leave space below for State Library use.

State Library reply:

☐ In Use

☐ Reserved ____ ahead of yours

☐ On order

☐ Not owned and not available through ILL

☐ Special loan for use in borrowing library only

☐ Substitute sent

☐ Cannot verify. More information needed

6824
10-1

State Library call number: QA76.6424 PRCUR, Dropped [handwritten; partly illegible]

Book author (last name first) OR
☐ Periodical, vol., number, and date
LIFFICK, BLAISE [ED.]

Book title OR periodical article author, title, pages
PROGRAMMING TECHNIQUES

Book edition

Publisher: BYTE PUBLICATIONS

Date of publication: 1978

This space for notes or further information

Date of request: 8/23/91

Not needed after

If material is not available, may OSL
☑ Reserve for you?
OR for a faster response,
☐ Substitute by author?
☐ Substitute by Subject? (explain subject)

State Library reply:
☐ In Use
☐ Reserved
_____ ahead of yours
☐ On order
☐ Not owned and not available through ILL
☐ Special loan for use in borrowing library only
☐ Substitute sent
☐ Cannot verify. More information needed

If material is not listed in OSL catalog, please supply the following information if available:

ISBN

LC #

Price

Source of Review

Verified in ☐ OSL MFC ☐ OSL MFCS ☐ OSL MBC ☐ Monthly Cat. ☐ ORULS
☐ NUC ☐ CBI ☐ BIP ☐ FCB ☐ Other

Vol., date, page OR fiche number for above verification

Name of patron or branch: CLIFF WELLS

Library Name and Address

O.S.C.I. LIBRARY
3405 DEER PARK DR., S.E.
SALEM, OR 97310

Library Phone ________ Library contact person ________

Please leave space below for State Library use.

Keep green and pink copies. Send yellow and white copies to OSL.

PUBLIC LIBRARY REQUEST TO OREGON STATE LIBRARY

...2-76 Rev. 4/86

the disadvantage of requiring that the stack pointer never be used for other purposes, such as a pseudo-index register, when interrupts are possible. The three interrupts possible on the 6800 are:

- Maskable Interrupt (IRQ). This interrupt occurs when a hardware signal causes a low state on the IRQ line of the processor. This line is always wired in a *wired or* configuration when multiple sources are used, so some form of polling or priority logic is needed to identify sources. When an interrupt occurs, a flag is set in the processor that prevents a second interrupt from interrupting the routine which processes the first to arrive.
- NonMaskable Interrupt (NMI). This interrupt is identical to the IRQ interrupt except that no masking of repeated interrupts occurs in the processor to prevent conflicts. As a result, without external logic to do the masking, only one interrupt source should be dedicated to this signal. Motorola intended this line to be used with the absolute highest priority external signal in a typical system: the signal that indicates a 110 VAC main power supply failure in a dedicated application system. The interrupt response routine in such a case typically would have enough time before the capacitors of the power supply discharge to save the state of the processor and prepare for later return of power. But the intended use does not mean the only use, and with proper care this interrupt line can be used for inputs as diverse as a direct memory address (DMA) controller or real-time clock.
- Software Interrupt (SWI). This interrupt occurs when a program executes a software interrupt instruction. The actions taken are exactly the same as those for the totally asynchronous NMI and IRQ hardware inputs. The only difference is that the SWI is not a true interrupt since it is programmed into the software at a fixed point. Whereas an interrupt, such as NMI or IRQ, can occur at any time relative to the execution of a program. Thus the SWI instruction is a call to an interrupt subroutine, with return implemented via a return from interrupt (RTI) instruction.

There is one further method of interrupting a process in the 6800 that is not characterized by the state saving needed to effect a true interrupt-style action. This is use of the reset (RES) line of the hardware. This form of interruption merely causes an unconditional branch to a restart location and is typically used to initialize the system or to recover from disastrous errors.

All four sources of interruption of the 6800 processor, IRQ, NMI, SWI, and RES, use a similar, indirect, vectored approach to locating the address of the desired routine. In the cases of IRQ, NMI, and SWI the desired routine is a subroutine which returns via an RTI instruction; in the case of RES the desired routine is the beginning of the software which gains control when the processor is restarted.

In each case, the processor uses a 2-byte address stored in the region from hexadecimal address FFF8 to FFFF in memory address space as the starting address for the desired routine. Thus, for example, suppose a source of an interrupt changes the state of the IRQ line, causing an IRQ interrupt. The processor first completes the previous instruction, as noted earlier. Then, instead of executing the next instruction, it executes the details of the built-in state-saving sequence. After state saving, the processor sends out address to memory for location FFF8, from which it obtains the high-order address of the interrupt routine. Then it sends out the address FFF9, from which it obtains the low-order address of the interrupt routine. It then branches to the interrupt routine at the address just obtained. A similar process occurs for the NMI response using the data contained in locations FFFC and FFFD as an address; for the SWI response using data contained in locations FFFA and FFFB as an address; and for the RES response using data contained in locations FFFE and FFFF as an address.

The MOS Technology 6502

This 8-bit processor is very similar to the 6800 in its processng of interrupts. There is no separate vector for a software interrupt as implemented in the 6800, so the 6502's interrupt vector region only includes nonmaskable interrupts (eg: FFFA and FFFB contain the address), reset (eg: FFFC and FFFD contain the address), and maskable interrupts (eg: FFFE and FFFF contain the address). The 6502's BRK instruction is similar to the 6800's SWI, except it uses the same vector location as the maskable interrupt IRG, rather than a separate address vector.

Interesting Uses

Now knowing about interrupts, what are their uses on the personal computer system, and what kinds of programming should we use with them? Probably a majority of users will not need to use interrupts at all, at least until they have several years programming experience. If you have an 8080, just be careful to write your programs around the critical interrupt locations in low memory addresses, in case sometime in the future you decide to start using them. If you have a 6800 and use a dedicated monitor such as JBUG of MIKBUG, much of your freedom to use interrupts is replaced by hardwired response vectors in ROM found at FFF8 to FFFF. Almost certainly if you plan on writing or using some type of operating system, the interrupt facilities will need to be used in the interrupt routines.

The use of interrupts for I/O operations probably will not be a major application except in cases of direct memory access or fast peripherals. Personal systems tend to be strongly oriented to a memory conservative type of programming, since the cost of the processor hardware is so low to begin with, and the slowness of I/O is not really a significant factor.

Real-time applications are likely to abound in small systems. The timers that are included in some systems often operate by allowing the program to load a desired number, which is then counted down (or added up, depending on the hardware) independent of the processor. When 0 is reached, the timer can generate an interrupt. This could be useful in such applications as keeping track of how long programs use the processor, allowing a player a limited amount of time to make a move in

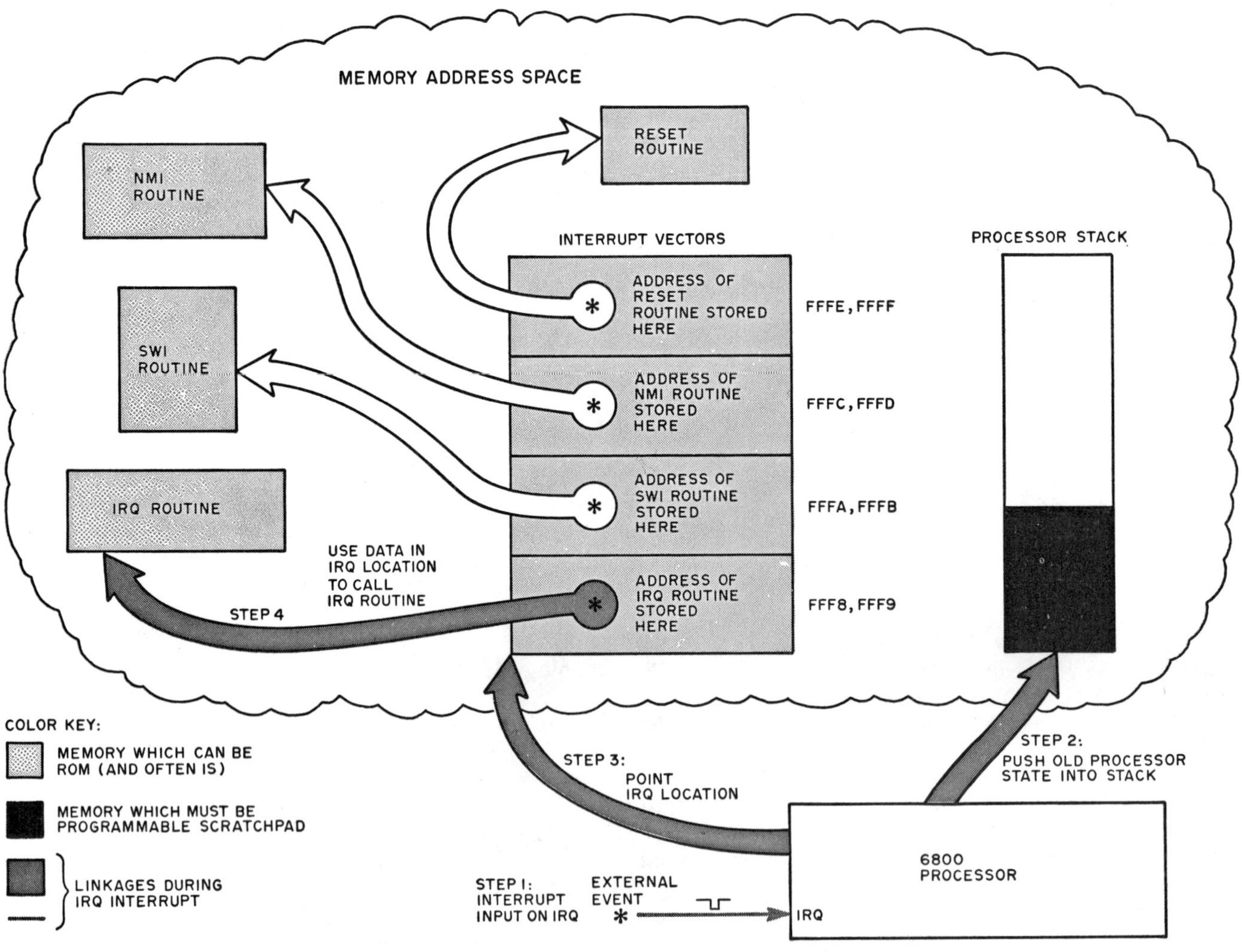

Figure 3: The 6800 processor's interrupt structure. This vectored interrupt method starts with an interrupt signal to the processor. In this example, IRQ occurs, so the processor generates a reference to the IRQ vector location at hexadecimal FFF8 and FFF9. The two-byte address at the IRQ vector location in turn points to the IRQ routine somewhere else in address space and as the last step in the process, the routine is called. As part of the special interrupt routine call, the old state information is pushed onto the stack.

games like *Star Trek*, generating time of day applications, and so on. A very interesting real-time application of interrupts is in the use of light pens on oscilloscope graphics displays. This is one use of computers that many hobbyists, upon seeing it operate for the first time, feel it just this side of magic. Actually, when you consider how the oscilloscope display is generated, the mechanism is very straightforward. You may deduce that the computer, or I/O device, must know where the beam of light is currently positioned on the scope's screen, or else it would be just a jumbled mess. Therefore, if a photosensitive device is placed close to the screen, an interrupt may be generated when the light beam strikes the cell. This interrupt may cause the location of the beam to be noted by storing the current values in the counters used to control the beam.

Another extremely interesting application is the emulation of hardwired instructions. If the processor allows software or illegal instruction interrupts, then software routines may be programmed to produce the same effect as if the desired instruction had actually been included in the silicon on the chip. For example, suppose that you frequently needed an instruction which would, for some unfathomable reason, add the contents of all the registers and output them to a teleprinter. You could set up a subroutine in each program that required this action. But if you found that you needed this instruction frequently in every program you ran on the machine, another way of implementing this routine would be to place into the running program's code something to cause an interrupt.

This interrupt would cause the interrupt routine to determine which action was desired, execute it, and then resume the interrupted program. Of course, the instruction would be executed much more slowly than if hardwired. Once the routine was finalized, it could be burned into read-only memory, and from then on it would always be available for the programmer's use.

The actual bit pattern inserted into the program to cause the interrupt varies with the processor. If there are unimplemented operation codes, then you may simply choose one and use it to signify the new operation from then on. If unimplemented operation codes do not exist or if they cause the machine to "hang up" and not interrupt, then a software interrupt, called a supervisor call on the IBM 370, may be used.

This is somewhat less pleasing, however, since the code on the program listing will always look the same (ie: a software interrupt) and make debugging a bit more difficult. The 6800's SWI instruction with its separate vector is ideally suited to this use. Obviously, a byte would have to be stored somewhere, signifying to the interrupt routine which operation was desired. In a 6800 this would be accomplished by following the SWI instruction with the appropriate 1-byte code and modifying the stack so that RTI returns control 1 byte past its normal point of return.

It is possible to reproduce a particular machine's entire instruction set on another entirely different machine in this manner. This is frequently called emulation, although the term is also used to describe this process being accomplished by microcode which, confusingly enough, is only remotely related to microprocessors.

Conclusion

We have seen that the use of interrupts allows computers to become more versatile than when they are dedicated to one program. Interrupts allow the machine to interact with the outside world, while at the same time allowing it to pursue its own interests. Interrupts are useful for accomplishing things in ways which, while perhaps more difficult to program initially, may be worthwhile in the ease of application.■

REFERENCES

1. *Intel 808 Microcomputer Systems User's Manual.* Intel Corporation, Santa Clara CA, July 1975.
2. *M6800 Systems Reference and Data Sheets.* Motorola Semiconductor Products Inc, Phoenix AZ.
3. *MCS6500 Microcomputer Family Programming Manual.* MOS Technology, Norristown, PA.

Optimization: A Case Study

William B Noyce

Whatever size computer one works with, there is usually pressure to make it perform a given task in less time or less memory. Optimization techniques are methods for accomplishing such speed or memory improvements. Usually the most effective changes to a program are algorithmic changes. These are changes to the strategy the program uses to achieve its result. An algorithmic change can reduce the time a program takes to run by 50% to 90%. For example, using the well-known quick sort or heap sort instead of a bubble sort to sort long lists can have this effect.

Sometimes, however, significant results can be achieved by *coding changes*, in which the modified program does essentially the same thing as the previous version, but in a better way. Most compilers perform optimizations of this type, such as keeping in a register any expression whose value is used more than once, rather than recomputing it whenever it is needed. Coding changes often exploit simple mathematical or logical identities.

This article follows through the step-by-step processes used to reduce by about 25% of the time and space taken by a small subroutine. The example subroutine is the "Novel 8 Bit Multiplication" by Christopher D Glaeser (July 1977 BYTE, page 142), that is reproduced in listing 1.

Coding changes are not effective at reducing the time taken by a program unless they are applied to the most heavily used parts of the program. If some part only accounts for 2% of the time used by the program, no optimizations applied only to this part can speed up the program by more than 2%. Usually, the most heavily used parts of a program are inside commonly used subroutines or deeply nested loops.

The eight instruction loop starting at LOOP in listing 1 acounts for about 80% of the time in the multiply subroutine. The loop works by testing, from right to left, bits of the number passed in C, and adding the number passed in D to the appropriate position on the partial product. The number whose bits are tested is called the multiplier, and the number that is added is called the multiplicand. The partial product is kept in HL, because it accumulates a 16-bit sum. Since the multiplicand needs to shift left, it is kept in DE, and XCHG instruction moves it into HL to be shifted. If we can eliminate the need to shift the multiplicand we can save the XCHG instructions and a little setup code.

The original loop computes:

$$2^0P_0+2^1P_1+2^2P_2+2^3P_3+2^4P_4+2^5P_5+2^6P_6+2^7P_7$$

where P_i = the multiplicand if bit i of the multiplier is 1, or 0 if the bit is 0. This expression is equivalent, by the distributive law, to:

$$((((((P_7\cdot 2+P_6)\cdot 2+P_5)\cdot 2+P_4)\cdot 2+P_3)\cdot 2+P_2)\cdot 2+P_1)\cdot 2+P_0$$

```
                 ; MULTIPLY C BY D, GIVING BC.
                 ; PRESERVES D,E,H,L.
                 ;
                 ; ORIGINAL PROGRAM BY CHRISTOPHER D GLAESER
                 ;
                 ;
                 ; 27 BYTES, ABOUT 512 CYCLES.
                 ;
0000 D5            MULT1:  PUSH D          ; SAVE REGISTERS
0001 E5                    PUSH H
0002 5A                    MOV E,D         ; MOVE MULTIPLICAND TO DE (LOWER)
0003 1600                  MVI D,0         ; AND CLEAR DE (UPPER)
0005 6A                    MOV L,D         ; CLEAR PRODUCT AREA
0006 62                    MOV H,D
0007 0608                  MVI B,8         ; LOOP COUNTER
0009 79                    MOV A,C         ; PUT MULTIPLIER WHERE IT CAN SHIFT

000A 1F            LOOP1:  RAR             ; TEST NEXT MULTIPLIER BIT
000B D20F00                JNC SKIP1
000E 19                    DAD D           ; ADD MULTIPLICAND
000F EB            SKIP1:  XCHG            ; SWAP DE WITH HL
0010 29                    DAD H           ; SHIFT MULTIPLICAND LEFT
0011 EB                    XCHG            ; SWAP BACK
0012 05                    DCR B
0013 C20A00                JNZ LOOP1       ; REPEAT 8 TIMES

0016 44                    MOV B,H         ; MOVE PRODUCT TO BC
0017 4D                    MOV C,L
0018 E1                    POP H           ; RESTORE REGISTERS
0019 D1                    POP D
001A C9                    RET             ; RETURN

                 $ EJECT
```

Listing 1: The starting point for this case study in optimization is a routine by Christopher D Glaeser, which appeared in July 1977 BYTE on page 142. This listing reproduces Christopher's multiplication algorithm, which takes 27 bytes of memory and about 512 cycles of the processor clock.

```
                 ; MULTIPLY C BY D, GIVING BC.
                 ; PRESERVES D,E,H,L.
                 ;
                 ; SHIFT PRODUCT INSTEAD OF MULTIPLICAND.
                 ; SHIFT MULTIPLIER LEFT INSTEAD OF RIGHT.
                 ;
                 ; 25 BYTES, ABOUT 448 CYCLES.
                 ;
001B D5            MULT2:  PUSH D          ; SAVE REGISTERS
001C E5                    PUSH H
001D 5A                    MOV E,D         ; MOVE MULTIPLICAND TO DE (LOWER)
001E 1600                  MVI D,0         ; AND CLEAR DE (UPPER)
0020 6A                    MOV L,D         ; CLEAR PRODUCT AREA
0021 62                    MOV H,D
0022 0608                  MVI B,8         ; LOOP COUNTER
0024 79                    MOV A,C         ; PUT MULTIPLIER WHERE IT CAN SHIFT

0025 29            LOOP2:  DAD H           ; SHIFT PRODUCT LEFT
0026 17                    RAL             ; TEST MEXT MULTIPLIER BIT
0027 D22B00                JNC SKIP2
002A 19                    DAD D           ; ADD MULTIPLICAND
002B 05            SKIP2:  DCR B
002C C22500                JNZ LOOP2       ; REPEAT 8 TIMES

002F 44                    MOV B,H         ; MOVE PRODUCT TO BC
0030 4D                    MOV C,L
0031 E1                    POP H           ; RESTORE REGISTERS
0032 D1                    POP D
0033 C9                    RET             ; RETURN

                 $ EJECT
```

Listing 2: By rearranging the code of the inner loop so that an equivalent operation is performed, some time can be saved. This, for an 8080, involves changing the order of shifting of the multiplier and using a double precision addition operation as the equivalent of a shift. This modified routine takes 25 bytes and executes in about 448 cycles.

This latter expression shows how we can shift the product left after every addition except the last, if we always add the multiplicand into the lower byte. If we added the multiplicand into the upper byte, we could shift the product to the right after every addition, but the 8080 has no 16-bit right-shift instruction. The change to shift the product left requires that we examine the leftmost multiplier bits first: the new inner loop appears in listing 2. Note that the product is shifted at the beginning of the loop; this is so it does not get shifted after the last time through.

Since the product is shifted left eight times, there is no need to clear its upper half initially with a MOV H, D instruction. Whatever garbage is in H will be shifted off and have no effect on the subroutine's result. But we can put these unused bits to work instead of wasting them. After *n* times through the loop there are $8 - n$ bits remaining in the multiplier and $8 - n$ unused bits in H, since the partial product occupies only $8 + n$ bits. The product and multiplier can coexist peacefully in HL, and every time the product is shifted, a bit of the multiplier falls out into the carry. We can thus eliminate the RAL instruction which shifted multiplier bits into the carry. The new subroutine appears in listing 3.

Where else can we save time or space? The user of the original subroutine obviously did not care whether the input values of registers A and C were preserved, but we do not use the registers in the loop. We can, however, save time and space by using these registers. Instead, program 3 uses B, D and E, and saves input values of D and E on the stack. Register pair DE was used as the multiplicand because we needed to use XCHG; DAD H; XCHG to shift it, but we no longer shift the multiplicand. Because we want our multiplicand in the lower byte of a register pair, we should use the number passed in C as the multiplicand and the number passed in D as the multiplier. This is legal because of the commutative law. Effectively, we save the MOV E, D which moves the multiplicand to the lower half of its register pair, and other instructions are changed. We can keep the loop counter in A, which is no longer needed for the multiplier. Now the subroutine no longer modifies D or E, so the PUSH D and POP D instructions may be deleted. The savings in stack space may or may not be important, depending on other parts of the

```
                     ; MULTIPLY C BY D, GIVING BC.
                     ; PRESERVES D,E,H,L.
                     ;
                     ; THE GREAT REGISTER SHUFFLE.  MULTIPLICAND IS IN BC,
                     ; MULTIPLIER IN H, AND LOOP COUNTER IN A.  DE IS NOT USED.
                     ;
                     ; 20 BYTES, ABOUT 385 CYCLES.
                     ;

004B E5              MULT4:  PUSH H        ; SAVE REGISTERS
004C 0600                    MVI B,0       ; CLEAR MULTIPLICAND HIGH BYTE
004E 68                      MOV L,B       ; CLEAR PRODUCT LOW BYTE
004F 62                      MOV H,D       ; MOVE MULTIPLIER TO HIGH PRODUCT AREA
0050 3E08                    MVI A,8       ; LOOP COUNTER

0052 29              LOOP4:  DAD H         ; SHIFT MULTIPLIER AND PRODUCT LEFT
0053 D25700                  JNC SKIP4     ; TEST A MULTIPLIER BIT
0056 09                      DAD B         ; ADD MULTIPLICAND
0057 3D              SKIP4:  DCR A
0058 C25200                  JNZ LOOP4     ; REPEAT 8 TIMES

005B 44                      MOV B,H       ; MOVE PRODUCT TO BC
005C 4D                      MOV C,L
005D E1                      POP H         ; RESTORE REGISTERS
005E C9                      RET           ; RETURN

                     $ EJECT
```

Listing 3: Having made the modifications of listing 2, the upper half of the HL register pair can initially contain arbitrary data. By actually using the most significant bits of HL, the product and multiplier can both be kept in this one register in a new version of the routine which takes 23 bytes and about 411 clock cycles.

```
                     ;MULTIPLY C BY D, GIVING BC.
                     ; PRESERVES D,E,H,L.
                     ;
                     ; KEEP MULTIPLIER AND PRODUCT TOGETHER IN HL.
                     ; 23 BYTES, ABOUT 411 CYCLES.
                     ;

0034 D5              MULT3:  PUSH D        ; SAVE REGISTERS
0035 E5                      PUSH H
0036 5A                      MOV E,D       ; MOVE MULTIPLICAND TO DE (LOWER)
0037 1600                    MVI D,0       ; AND CLEAR DE (UPPER)
0039 6A                      MOV L,D       ; CLEAR LOW PRODUCT AREA
003A 61                      MOV H,C       ; MOVE MULTIPLIER TO HIGH PRODUCT AREA
003B 0608                    MVI B,8       ; LOOP COUNTER

003D 29              LOOP3:  DAD H         ; SHIFT MULTIPLIER AND PRODUCT LEFT
003E D24200                  JNC SKIP3     ; TEST A MULTIPLIER BIT
0041 19                      DAD D         ; ADD MULTIPLICAND
0042 05              SKIP3:  DCR B
0043 C23D00                  JNZ LOOP3     ; REPEAT 8 TIMES

0046 44                      MOV B,H       ; MOVE PRODUCT TO BC
0047 4D                      MOV C,L
0048 E1                      POP H         ; RESTORE REGISTERS
0049 D1                      POP D
004A C9                      RET           ; RETURN

                     $ EJECT
```

Listing 4: By doing "the great register shuffle," further improvement can be accomplished by passing parameters in registers. This version chips away at time requirements and requires only 385 cycles, with 20 bytes of code.

```
                     ; MULTIPLY C BY D, GIVING BC.
                     ; PRESERVES D,E,H,L.
                     ;
                     ; LOOP IS PARTIALLY UNROLLED.
                     ;
                     ; 28 BYTES, ABOUT 325 CYCLES.
                     ;

005F E5              MULT5:  PUSH H        ; SAVE REGISTERS
0060 0600                    MVI B,0       ; CLEAR MULTIPLICAND HIGH BYTE
0062 68                      MOV L,B       ; CLEAR PRODUCT LOW BYTE
0063 62                      MOV H,D       ; MOVE MULTIPLIER TO HIGH PRODUCT AREA
0064 3E04                    MVI A,4       ; LOOP COUNTER (HALF NORMAL SIZE)

0066 29              LOOP5:  DAD H         ; SHIFT MULTIPLIER AND PRODUCT LEFT
0067 D26B00                  JNC SKIP5A    ; TEST A MULTIPLIER BIT
006A 09                      DAD B         ; ADD MULTIPLICAND
006B 29              SKIP5A: DAD H         ; -- REPEAT LOOP AGAIN --
006C D27000                  JNC SKIP5B
006F 09                      DAD B
0070 3D              SKIP5B: DCR A
0071 C26600                  JNZ LOOP5     ; REPEAT 4 TIMES

0074 44                      MOV B,H       ; MOVE PRODUCT TO BC
0075 4D                      MOV C,L
0076 E1                      POP H         ; RESTORE REGISTERS
0077 C9                      RET

                     $ EJECT
```

Listing 5: After virtually exhausting straight-forward improvements of the looping methods, the only further improvements possible come from unrolling the loop into larger amounts of program memory. This version partially unrolls the multiplication loop, takes 28 bytes of memory and about 325 cycles.

```
LOC  OBJ          SEQ          SOURCE STATEMENT

                  150 ;MULTIPLY C BY D, GIVING BC.
                  151 ; PRESERVES D,E,H,L.
                  152 ;
                  153 ; LOOP IS FULLY UNROLLED.
                  154 ;
                  155 ; 49 BYTES, ABOUT 258 CYCLES.
                  156 ;
                  157
0078 E5           158 MULT6:  PUSH H        ; SAVE REGISTERS
0079 0600         159         MVI B,0       ; CLEAR MULTIPLICAND HIGH BYTE
007B 68           160         MOV L,B       ; CLEAR PRODUCT AREA LOW BYTE
007C 62           161         MOV H,D       ; MOVE MULTIPLIER TO PRODUCT AREA HIGH BYTE
                  162
007D 29           163         DAD H         ; SHIFT MULTIPLIER AND PRODUCT LEFT
007E D28200       164         JNC SKIP6A    ; TEST A MULTIPLIER BIT
0081 19           165         DAD D         ; ADD MULTIPLICAND
0082 29           166 SKIP6A: DAD H         ; -- REPEAT LOOP 7 MORE TIMES --
0083 D28700       167         JNC SKIP6B
0086 19           168         DAD D
0087 29           169 SKIP6B: DAD H
0088 D28C00       170         JNC SKIP6C
008B 19           171         DAD D
008C 29           172 SKIP6C: DAD H
008D D29100       173         JNC SKIP6D
0090 19           174         DAD D
0091 29           175 SKIP6D: DAD H
0092 D29600       176         JNC SKIP6E
0095 09           177         DAD B
0096 29           178 SKIP6E: DAD H
0097 D29B00       179         JNC SKIP6F
009A 09           180         DAD B
009B 29           181 SKIP6F: DAD H
009C D2A000       182         JNC SKIP6G
009F 09           183         DAD B
00A0 29           184 SKIP6G: DAD H
00A1 D2A500       185         JNC SKIP6H
00A4 09           186         DAD B
                  187 SKIP6H:               ; -- END OF UNROLLED LOOP --
00A5 44           188         MOV B,H       ; MOVE PRODUCT TO BC
00A6 4D           189         MOV C,L
00A7 E1           190         POP H         ; RESTORE REGISTERS
00A8 C9           191         RET
                  192
                  193         END
```

Listing 6: Perhaps the ultimate 8-by-8 multiply short of a memory intensive full table lookup of answers is this fully unrolled version which expands the memory requirements to 49 bytes, but cuts the time requirements to 258 cycles for nearly 50% savings relative to the time requirement of the original program.

program in which the subroutine appears, but there is a significant saving in time and program size. The final version of the subroutine appears in listing 4. It is 20 bytes long, compared with 27 bytes for the original routine, and takes about 393 cycles, compared with about 525 cycles for the original routine. A million multiplications with a typical 8080 processor's clock would take about four minutes, 20 seconds with the old version and about three minutes, 15 seconds with the new.

If this is not fast enough, we can speed up the routine still further, by *unrolling* the loop, replicating its instructions as shown in listings 5 and 6. This eliminates some or all of the time taken by the DCR A and JNZ LOOP instructions which control is only executed four times instead of eight times, and in listing 6 there is no loop control at all. These speedup techniques cost memory, however, and tend to make the code more confusing. It is common to have to trade memory for speed, and which is more important depends on the particular program. With the long program, our million multiplications would take only about 2 minutes, 13 seconds, just over half as long as the original program.■

Low-Level Program Optimization:

Some Illustrative Cases

James Lewis

A program or subroutine can usually be modified so that it requires less time or space for execution. This observation about optimization suggests that a program or subroutine can usually be changed, so that it either runs faster or takes up less memory space, and one can often accomplish both at the same time.

Programs can be optimized for other things, such as readability, maintainability, structure, etc. This article, however, stresses optimization for time and space. If a program written for a microprocessor can be made shorter using space optimization, less memory can be used, or more functions can be packed into the same memory. Either way, optimization pays off. If the program can be made to run faster, more functions can be performed in the same amount of time. In fact, optimization can make the difference between whether or not an application of a microprocessor is feasible.

A distinction can be made between two types of optimization techniques. One is code optimization and the other is algorithmic optimization. Code optimization involves concentrating on the structure of the actual code on a low level. This includes such operations as recording instruction sequences and combining two instructions into one instruction. Algorithmic optimization is on a high level and involves rethinking the whole approach to a program or section of a program. This is much more general and powerful than code optimization, but its rules cannot easily be written down. It takes an experienced programmer or system designer to perform algorithmic optimization effectively. Examples of code-optimization tricks will be given below.

In the event that a program cannot be modified so that both space and time are lessened, there is usually the possibility of a trade-off. That is, if space is decreased, time will increase, and if time is decreased, space will increase. Only the particular situation can determine which route to take.

How much optimization is possible? Experience has shown that upon careful analysis a first draft program can typically be reduced by as much as 50% or more in terms of memory space. Time optimization is another story. Some programs can be accelerated at the expense of using more memory. However, significant time reductions can usually be made at little expense of memory; in fact, there may even be a savings of memory.

How much optimization should be done? In the process of optimizing a program, it becomes harder and harder to discover more program reductions. How far one should go depends on the relation between the cost of the programmer's time and the savings due to optimizations.

The process of optimization has fringe benefits. In analyzing a program, the programmer gains a clearer picture of how it works and often finds bugs. It is clear that a good software engineer should spend some time optimizing code.

Before discussing the techniques themselves, it should be pointed out that not all of the ideas mentioned are always beneficial. For example, one of the tricks reduces the elegance of the subroutine structure. If this type of elegance is desired, perhaps the trick should not be used.

The ideas presented are applicable to most microprocessors. They are intended for use on assembly-language programs, although some of them apply to other languages. An English assembly language is used in the examples for generality. Note that the command CALL SUB means push the return address on the stack and then jump to the subroutine.

The code-optimization examples will usually be presented in the following format:

Title	
Description of optimization technique	
Example of program before optimization	The same program shown after optimization

Returning a Call	
If a call to a subroutine is followed by a return instruction, the two instructions can be replaced by a jump to the subroutine.	
CALL ARNOLD RETURN	JUMP ARNOLD

Endless Subroutine	
If the last line of a subroutine is a jump to another subroutine, as in the first example, one can often position the subroutine which is jumped to direclty below the jump instruction, so that the jump instruction is not needed.	
JUMP BETTY CINDY: LOAD X . . . RETURN BETTY: STORE X . . . RETURN	BETTY: STORE X . . . RETURN CINDY: LOAD X . . . RETURN

Expanded Loop	
To increase the speed of an important loop, one can expand the loop either partially or wholly at the expense of space. This works best when the loop has a fixed number of iterations that is relatively small.	

```
        LOAD IMMEDIATE 10
LOOP:   CALL DANNY
        CALL EDDY
        DECREMENT
        JUMP IF NOT ZERO LOOP
```

```
LOAD IMMEDIATE 5
LOOP:   CALL DANNY
CALL EDDY
CALL DANNY
CALL EDDY
DECREMENT
JUMP IF NOT ZERO LOOP
```

Passing Fixed Data	
If a block of data has to be passed to a subroutine, rather than setting up and passing a pointer to the data, put the data directly following the call and rewrite the subroutine to look for the data at the return address. This may involve more code in the data processing subroutine, but can pay off in many cases. The subroutine must compute a new return address that follows the data, and use this altered return address instead of the original.	

```
        LOAD ADDRESS OF DATA
        CALL FARRAH
            .
            .
            .
DATA:   BYTES 36,24,36
```

```
        CALL FARRAH
DATA:   BYTES 36,24,36
```

Power of Two	
Short tables that have more than 1 byte per entry are easier to work with if the number of bytes per entry is a power of 2. This may waste some space in the table, but may save more space and also time in the code which handles the table. Computing an offset into a table that is a power of 2 can be done with a series of shifts instead of the integer multiplication that would otherwise be required.	

```
TABLE:  BYTES 36,24,26
        BYTES 36,22,37
        BYTES 38,23,38
        BYTES 35,20,34
```

```
TABLE:  BYTES 36,24,26,00
        BYTES 36,22,37,00
        BYTES 38,23,38,00
        BYTES 35,20,34,00
```

Use the Stack
Instead of saving temporary values at some memory location, they can often be saved on the stack. This usually holds true, even when manipulating data on top of the stack. The details are too machine dependent to give an example, but some of the newer microprocessors recognized this by having more than one hardware-implemented stack pointer.

Combine Instructions	
It is sometimes easy to miss the possibility of combining instructions. One situation which can be missed is when one can combine a symbolic value with a constant at assembly time rather than at execution time.	
LOAD IMMEDIATE ADDRESS ADD IMMEDIATE 1	LOAD IMMEDIATE ADDRESS +1

Multiple Additions

Normally, several ADD IMMEDIATE instructions in a row would be a bad idea. In a frequent situation, however, it can be very useful. Suppose one wants to pass a number to a subroutine and have the subroutine return 1, 2, or 3, depending on whether the passed number was 5, 12, or 13 respectively. Note that the optimization shown is of space at the expense of some time.

```
      COMPARE IMMEDIATE WITH 5
      JUMP IF EQUAL TO ONE
      COMPARE IMMEDIATE WITH 12
      JUMP IF EQUAL TO TWO
      LOAD IMMEDIATE 3
      RETURN
ONE:  LOAD IMMEDIATE 1
      RETURN
TWO:  LOAD IMMEDIATE 2
      RETURN
```

```
      COMPARE IMMEDIATE WITH 5
      JUMP IF EQUAL TO ONE
      COMPARE IMMEDIATE WITH 12
      JUMP IF EQUAL TO TWO
      ADD IMMEDIATE -6
ONE:  ADD IMMEDIATE 6
TWO:  ADD IMMEDIATE-10
      RETURN
```

[Editor's note: *The techniques presented here tend to produce nonstructured programs. The programmer must make a choice between readable structured code and speed optimized code. Structured-programming techniques are recommended for all programs not requiring crucial space and time specifications . . .* **RGAC]** ■

Queuing Theory, The Science of Wait Control

Part 1: Queue Representation

Len Gorney

How many times have you waited in a line? Do you always get to a supermarket checkout counter without having to wait? Is the pump at the gas station always open and ready for you as you drive into the service area? It's difficult to imagine anyone going anywhere and not having to wait in a line.

Since we are computer oriented, we should define a waiting line by its proper name — that is, a queue.

A queue is a waiting line controlled by some service mechanism. A customer enters a queue at the *tail* of the queue, waits in line until he or she arrives at the *head* of the queue, is serviced at the head of the queue, and, finally, leaves the queue. At the supermarket a customer pushes a cart to one of the lines formed at the checkout area and waits in a line until finally arriving at the cash register at the head of that line. After checking out the purchases, that customer leaves the queue.

Queue Examples

Other examples of queues can be found in many areas of our everyday lives. The supermarket checkout queue is a commercial type of queuing system. Other commercial queues include the bank teller queue, the barbershop queue, the gas station queue, etc. The field of transportation is not without its share of queues: traffic lights, turnpike toll booths, airport runways, loading and unloading docks are but a few examples.

Of course, we have personal queues. How about that shelf of books you're planning to read some day?

Let's Have Order

A queue is defined as a waiting line, and since a waiting line has both a beginning (ie: tail) and an end (ie: head), a queue must also have both these properties.

The head and tail idea implies that customers entering (ie: being inserted) or leaving (being deleted) must follow a definite ordering scheme as members of the queue. This ordering scheme is defined as the dispatching discipline of the queue.

The usual dispatching discipline of a queue is known as *first-in, first-out* or FIFO. An orderly queue exhibits this scheme. The first person entering the queue is the first person to receive service, and the last person entering the queue is the last person to receive service. Any person entering after the first but before the last must spend some

Listing 1: Simple BASIC simulation of a row queue. Pseudo-random-number generation is done to ensure that the queue simulation works correctly as described in the text. A sample run of the program is also shown.

```
1000        DIM Q(5)
1001   REM
1002   REM  INITIALIZE QUEUE TO EMPTY STATE
1003   REM
1010        FOR J2 = 1 TO 5
1020        Q(J2) = -9
1030        NEXT J2
1031   REM
1032   REM  INITIALIZE TAIL TO HEAD OF QUEUE
1033   REM
1040        T = 5
1041   REM
1042   REM  START OF MAIN SIMULATION LOOP
1043   REM
1050        FOR J2 = 1 TO 15
1051   REM
1052   REM  GENERATE A RANDOM NUMBER TO DETERMINE
1053   REM  AN INSERTION WHEN N < = 5
1054   REM  A DELETION WHEN N> = 6
1055   REM
1060        N = INT  (RND (1) * 10 ) + 1
1070        PRINT "NUMBER ="; N;
1080        IF N < =5 GOSUB 1170
1090        IF N > = 6 GOSUB 1240
1091   REM
1092   REM  PRINT QUEUE CONTENTS
1093   REM  PRINT TAIL POINTER VALUE
1094   REM
1100        PRINT "QUEUE=";
1110        FOR J3 = 1 TO 5
1120        PRINT Q(J3);
1130        NEXT J3
1140        PRINT "TAIL="; T
1141   REM
1142   REM  END OF MAIN SIMULATION LOOP
1143   REM
1150        NEXT J2
1160        STOP
1161   REM
1162   REM    I N S E R T I O N   R O U T I N E
1163   REM
1164   REM  WHEN T= 0 QUEUE IS FULL, I.E. OVERFLOW
1165   REM  ELSE, INSERT N AT TAIL AND DECREMENT TAIL
1166   REM
1170        IF T = 0 GOTO 1220
1180        PRINT " INSERTION";
1190        Q(T) = N
1200        T = T - 1
1210        RETURN
1220        PRINT " OVERFLOW";
1230        RETURN
1231   REM
1232   REM    D E L E T I O N   R O U T I N E
1233   REM
1234   REM  WHEN T= 5 QUEUE IS EMPTY, I.E. UNDERFLOW
1235   REM  ELSE, DELETE N AT HEAD OF QUEUE
1236   REM  AND MOVE REMAINING ITEMS TOWARD HEAD
1237   REM
1240        IF T = 5 GOTO 1350
1250        PRINT " DELETION";
1260        T = T + 1
1270        FOR J4 = 5 TO T STEP -1
1280        IF J4 = 1 GOTO 1330
1290        J5 = J4 - 1
1300        Q(J4) = Q(J5)
1310        NEXT J4
1320        RETURN
1330        Q(1) = -9
1340        RETURN
1350        PRINT " UNDERFLOW";
```

time waiting in the queue before service may be rendered.

The first-in, first-out discipline is but one of many ordering schemes that queues follow. Other servicing disciplines include last-in, first-out (eg: a stack of dishes), a priority queue and shortest line first or longest line first. These are multiple-queuing systems and will be discussed later.

Queue Representation

How can we represent a queue as part of a computer program? The following piece of BASIC coding, a one-dimensional array, could be used to represent a queue in a computer program:

10 DIM A(100).

A queue is nothing more than a special purpose one-dimensional array. Just as the ordinary one-dimensional array is represented as a single row or a single column structure *n* locations long or deep, the queue can be represented as a single row structure *n* locations long.

Over and Under

When an array is dimensional to 100 locations, the program cannot access the 104th or −36th location. These integer values are not within the boundaries of the dimensioning statement. If the program attempts to address out of range locations during execution of the program, an *overflow* or *underflow* condition occurs. Overflow occurs when a location greater than that given in the dimensioning statement is addressed. Likewise, underflow occurs when a negative subscript is given as an addressing value.

Some BASIC interpreters allow for addressing location 0 of an array. If an array is dimensioned to 100 locations, the actual number of legally addressable locations is 101 (by counting location 0 as the first available location).

The program listings in this article do not take advantage of this extra available array location. The first available location is always array location 1, and the last available location is equal to the integer value given in the dimensioning statement.

Let's get back to overflow and underflow as these conditions apply to queues. If we assume that our queuing program will not address a location above or below those given in the dimensioning statement, overflow and underflow take on a somewhat different meaning.

A queue overflow occurs when the program attempts to insert an item into our queue and the queue is filled to its capacity. Underflow in a queue structure occurs when the program attempts to delete an item from the queue, but there are no items in the queue.

Queue Operations

Items in an ordinary one-dimensional array can have many operations performed on them. A program can insert items anywhere within the array, and items can be removed from any legal location within the array. Items can be examined and left in place or moved to any location within an array.

A queue can have only two operations performed upon its items. The first of these allowable operations is the insertion of an item into the queue. This insertion can be done only at the tail of the queue. The second operation allows for deletion. Deletion is done only at the head of the queue.

The Simple Row Queue

The program shown in listing 1 is a simulation of a *row* queue. (See figure 1.) The mechanics of a row queue follow the definitions we have seen so far.

The row queue has its tail at location 1 of array Q, while its head is at location 5 of array Q. The choice of these locations for tail and head is arbitrary. I chose this scheme because it is easier to output the queue during execution of the program in a normal left-to-right reading fashion.

The head (ie: service facility area) of the queue of listing 1 is always at location Q(5). The tail of the queue (ie: the location in the queue where items will be inserted) moves from location 5 toward location 0 or array Q as items are inserted into the queue. When items are deleted, the tail of the queue moves from its present value toward location 5.

The tail of the row queue is indicated by a tail pointer — variable T. When T is 5 the queue is empty, that is, there are no items in the queue. When T is 0 the queue is filled to its capacity and no insertions can be made without causing an overflow condition.

To simulate the action of a queue properly, listing 1 generates pseudorandom numbers to determine queue in-

Listing 1 continued:

```
1360        RETURN
1370  END

RUN
NUMBER= 7  UNDERFLOW  QUEUE=-9   -9 -9 -9 -9 TAIL= 5
NUMBER= 3  INSERTION  QUEUE=-9   -9 -9 -9  3 TAIL= 4
NUMBER= 7  DELETION   QUEUE=-9   -9 -9 -9 -9 TAIL= 5
NUMBER= 4  INSERTION  QUEUE=-9   -9 -9 -9  4 TAIL= 4
NUMBER= 1  INSERTION  QUEUE=-9   -9 -9  1  4 TAIL= 3
NUMBER= 3  INSERTION  QUEUE=-9   -9  3  1  4 TAIL= 2
NUMBER= 2  INSERTION  QUEUE=-9    2  3  1  4 TAIL= 1
NUMBER= 5  INSERTION  QUEUE= 5    2  3  1  4 TAIL= 0
NUMBER= 2  OVERFLOW   QUEUE= 5    2  3  1  4 TAIL= 0
NUMBER= 8  DELETION   QUEUE=-9    5  2  3  1 TAIL= 1
NUMBER= 7  DELETION   QUEUE=-9   -9  5  2  3 TAIL= 2
NUMBER= 8  DELETION   QUEUE=-9   -9 -9  5  2 TAIL= 3
NUMBER= 3  INSERTION  QUEUE=-9   -9  3  5  2 TAIL= 2
NUMBER= 4  INSERTION  QUEUE=-9    4  3  5  2 TAIL= 1
NUMBER= 9  DELETION   QUEUE=-9   -9  4  3  5 TAIL= 2
```

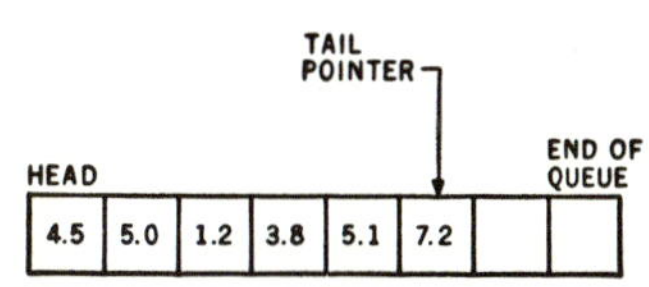

Figure 1: Simple row queue. This type of queue has a stationary head and a moving tail. As data items are deleted from the head, all of the data items in the queue are moved toward the head, and the tail pointer is decremented by 1. As more data is entered into the queue as the tail, the location of the tail pointer is incremented by one location.

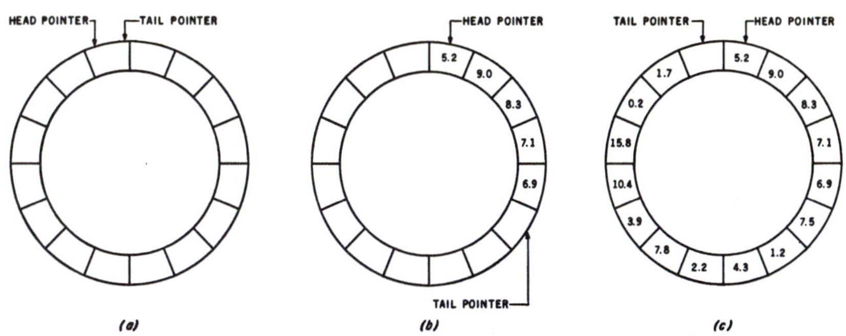

Figure 2: Circular queue in three states of use. Figure 2a is an empty queue, in which the head pointer and the tail pointer point to the same location in the queue. Figure 2b shows a partially filled circular queue. The tail pointer moves ahead of the head pointer as data items are added to the queue. As an item is deleted, the head pointer moves towards the tail pointer. Figure 2c shows a full queue. In this state the tail pointer has caught up with the head pointer. Note that one location in the queue will be left empty. If this were not done, the next item added to the queue would make the head and tail pointers point to the same location, which would seem to indicate that the queue was empty.

Listing 2: BASIC listing for a circular simulation. Lines 1900 through 2100 are the insertion routine; lines 2110 through 2270 are the deletion routine. A sample run of the program is shown at the end of the listing.

```
1000        DIM Q(5)
1001  REM
1002  REM   INITIALIZE QUEUE TO EMPTY STATE
1003  REM
1010        FOR J2 = 1 TO 5
1020        Q(J2) = -9
1030        NEXT J2
1031  REM
1032  REM   INITIALIZE HEAD AND TAIL POINTERS
1033  REM   TO HEAD OF QUEUE LOCATION
1034  REM
1040        H = 5
1050        T = 5
1051  REM
1052  REM   START OF MAIN SIMULATION LOOP
1053  REM
1060        FOR J3 = 1 TO 10
1061  REM
1062  REM   GENERATE A RANDOM NUMBER TO DETERMINE
1063  REM   AN INSERTION WHEN N < = 5
1064  REM   A DELETION WHEN N > = 6
1065  REM
1070        N = INT ( RND (1) * 10 ) + 1
1080        IF N < = 5 GOSUB 1900
1090        IF N > = 6 GOSUB 2110
1091  REM
1092  REM   PRINT QUEUE CONTENTS
1093  REM   PRINT TAIL AND HEAD POINTER VALUES
1094  REM
1100        FOR J4 = 1 TO 5
1110        PRINT Q(J4);
1120        NEXT J4
1130        PRINT " TAIL AT"; T; " HEAD AT"; H
1131  REM
1132  REM   END OF MAIN SIMULATION LOOP
1133  REM
1140        NEXT J3
1150        STOP
1151  REM
1152  REM     I N S E R T I O N   R O U T I N E
1153  REM
1154  REM   CHECK TAIL AND HEAD POINTER VALUES
1155  REM
1900        IF H = T GOTO 1970
1910        IF H < GOTO 2030
1920        IF T> = 1 GOTO 2030
1930        IF H = 5 GOTO 2080
1931  REM
1932  REM   INSERT ITEM AT Q(H)
1933  REM   SINCE QUEUE IS EMPTY
1934  REM
1940        Q(5) = N
1950        T = 4
1960        GOTO 2050
1970        IF T <> 0 GOTO 2000
1971  REM
1972  REM   RESET POINTERS TO HEAD OF QUEUE
1973  REM
1980        H = 5
1990        T = 5
1991  REM
1992  REM   CHECK IF Q(T) EMPTY FOR POSSIBLE INSERT
1993  REM
2000        IF Q(T) <> -9 GOTO2080
2010        H = 5
2020        T = 5
2021  REM
2022  REM   NORMAL TAIL INSERTION
2023  REM
2030        Q(T) = N
2040        T = T - 1
```

sertion or deletion. The importance of randomness in proper queue operation is explained later.

Before you execute the program in listing 1, run through its operations with pencil and paper. This approach will show you how the program will *run* before the actual operation is simulated by the computer. This method will also clarify the mechanics of a simple row queue operation.

The Circular Queue

A major disadvantage of our simple row queue is the fact that items must be moved toward the head of the queue after each deletion. *[**Editor's Note:** This is not true, however for all implementations of a row queue. Often, the pointers indicating the head and tail of the row queue are moved instead of all the data inside the queue . . .* **RGAC***]* The loop in line numbers 1370 thru 1400 of listing 1 accomplishes this move. If we're trying to represent a queue simulation in a computer program, why not use some programming techniques to take advantage of decreasing execution time and thereby eliminate some of the unwieldy code?

The circular queue, figure 2, is also represented as a special-purpose, one dimensional array. The simple row queue has a pointer to keep track of the location where the next item insertion was to take place. The circular queue also has this tail pointer.

The difference between the row and circular queue lies in the addition of another pointer to indicate the location of the head of the queue. The simple row queue always has its head at the last available location of the array Q. The circular queue structure can have its head anywhere within the queue.

Circular Queue Representation

The circular queue operates in the same manner as the simple row queue. Items are still inserted into the location given as the tail point location of array Q.

The major difference is in the way which the program controls the head location of the queue. A new variable for head pointer called H points to the array location which holds the item ready for deletion.

An item is inserted into the queue at the location pointed to by the tail pointer. After this insertion, the pointer is moved by one location in readiness for another insertion. When an item is deleted, the head pointer comes into play. In the simple row queue, the head is always at the last available location. In the circular queue, the head of the queue is defined by the value of the head pointer variable H. After an item is deleted, the head pointer is moved one location toward the value of the tail pointer. In this structure, data items remain stationary; only the pointers vary, indicating relative positions of the tail and the head of the queue.

This queue structure is clearly advantageous when we're dealing with long queues. If a row queue is filled to its capacity and an item is deleted, every remaining item has to be moved one at a time toward the stationary head of the row queue. The circular queue moves the head pointer by only one location, thereby cutting program execution time.

The tradeoff is time versus space. The circular queue program is longer than the simple row queue; however, the time to execute the circular queue routine is shorter since the majority of code execution in the simple row queue is during the moving of the items after a delete operation.

In the circular queue, the tail pointer chases the head pointer during insertions. During deletions, the head pointer chases the tail pointer.

When the circular queue is filled to capacity, the head and tail pointers are at adjacent locations. No more items may be inserted simply because there is no more available space to fit an item into the queue. An overflow condition occurs if an insertion is attempted on a filled queue.

An underflow occurs when the queue is empty and a deletion is attempted. An empty circular queue is one in which the tail and the head pointers are at the same location in the array Q.

The program given in listing 2 simulates a circular queue. Again, a pencil and paper method of initial execution may prove helpful. After the mechanics of this structure are understood, then execute the program.

This completes our discussion of two different types of queues and their representation in a computer. In part 2 we will consider queues in the world around us and fit them into the structures already developed.■

Listing 2 continued:

```
2050        PRINT " "
2060        PRINT "ARRIVAL"
2070        RETURN
2080        PRINT" "
2090        PRINT "OVERFLOW"
2100        RETURN
2101  REM
2101  REM   D E L E T I O N   R O U T I N E
2103  REM
2104  REM   CHECK POINTER VALUES FOR POSSIBLE DELETE
2105  REM
2110        IF H = T GOTO 2150
2101        IF H > 0 GOTO 2190
2130        H = 5
2140        GOTO 2180
2150        IF H <>0 GOTO 2180
2160        H = 5
2170        T = 5
2171  REM
2172  REM   DELETE FROM Q(H) HAS AN ITEM
2173  REM   ELSE, QUEUE IS EMPTY, I.E. UNDERFLOW
2174  REM
2180        IF Q(H) = -9 GOTO 2240
2190        Q(H) = -9
2200        H = H - 1
2201  REM
2202  REM   RESET POINTERS FOR NEXT DELETE
2203  REM
2210        IF H <> 0 GOTO 2260
2220        H = 5
2230        RETURN
2240        PRINT " "
2250        PRINT "UNDERFLOW"
2260        RETURN
2270  END

RUN

ARRIVAL
-9  -9  -9  -9   3  TAIL AT 4 HEAD AT 5

ARRIVAL
-9  -9  -9   2   3  TAIL AT 3 HEAD AT 5

ARRIVAL
-9  -9   4   2   3  TAIL AT 2 HEAD AT 5
-9  -9   4   2  -9  TAIL AT 2 HEAD AT 4

ARRIVAL
-9   5   4   2  -9  TAIL AT 1 HEAD AT 4

ARRIVAL
 3   5   4   2  -9  TAIL AT 0 HEAD AT 4

ARRIVAL
 3   5   4   2   1  TAIL AT 4 HEAD AT 4

OVERFLOW

 3   5   4  -9   1  TAIL AT 4 HEAD AT 3

ARRIVAL
 3   5   4   3   1  TAIL AT 3 HEAD AT 3
```

Queuing Theory, The Science of Wait Control

Part 2: System Types

Len Gorney

In part 1 we discussed the computer implementation of *row* and *circular* queues. Now, let us take a look at the strucutre of queues in the real world and see if they can be fitted to our previous programs. In the following discussion, the word *queue* refers to the waiting line in the system. The word *facility* refers to the service facility area located at the head of the queue.

System Types

There are four general types of queuing structures. The first, and simplest, is the single-queue single-facility system shown in figure 3. In this structure, there is one waiting line and one service area to be studied. A one-pump gas station with one entrance is a real world example of this system.

We can extend this system to the single queue multifacility system shown in figure 4. In this structure, customers line up in a single waiting line and are serviced at the first of a series of facilities. Upon departure from the first facility, the customers immediately enter another queue to await their turn at the second service facility. This insertion and deletion continues until the customer is eventually deleted from the last facility and consequently the entire system. This structure is not unlike a cafeteria where you first line up for a sandwich, then line up for dessert, then for a drink, and finally, for the cash register.

Another basic queue structure is a multiqueue single facility system shown in figure 5. This is the type of structure you see at a typical supermarket checkout counter area. Customers arrive at the queue with their purchases and choose one of many waiting lines. Each service facility offers the same service, that is, checking out the purchases, but each line holds different customers.

The multiqueue multifacility system in figure 6 is a combination of the previously mentioned structures. A number of initial queues feed into a series of facilities. When a customer enters a particular queue, that customer travels from each facility within that subsystem until the eventual deletion from the system. Once a customer is entered into a subsystem, that customer causes that subsystem to behave as does the single queue multifacility queue system.

Any waiting line can be fitted to one of the four queue structures just mentioned. Try it the next time you're waiting in a line.

After we are able to define the type of queue we have, the problem of analyzing the structure and arriving at answers

Note: The numbering of the figures and listings is continued from part 1.

most important in queuing problems is our next step. At this time we will not concern ourselves with the difference between a single server or a multiserver queue. The former represents a grocery store checkout counter arrangement where customers enter any line — usually the shortest or the fastest moving. The latter fits into the situation at a barbershop. One long line feeds into a large service area where a number of barbers (ie: the servers) wait for you to come to them.

Let's imagine a one-pump gas station. At the start of the day, the operator (ie: server) opens the pump and waits for the first customer of the day to arrive. After some period of time, the first customer arrives and immediately drives up to the pump for service. This lucky first customer has no waiting time since the facility at the head of the queue is open and free of previous customers. The customer requires some period of time for service, and upon completion of this serving time leaves the system. The operator sits back and waits for the next customer to arrive.

The second customer arrives, is immediately served, and leaves the system. If the only time a customer spends in a queue is the time required for service, no queue forms. What we need for a queue to form is to have customers arrive while there is a customer being serviced. Then a line will form with waiting customers. The queue will form based entirely upon the service requirements of the customer at the service area.

Randomness

A pure queuing problem requires that customer arrival and service times be different. In other words, while a customer is being serviced, other customers enter the system at random

Figure 3: A single-queue single-facility system with one waiting line and one service area.

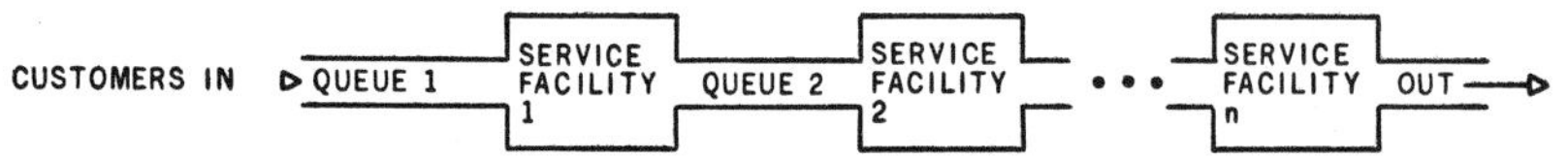

Figure 4: Single-queue multifacility system, in which the customer waits in a queue to use a facility, then waits in another queue for the second facility, and so on until all service facilities have been used.

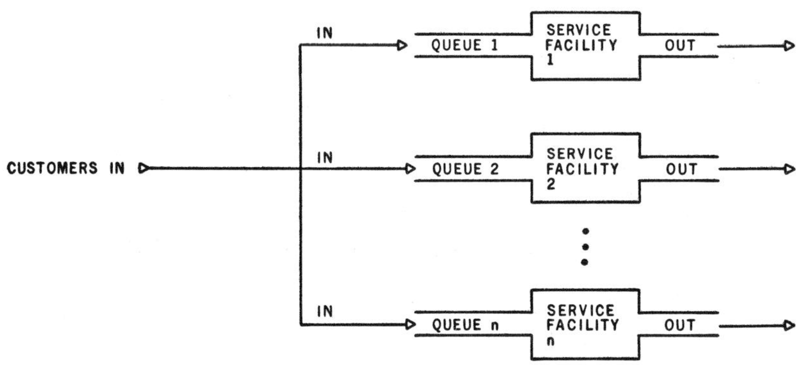

Figure 5: Multiqueue single-facility system. An example of such a system is the supermarket checkout area. The checkout area has several service facilities, each with a corresponding queue, that all offer the same service.

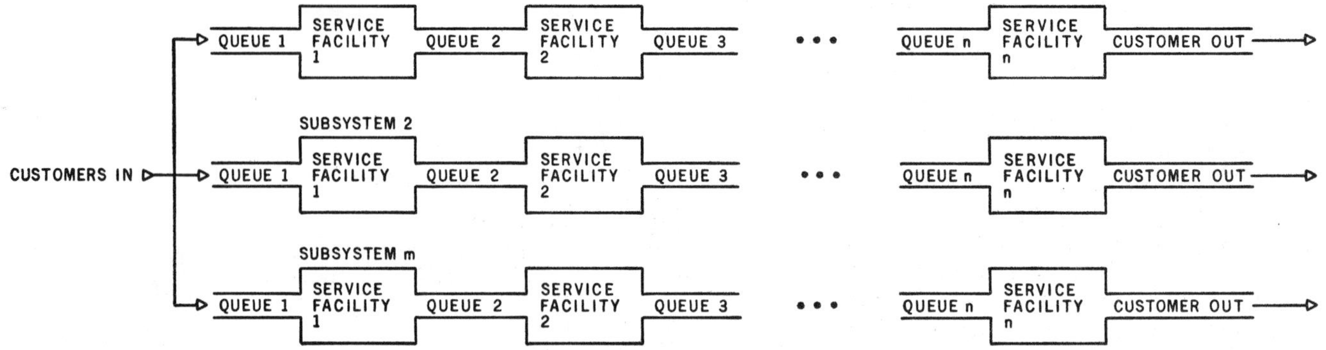

Figure 6: Multiqueue, multifacility system. This system has a number of initial queues feeding into a series of facilities. A customer entering a particular queue stays within that particular subsystem until leaving the system.

intervals during the simulation period to form a queue.

Formally speaking, the randomness of these arrivals follows a *Poisson distribution* and exponential interarrival times. Basically, this means that an arrival has an equal chance of arriving at the tail of the queue at any time during the simulation period of the problem. Typical nonqueue structures do not exhibit this random criterion. For example, a movie theater line is not a good queue problem because arrivals usually bunch up in a period 10 to 15 minutes before the new show starts. Therefore, during the simulation period, randomness is a key ingredient. Randomness causes the queue to lengthen and to shorten bases only on the service requirements of each customer.

Usually a customer must wait in a line at any business establishment before receiving the desired service. How the businessman treats these waiting customers is of prime importance as to the success or failure of most businesses. A typical customer will take one of the following actions when faced with a waiting line. The first action is to just wait in the line until service arrives. Once in line, that customer will remain in line until the end. The businessman has little worry over this customer because this customer will eventually be serviced and some profit will be realized.

A second alternative open to a waiting customer is for that customer to jockey from line to line. How many times have you seen this customer arrive at one queue, wait for a short period of time, move to another queue, wait again, then move again, and so on. This situation exists in the multiqueue system as is evidenced in a bank or large supermarket with many service facilities available for customer use.

The previous two actions should cause little concern. The customer remains in the system and will eventually be served, thereby yielding the business some profit. However, what happens when the customer leaves the system after entering or refuses to enter the system initially?

If a customer has entered the system and leaves before being serviced, that customer has reneged. This situation occurs quite often when the waiting lines are moving at a rate far too slow for the customers within the lines. The customer and possible profits are lost to the businessman when a customer's action takes him or her on this route.

Listing 3: BASIC program that simulates a single-queue single-facility system such as a one-pump gas station. The program incorporates several functions discussed in part 1.

```
1000 DIM Q(10)
1010 PRINT "MINUTES TO RUN SIMULATION=";
1020 INPUT M
1030 PRINT "MAXIMUM ARRIVALS/UNIT TIME=";
1040 INPUT A2
1050 PRINT "MINIMUM SERVICE TIME=";
1060 INPUT S2
1070 PRINT "MAXIMUM SERVICE TIME=";
1080 INPUT S3
1090 PRINT "QUEUE LENGHT=";
1100 INPUT H2
1110 PRINT "INPUT 1 FOR RUNNING OUTPUT, ELSE INPUT 0";
1120 INPUT P
1130 C = 0
1140 C2 = 0
1150 C3 = 0
1160 C4 = 0
1170 M2 = 0
1180 M3 = 0
1190 S4 = 0
1200 H = H2
1210 T = H2
1220 FOR J2 = 1 TO H2
1230 Q(J2) = -9
1240 NEXT J2
1250 Q(T) = 0
1260 T = T - 1
1270 GOSUB 1610
1280 FOR J = 1 TO M
1290 FOR J2 = 1 TO H2
1300 IF Q(J2) = -9 THEN 1330
1310 C = C + 1
1320 Q(J2) = Q(J2) + 1
1330 NEXT J2
1340 C2 = C2 + C
1350 IF C <= C3 THEN 1370
1360 C3 = C
1370 C = 0
1380 IF P = 0 THEN 1410
1390 PRINT "PICTURE OF QUEUE AFTER"; J;"MINUTES"
1400 GOSUB 1680
1410 IF Q(H) < M3 THEN 1520
1420 M2 = M2 + M3
1430 C4 = C4 + 1
1440 S4 = S4 + S
1450 IF P = 0 THEN 1470
1460 GOSUB 1730
1470 GOSUB 2110
1480 GOSUB 1610
1490 IF P = 0 THEN 1520
1500 PRINT "PICTURE OF QUEUE AFTER DELETE"
1510 GOSUB 1680
1520 A3 = 1
1530 A = INT (RND(1) * A2)
1540 IF A3 > A THEN 1580
1550 GOSUB 1900
1560 A3 = A3 + 1
1570 GOTO 1540
1580 NEXT J
1590 GOSUB 1730
1600 STOP
1610 S = INT(RND (1) * (S3 - 9)
1620 IF Q(H) = -9 THEN 1640
1630 Q(H) = 0
1640 M3 = Q(H) + S
1650 IF P = 0 THEN 1670
1660 PRINT "REQUIRED SERVICE TIME=";S
1670 RETURN
1680 FOR J2 = 1 TO H2
1690 PRINT Q(J2);
1700 NEXT J2
1710 PRINT "TAIL=";T;" HEAD=";H
1720 RETURN
```

```
1730 PRINT C4; " FULLY SERVED CUSTOMERS IN";J;"MINUTES"
1740 PRINT "MAXIMUM CUSTOMERS QUEUED=";C3
1750 M5 = M2/C4
1760 PRINT "AVERAGE WAIT TIME=";M5
1770 S5 = S4/C4
1780 PRINT "AVERAGE SERVICE TIME=";S5
1790 C5 = C2/J
1800 PRINT "AVERAGE NUMBER OF QUEUED CUSTOMERS="; C5
1810 RETURN
1850 REM
1860 REM   I N S E R T I O N   R O U T I N E
1870 REM
1880 REM  CHECK TAIL AND HEAD POINTER VALUES
1890 REM
1900      IF H = T GOTO 1970
1910      IF H < T GOTO 2030
1920      IF T >= 1 GOTO 2030
1930      IF H = H2 GOTO 2080
1931 REM
1932 REM  INSERT ITEM AT Q(H)
1933 REM  SINCE QUEUE IS EMPTY
1934 REM
1940      Q(H2)=0
1950      T=H2-1
1960      GOTO 2050
1970      IF T <> 0 GOTO 2000
1971 REM
1972 REM  RESET POINTERS TO HEAD OF QUEUE
1973 REM
1980      H=H2
1990      T=H2
1991 REM
1992 REM  CHECK IF Q(T) EMPTY FOR POSSIBLE INSERT
1993 REM
2000      IF Q(T) <> -9 GOTO 2080
2010      H=H2
2020      T=H2
2021 REM
2022 REM  NORMAL TAIL INSERTION
2023 REM
2030      Q(T)=0
2040      T=T-1
2050      IF P = THEN 2070
2060      PRINT "ARRIVAL"
2070      RETURN
2080      IF P=0 THEN 2100
2090      PRINT "OVERFLOW"
2100      RETURN
2101 REM
2102 REM   D E L E T I O N   R O U T I N E
2103 REM
2104 REM  CHECK POINTER VALUES FOR POSSIBLE DELETE
2105 REM
2110      IF H=T GOTO 2150
2120      IF H>0 GOTO 2190
2130      H=H2
2140      GOTO 2180
2150      IF H<>0 GOTO 2180
2160      H=H2
2170      T=H2
2171 REM
2172 REM  DELETE FROM Q(H) IF Q(H) HAS AN ITEM
2173 REM  ELSE, QUEUE IS EMPTY, I.E. UNDERFLOW
2174 REM
2180      IF Q(H)= -9 GOTO 2240
2190      Q(H)= -9
2200      H=H-1
2201 REM
2202 REM  RESET POINTERS FOR NEXT DELETE
2203 REM
2210      IF H <>0 GOTO 2260
2220      H=H2
2230      RETURN
2240      IF P=0 THEN 2260
2250      PRINT "UNDERFLOW"
2260      RETURN
2270 END
```

The last, and most damanging to the businessman, is the situation where a customer does not initially enter the system. When a customer sees a long and slow moving line, that customer usually balks. This customer is surely lost because he does not even give the businessman a chance at the very outset.

Since time is money, the important questions relating to queuing systems must be solved with relation to the time involved in waiting and servicing customers.

What is the maximum amount of time a customer waits in a line? What is the average amount of time all the customers are expected to wait in line before being served and deleted? What is the maximum amount of service time for any one customer during a typical period of time? Any measurement involving customer waiting time and customer service time is vital to the success or failure of a business.

A Queuing Problem

The program shown in listing 3 is that of a typical queuing problem utilizing the circular queue as the queuing structure. What we may have here is a hypothetical one-pump gas station. The system will therefore be described as a single-queue single-facility structure.

Past experience gives us some of the input parameters required for the problem solution. For example, our queue is dimensioned to ten locations, so only ten cars can fit in our service area. This parameter can be adjusted using input parameter questions at the beginning of the program. In addition to the queue length, the program asks for the minimum and maximum typical service times. The arrivals per unit time determine how many customers are arriving each minute during the simulation. The simulation is halted after the first parameter value is reached, namely, the amount of time to run the model.

Conclusion

For the serious reader, the list of reference material includes those texts that place a good emphasis on queuing theory. After digesting the ideas in this article, plunge into these texts. Now I can return to my reading queue and get to those lines of books and articles waiting on my bookshelf. I'm sure that somewhere a line is waiting for you! ■

BIBLIOGRAPHY

1. Cooper. *Introduction to Queueing Theory.* Macmillan, New York, 1972.

2. Cox, Smith. *Queues.* John Wiley and Sons, New York, 1961.

3. Gross, Harris. *Fundamentals of Queuing Theory.* John Wiley and Sons, New York, 1974.

4. Harrison. *Data Structures and Programming.* Scott, Foresman, Glenview IL, 1973.

5. Hilier, Lieberman. *Operations Research.* Holden-Day, San Francisco, 1974.

6. Siemens, Marting. Greenwood, *Operations Research.* Macmillan, New York, 1973.

7. Wagner. *Principles of Operations Research.* Prentice-Hall, Englewood Cliffs NJ, 1975.

An Introduction to BNF

W D Maurer

BNF is a standardized method of abbreviating certain statements which are made about a programming language when it is being strictly defined, as in a programming manual. As such, BNF bears an analogy to the use of algebra in order to simplify certain statements which are made about physical and mathematical quantities. Thus the statement that the volume of a sphere is equal to four-thirds the cube of the radius times the ratio of the circumference of a circle to its diameter may be abbreviated as:

$$V = \frac{4\pi r^3}{3}$$

In order to make abbreviations such as the one above, we set up various conventions. For example:

1. The quantities in the statement are represented by single letters; thus, V stands for the volume.
2. Squares, cubes, and other powers are represented by superscript notation; thus, r^3 is the cube of r.
3. Certain fixed quantities which appear very often have standard names; thus, the ratio of the circumference of a circle to its diameter is always denoted by π.
4. Two single letters written together signify "times"; thus, πr means π times r. (This rule must be amplified in order to specify clearly that πr^3 means π times the cube of r, and not the cube of πr; and to make clear that it also applies to numbers, so that 4π means 4 times π.)

We shall now set up a number of similar conventions in order to abbreviate statements made about programming languages. For example, consider the following sentence:

A GO TO Statement in FORTRAN consists of the word GO TO followed by a statement number.

We may abbreviate this in BNF as follows:

< GO TO statement > :: =
'GO TO' < statement number >

In doing this we have implicitly set up the following conventions:

1. The signs < and >, which also stand for "less than" and "greater than" but in this context are called *angle brackets,* enclose the name of some "quantity" which we wish to define in the programming language. We call such a "quantity" a *syntactical variable.*
2. The special sign :: = means "is defined as." This comes from ALGOL, in which the sign := is the replacement symbol, used in statements such as A: =B (ie: set A equal to B).
3. The words "followed by" may be omitted, just as "times" may be omitted in algebra.

There is a further analogy between BNF and algebra. When we write 'GO TO' <statement number>, we mean the words GO TO followed by *any* statement number. This is very much like writing 3x to mean 3 times the value of x, whatever it happens to be. Here, x is a variable, but 3 is a constant. Similarly, the phrase < statement number > is a syntactical variable, and may stand for any of various statement numbers; but 'GO TO' always stands for the same thing, and may thus be called a *syntactical constant.* Syntactical constants are subject to another rule:

4. A syntactical constant is enclosed in quotes.

This last rule, incidentally, is not always followed. The single quote character ' is actually meaningful in some programming languages, and its use in programming-language definition would cause confusion here. Of course, we can always use the double quote " instead of the single quote, unless the programming language uses both of these symbols (like SNOBOL, for instance). But sometimes even when there is no confusion, the quotes are omitted for the sake of brevity.

It is clear, of course, that statements about programming languages may be abbreviated even further. We might write G → 'GO TO' S, thus incorporating the use of single letters for variables, as is done in algebra. In fact, this type of abbreviation is used extensively in the theory of context-free languages. (See references 2 and 3 for two interesting applications of this theory and this type of abbreviation to programming languages.) The trouble with abbreviating this far is that now the abbreviation is not self-contained. We must still make some statement such as "where S stands for a statement number." In contrast, the BNF rules which we define here permit the entire syntax, or "grammar rules" of a language, to be specified in a precise manner, using no other information than that contained in the BNF rules themselves. The semantics, or "meaning" of the language, must still be specified separately; and at this time there is no easy and fairly universal way to specify semantics, although attempts have been made. (See references 2 and 4.)

Rules in BNF may be extremely simple. We may write:

< statement number > :: =
< unsigned integer >

to specify that the syntactical variable "statement number" takes the same form as the syntactical variable "unsigned integer." This is often convenient when several syntactical variables have the same form. In most languages, for example, simple variable names, array names, and function (or subroutine or procedure) names all follow the same rules about starting with a letter, etc, and we define each of them to be the same as the syntactical variable < identifier >.

Sometimes, in a definition of this type, there will be more than one alternative. For example, let us make a definition of "integer" not restricted to unsigned integers. If we already know what an unsigned integer is, we may use the following:

> *An integer is an unsigned integer optionally preceded by a plus or a minus sign.*

The conventions which we have used thus far do not allow for the words *optionally* or *preceded by,* although *followed by* is permitted. Therefore, let us make an equivalent definition, which is slightly longer:

> *An integer is either: (1) an unsigned integer; or (2) a plus sign followed by an unsigned integer; or (3) a minus sign followed by an unsigned integer.*

Now all we need is a symbol for "or." The symbol we use is the vertical line |. Thus our abbreviated definition is:

<integer> :: = <u.i.> | '+' <u.i.>
| '−' <u.i.>

where we have used "u.i." for unsigned integer" in order to keep the definition from running off the end of the line. Actually, this precaution is not necessary. Rules in BNF, just like statements in ALGOL, may run to several lines, and position on a given line is immaterial, although, in practice, a definition will be started at the beginning of a new line. Thus:

<integer> :: = <unsigned integer>
| '+' <unsigned integer>
| '−' <unsigned integer>

is a self-contained BNF rule equivalent to the one given above.

The vertical line is often used for "lowest-level" definitions, in which a syntactical variable is being defined as any one of a certain collection of characters. Thus:

<digit> :: ='0'|'1'|'2'|'3'
|'4'|'5'|'6'
|'7'|'8'|'9'

is a very common definition. Note that this defines only a single digit, not an arbitrary integer; 63, for example, is not a digit by this definition. We may, if we wish, define "letter" in the same way, as any one of the twenty-six letters of the alphabet. We may even define "alphanumeric character" as any one of thirty-six different symbols, although what is usually done is to define "letter" and "digit" first, and then to define:

<alphanumeric character> :: =
<letter>
|<digit>

The definition of an integer, or of an identifier, is slightly more complex. An unsigned *two-digit* integer may be defined very simply:

<unsigned two-digit integer> :: =
<digit><digit>

Similarly, an identifier containing exactly two characters may be defined:

<2-character identifier> :: =
<letter><alphanumeric character>

Extensions to three characters, four characters, etc, are easy enough to visualize; and now, using the vertical line and a few auxiliary abbreviations, we may put together a definition of an identifier which has six characters or less. (See figure 1.) In a similar way, we may construct a definition of an unsigned integer containing at most eleven digits, or however many digits are permitted on a given computer.

This kind of construction, however, fails when we do not wish to put *any* limit whatsoever on the number of digits in an unsigned integer or on the number of characters in an identifier. In addition, it is overly cumbersome even in the form given above. Therefore, we must call on some new resource. This has actually been done, historically, in two different ways. One way is designed for languages such as ALGOL, LISP, and SNOBOL, in which most constructions do not have length limitations. The other way is intended for FORTRAN and for simplified versions of ALGOL, as well as for various other languages, in which length limitations do exist. We shall consider these in historical order.

The response of the ALGOL group to this problem was to use the resources of mathematics, which rescue us (as they do so often) with what looks like magic. The trick is to use *recursive* definitions, which use the quantity being defined in the definition itself. Consider, for example, the following definition:

<unsigned integer> :: =
<digit><unsigned integer>
|<digit>

Those without a background in mathematical logic may need a considerable amount of time to convince themselves that this definition of "unsigned integer" defines that syntactical variable, in a perfectly valid manner, to be a sequence of digits of any length whatsoever. The argument goes as follows:

1. A digit is an unsigned integer by the above definition.
2. A two-digit number is a digit followed by another digit, and the second digit, by the sentence above, is an unsigned integer. Therefore a two-digit number is an unsigned integer.
3. A three-digit number is a digit followed by a two-digit number; a two-digit number is an unsigned integer by the previous sentence; therefore, a three-digit number is an unsigned integer.
4. A four-digit number is a digit followed by a three-digit number, and so on; the argument may thus be extended indefinitely, with each sentence being used in the proof of the next.

<an> :: =<alphanumeric character>
<identifier> :: =<letter>
|<letter><an>
|<letter><an><an>
|<letter><an><an><an>
|<letter><an><an><an><an>
|<letter><an><an><an><an><an>

Figure 1: An identifier which has six characters or less.

Another common recursive definition is:

<identifier> :: = <letter>
| <identifier> <letter>
| <identifier> <digit>

This one is actually easier to understand if the last two alternatives are combined into a single alternative, < identifier >< an >, where < an > means "alphanumeric character" and is defined as either a letter or a digit. Using this syntactical variable, we may rewrite the definition of an identifier as:

<identifier> :: = <letter>
| <identifier> <an>

That this constitutes a valid definition may be seen as follows:

1. A letter is an identifier by the above definition.
2. An identifier with two characters consists of a letter, which is an identifier, followed by an alphanumeric character. Therefore, by the second part of the above definition, it is an identifier.
3. An identifier with three characters consists of an identifier with two characters followed by an alphanumeric character. Therefore, by the definition above, it is an identifier. This argument may then be extended to identifiers with four, five, or any number of characters.

Note that this definition of an identifier involves various other identifiers whose names are contained within it. Thus the word TAU is an identifier partly because T is an identifier and so is TA. This fact may lead to confusion because we are constantly reminded, when studying programming languages, that the individual characters in an identifier have no separate meaning. Thus TAU is not (by definition) T times A times U, or TA times U, or T times AU. Nevertheless, TAU is a properly *formed* identifier because T and TA are — just as 2PI is *not* a properly formed identifier because 2 and 2P are not.

Still another common recursive definition is:

<argument list> :: =
<expression>','<argument list>
| <expression>

This defines an argument list to be a series of expressions separated by commas. It may be used in various ways; for example, the BNF rule:

<function reference> :: =
<function name>'('<argument list>')'

is one way of defining a function reference (ie: a use of a function, such as SIN(T*U − B) or ATAN2(X2 − X1,Y2 − Y1).

The justification for the definition of an argument list is:

1. A single expression is an argument list.
2. Two expressions separated by one comma may be thought of as the first expression followed by a comma followed by an argument list, namely the second expression. Therefore, this is an argument list.
3. Three expressions separated by commas may be thought of as the first expression followed by a comma followed by what remains — namely, the second and third expressions separated by a comma. This much is an argument list, by the sentence above. Therefore, three expressions separated by commas constitute an argument list. The same argument may be used for four, five, etc, expressions separated by commas.

The recursive examples given above are written in what may be called *pure* BNF. The alternative is to add some new conventions to BNF which take care of the recursive cases. This brings us to the second possible response to the problem of representing sequences in BNF. For example, an unsigned integer which is a sequence of from one to thirteen digits might be written:

<unsigned integer> :: = <digit>$_{1}^{13}$

and an unsigned integer which is a sequence of an arbitrary number of digits (at least one) might be written:

<unsigned integer> :: = <digit>$_{1}^{\infty}$

Similarly, an identifier of arbitrary length is given by:

<identifier> :: =
<letter>
<alphanumeric character>$_{0}^{\infty}$

Thus a subscript after any syntactical variable stands for a minimum number of repetitions, while a superscript after such a variable stands for a maximum number of repetitions.

The use of subscripts and superscripts in this way solves two problems at once. It makes syntactical variables whose lengths are strictly bounded much easier to represent in BNF. Also, by replacing many of the recursive uses of BNF with nonrecursive uses, it frees the user from having to "think out" these recursive defintions. Nevertheless, the subscript notation does not allow us to eliminate *all* recursion. This will become clear in the examples which we now consider, in which expressions are defined in BNF.

There are many types of expressions in programming languages. In ALGOL we have conditional expressions, relational expressions, and Boolean expressions, in addition to the standard simple arithmetic expression. Some of these are easy to define in terms of others. For example, a relational expression (such as P>Q in an *if* statement) is defined by:

<relational expression> :: =
<arithmetic expression>
<relational operator>
<arithmetic expression>

where a relational operator may be any one of the six relations (eg: greater than, less than, etc) expressed in a manner which depends on the language used. In any sort of expression containing operators and possibly nested parentheses, however, the definition will be much more complex. We shall indicate here how to define simple arithmetic expressions in BNF; the basic technique used here may be used in other kinds of expressions.

What is a simple arithmetic expression? Clearly it is *not* simply any combination of identifiers, constants, operators, and parentheses. We may specify certain rules (eg: the parentheses have to balance, an operator cannot be the last character in the expression, etc) but it is difficult to know when we have specified all of them. One key to defining expressions is obtained by means of the *precedence rules*. You have probably seen these, although possibly not by this name; these are the rules that specify that multiplication is performed before addition, and the like. Thus in order to evaluate an expression (without parentheses) there are three basic steps:

1. Perform all the exponentiations.
2. Perform all the multiplications and divisions.
3. Perform all the additions and subtractions.

We shall incorporate these steps into our definition of an expression by defining four separate syntactical variables; primary, factor, term, and expression. Factors are made up of primaries; terms are made up of factors; and expressions are made up of terms. Thus, performing all the exponentiations in an expression corresponds to grouping the primaries into factors, and similarly for the other two steps mentioned above.

In order to define a factor as a collection of primaries separated by exponentiation signs, we note that this is similiar to defining an argument list as a set of expressions separated by commas. We need only substitute "exponentiation sign" for "comma," and "primary" for "expression." Thus the definition is:

<factor> :: = <primary>'↑'<factor>
|<primary>

We could also rewrite this definition in the other mode:

<factor> :: = <primary>
['↑'<primary>]$_0^\infty$

In other words, a factor is a primary followed by any number of occurrences, including none, of an up-arrow (↑) followed by another primary. This illustrates another feature of extended BNF: the use of *square brackets,* the signs [and]. Square brackets in BNF serve roughly the same function as parentheses do in algebra, and the use of square brackets in BNF is sometimes called *factoring.*

We continue our definition of an expression by defining a term as a collection of factors separated by multiplication and division signs. One way to do this is to define a "multiplication operator," or "mulop," as *either* * or /. The definition can then take the same form as before (here we illustrate only the recursive formulation):

<term> :: = <factor>
<mulop><term>
|<factor>

An expression would then be defined in a similar way, using "adop" for either + or − :

<expression> :: =
<term><adop><expression>
|<term>

where we have used "expression" as

short for "simple arithmetic expression." Alternatively, both of these could be written out:

```
<term> :: = <factor>'*'<term>
   |<factor>'/'<term>
   |<factor>
```

```
        <expression> :: =
     <term>'+'<expression>
     |<term>'−'<expression>
             |<term>
```

The only question remaining is what we mean by "primary." This differs from one language to another; roughly speaking, a primary is one of the "elementary" constructions which are connected by the operators, such as a constant, a variable, a subscripted variable, or a function reference. There is always, however, one special type of "primary" which takes care of parentheses.

Up to now we have considered only expressions without parentheses. In one sense, when we introduce parentheses into an expression, we sometimes violate the precedence rules upon which we have built the entire preceding construction. Thus in the expression:

A − B*C/(D − E)

we do *not* perform all the multiplications and divisions first. In fact, the subtraction D − E must be performed before the division of C by the result.

This expression, however, may also be thought of as:

A − B*C/F

where F stands for (D − E). In this new expression, we do perform all the multiplications and divisions before the additions and subtractions. The process of substituting F for (D − E) may suggest to us that *an expression in parentheses can be treated as if it were a single primary*. This is also true for more than one level of parentheses. Thus, the expression:

A + B*(C − D*(E + F/G) − H) + I

may be thought of as the expression:

A + B*J + I

where J stands for the expression:

C − D*K − H

in which K stands for the expression E + F/G. In each of these three expressions — E + F/G, C − D*K − H, and A + B*J + I — the precedence rules apply; and the last two of these contain primaries (K and J) that take the form of an entire expression in parentheses. The BNF description of an expression is now completed by adding this form of a primary to the definition. Thus:

```
<primary> :: = <constant>
        |variable>
     |<array reference>
   |<function reference>
     |'('<expression>')'
```

is a sample definition of a primary in which the syntactical variables "constant," "variable," etc, should be further defined according to the rules of the particular language under consideration.

One final and important fact about BNF is that although widely used, it is *not* universal enough to describe the syntax of every well-known programming language. In particular Common Business Oriented Language (COBOL) contains certain constructions which are not amendable to BNF. The formal definition of the PL-I language as shown in reference 5, is made according to a separate set of abbreviation conventions which are similar, but not identical, to BNF.■

REFERENCES

1. Naur, P, ed. "Report on the Algorithmic Language ALGO 60" *Communications of the ACM,* volume 3, May 1960, pages 299 thru 314.
2. Knuth, D E. *"Semantics of Context-Free Languages." Math Systems Theory,* volume 2, number 2; 1968, pages 127 thru 145.
3. Knuth, D E. *On the Translation of Languages from Left to Right.* Inf Contr volume 8, Oct 1965, pages 607 thru 639.
4. Wirth, N, and H. Weber. "Euler, A Generalization of ALGOL, and Its Formal Definition." *Communications of the ACM,* volume 9 January and February 1966, pages 13 thru 25 and 89 thru 99.
5. IBM Form C28-6571-4. *IBM Systems/360 Operating System, PL-I: Language Specifications.*

Aids for Hand-Assembling Programs

Erich A Pfeiffer PhD

Resident assembler programs and interpreters for high-level languages are available increasingly for microcomputer systems based on the more popular microprocessors. Nevertheless, many operators of small microcomputer systems are unable to use such programs because their systems are not large enough to support them. Unless they are lucky enough to have access to a time-sharing service or to some larger computer which supports a cross assembler, their only way of developing a usable object program is to assemble it by hand.

While the mere idea of such an endeavor might horrify any programmer who is used to working with large machines, the hand assembly of shorter programs for 8-bit microprocessors actually is not very difficult. It has been my experience that the assembly of programs can be greatly simplified and the likelihood of errors can be reduced by using some simple aids in the assembly process.

One of these aids is in the form of hardware and consists of a special program assembly form. The software aids are several short utility routines which run even on the smallest microcomputer systems. Development of the assembly method described in this article is based on experience gained from working with programmable calucators of the keyboard language type. Matt Biever of the Pro-Log Corporation has long been advocating some of the techniques that I am using. The article's assembly method is used for program development for a KIM-1 microcomputer. It can be adapted easily for other microcomputer systems as long as they use an 8-bit processor. The assembly method will be demonstrated with a sample program.

Before writing a program, it is a good idea to put down in writing what the program is supposed to do. Such a program description, as shown in listing 1, might state any limitations on the magnitude of variables used or might indicate what happens if these limitations are exceeded.

The next step is to develop a concept of the program in the form of a flowchart as in figure 1. While the symbols used in such charts are standardized, the chart's degree of detail is a matter of personal preference. From program descriptions and flowcharts, one can determine how many memory locations or registers will be necessary to store data and temporary results. These

BRAVEC

The program takes a 16-bit number ORigin and adds 2 to it. The new number then is subtracted from another 16 bit number, DEstination. The difference, which may be positive or negative, in two's complement, is stored in POINTL. The difference is also examined to determine if it is larger than +127 (if positive) or smaller than −127 (if negative). If this is the case, FF is loaded into POINTH; otherwise 00 is loaded. POINTH and POINTL are then displayed by transferring control to the (KIM) operating system.

Listing 1: Program description for BRAVEC. This description should be the first step taken when writing a program.

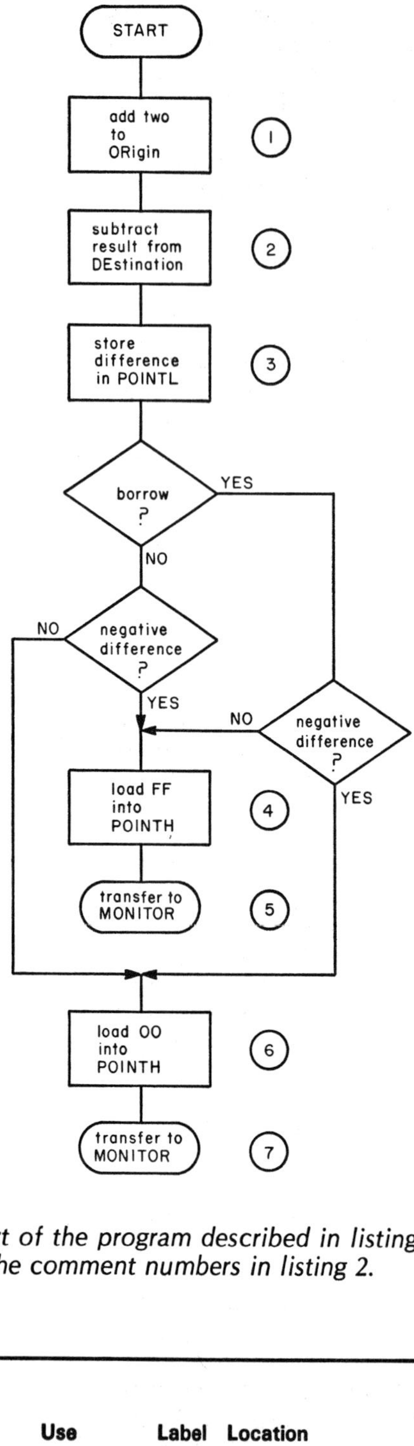

Figure 1: Flowchart of the program described in listing 1. The circled numbers refer to the comment numbers in listing 2.

Use	Label	Location
ORigin	ORLO ORHI	0000 01
DEstination	DELO DEHI	02 03
"open cell"	POINTL POINTH	FA from listing of FB KIM monitor
Transfer to KIM monitor	START	1C4F from listing of KIM monitor

Table 1: Program register table for program BRAVEC. This table contains all descriptions of all memory locations used by the program.

locations should be written in the program register table as shown in table 1. This table also contains the addresses of subroutines or registers of the monitoring system that are called by the program, or of peripheral interface adapter (PIA) registers that will be addressed. The table is similar to the symbol table printed by the computer during the machine assembly of a program.

After a program description is developed the actual writing of the program can begin. The programmer, who writes a symbolic listing for machine assembly, arranges a program in the form of lines. Each line is successively numbered, contains one mnemonic for an operation, unless it is an "all comment" line, and later will be punched into one punch card for computer entry. Because the operation described by the mnemonic can have a length of one, two or three bytes, each line eventually results in one, two, or three machine instructions. Therefore, there exists no simple relation between the line number and the address at which the machine code is stored in the computer memory. For the hand assembly of programs, it is advantageous to use a different format for the program listing in which there is a one-to-one relationship between program line and memory location. The writing of the symbolic program and the assembly into machine code is greatly simplified by the use of a special program-assembly form. The form I developed for our KIM-1 system is shown in listing 2. (Similar forms are available from the Pro-Log Corporation; order NrCF-1.) Each line of the coding form corresponds to one memory location with the least significant hexadecimal digit of the address preprinted in the ADD column. The form can be used with any computer system that uses a hexadecimal machine code. For octal notation, a different layout is advantageous.

The programmer starts writing a program by adding the other digits of the program-starting address in the ADD and Page columns. It should be noted that the Page column refers to memory pages while the Page-of heading indicates pages of coding forms. The program is written by entering the mnemonic of the first instruction into the MNE column of line 0. Many of the instructions of a microprocessor can occur in more than one addressing mode. During machine assembly, the assembler program deducts the addressing mode from the format of the operand or the definition of a symbol. When hand-assembling a program it is advantagous to specify the addressing mode in the Mode column. Immediate mode addressing is commonly indicated by the symbol #. For other addressing modes, suitable abbreviations of the column headings in the programmer's reference card should be used. For operations which have only one addressing mode, the Mode column is left empty. The addressing mode determines how many address bytes will have to follow the op code byte. After filling in the Mode column, the programmer should cross out the appropriate number of lines in the MNE column. This reserves the corresponding memory locations for the address or operand part of the instruction.

The Label column will carry an entry for two conditions only:

- if the line contains the start of a subroutine
- if the line is the destination of a conditional or unconditional jump or branch instruction

While assembly programs sometimes put certain limitations on the choice of labels, any suitable word or letter and number combination can be used as a label for hand assembly. However, it makes sense to pick a word or abbreviation that indicates what the subroutine or branch destination is doing in the program (ie: "WAITLOOP," "COUNT," or simply "LOOP 7").

The next column to fill in is the one with the heading Operand. When writing programs for machine assembly, the programmer enters a symbolic label in this field and leaves it up to the assembly program to figure out what to do with it. When writing for hand assembly, the programmer can make the task easier by being a bit more specific. The operand can be one of the following things:

1. In the immediate addressing mode, it is simply the number that is to be entered by the operation. Rather than give this number a symbolic name which is defined somewhere in a symbol table, it is much easier to enter it directly in the Operand column. One has to be careful to remember which number system is being used. A number without a prefix indicates decimal notation. The prefix % indicates binary notation. A bit mask for bit 2 and 0, for example, would have the operand % 0000 0101. If the number is in hexadecimal form, the prefix $ would normally be used, but in this case it is much simpler to enter the hexadecimal number directly in the OPC column of the following line.

2. With a jump or branch instruction, the operand symbol indicates the destination of the operation. The operand of such an operation must have a counterpart in the label column somewhere in the program. The only exception is when the program calls subroutines that are stored in read-only memory, as I do frequently with subroutines of the KIM monitoring system. In this case, the operand symbol has to have a counterpart in the stored program.

3. With any other memory referenced instruction, the operand must symbolize a memory location. I have found it useful to think of these locations as registers even though, unlike the registers of the processor, they are physically located somewhere in memory. As a matter of fact, their location, if possible, is in page 0 of the memory to take advantage of the shorter addressing mode. For registers used in stock subroutines, I have assigned locations which begin at the upper end of page 0 and work their way downward. They are listed in a master register list and care has been taken that subroutines that are likely to be used in the same program do not occupy the same register addresses. The symbolic names for registers that will be used in the main program are noted in a program register table with the addresses to be assigned later. (See table 1.) The symbols again should be words or abbreviations which indicate the meaning of the data contained in the register, such as STARLO to mean starting address, low-order byte.

The column N of the program assembly form can be used to indicate the number of cycles it takes to execute the instruction. This is necessary, for example, to determine the time of timing loops. In most cases, however, this column will be left empty.

Finally, the Comment column should be used to explain the function of the operation listed in the current line and sometimes some following lines. While this information may not be needed by the programmer, it is a tremendous help for any other person trying to understand what the program is doing. If the program has been flowcharted first, which is highly recommended for all but

Listing 2: Program listing of BRAVEC using the author's hand-assembly form for the KIM-1. This form can be used with any hexadecimal based microprocessor.

Program: BRAVEC
Page 1 **of** 2 **Date:** **Programmer:**

Page	ADD	OPC	Label	MNE	Mode	Operant	N	Comment
00	0Ø		ORLO					DATA REGISTERS
	1		ORHI					
	2		DELO					
	3		DEHI					
	4	18		CLC				①
	5	49		LDA	#	2		
	6	02		/				
	7	65		ADC	Z	ORLO		
	8	00		/				
	9	90		BCC		NELO		
	A	02		/				
	B	E6		INC	Z	ORHI		
	C	01		/				
	D	85	NELO	STA	Z	ORLO		
	E	00		/				
	F	38		SEC				②
	1Ø	A5		LDA	Z	DELO		
	1	02		/				
	2	E5		SBC	Z	ORLO		
	3	00		/				
	4	85		STA	Z	POINTL		③
	5	FA		/				
	6	A5		LDA	Z	DEHI		②
	7	03		/				
	8	E5		SBC	Z	ORHI		
	9	01		/				
	A	A5		LDA	Z	POINTL		
	B	FA		/				
	C	90		BCC		NEG		
	D	09		/				
	E	10		BPL		OUT		
	F	09		/				

VA-BECC Program Assembly Form

the shortest programs, the comment can simply be a number which refers to an equally numbered symbol on the flowchart.

In this way, the programmer works down the lines of the program-assembly form. Every time a 0 is encountered in the ADD column, he adds the most significant bit. If that addition makes the ADD column, it is also advanced. Eventually the program will be completed and the hand assembly can begin. Like the computer, I do this in a number of passes.

The first pass is the easiest one. Using a listing of the instruction set, or the programmer reference chart, the mnemonic and the entry in the Mode column are used to look up the op code of the instruction, which is entered into the OPC column of the line. A frequent error during this operation is to mistake an 8 for a B or vice versa, and I double check op codes with these symbols. The programmer's reference cards supplied by the manufacturers, although they fit nicely into a shirt pocket, were apparently not intended for use by progammers over 40 years of age. The listing of the instruction set in the data sheets or system manuals is usually printed in a more reasonable letter size.

The second step is to assign absolute addresses to the symbols of the program register list. First, all registers and their addresses used in stock subroutines to be called by the program are transferred from the master register list to the program register list. Then absolute addresses are assigned to all other registers listed, making sure that no duplication occurs. Registers which contain the low-order and high-order bytes of numbers, or registers which contain successive bytes if multiple precision operations are used, have to be arranged in such a way that their absolute addresses are adjacent in increasing order (STARLO = B3, STARHI = B4).

With the completed program register list one can go over the program again. For each memory referenced instruction other than branch and jump instructions, the program register list will contain an absolute address for the symbol in the operand column. This hexadecimal number is now entered into the OPC column of the following line. For registers located outside of page 0 (such as the registers in PIAs) the address will be entered in two lines, and care has to be taken to enter the low-order byte first, followed by the high-order byte. During this pass I also check all lines with a # in the Mode column and, if necessary, convert the binary or decimal operand into hexadecimal notation which is entered in the OPC column of the following line. With this step completed, the OPC column should show a hexadecimal number in most lines. The next step is to pass over the program again.

Any line with an open OPC column where the menemonic indicates a branch instruction will require that the branch vector for the relative addressing mode be calculated. For short forward branches this poses no problem because the offset can easily be counted off by beginning at the second line following the one which contains the branch instruction, and continuing to the line which has the corresponding symbol in the label column. For longer branches and especially backwards branches, if memory pages are crossed it is very easy to make a mistake and miss by one count in either direction. I have found it advantageous to let the microcomputer perform this operation because, after all, it is much better in hexadecimal calculations than any programmer.

The example program BRAVEC receives the origin and destination of a branch and calculates the branch vector in two's complement notation. A flag is set if the relative addressing range is exceeded. The program is loaded from cassette tape beginning at memory location 0000. Loading begins here because this location in the KIM-1 system can be addressed easily by pressing the space bar of the connected terminal. The first four locations are actually data registers into which the low- and high-order bytes of origin and destination of the branch are entered.

When the program is executed beginning at location 0004, it displays or prints the branch vector in two's complement as the low-order byte of the address field. The high-order byte of this field normally shows 00, while FF indicates that the reach of the relative addressing mode has been exceeded.

While the program, as listed, is written for the 6502 microprocessor, only instructions that have an equivalent in the instruction set for the 6800 were used. The program, therefore, can be converted easily. However, the registers POINTHI and POINTLO, which are displayed as an address in the light-emitting diode (LED) display of the KIM-1 microcomputer, are specific for this system. For other computers, the user will have to find another way of displaying the result of the calculation.

Listing 2 continued:

Program: BRAVEC
Page 2 **of** 2 **Date: Programmer:**

Page	ADD	OPC	Label	MNE	Mode	Operant	N	Comment
	2Ø	A9	FLAG	LDA	#	$FF		(4)
	1	FF						
	2	85		STA	Z	POINTH		
	3	FB						
	4	4C		JMP	ABS	START		(5)
	5	4F						
	6	1C						
	7	10	NEG	BPL		FLAG		
	8	F7						
	9	A9	OUT	LDA	#	00		(6)
	A	00						
	B	85		STA	Z	POINTH		
	C	FB						
	D	4C		JMP	ABS	START		(7)
	E	4F						
	F	1C						
	Ø							
	1							
	2							
	3							
	4							
	5							
	6							
	7							
	8							
	9							
	A							
	B							
	C							
	D							
	E							
	F							

VA-BECC Program Assembly Form

After all branch vectors have been calculated in this fashion and entered in the appropriate lines, the only open spaces in OPC column should be the address parts of jump instructions. For jumps within the main program it is easy to find the line with a matching entry in the label column and to enter the address of this line into the OPC columns of the lines following the one containing the jump instruction. For subroutines called from read-only memory, the address has to be looked up in the subroutine listing.

Stock subroutines which have been written on some other occasion and which can be loaded from magnetic or paper tape frequently can be used. Normally such subroutines will be tacked on after the last memory location occupied by the main program. The KIM-1 system has a relocating loading routine for loading from magnetic tape. If this feature is not available, some area in the memory should be set aside into which the subroutines are loaded. A move program then can be executed to pull up the subroutine. For the 6502 processor, I use a program called MOVBLO which requires only fourteen program steps due to one very convenient addressing mode of this processor.

Unless one is very pressed for memory space, it is a good idea to have all subroutines start in lines with a 0 as the least significant digit because it is easier to keep track of the starting address after relocation. In order to be relocatable, a subroutine may not contain any absolute jump instructions and only relative addressing within the subroutine is permitted.

After the last addresses for the stock subroutines have been entered in the program assembly form, the hand assembly is completed. I have never clocked the operation, but by following the methods described, it goes much faster than one would expect . With all op codes being listed in a single column it is much easier to enter them into the machine, either from a hexadecimal keyboard or from the keyboard of a terminal. This is another occasion in which operator errors can easily occur and I proofread all programs after entry. This operation is again greatly simplified by the use of the assembly form which shows address and op code in adjacent columns.

The assembly method and the assembly aids described have been in use for several months and have been found to greatly reduce the likelihood of assembly errors. Unfortunately, this method does not protect from programming errors, and the debugging of the program still is a time consuming but necessary step to follow the assembly of a program.■

An Introduction to Polish Postfix Notation

D Wilson Cooke

We are living in an age of machines, and we must often adjust our ways to the ways of machines if we are to get along with the big black boxes. Communication of mathematical expressions to a computer or pocket calculator must be done in a form that the machine understands. This article discusses one aspect of this man-machine communication: Polish notation.

In high school algebra we learned to evaluate mathematical expressions such as $a^2 + b(c - a)$. This sort of algebraic notation, called infix notation, has been in wide use for many years. It has served us well, and it is the only notation that most people know. Many of the better scientific pocket calculators have keys for entering parentheses so that the user can calculate complex mathematical expressions using this popular standard notation. Many high-level computer languages such as BASIC, FORTRAN, ALGOL, PL/I, etc, permit the programmer to write rather complex math expressions involving several operations and several variables using infix notation.

There is a form of notation called Polish notation or reverse Polish notation (RPN) which is generally more efficient for computer processing. The name "Polish" is in honor of the Polish mathematician, Jan Lukasiewicz, who introduced this alternate form of notation in the late 1920s. Some pocket calculators, like the Hewlett-Packard scientific calculators, use reverse Polish, or Polish postfix, notation. I will define this term later.

Characteristics of Standard Algebraic Notation

Standard algebra expressions have two characteristics which distinguish them from Polish expressions:

1. In infix notation, the operation symbol, or operator, is written between the symbols representing the variables, or operands. Thus, $a + b$ means the sum of b added to a; $a - b$ means the difference of b subtracted from a; $a \uparrow b$ means the result of raising a to the b power, and so on. We have all learned the shorthand way of writing products, which looks like "ab," and raising to a power, which looks like "a^b," but this notation is not generally used in computer languages. The operator must be included with the operands.

2. Infix notation expressions involving mixed operations are always calculated in a definite order of precedence. For example:

- Expressions in parentheses are evaluated first and treated as a single term.
- Raising to a power (↑) is always the

Infix Notation	Polish Notation	Evaluation
A+B−C	AB+C−	1
A*B+C*D	AB*CD*+	26
A+B↑2*C	AB2↑C*+	38
A*B/C	AB*C/	1.5
A*B+A*(B*D+C↑E)	AB*ABD*CE↑+*+	68
A*B−C+D/E	AB*C−DE/+	2.83333
A*(B−C)+D/E	ABC−*DE/+	−1.16667

Table 1: *Comparison of infix and Polish notation for several expressions. In this case A=2, B=3, C=4, D=5 and E=6.*

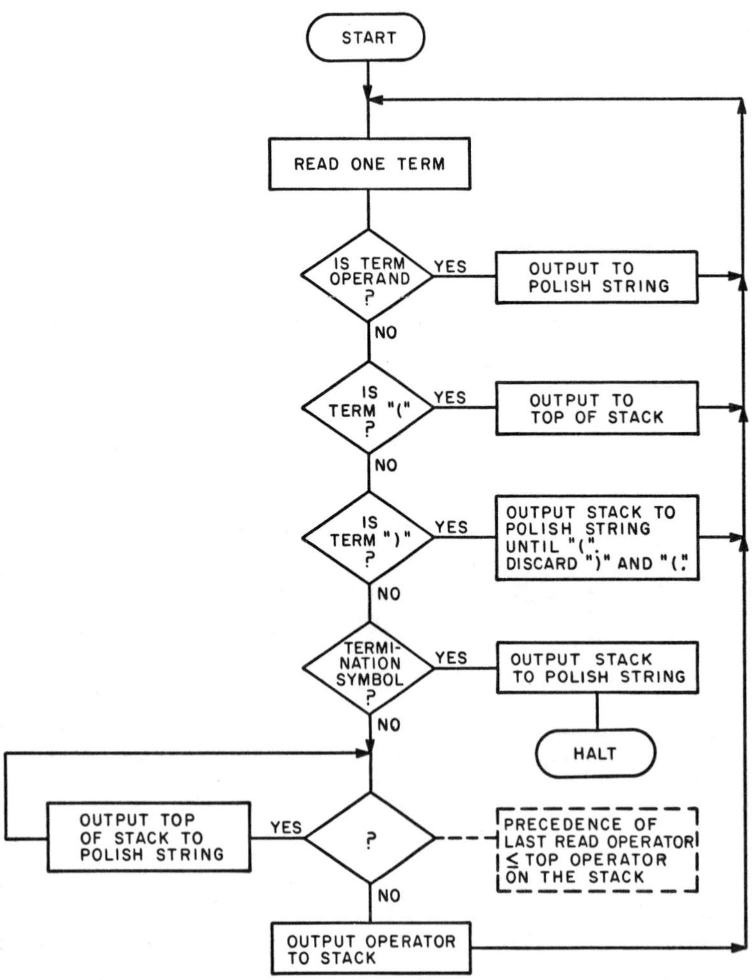

Figure 1: *Flowchart for the step-by-step conversion of an infix notation expression to a Polish notation string.*

first operator to be performed.

- Multiplications and divisions (*,/) are performed next.
- Additions and subtractions (+, −) are performed last.
- Within a sequence of multiplications or divisions containing no parentheses, evaluation is from left to right.
- Within a sequence of additions or subtractions containing no parentheses, evaluation is from left to right.

Using these characteristics of infix notation, we can construct a correct and unambiguous evaluation of every expression, no matter how complex. Consider the expression:

$$x=(ab-c(b-a)^3)/(d+b)$$

This would be coded in BASIC as:

LET X = (A*B−C*(B−A)↑3)/(D+B).

The BASIC statement is an instruction to evaluate the expression to the right of the equal sign according to the rules stated earlier, and to then store the result as X. The evaluation proceeds as follows:

- Because of the parentheses, A is subtracted from B, and D is added to B. Each result is stored temporarily.
- The result of B − A is then raised to the third power, (ie: it is multiplied by itself three times).
- The result from step 2 is multiplied by C; also, A and B are multiplied together.
- The second of the two results from step 3 is subtracted from the first because of the parentheses.
- This result is divided by the second result of step 1.

The evaluation is complete, and the final result is written as X. It is important that both the mathematics student and the computer programmer understand this procedure if correct results are to be obtained. (I have seen many incorrect answers on test papers because students failed to apply the rules of procedures correctly.) If we let A = 2, B =3, C = 4 and D = 5, the final result for X should be 0.25.

Polish Notation Characteristics

Infix notation is important because it

is universally used from elementary school onward. It is a "people-oriented" way of writing mathematical expressions. Readers with only a casual interest in computation on a computer with a high-level language, or the majority of pocket calculators available today, will find this notation entirely adequate. If, however, one is curious to learn more about the inner workings of computer logic, a study of Polish notation is in order. Hewlett-Packard points out that Polish notation is the most efficient machine processing notation available today. Most computer-language compilers will convert infix expressions to Polish expressions prior to the conversion to machine language for evaluation.

There are several different forms of Polish notation in use, but all are based on the same principles. This article will treat only one version: Polish postfix (RPN) notation. Polish notation differs from infix in the two characteristics outlined earlier, namely the order of operators and operands, and the hierarchy of precedence.

Operators are written after operands. Thus AB+ means the sum of B added to A; AB− means the difference of B subtracted from A; AB* means the product of A multiplied by B; AB/ means the quotient of A divided by B; and AB↑ means A raised to the B power.

In expressions involving mixed operations, evaluation proceeds from left to right. No parentheses are used and there is no precedence of operations.

Since this notation is unfamiliar to many people, several examples of expressions in both infix and Polish notation along with numeric results are presented in table 1. The mechanism for conversion from infix to Polish form is a formal procedure which requires the use of temporary storage of certain operation symbols, always keeping in mind the order of precedence in infix notation. As each character is read from left to right, a decision is made either to write it as output on the Polish string or to store it for later use. The storage medium is a stack or push down-list. It is sometimes called a last-in first-out (LIFO) memory. The stack is a sequence of memory locations in which new items can be added only from one end pushing all other items down one location. Items are removed from the same end raising all other items in the stack.

A physical illustration of a push-down stack is seen in many restaurants where dishes are put in a well with a spring-loaded bottom. As a new dish is added, all others shift down one position. As a

Character Number	Stack	Polish String	Comments
1	empty	A	operand;
2	*	A	operation symbol is put on top of stack;
3	*	AB	operand;
4	+	AB*	+ operation has less precedence than * on top of stack. * is output to Polish string and + is put on top of stack;
5	+	AB*A	operand;
6	*+	AB*A	* operation has more precedence than + on top of stack * is put on top pushing + down.
7	(*+	AB*A	put parenthesis on stack;
8	(*+	AB*AB	operand;
9	*(*+	AB*AB	* operation has more precedence than (on top of stack. * is put on top pushing (down;
10	*(*+	AB*ABD	operand;
11	+(*+	AB*ABD*	+ operation has less precedence than * on top of stack. * is output to Polish string and test is repeated. + is greater than (so + is output to Polish string;
12	+(*+	AB*ABD*C	operand;
13	↑+(*+	AB*ABD*C	↑ operation has more precedence than + on top of stack. ↑ is put on top of stack;
14	+(*+	*AB*ABD*CE*	*operand;*
15	*+	AB*ABD*CE↑+	), all operators on stack are output up to (, (is discarded;
16	empty	AB*ABD*CE↑+*+	no more characters. all operators are output to the Polish string and evaluation is complete;

Table 2: *Step-by-step evaluation of the expression A*B+A*(B*D+C↑E). The stack contents at any stage are listed from left to right with the top of the stack at the left.*

dish is removed, all other dishes move up one location. The last dish put on the stack is the first to be removed.

Conversion of infix to Polish notation proceeds as follows:

- Read the infix expression from left to right one character at a time.
- Put operands (ie: variable or numbers) directly into the Polish string.
- Push all left parentheses temporarily onto the stack.
- Check all operators read for order of precedence in comparison with the operator on the top of the stack.

The order of precedence is as follows:

- ↑ is greater than * or /, which are greater than + or −, which are greater than (.
  a. If the operator last read is greater in precedence than the operator on the top of the stack, it is pushed onto the stack.
  b. If the operator last read is not greater in precedence than the operator on the top of the stack, the stack top is placed in the Polish string, and the test is repeated until this is no longer true. The operator last read is then put on the stack.
- When a right parenthesis is encountered, all operators on the stack are sent to the string, starting with the top, until a left parenthesis is encountered. This is discarded.
- When a terminating character indicates that the end of the infix expression has been read, the entire contents of the stack is output to the Polish string, starting with the top.

Figure 1 presents these rules in flowchart form, and table 2 shows a step by step conversion of the expression:

A * B + A * (B * D + C ↑ E)

into Polish notation. Following each step in table 2 along with the rules above (or the flowchart) should help the reader to understand the rules.

When an expression involves some function such as sine, square root, logarithm or arc tangent, a subroutine is usually called to execute the function after the Polish string is evaluated. One may write the name of the function at the end of the Polish string to indicate this.

Once a Polish string is obtained, it is reasonably easy to read the string from left to right and generate assembler code for computer processing, or to

```
LOAD A          ; A is loaded into the accumulator
MULT B          ; contents of accumulator multiplied by B
STORE TEMP 1    ; contents of accumulator stored temporarily
LOAD A          ; A is loaded into the accumulator
STORE TEMP 2    ; contents of accumulator stored temporarily
LOAD B          ; B is loaded into the accumulator
MULT D          ; contents of accumulator multiplied by D
STORE TEMP 3    ; contents of accumulator stored temporarily
LOAD C          ; C is loaded into the accumulator
EXPN E          ; contents of accumulator raised to E power. This most likely will be a subroutine call of
                some sort
ADD TEMP 3      ; contents of TEMP 3 added to accumulator
MULT TEMP 2     ; contents of accumulator multiplied by TEMP 2
ADD TEMP 1      ; contents of TEMP 1 added to the accumulator; The accumulator now contains the final
                result
```

Table 3: *Hypothetical assembly code listing for the Polish notation string AB*ABD*CE↑+*+. The terms were chosen for clarity rather than for any particular assembler. The storage locations TEMP1, TEMP2, and TEMP3 could be located in programmable memory; ideally, they would be part of a push-down stack. Note that the locations are used in the reverse order from the way they were created. Polish notation pocket calculators have a push-down stack available. Loading is usually done with an ENTER key.*

read and enter numbers in a pocket calculator following the instructions supplied by the manufacturer. Table 3 presents a hypothetical assembler translation of the Polish string AB*ABD*CE↑+*+ obtained in table 2. It is impossible to evaluate this expression as written on the HP−45 because of limited stack capacity, but a slight modification of the expression to eliminate the need for three temporary storage locations in the stack will solve this problem. Had the original infix expression been written as (B*D + C↑E)*A + A*B prior to translation to the Polish string BD*CE↑+A*AB*+, the need for three temporary stack storage locations would have been eliminated, and the HP−45 could have handled the expression. The lesson is that if you are using a computer or calculator with limited stack capacity, write your algebra to keep a minimum of storage locations.

A word should be said about the unary minus sign. The expression −A is interpreted to mean the additive inverse or opposite of A and the "−" is not a subtraction sign. A new symbol could be invented to distinguish this from subtraction, but this is not necessary. We can interpret −A as meaning either −1*A, where −1 is the number negative one, or we can interpret −A as meaning to add the additive inverse of A. An application of a little high school algebra theory will usually clear up the problem quickly.

It is generally not necessary for the average computer user to become an expert at quick translation of complex infix expressions into Polish expressions. After all, computers were invented to do routine work of this sort and free the mind for creative thinking. Anyone who already has a compiler for his computer has the ability to make the necessary translation from infix notation to machine language.

Compiler design differs from machine to machine, but the design philosophy is similar. If your computer is without a compiler, it might be interesting to write a program that will perform the necessary translations. If a programmer knows how his compiler works, he can use this knowledge to write his expressions so that they will compile in the most efficient machine-language code.

It is beyond the scope of this article to go into the area of compiler design, but I hope it has helped the reader to understand mathematics notation and the use of Polish notation. We will not soon abandon our standard algebra notation in favor of something else. This generation and the next will undoubtedly be raised on infix notation. But who knows? Your grandchild may come home from first grade some day and ask you if 2 2 + is really 4.■

Microprocessor Memory Testing

Larry Lee

Semiconductor memory certainly dominates the memory market when it comes to microprocessors. It is cheap, readily available in a wide variety of sizes, speeds, packages, etc, and it is easy to use. It also possesses good reliability characteristics once the initial "burn in" failures are weeded out. Finding these failures is absolutely essential if your system is to operate reliably, or even operate at all. If the memory is not 100 percent functional, then the system cannot be expected to perform as planned.

Memory failures can be very difficult to find. How do you find a memory chip that is pattern sensitive, or one whose access time is a little slow sometimes? If you have a high performance integrated circuit tester available you can screen out the obviously defective parts rapidly; but, however good integrated circuit testers may be, they are not perfect. Some chips that work fine on the tester may not work in your system. There could be several reasons for this: your system may have more noise than the tester; the input voltages may be different; the timing could be significantly different. The only test that really counts is whether or not the chips work correctly in your system.

If you use large quantities of programmable memory, then it would probably be worth your while to invest in a good integrated-circuit tester. But if you only use small quantities of memory chips, it would definitely not pay to invest $50,000 or more in a high-performance integrated-circuit tester. In this case there are three alternatives:

1) Pay a little more and have the manufacturer test the chips.
2) Find an independent company with the proper tester and pay them to test the parts.
2) Develop a few short programs for your microprocessor and test them yourself.

The way I have found to be most effective in testing semiconductor memory is to plug the chips into the memory board and let the processor do the testing. This way the memory is tested in its actual operating environment. Note that this works only if the processor, address bus, data bus and control bus are known to be 100% functional. If any of the test-system components are faulty, then the concept of a self-testing system will not work. This kind of testing also requires some memory that is assumed to be good in order to hold the test program.

What do you test? Basically, you test the memory chips to see if they will accept and retain data that is given to them by the processor. How do you do it? The obvious answer is to write something into memory, and then read it to make sure that it was written properly and is readable. Using the concept of system self-test, the easiest way to check all the locations in a memory is to write a program to lay down a known pattern through memory, and then read

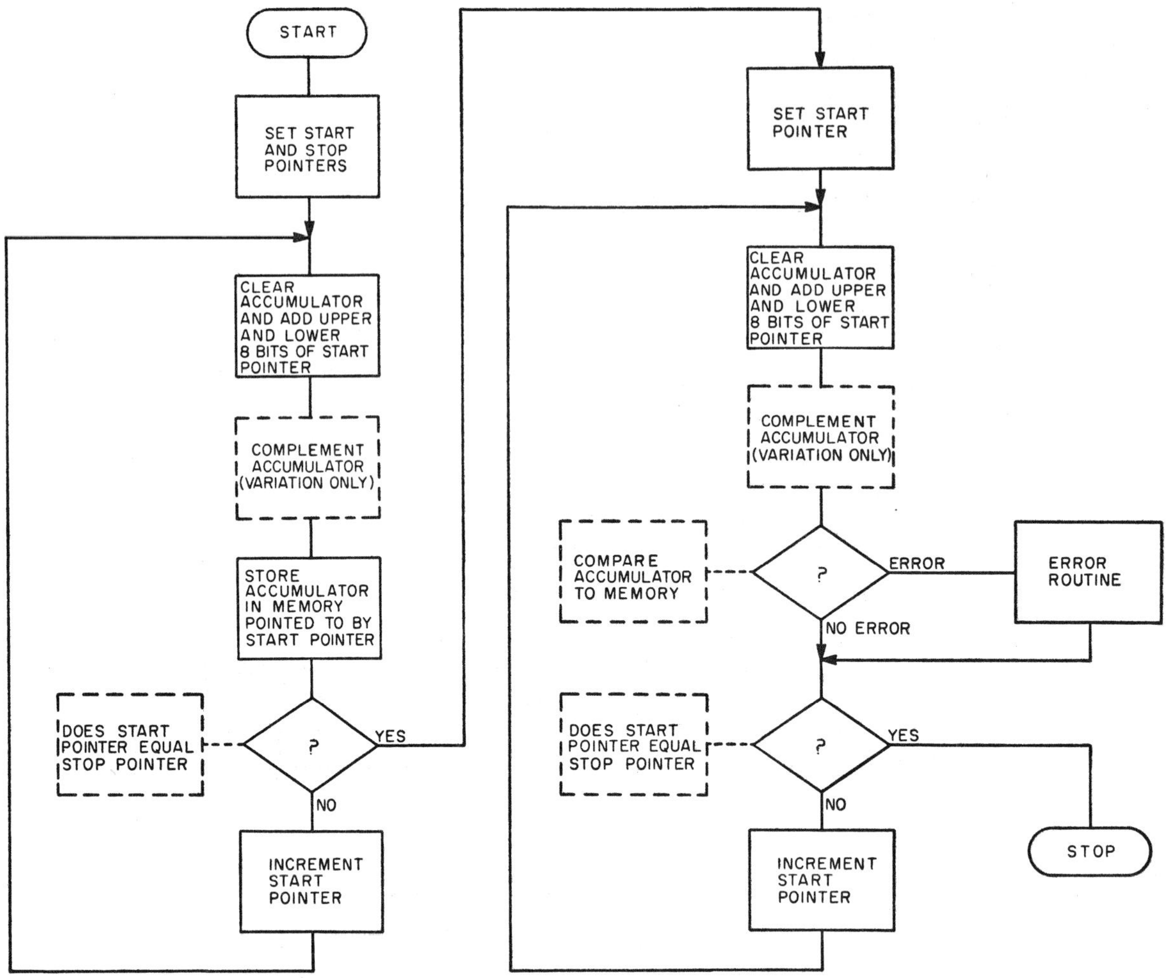

Figure 1: *Flowchart for test 1 and its variation.*

the pattern back. It would then be little problem to output a list of all incorrect locations on your display device. But what pattern do you write into memory? This is an important decision since some patterns are better than others at finding errors. The easiest pattern to run might be to write all 1s, read that, then write all zeros and read that. This type of test would find three kinds of errors: gross chip failure; a bit or bits stuck at logical 1; a bit or bits stuck at logical 0. This test also might find gross access time failures. But it probably would not discover chips that were a little slow due to the nature of the data stored in them. In addition, this test would not find adjacent bit failures, another common type of error. This failure occurs when two bits appear to be "stuck" together. This type of failure can be due to metalization shorts on the chip, leakage from one memory cell to another through the substrate, or moving an address line while the read/write input is in the write mode. One way of detecting this type of failure is to fill the chip with all zeros, then change one location at a time to a one. After one bit is changed the entire memory is read to ensure that only one location has changed.

Another type of memory chip failure is the thermal related failure. Usually chips fail when they heat up excessively (although it is possible that they might not work right until they warm up a little). There are basically two kinds of thermal related failure: access time failure and loss of data. Access time failures stem from the fact that as the chip temperature rises the access time increases. Loss of data failures occur because internal chip thresholds and voltage levels shift with changes in temperature, resulting in a memory cell or cells becoming unable to retain data. Both of these failures can be extremely difficult to find. It could take hours for the problem to show up, as soon as you power down to check or change something, the chip could cool down enough to make the problem disappear for another half hour or so. One solution to this type of failure might be to put a

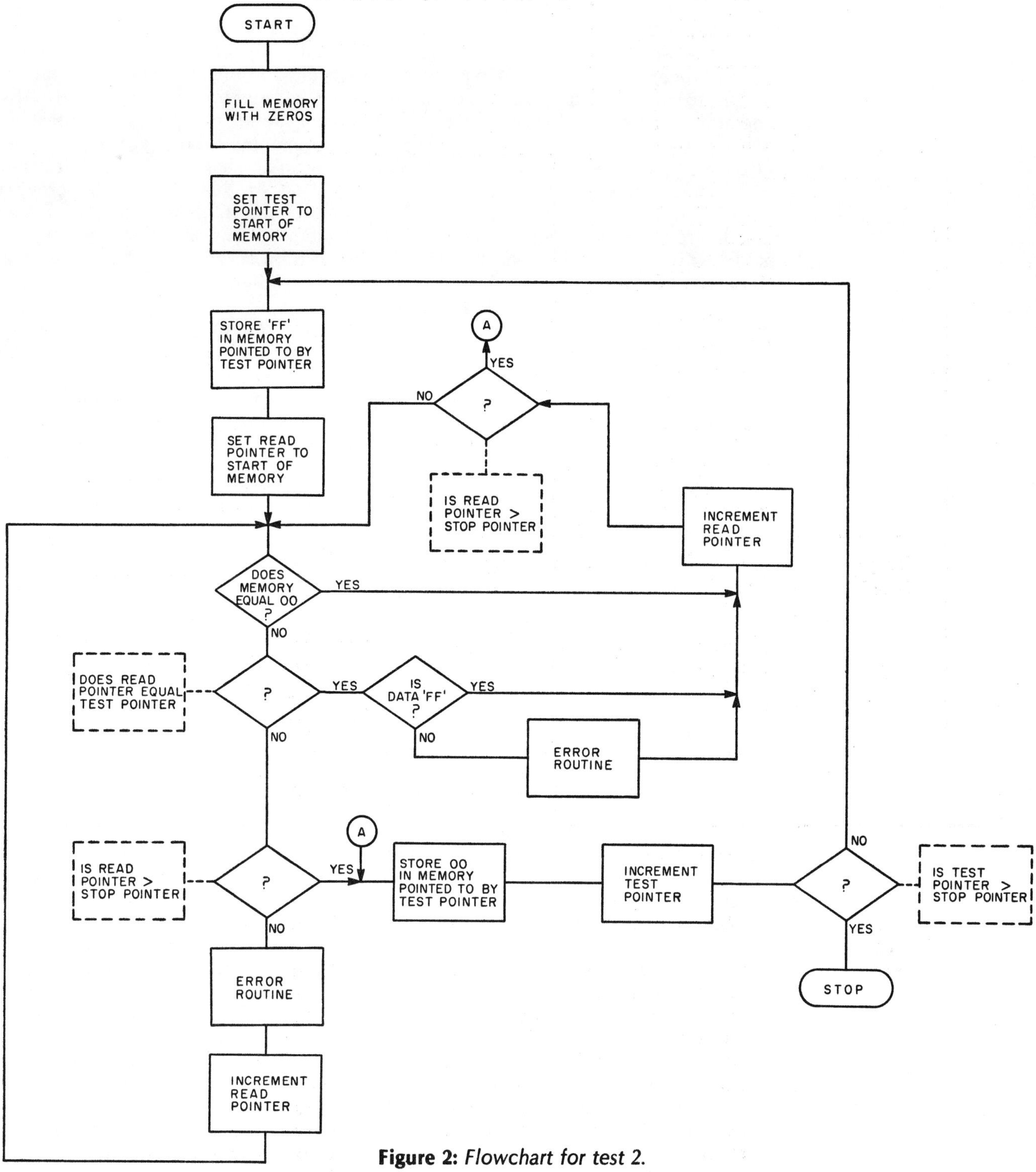

Figure 2: *Flowchart for test 2.*

small fan somewhere in your system where it can blow cool air over your memory. This should circumvent the problem and definitely would prolong chip life.

In the program I run there are two basic tests, with a variation of each. The first test, as flowcharted in figure 1, runs in about ten seconds for 8 K bytes on an 8008. It finds gross chip failures, bits stuck at 1 or 0, most adjacent bit failures and some access time failures. The second test, which is flowcharted in figure 2, runs in about six hours for 8 K bytes and finds adjacent bit and thermal related failures.

The first test scans through memory twice. The first pass is used to generate and write a pattern through memory. The second pass is used to verify that the pattern remains correct in memory. The algorithm for this test is as follows: there are two 16-bit pointers maintained in the processor's registers. One pointer is set to the starting location of the memory to be tested. The other is set to the last location to be tested. The upper and lower eight bits of the address in the start pointer are added together and the result is stored in the memory location pointed to by the start pointer. The start and stop pointers are compared. If they are equal, then something has been written into every location and it is time to branch to the read routine. If the two pointers are not equal, then increment the start pointer and branch back to the add step.

The read routine consists of setting the start pointer back to the start of memory to be tested, adding the upper and lower eight bits of the address in the start pointer together, and comparing the result with the contents of memory pointed to by the start pointer. If the two are not the same, then there is an error and the program should branch to an error routine. If they are the same, then compare the start pointer to the end pointer. If these pointers are equal, then the test is complete and control should be transferred to the system monitor or to the next test. If not equal, then increment the start pointer and branch back to the add step.

A useful variation of this test if as follows: after adding the upper and lower eight bits of the start pointer, store the complement of the result in memory and continue as before. The read routine would be identical to the first read routine, except that the program would check for the complement cf the sum of the upper and lower eight bits of the start pointer. Together these test programs check every bit in memory for a one and a zero.

It is possible for errors to slip through the test just presented, but it is very unlikely that any defective memory chips would get through the next test undetected. The first part of this test (refer to figure 2) starts out by filling memory with all 0s and putting a hexadecimal FF in the first location to be tested. The program then verifies that the FF is in memory correctly and that all other locations still contain 0s. After this is done, the program writes hexadecimal 00 in the previous address location and hexadecimal FF in the next location. It then checks the previous location for 00, the next for a hexadecimal FF and all other address locations for a hexadecimal 00. The program then continues this procedure as it marches a hexadecimal FF through memory, stopping when the test pointer is greater than the stop pointer. Note that at any time there is only one location in memory that contains a hexadecimal FF. The variation of this test is to fill the memory with ones and march hexadecimal 0s through in the same way as just described.

This test and its variation can take hours to run, depending on processor speed and memory size, and is intended to be run either whenever you add new memory to a system or if you suspect a memory problem. Because of its speed, the test flowcharted in figure 1 can be run at almost any time. Some appropriate times to run this test might be whenever you power up the system or just before you run an important program.

Whenever any of the tests detects an error it should immediately call the error routine. The purpose of the error routine is to give the operator as much information as possible about the error, such as the error data, the data that should have been there and the address of the error. After the error message is complete, the processor should continue testing from the next location. The error routine should not affect the test routine. An error counter might be included to stop the test if too many errors are detected.

By spending a little time writing a few fairly simple test programs, you can save a lot of time and trouble debugging your system. Not only will you find memory problems faster, but you will have more confidence that your system will run as planned.■

An Algorithm for Drawing Lines

Louis J Cesa
Eduardo Kellerman
Robert B Hitchcock Sr

This article describes an algorithm that generates, in sequence, the points that best approximate a straight line between two endpoints in an integer coordinate system. The algorithm makes no use of multiplication or division. Thus, it is particularly suitable for implementation in microprocessors which do not support these operations. In addition, no calculation generated by the algorithm exceeds 1.5 times the larger of the horizontal or vertical distance between endpoints, a value that is exceeded by all other algorithms known to the authors. This means that this algorithm can be used without overflow on as large as a 170 by 170 grid using 8-bit arithmetic only.

Given the coordinates (X1,Y1) and (X2,Y2) for the two endpoints of the line to be drawn, the algorithm computes the points that best approximate the straight line. It generates the points starting with (X1,Y1) and ending with (X2,Y2) as follows:

STEP 1: Set R = 0
  DX = |X2 − X1|
  DY = |Y2 − Y1|
  X = X1
  Y = Y1
STEP 2: Output X, Y (next point).
STEP 3: If DX<DY then go to STEP 10.
STEP 4: If X = X2 then stop.
STEP 5: Change X : If X2>X1 then increment X by 1.
  If X2<X1 then decrement X by 1.
STEP 6: Set R = R + DY.
STEP 7: Decide if Y is to be changed:
  If R<DX − R then go to STEP 2.
STEP 8: Change Y: If Y2>Y1 then increment Y by 1.
  If Y2<Y1 then decrement Y by 1.
STEP 9: Set R = R − DX then go to STEP 2.
STEP 10: If Y = Y2 then stop.
STEP 11: Change Y: If Y2>Y1 then increment Y by 1.
  If Y2<Y1 then decrement Y by 1.
STEP 12: Set R = R + DX.
STEP 13: Decide if X is to be changed:
  If R<DY − R then go to STEP 2.
STEP 14: Change X: If X2>X1 then increment X by 1.
  If X2<X1 then decrement X by 1.
STEP 15: Set R = R − DY, then go to STEP 2.

As an example, let's set point (X1,Y1) = (0,0) and point (X2,Y2) = (9,3). The result of executing the algorithm is as follows:

```
POINTS            PLOT

 0,0
 1,0      Y↑3            XX
 2,1        2        XXX
 3,1        1   XXX
 4,1        0XX
 5,2         0123456789
 6,2
 7,2                 X →
 8,3
 9,3
```

■